Europäischer Gottesdienstatlas

European Atlas of Liturgy

Europäischer Gottesdienstatlas
European Atlas of Liturgy

Protestantische Perspektiven auf den Gottesdienst
Protestant Perspectives on Worship Services

Im Auftrag der Gemeinschaft Evangelischer Kirchen in Europa herausgegeben von Jochen Arnold und Adél Dávid

By order of the Council of the Community of Protestant Churches in Europe edited by Jochen Arnold and Adél Dávid

EVANGELISCHE VERLAGSANSTALT
Leipzig

Bibliographische Information der Deutschen Nationalbibliothek
Die Deutsche Nationalbibliothek verzeichnet diese Publikation
in der Deutschen Nationalbibliographie; detaillierte bibliographische
Daten sind im Internet über http://dnb.dnb.de abrufbar.

Printed in Germany

Das Buch wurde auf alterungsbeständigem Papier gedruckt.

Cover: Kai-Michael Gustmann, Leipzig
Coverbild: Kai-Michael Gustmann, unter Verwendung eines Fotos
von © steuccio 79 – Fotolia.com
Satz: Steffi Glauche, Leipzig
Druck und Binden: Hubert & Co., Göttingen

ISBN 978-3-374-05663-7
www.eva-leipzig.de

Michael Bünker

Vorwort

»Die GEKE ist vor allem gottesdienstliche Gemeinschaft«. Mit dieser Feststellung im Bericht des Präsidiums an die 6. Vollversammlung der GEKE im Jahr 2006 in Budapest[1] wurde auf zentrale Einsichten der »Leuenberger Konkordie« zurückgegriffen und zugleich eine Zukunftsperspektive eröffnet. Die Konkordie sieht den Grund der Kirchengemeinschaft im gemeinsamen Verständnis des Evangeliums (LK 6), dessen rechtes Verständnis seit der Reformation in der Lehre von der Rechtfertigung zum Ausdruck gebracht wird (LK 8)[2]. Das führt die Kirchenstudie von 1994 »Die Kirche Jesu Christi« dann weiter aus: »Indem Menschen die rechtfertigende Gnade Gottes in Jesus Christus durch den Heiligen Geist empfangen, werden sie zur Gemeinschaft verbunden.«[3] Diese Gemeinschaft orientiert sich an Gottes Wort im biblischen Zeugnis, sie bezeugt und verkündigt das Evangelium und feiert die Sakramente. In der gottesdienstlichen Gemeinschaft kommt also der Grund der Kirchengemeinschaft ebenso zum Ausdruck wie die Vielfalt der Sprachen und Formen, die die Traditionen der evangelischen Kirchen herausgebildet haben. Es ist die versöhnte Vielfalt, die die Einheit der Kirchengemeinschaft kennzeichnet.

---

1 Wilhelm Hüffmeier / Martin Friedrich (Hrsg.), Gemeinschaft gestalten – Evangelisches Profil in Europa, Texte der 6. Vollversammlung der Gemeinschaft Evangelischer Kirchen in Europa – Leuenberger Kirchengemeinschaft – in Budapest, 12. bis 18. September 2006, Frankfurt a. M. 2007, 189.

2 Michael Bünker / Martin Friedrich (Hrsg.), Konkordie reformatorischer Kirchen in Europa (Leuenberger Konkordie), Leipzig 2013.

3 Michael Bünker / Martin Friedrich (Hrsg.), Die Kirche Jesu Christi, Leuenberger Texte 1, Leipzig 2012[4].

Erste gottesdienstliche Projekte der GEKE widmeten sich der Erarbeitung von liturgischem Material für einen »Leuenberg Sonntag« und der Herausgabe von liturgischen Texten, in denen die Vielfalt des evangelischen Gottesdienstes erfahren werden konnte.[4] Im Jahr 2003 wurde ein Liturgiebeauftragter des Rates der GEKE berufen. Diese Aufgabe hat von 2003 bis 2012 Peter Bukowski wahrgenommen. Er widmete sich zwei Projekten: Einmal der Einrichtung eines eigenen Liturgie-Bereiches auf der Website der GEKE und dann der Erarbeitung und Herausgabe eines vielsprachigen Gesangbuches, das unter dem Titel »Colours of Grace« im Jahr 2006 erschienen ist.[5]

Der Gottesdienst als zentraler Arbeitsbereich der GEKE wurde seit der 7. Vollversammlung in Florenz 2012 kontinuierlich verstärkt. Jochen Arnold übernahm die Aufgabe des Liturgiebeauftragten, unterstützt durch Adél Dávid, die in der Geschäftsstelle für den Bereich »Gottesdienst und Liturgie« tätig ist. Konsultationen der Gottesdienstbeauftragten der GEKE-Mitgliedskirchen wurden organisiert. Gottesdienstentwürfe für gemeinsame Feiern mit gesamteuropäischer Ausrichtung z. B. zur Erinnerung an den Ausbruch des Ersten Weltkriegs (August, 2014) sind erarbeitet und umgesetzt worden. Für das Jahr des Reformationsjubiläums 2017 wurden ein Gebetbuch[6] veröffentlicht und ein eigener Reformationslied-Wettbewerb mit beachtlicher Beteiligung[7] durchgeführt. Die Südosteuropa-Regionalgruppe der GEKE hat sich über mehrere Jahre dem Thema »Gottesdienst« gewidmet. Das Ergebnis ihrer Beratungen[8] und ihres Austausches wurde der Vollversammlung in Florenz vorgelegt. Die

---

4 Peter Bukowski/ Susanne Labsch/ Helmut Schwier (Hrsg.), »Wir freuen uns über die Vielfalt der Kirchen …«, Wuppertal/Berlin 2003.

5 Peter Bukowski u. a. (Hrsg.), Colours of Grace, Gesangbuch der Gemeinschaft Evangelischer Kirchen in Europa (GEKE), München 2006.

6 Adél Dávid/ Jochen Arnold (Hrsg.), Fröhlich in dir. Gemeinsam glauben und beten in Europa, Wien 2016.

7 Jochen Arnold (Hrsg.), We hymn you. Lieder für Europa aus dem Reformationslied-Wettbewerb der GEKE, Wien 2017.

8 Michael Bünker/ Michael Martin (Hrsg.), Bleibe in der Zeit. Evangelischer Gottesdienst in Süd-Mittel-Osteuropa zwischen Bewahrung und Veränderung. Eine Studie anhand von Fallbeispielen, erarbeitet von der Regionalgruppe Südosteuropa im Auftrag der GEKE, Wien 2012.

Vollversammlung hat die Studie als einen beispielhaften Beitrag zur liturgischen Arbeit in der GEKE und als gelungene Umsetzung gewürdigt und den Mitgliedskirchen als Anregung zur Weiterarbeit empfohlen.

Der reiche Schatz der unterschiedlichen Liturgien und Gottesdienstformen, wie er in den Kirchen der GEKE gegeben ist, ist noch lange nicht ausgeschöpft. Neu dazu kommen die Herausforderungen, die sich durch die Migration und andere Veränderungen in Kirche und Gesellschaft auch für das gottesdienstliche Leben der evangelischen Kirchen in Europa stellen. Die Treue zum Bewährten und der Mut zu neuen Wegen verbinden sich auf fruchtbare Weise. Der Gottesdienst als permanente Gestaltungsaufgabe dient der Vertiefung der Kirchengemeinschaft, die auch auf diesem Weg selbst immer mehr Kirche wird. Denn die Kirche – so Martin Luther[9] – ist nichts anderes als die Versammlung derer, die ihres Herrn Stimme hören und ihm antworten durch ihr Gebet und ihren Gesang.

Die grundlegende Einsicht der Kirchengemeinschaft als Gottesdienstgemeinschaft, die seit Jahren durchgeführte liturgische Arbeit und die neuen Möglichkeiten und Herausforderungen für das gottesdienstliche Leben der Kirchen haben die Zeit reif werden lassen für einen evangelischen »Europäischen Gottesdienstatlas«. Er vereint den Blick auf die Vielfalt mit den neuen Impulsen, die in den Kirchen entwickelt und erprobt werden. Beides kann zur fruchtbaren Anregung dienen. So danke ich allen, die zu diesem Gottesdienstatlas einen Beitrag beigesteuert haben, vor allem aber Jochen Arnold und Adél Dávid, die federführend das Gesamtprojekt durchgeführt haben. Mit dem Gottesdienstatlas liegt der 8. Vollversammlung der GEKE ein Buch vor, das den gegenwärtigen Stand dokumentiert und zugleich und noch mehr in die Zukunft weist.

---

[9] Martin Luther, Schmalkaldische Artikel III,12 und Predigt zur Einweihung der Schlosskapelle in Torgau vom 5. Oktober 1544.

Michael Bünker

PREFACE

»The CPCE is above all a worshipping community«. This statement in the Presidium's report to the 6th General Assembly of the Community of European Churches in Europe, held in Budapest in 2006,[1] was drawn from central insights of the Leuenberg Agreement and, at the same time, opens a perspective on the future. The Agreement sees the basis of church fellowship in »the common understanding of the Gospel« (LA 6), the true understanding of which has since the Reformation been expressed in the doctrine of justification (LA 8)[2]. The study »The Church of Jesus Christ« (1994) then went further: »In receiving the justifying grace of God in Jesus Christ through the Holy Spirit people are bound together in community.«[3] This community is oriented to God's word in biblical witness, it testifies to and proclaims the gospel and celebrates the sacraments. The worshipping community therefore not only expresses the foundation on which CPCE is built but also the variety of languages and forms that have developed through the traditions of Protestant churches. CPCE's unity is marked by reconciled diversity.

The first CPCE worship projects focused on compiling materials for a »Leuenberg Sunday« and editing liturgical texts manifesting the variety

---

1 WILHELM HÜFFMEIER / MARTIN FRIEDRICH (Hrsg.), Gemeinschaft gestalten – Evangelisches Profil in Europa, Texte der 6. Vollversammlung der Gemeinschaft Evangelischer Kirchen in Europa – Leuenberger Kirchengemeinschaft – in Budapest, 12. bis 18. September 2006, Frankfurt a. M., 2007, 189.

2 MICHAEL BÜNKER / MARTIN FRIEDRICH (eds.), Agreement between Reformation Churches in Europe (Leuenberg Agreement), Leipzig, 2013.

3 MICHAEL BÜNKER / MARTIN FRIEDRICH (eds.), The Church of Jesus Christ, Leuenberger Texte 1, Leipzig, 2012[4].

of Protestant worship.[4] In 2003 the Council appointed a CPCE liturgy advisor. Peter Bukowski took on this office from 2003 to 2012. He invested a lot of energy in two projects: first, establishing a separate area for liturgy on the CPCE website, and then compiling and editing a multilingual hymnbook that appeared in 2006 entitled »Colours of Grace«.[5]

Since the 7th General Assembly in Florence in 2012, worship has continually grown into a central area of CPCE's activity. Jochen Arnold took on the task of liturgy advisor, supported by Adél Dávid, who is responsible in the head office for »Worship and Liturgy«. They organised consultations with the worship convenors of the CPCE member churches. Orders of worship for joint celebrations with an all-European character have been designed and put into practice. We published a prayer book[6] for the 500th anniversary of the Reformation in 2017 and organized our own competition to write Reformation hymns and songs, with a pleasing number of entries.[7] CPCE's Southeast Europe Group has been dedicating itself to the topic of worship for many years. They presented the results of their discussions[8] and exchanges to the General Assembly in Florence. The General Assembly expressed appreciation of the Anchor in Time, calling it an exemplary contribution to liturgical work in the CPCE and a successful accomplishment. It recommended the study to the member churches for further development in their own contexts.

The rich treasure of different liturgies and worship forms present in CPCE churches has yet to be fully explored. Migration and other changes in the church and society now pose new challenges, and also engage the

---

4 PETER BUKOWSKI/SUSANNE LABSCH/HELMUT SCHWIER (eds.), »Wir freuen uns über die Vielfalt der Kirchen ...«, Wuppertal/Berlin, 2003.

5 PETER BUKOWSKI ET AL. (eds.), Colours of Grace, Hymnbook of the Community of Protestant Churches in Europe (CPCE), Munich, 2006.

6 ADÉL DÁVID/JOCHEN ARNOLD (eds.), Fröhlich in dir. Gemeinsam glauben und beten in Europa, Vienna, 2016.

7 JOCHEN ARNOLD (ed.), We hymn you. Lieder für Europa aus dem Reformationslied-Wettbewerb der GEKE, Vienna, 2017.

8 MICHAEL BÜNKER/MICHAEL MARTIN (eds.), Anchor in Time. Protestant Worship in Southern, Central and Eastern Europe between Conservation and Change. A study based on case studies by the Southeast Europe Group on behalf of CPCE, Vienna, 2012.

worship life of Protestant churches in Europe. We are witnessing a fruitful merging of loyalty to tradition and the courage to take new paths. Worship is an ongoing planning exercise that enables us to deepen church communion in the CPCE, which is becoming more and more profound through worship. After all, said Martin Luther,[9] the church is no less than the assembly of those who hear the voice of their Lord and respond to him through their prayers and singing.

The fundamental insight of the CPCE as worship community, the years of liturgical work and the new possibilities and challenges to the worship life of the churches – all this means that the time is ripe for a Protestant »European Atlas of Liturgy«. It focuses our attention on the variety, and the new ideas being developed and tried out in the churches. All this can give fruitful inspiration. My thanks go to everyone who has contributed to this Atlas of Liturgy, above all to Jochen Arnold and Adél Dávid, the facilitators of the whole project. The Atlas of Liturgy presented on the occasion of the 8th CPCE General Assembly maps out the liturgy scene and, even more importantly, will be a guide to the future.

---

[9] Martin Luther, Schmalkaldic Article III, 12 and sermon at the consecration of Torgau castle chapel, 5 October 1544.

Inhalt/Content

II Examples of good practice/Beispiele guter Praxis

Jochen Arnold / Adél Dávid

Einleitung

Zwischen theologischer Identität und liturgischer Vielfalt

Bleibe in der Zeit – mit diesem Titel hat die Südosteuropagruppe der GEKE über die Herausforderungen rund um den Gottesdienst in Mittel- und Osteuropa eine Studie anhand von Fallbeispielen veröffentlicht (2012). Die 7. Vollversammlung in Florenz hat den Wunsch geäußert, auch in anderen Ländern von Europa eine Bestandsaufnahme auf diesem Themengebiet zu machen. Dies ist umso naheliegender, weil die Mitgliedskirchen der GEKE immer wieder zum Ausdruck bringen, dass sie von einer europäischen protestantischen Organisation vor allem Vernetzung und Informationsfluss erwarten. Vieles liegt ja schon bereit, doch das gegenseitige Kennenlernen der Ergebnisse der liturgischen Forschungen und Praxisbeispiele ist oft durch sprachliche Barrieren oder auch durch die Begrenztheit der beruflichen Netzwerke auf das eigene Land erschwert.

Die vorliegende Publikation möchte einen – keineswegs vollständigen – Einblick in die Konzeption und Geschichte, Reflexion und Praxis des Gottesdienstes in einzelnen Mitgliedskirchen geben. Alle Mitgliedskirchen wurden eingeladen, über aktuelle Fragen des gottesdienstlichen Lebens einen Beitrag zu schreiben. Ebenfalls haben wir gebeten, Beispiele guter Praxis, die die Kirchen für sich entdeckt haben, mit der europäischen Leserschaft zu teilen. Wir freuen uns, dass sich mehrere Landeskirchen der EKD, die Schweizer Reformierten, die Lutherische Kirche in Estland, die Dänische Volkskirche, die Waldenserkirche in Italien, die Methodistische Kirche in Deutschland, die Evangelische Kirche A.B. in Österreich, die United Reformed Church sowie die Church of Scotland angesprochen fühlten und Autorinnen und Autoren aus ihrem Kontext vorgeschlagen haben. Den Verfasserinnen und Verfassern der Aufsätze danken wir für ihre engagierte ehrenamtliche Mitarbeit.

Gottesdienst stiftet Identität. Ganz persönlich und auch für die kirchliche Gemeinschaft. Jochen Arnold, Direktor des Michaelisklosters Hildesheim in der Landeskirche Hannovers und Liturgiebeauftragter der GEKE, arbeitet eine Theologie des evangelischen Gottesdienstes im ökumenischen Kontext aus, die sich aus der Gewissheit der Annahme durch Gott (Rechtfertigung) herleitet. Elementar sind für ihn Dialogizität und Verständlichkeit des Gottesdienstes zum einen sowie seine verändernde Kraft zum anderen. Arnold folgt den Spuren Martin Luthers und versteht den Gottesdienst als Zuwendung des liebenden Gottes auf Augenhöhe in Wort, Sakrament, Musik und Segen, der die Antwort des Menschen mit Herzen, Mund und Händen folgt. Arnold spiegelt diese Aussagen an aktuellen Fragestellungen und kulturellen Herausforderungen. Dazu gehört die Suche nach einem gastfreundlichen, möglichst inklusiven Gottesdienst, der viele Menschen erreichen will und deshalb um eine zeitgenössische Gestalt von Sprache und Musik ringt. Wie können wir Christus im Zentrum haben und zugleich auch an den Rändern präsent sein, wie gelingt es nahe bei Gott und nahe bei den Menschen zu sein?

Das Abendmahlverständnis von John Wesley und die Praxis der methodistischen Kirchen haben der GEKE-Gottesdienstkonsultation in Wien 2016 erfrischende Impulse gegeben und werden in der 8. Vollversammlung im Basel auch im Rahmen einer Themengruppe im Mittelpunkt stehen. Holger Eschmann, Praktischer Theologe an der theologischen Hochschule der EmK in Reutlingen, beschreibt Grundlinien einer methodistischen Theologie des Gottesdienstes, indem er zunächst die hochkirchlichen, freikirchlichen und spezifisch südwestdeutschen Wurzeln seiner Kirche benennt. Ganz im Sinne Wesleys legt sie Wert darauf, dass das Abendmahl häufig gefeiert wird und für alle, auch für Ungetaufte, offen ist (open table). »Eingeladen ist, wer nach der Gnade Gottes sucht«. Im Blick auf die anstehende (deutsche) Gottesdienstreform akzentuiert Eschmann u. a. die aktive Beteiligung der Gemeinde, die gesellschaftliche Relevanz des Gottesdienstes und seine Öffnung für verschiedene Lebens- und Frömmigkeitsstile. Theologische Elementarisierung und sinnliche Vertiefung sind das Gebot der Stunde. Die Grundstruktur des Gottesdienstes soll den vierfachen Schritt von Ankommen – Hören – Teilen – Weitergehen abbilden.

Qualität im Gottesdienst – dieses Thema war lange Zeit ein Tabu unter Theologen, weil es zu sehr an die ökonomische Welt gebunden schien. Folkert Fendler, langjähriger Leiter des EKD-Zentrums für Qualitätsentwicklung im Gottesdienst, setzt sich dagegen dezidiert theologisch ein und bestimmt den Gottesdienst als göttliche Gabe und menschliche Aufgabe. Im Blick auf den Qualitätsbegriff unterscheidet er einen umgangssprachlichen, ökonomischen und philosophischen Zugang. Das sogenannte 3-G-Modell akzentuiert drei theologische Leitmotive für die Gottesdienstgestaltung und -wahrnehmung: **G**eheimnis, **G**ewissheit bzw. **G**emeinschaft. Das Modell der »vier Wirkfelder« betrachtet das gottesdienstliche Ereignis als »selbstwirksam« unter den Aspekten existenzielle Erfahrung, Sinndeutung, Handlungsorientierung und Beziehung. Fendler nimmt aber auch Einsichten aus dem Qualitätsmanagement auf. Dazu gehört u.a. das sogenannte Kano-Modell mit der gestuften Trias von Grundanforderungen, Leistungserwartungen und Begeisterungsfaktoren.

Olivier Favrod stellt die liturgische Tradition und eine Situationsanalyse der französischsprachigen Schweiz (Kanton Vaud) vor. Die Gemeinden sehen sich vor der Herausforderung, Formen des Gottesdienstes auszudifferenzieren und zu erneuern. Dies beginnt mit einer Anfrage an die eigene Haltung zum Gottesdienst und die Entwicklung einer neuen Einladungskultur. Dazu gehört eine genauere Wahrnehmung der Adressaten und eine bessere Öffentlichkeitsarbeit sowie eine Ausdifferenzierung der sprachlichen Mittel, auch gestisch und symbolisch. Die Musikstile sind einer Prüfung zu unterziehen, generationenübergreifende Angebote erscheinen ebenso wichtig wie eine höhere Beteiligung der Gemeinde in der Vorbereitung und Durchführung.

Monika Hautzinger und Ulrike Beichert, Gottesdienstberaterinnen in Baden, zeigen uns, wie die Badische Landeskirche in Zeiten geringer werdender Ressourcen ihr gottesdienstliches Leben an die neue Situation anzupassen sucht. Durch ein regionales Konzept und örtliche Schwerpunktsetzungen entstehen neue Gottesdienstangebote an anderen Orten, zu anderen Zeiten und mit neuen Formaten. Wichtige Einsichten des Veränderungsprozesses sind u.a., dass ein regionales Gottesdienstkonzept kein Zufall ist, sondern von den Verantwortlichen gewollt sein muss. Dann eröffnen sich Möglichkeiten, die Adressaten besser in den Blick zu nehmen und sie auch selbst an den Veränderungsprozessen zu beteiligen: »aus Betroffenen Beteiligte machen«.

Ob Besucher den Gottesdienst als gut erleben, hängt wesentlich an der Musik und den Liedern. Stephan Goldschmidt, langjähriger Referent für Gottesdienst in der EKD und Geschäftsführer der Liturgischen Konferenz, beschreibt aktuelle empirische Untersuchungen und fordert, das bestehende Repertoire durch neue Lieder, anknüpfend an die Hörgewohnheiten der Menschen, zu erweitern. Seine Erfahrungen kommen aus der Arbeit am Gesangbuch freiTöne, das anlässlich des Kirchentags 2017 in Berlin/Wittenberg erschienen ist. Qualitätskriterien sind für ihn u.a. die Aspekte Innovation und Singbarkeit. Eine bessere Vermittlung der neuen Lieder im Gottesdienst, gestützt durch didaktische Hilfen und moderne Begleitsätze, stehen ebenso auf seiner »Wunschliste« wie eine Digitalisierung des Materials und die Öffnung des Repertoires für internationale Lieder.

Zweifellos ist es eine der größten aktuellen Herausforderungen in Europa, dass Menschen – sei es freiwillig oder weil sie vertrieben wurden – nicht ihr ganzes Leben in dem Land verbringen, wo sie geboren wurden. In der neuen kulturellen und sprachlichen Umgebung eine spirituelle Gemeinschaft zu finden geht leichter, wenn Gottesdienste offen, interkulturell und mehrsprachig gefeiert werden. William Jourdan, Pastor der Waldenserkirche, diskutiert Chancen und Herausforderungen mehrsprachiger Gottesdienste am Beispiel einer Gemeinde in Norditalien, die sich hauptsächlich aus Italienern und ghanaischen Migranten zusammensetzt. Wie konnte es gelingen, dass Menschen die mit der Muttersprache verbundenen Wurzeln ihres Glaubens bewahren und zugleich neue Wurzeln schlagen? Die theologische Kunst besteht für ihn darin, einen integrativen Mittelweg zu finden. So gewann die Darbringung der Gaben mit fröhlichem Tanz als Ausdruck der Dankbarkeit vor Gott eine neue Bedeutung für die Italiener. Außerdem gelang eine alle ansprechende Durchmischung der Musik durch die Erweiterung des Repertoires mit afrikanischen Liedern und durch gute englische Übersetzungen zu italienischen Melodien.

Katrin Kusmierz, Theologin am Kompetenzzentrum für Liturgik der Universität Bern, stellt die Entwicklung der Abendmahlsfeier in der deutschsprachigen Schweiz aus den letzten ca. 100 Jahren vor. Zu Beginn des 20. Jh. bestand der Abendmahlsteil aus Ermahnung, Beichte, Vergebungszusage, Einsetzungsworte, Gebet, Kommunion und Dankgebet. Diese typisch »oberdeutsche« Variante hat sich dann ausdifferenziert; 1983 finden sich 14 verschiedene Formen in Gebrauch. Ziel des 1998 erschienenen Gesangbuchs und der Liturgie-Kommission war es, einen gemeinsamen Rahmen zu schaffen und zugleich viel Freiheit zur Gestaltung zu ermöglichen. Insgesamt wurde ein Fünf-Schritte-Modell eingeführt (Sammlung – Anbetung – Verkündigung – Fürbitte – Segen), in das die Eucharistie hier und dann zu integrieren ist. Im Gegensatz zu 1911 steht das Sündenbekenntnis am Beginn des Gottesdienstes. Die Abendmahlsliturgie selbst akzentuiert die narrativen und doxologischen Teile stärker, um den »Staub der ständigen Ermahnung und Moralisierung« wegzuwischen. Außerdem soll die Mahlfeier im sonntäglichen Gottesdienst integriert und nicht mehr im Anschluss gefeiert werden. Die Herrenworte heißen nicht mehr Worte der Einsetzung, sondern Abendmahlsbericht. Damit wird ihr narrativer Charakter ebenso betont wie die Überzeugung, dass diese Worte selbst nicht etwas automatisch bewirken. Aktuelle Überlegungen gehen in Richtung einer Öffnung hin zum eucharistischen Typ der Messe und einer stärkeren Einbettung des Vaterunsers in die Abendmahlsfeier. Insgesamt begrüßt Kusmierz die Entwicklung, weil die Schweizer Abendmahlsliturgie durchlässig ist für unterschiedliche theologische Gewichtungen und dafür offen, aktuelle Kontexte bzw. musikalisch-stilistische Gestaltungen aufzunehmen.

Phill Mellstrom, zuständig für Gottesdienstentwicklung in der Church of Scotland, stellt das Konzept »Partizipativer Gottesdienst« vor. Partizipation ist konstituierender Bestandteil des evangelischen Gottesdienstverständnisses, also keine Option, die man entweder wählen oder auf die man verzichten kann. Die aktive Beteiligung der Gemeinde (vgl. auch das II. Vat. Konzil mit dem Ausdruck *participatio actuosa*) hat in Schottland mehrere Gottesdienstformen ins Leben gerufen – für Erwachsene ebenso wie für Kinder. Wesentlichen Anteil haben dabei der Dialog mit den Künsten und eine zeitgenössische Kirchenmusik. Lieder sollen mit dem Alltag verbunden sein und die Nöte der Menschen zur Geltung bringen. Sie sollen so angeleitet sein, dass aktive Partizipation möglich wird. Im Aufsatz stellt der Autor auch Projekte und Modelle seiner Kollegen dar: Peter Johnston, Darren Phillip, Jo Love, Michelle Browns und Pam Mellstrom. In allem zielt dieser Ansatz auf die vitale wechselseitige Befruchtung von Gottesdienst und Spiritualität, von Sonntag und Alltag.

Die United Reformed Church ist eine Kirche in Großbritannien, die sich aus unterschiedlichen Kirchen zusammensetzt. Sam Richards and Simon Peters stellen vor, wie diese Kirche gleichzeitig Vielfalt schätzt und ein gemeinsames Ziel vor sich hat: In der Nachfolge Jesu stehen und auch andere dazu einladen. Das geschieht in einem komplexen Lebenszusammenhang der Kirche, wo Gottesdienst nicht die einzige Komponente ist, aber eine wichtige Rolle spielt. Dabei sind alle Generationen gleich wichtig, und zwar nicht nur im Nebeneinander, sondern auch im Miteinander.

Am Ende des ersten Teils stehen zwei Aufsätze aus zwei Minderheitenkirchen. Kaido Soom, Lehrer für praktische Theologie an der Universität Tartu präsentiert die Geschichte des estnischen lutherischen Gottesdienstes und seiner Agenden von der Reformationszeit bis in die Gegenwart. Darin werden theologische Weichenstellungen und politische Kontexte in gleicher Weise deutlich. Schlüsselfigur der Reformation war Johann Briesmann, der in seiner Gottesdienst-Ordnung, basierend auf dem Messformular, weite Teile auf Deutsch und Latein vorsah. Weitere Stationen waren die am schwedischen Handbuch angelehnte Liturgie von 1699 und eine Agende von 1834, die u. a. Spuren der Rezeption der Preußischen Agende zeigt (z. B. Kyrie – Absolution – Gloria). Nach der Unabhängigkeit von Estland 1991 arbeitete man bis 2007 an einem neuen Handbuch in guter Kooperation mit den Nachbarn aus Finnland. Allerdings fand das neue Gottesdienstbuch keine Zwei-Drittel-Mehrheit unter den Ordinierten. So kam es 2009 zu dem Kompromissvorschlag, dass zwei Agenden gleichzeitig benutzt werden könnten, eine ältere von 1951 (Uppsala) und die neue. Sie enthält vier Teile auf 1700 Seiten: handbook of services, handbook of readings, handbook of ceremonies, und handbook of blessings and consecration. Dabei können einzelne Teile bausteinartig ausgetauscht werden. Die Vielfalt scheint inzwischen gut anzukommen.

Hannelore Reiner, geistliche Oberkirchenrätin i. R. der Evangelischen Kirche A.B. in Österreich, schreibt darüber, wie die Österreichische Kirchengeschichte, eine Geschichte der Verfolgungen und Geheimprotestantismus, im Kirchenbau und in der Liturgie ihre Spuren hinterlassen hat. Eine aufregende Spurensuche in der Diaspora mit zahlreichen interessanten Einblicken. Dazu gehört u. a., dass schon im 17. Jahrhundert nichtordinierte Männer und Frauen Hausandachten hielten und sich für die Weitergabe des Glaubens in protestantischer Tradition bis heute verantwortlich fühlen. Ein weiterer Faktor für die Genese österreichischer Liturgie ist die Verschmelzung mit schlesischen, bayerischen und württembergischen Traditionen, die sich durch den »Import« der Geistlichen aus den benachbarten Ländern erklärt. Dazu gehört auch ein an das bayerische angelehnte Gesangbuch von J.E.Koch (1856). Nach dem 2.Weltkrieg wuchs die österreichische Kirche durch die Flüchtlingsbewegungen stark an. Auch hier kam es wieder zu einer spirituellen Durchmischung, zu einer Übernahme katholischer Kirchenbauten durch ev. Gemeinden und zu echten Neugründungen. Die »alte Widerstandskraft« der österreichischen Protestanten drückt sich darin besonders aus.

Die Gottesdienstlandschaft in Europa ist unglaublich reich. Der zweite Teil des vorliegenden Gottesdienstatlas will ein Stück dieses Reichtums an ausgewählten Beispielen der guten Praxis aufzeigen. Schon längst ist es eine Selbstverständlichkeit, bei der Gestaltung der einzelnen Gottesdienste aber auch bei konzeptuellen Entscheidungen über das Gesamtangebot einer Kirchengemeinde und einer Region auf den eigenen Kontext zu achten. So entstehen über den gewöhnlichen Sonntagsgottesdienst um 10 hinaus Modelle, die auch Menschen erreichen wollen, die sich eine Gemeinschaft und einen Ort der Begegnung mit Gott wünschen, sich aber im konventionellen Gottesdienst nicht zu Hause fühlen.

In Kopenhagen hat die Domkirche auch denen etwas zu bieten, die am Wochenende in der Nacht unterwegs sind. Signe Malene Berg, dänische Pastorin, stellt das Konzept Churchnight vor. Hier treffen sich Theologie und Kunst, Traditionelles und Zeitgenössisches. Menschen sind eingeladen, im Kirchenraum zu verweilen und sich mit dem Evangelium auseinanderzusetzen – mitten in der Nacht, unterwegs zu einer Party oder in eine Bar, und zwar in der Begegnung mit zeitgenössischen Kunstwerken und Musik. Von biblischen Sätzen inspirierte Installationen stehen in der Kirche und laden zur Reflexion ein. Gebete und meditative Texte, die die Besucher der Churchnight geschrieben haben, sind in einem eigenen Buch publiziert worden.

Das 350-jährige Jubiläum der Kirchweihe hat eine Gemeinde in Stollberg, Deutschland inspiriert, den Kirchenraum in ungewohnter Weise mit Leben zu erfüllen. Ein Geburtstagsfest mit Torte, Geschenk, Festrede und Tanz. Und doch wurde hier gleichzeitig ein Gottesdienst gefeiert. Darüber berichtet Pfarrerin Christiane Dohrn.

Pfarrer Gunnar Garleff zeigt gelungene Beispiele aus der Heidelberger Friedenskirche, wie der Kirchenraum nicht nur als Kulisse, sondern auch als Komponente der Gottesdienstplanung und -feier wirksam sein kann. Hier spielen außerbiblische Texte und Lebenswirklichkeit der Gottesdienstbesucher eine wichtige Rolle, sodass Profanes und Sakrales, Kirche und Welt, ganz im reformatorischen Sinne eine Einheit bilden.

Im überwiegend katholischen Österreich steht die evangelische Kirche A.B. (lutherisch) vor der Herausforderung, Kindern der 2. Schulstufe – also wenn die katholischen Kinder Firmung feiern – ein vergleichbares und doch typisch evangelisches Ritual anzubieten. Das Geheimnisfest ist eine Initiative, die Pfarrerin Margit Geley in Salzburg ins Leben gerufen hat. Kinder bekommen die Möglichkeit, sich den Geheimnissen des Glaubens gemeinsam anzunähern, sie zu entdecken. Das geschieht durch Gespräche wie durch Rituale im Rahmen aber auch außerhalb des Gottesdienstes. Der Lernprozess dauert ein ganzes Schuljahr und wird mit einer Segenshandlung abgeschlossen.

Eine Initiative der badischen Kirche hat das Ziel, wieder mehr Bewusstsein für das Glockenläuten zu schaffen. Martin Kares stellt die einschlägigen, von ihm verfassten Broschüren vor, in denen u. a. auch Anleitungen zum Gebet im Einklang mit den Glocken Platz finden. Das Projekt hat auch einen digitalen Teilbereich: Jugendliche sammeln Glockengeläut in ganz Deutschland und speichern die Tonaufnahmen in einer digitalen Datenbank. So kann eine alte Tradition auch die junge Generation erreichen, neu bewegen und begeistern.

Ebenfalls eine alte Tradition wird im zweiten Beitrag von Holger Eschmann vorgestellt. Die Feier zur Erneuerung des Bundes mit Gott ist eine Liturgie, die auf John Wesley (1747 bzw. 1755) zurückzuführen ist und seitdem fast unverändert in methodistischen Gemeinden gefeiert wird, z. B. beim Jahreswechsel. Er ist notwendigerweise mit einer Abendmahlsfeier verbunden. Einzelne Bausteine lassen sich auch auf andere Gottesdienste übertragen.

Ein gelungenes Beispiel des ökumenischen Zusammenspiels zeigt uns der Aufsatz von Duncan McLaren und Susan Mansfield aus Schottland. Refugio, eine kontemplative Abendmahlfeier, ist bestimmt von der ignatianischen Spiritualität und der protestantischen Abendmahlspraxis. Hinter diesem Format steht der Gedanke, dass das Abendmahl nicht das Eigentum einzelner Denominationen ist, sondern ein gemeinsames Gut der ganzen Kirche.

Das Buch wird mit drei guten Beispielen aus dem Schweizerischen Evangelischen Kirchenbund abgeschlossen. Susanna Meyer, theologische Mitarbeiterin im Kanton Bern-Jura-Solothurn, stellt ein Gottesdienstmodell aus Bern vor, das vom Stationenweg der Thomasmesse inspiriert worden ist und speziell die Altersgruppe der 40–60-Jährigen anspricht.

Der von Lisbeth Zogg Hohn beschriebene Gottesdienst setzt sich zweifach mit dem Thema Generationen auseinander. Die Liturgie ist bewusst so konzipert, dass sich Jung und Alt angesprochen fühlen kann und noch mehr: Alle Altersgruppen bekommen im Verkündigungsteil auch eine Stimme. Die Erzählung, der neben dem biblischen Text eine große Rolle zukommt, stammt aus einem Kinderbuch und thematisiert die gemeinsame Suche von zwei Generationen nach Licht und Freude. In einer Zeit, in der Kirche oft die Differenzierung des Angebots anstrebt, ist dieser Beitrag ein gelungenes Beispiel dafür, dass ein generationsübergreifender Gottesdienst doch möglich ist.

Der letzte Gottesdienst bietet einen Einblick in die Gottesdienstkonsultation der GEKE in 2016 in Wien. Hier haben die Teilnehmenden miteinander die Emmaus-Liturgie aus der Schweiz gefeiert. Dieses Gottesdienstmodell zeigt, dass neben den Einsetzungsworten auch andere Geschichten der Tischgemeinschaft für eine Abendmahlfeier inspirierend sein können. Auch bei diesem Gottesdienst war der Kirchenraum eine wichtige Komponente des Geschehens: Krypta, Kirchenschiff und Altartisch waren Stationen der Wanderung der Gottesdienstbesucher, die symbolisch wie die Emmaus-Jünger mit Jesus unterwegs waren.

Zum Schluss ist noch die Frage der Sprachen dieser Publikation zu erwähnen. Im ersten, eher theoretischen Teil des Buches haben wir uns dafür entschieden, die Texte nur auf Englisch abzudrucken, in der *lingua franca* unserer Zeit. So sind die Texte teilweise Übersetzungen aus dem Französischen, Estnischen oder Deutschen. Im zweiten Teil mit den Praxisbeispielen schien es uns wichtig, die Originalsprache der Beiträge beizubehalten. Falls sie nicht Englisch war, haben wir noch eine englische Übersetzung daneben gestellt. Eine Übersetzung ist auch immer ein Risiko, dass etwas wichtiges verloren geht – bei Texten von Gottesdiensten, die oft dichterisch und emotional sehr aufgeladen sind, ist es vielleicht noch mehr so. Einige Modelle arbeiten mit Texten aus der Belletristik oder Publizistik, Teile der Liturgie sind fast schon moderne Kunstwerke. Diese waren besonders herausfordernd. An dieser Stelle sei den Übersetzerinnen Dorothea Beck, Elaine Griffiths, Rosemary Selle und Julia Teschner herzlich gedankt! Eine weitere Herausforderung bei den Übersetzungen waren die Lieder in den Gottesdiestmodellen. Es nützt nicht viel, die Titel der Lieder ins Englische zu übersetzen. So haben wir in den Übersetzungen nur den Hinweis stehen lassen, dass an dieser oder jener Stelle ein Lied gesungen wird. Bei der Übernahme und Umsetzung der Ideen im eigenen Kontext – was die Herausgeber erfreuen würde – können und sollen die Leser im Liedschatz der eigenen Kirche und Sprache ein passendes Lied finden.

Wir wünschen eine gute Reise durch die europäische Gottesdienstlandschaft, viel Freude beim Entdecken von verborgenen und manchmal überraschenden Schätzen. Wie jede Reise soll auch diese nach dem Ankommen zu Hause neue Inspiration und Motivation in den Alltag bringen.

Jochen Arnold / Adél Dávid

Introduction

Between Theological Identity and Liturgical Diversity

Anchor in Time is a study presented in 2012 by CPCE's Southeast Europe group on worship-related challenges in Central and Eastern Europe, on the basis of case studies. The 7th General Assembly in Florence expressed the wish to take stock of the general situation in this field. This is understandable as the CPCE member churches often say that they primarily expect access to networks and a flow of information from a European Protestant organisation. A great deal of material is already available, yet it is often hard to get to know the results of liturgical research and practical examples due to language barriers or because relevant professional associations are limited to our own country.

The present publication aims to give a – by no means complete – insight into the conception and history of worship in individual member churches, into their thinking in this regard and also the way they hold services. All member churches were invited to write an article on current issues in worship life. We likewise asked them to share examples of good practice with a European readership. It was very pleasing to receive responses from several EKD member churches, the Swiss Reformed, the Estonian Evangelical Lutheran Church, the Evangelical Lutheran Church of Denmark, the Waldensian Church in Italy, the Methodist Church in Germany, the Evangelical Church of the Austrian Confession, the United Reformed Church and the Church of Scotland. They suggested authors from their church context, to whom we are very grateful for their articles and honorary cooperation.

Worship creates identity. Quite personally and also for ecclesial communion. Jochen Arnold, CPCE liturgy convenor, is director of the Centre for Worship and Music at the Michaelískloster Hildesheim, which belongs to the Evangelical Lutheran Church of Hanover. He is working on a theology of the Protestant worship service in an ecumenical context, a theology based on the certainty of acceptance by God (justification). For him, a service must, on the one hand, be dialogical and comprehensible and, on the other, have transforming power. Following the traces left by Martin Luther, Arnold understands worship as what happens when a loving God turns to the congregation in word, sacrament, music and blessing, to which people respond with hearts, mouth and hands. Arnold reflects on these statements with the aid of current issues and cultural challenges. That includes the search for a hospitable, inclusive service, which seeks to reach many people and so struggles to find a contemporary form of language and music. How can we put Christ in the centre and at the same time be present at the margins? How can we manage to be close to God and close to people?

John Wesley's understanding of Holy Communion and the practice of the Methodist Churches were a breath of fresh air at the CPCE Liturgy Consultation in Vienna in 2016 and will be the topic of a theme group at the 8th General Assembly in Basel. Holger Eschmann, a practical theologian at the Methodist School of Theology in Reutlingen, describes basic lines of a Methodist theology of worship by first naming the high-church, free-church and specific southwest German roots of his church. In the spirit of Wesley it attaches importance to frequent celebrations of communion and an open table for all, including those who have not been baptised. »Anyone seeking God's grace is invited.« With respect to the upcoming service reform, Eschmann particularly underlines the active participation of the congregation, the social relevance of the worship service and its opening to different styles of life and piety. The important thing is to focus on clear theological elements and deepen sensory awareness. The basic structure of the service is to be the four steps of Gathering – Listening – Sharing – Going Forth.

Quality in worship – this topic was long a taboo among theologians, because it seemed too closely linked to the world of business. Folkert Fendler, the long-time director of the EKD Center for Quality Development in Worship Services, takes decided issue with this on theological grounds, defining worship as a divine gift and a human task. Regarding the concept of quality he distinguishes a colloquial, economic and philosophical approach. The 3-C model accentuates three theological leitmotifs for worship planning and experience: **C**ertainty of hope, **C**ommunity of love and **C**elebration of mystery. The model of the »four effects« regards the worship event as happening from the angles of interpreting meaning, orienting action, experiencing profound emotions and experiencing relations. Fendler also takes up insights from quality management. They include the Kano Model with the triple process of basic expectations, expectations regarding performance and enthusiasm factors.

Olivier Favrod presents the liturgical tradition and a situation analysis of French-speaking Switzerland (Canton Vaud). The parishes are faced with the challenge of differentiating and renewing their forms of worship. This process starts with a question to a person's own attitude to worship and the development of a new culture of invitation. That includes a closer observation of the group of persons to be reached and better public relations, along with a variety of language, gestures and symbols. Styles of music must be examined and cross-generational offerings seem important, not to mention a high involvement of the congregation in planning and conducting the services.

Monika Hautzinger and Ulrike Beichert, both worship advisors in the Protestant Church in Baden, show us how this church is trying to adapt its worship life to the new situation in times of dwindling resources. Through a regional approach and local priorities, new worship offerings are arising in other places, at different times and with new formats. Important insights in the process of change include the fact that a regional approach to planning worship services is no accident – those responsible have to embrace it. Then it will offer opportunities to better focus on the worshippers and involve them in the change process »so that they can move from a more passive role to become agents of change«.

Whether church-goers think it is a good service will depend to a great extent on the music and hymns. Stephan Goldschmidt, long-standing EKD spokesperson on worship and executive secretary of the Liturgy Conference, describes current empirical studies, urging that the existing repertoire be extended by new songs familiar to people's listening habits. His experience comes from work on the song book freiTöne, which was published for the 2017 Kirchentag in Berlin/Wittenberg. Quality criteria, in his view, include the aspects of innovation and singability. His wish list includes better presentation of new songs in services, supported by teaching aids and modern accompaniments. In addition, he argues for more digitised material and for opening the repertoire up to international songs and hymns.

It is doubtless one of the greatest current challenges in Europe that people – whether they left of their own free will or were displaced – do not spend their whole life in the country where they were born. Finding a spiritual community in the new cultural and linguistic surroundings is easier when services are open, intercultural and multilingual. William Jourdan, a young pastor of the Waldensian Church, discusses opportunities and challenges of multilingual services on the example of a church in Northern Italy that is mainly made up of Italians and migrants from Ghana. How was it possible for people to preserve the roots of their faith linked to their mother tongue and, at the same time, to put down new roots? In his view, the theological art is to find an integrative middle way. Bringing gifts as an expression of gratitude to God gained new importance for the Italians when this was accompanied by joyful dancing. Furthermore, church members managed to mix elements of music and words to please everyone, expanding the standard repertoire with African songs or with good English translations sung to Italian tunes.

Katrin Kusmierz, theologian at the competence centre for liturgy at Bern University, presents the development of Holy Communion in German-speaking Switzerland over the last approx. 100 years. At the beginning of the 20th century the communion part consisted of exhortation, confession, the promise of forgiveness, the words of institution, prayer, communion and thanksgiving. This typically »upper German« variant then began to vary; 1983 saw 14 different forms in use. The aim of the Liturgy Commission with the hymn book that appeared in 1998 was to create a common framework and at the same time enable scope for free choice. A five-step model was introduced (gathering – worship – proclamation – intercessions – blessing), into which the Eucharist is to be occasionally integrated. By contrast to 1911, the confession of sins is at the beginning of the service. The communion liturgy itself gives greater emphasis to the narrative and doxological parts in order to free the liturgy of the »dust of admonition and moralizing«. Furthermore the communion is to be integrated into Sunday services and no longer celebrated afterwards. The Lord's words are no longer called the words of institution but »the account of the Lord's Supper«. That underlines its narrative character as well as the belief that these words themselves do not automatically cause anything to happen. Current thinking is moving towards a eucharistic form and a greater focus on the Lord's Prayer in the Lord's Supper. Kusmierz welcomes this development because the Swiss communion liturgy is permeable to different theological emphases and thus open to taking in current contexts or musical styles.

Phill Mellstrom, responsible for worship development in the Church of Scotland, presents the concept of »participatory service«. Participation is – derived from *leiturgia*, the Greek word for service – a constituent part of a service, not an option to take in or leave out. The active participation of the congregation (see also the Second Vatican Council with the expression *participatio actuosa*) has called forth several forms of service in Scotland – for adults and also for children. A lot of space is given to dialogue with the arts and contemporary church music. Hymns are meant to be linked to daily life and to bring out people's needs. Services should be patterned to enable active participation. The author includes descriptions of colleagues who were responsible for individual projects and models: Peter Johnston, Darren Phillip, Jo Love, Michelle Browns and Pam Mellstrom. All in all, this approach aims for a lively cross-fertilisation of worship and spirituality, of Sunday and every day.

The United Reformed Church is one of several churches stemming from different traditions in the United Kingdom. Sam Richards and Simon Peters explain how it values diversity at the same time as focusing on the common aim of following Jesus and inviting others to do the same. This takes place in a complex web of life circumstances within the church, where celebrating worship is not the sole aspect but plays a significant role. All generations are equally important, as they live alongside and engage with one another in this both multigenerational and intergenerational community.

The first part concludes with two essays from two minority churches. Kaido Soom, who teaches practical theology at Tartu University, presents the history of the Estonian Lutheran service and its books of worship from Reformation times to the present day. They illustrate changes of theological direction and political contexts in an equal manner. A key Reformer was Johann Briesmann, who used extensive passages in German and Latin in his order of service, basing it on the mass. Other milestones were the liturgy analogous to the Swedish handbook of 1699 and a book of services from 1834, which shows traces of the reception of the Prussian book of services (e. g. Kyrie – Absolution – Gloria). After Estonia regained its independence in 1991 liturgists worked until 2007 on a new handbook in good cooperation with the neighbours from Finland. However, the new service book did not receive a two-thirds majority among the ordained ministers. In 2009 they reached a compromise that two books of services should be used at the same time, an older one from 1951 (Uppsala) and the new one. It consists of four parts on 1700 pages: a handbook of services, handbook of readings, handbook of ceremonies, and handbook of blessings and consecration. Individual parts can be moved around like building blocks. The variety seems to have been well received by congregations.

Hannelore Reiner, a retired senior church official responsible for worship in the Evangelical Church of the Augsburg Confession in Austria, writes on how Austrian church history, marked by persecutions and crypto-Protestantism, left its traces in church buildings and the liturgy. This gives rise to an exciting search for clues in the diaspora with many interesting insights. They include the fact that, as early as in the 17th century, non-ordained men and women led house devotions and that lay people feel responsible for handing on the faith in Protestant tradition to this day. A further factor for the genesis of Austrian liturgy is the merging of Silesian, Bavarian and Württemberg traditions, which can be explained by the »importing« of clergy from neighbouring countries. A Bavarian-style hymnbook was likewise imported by J. E. Koch (1856). After the Second World War, the Austrian church expanded greatly through the inflow of refugees. Here too there was a spiritual mix, with Protestant congregations taking over Catholic buildings and founding new congregations. This particularly expresses the »old power of resistance« of the Austrian Protestants.

The worship landscape in Europe is incredibly rich and varied. The second part of our Atlas seeks to express part of this wealth through selected examples of good practice. It has long been normal to pay attention to one's own context not only in devising the individual services but also in the conceptual decisions about the whole worship programme of a parish and a region. Consequently, going beyond the usual Sunday service at 10am, we are seeing the emergence of models that try to reach people who wish for a place to encounter God but do not feel at home in a conventional service.

In Copenhagen the cathedral church has something to offer those who are around at night over the weekend. Signe Malene Berg, a Danish pastor, presents the »Churchnight« idea. Here theology meets art, the traditional meets the contemporary. People are invited to stay a while in the church and engage with the gospel – in the middle of the night, on the way to a party or a bar with the aid of contemporary art and music. Installations inspired by biblical phrases stand in the church and invite the viewer to reflect on them. Prayers and meditative texts written by the visitors to the Night Church have been published in a book.

The 350th anniversary of the church's consecration inspired a parish in Stollberg, Germany, to fill the church with life in an unusual way. It held a birthday party with cake, gifts, speeches and dancing – that was a worship service at the same time. Christiane Dohrn reports on this.

Gunnar Garleff shows successful examples from the Friedenskirche (peace church) in Heidelberg, of how the church space can be not a setting but a substantive component of worship planning and celebration. Non-biblical texts and the life reality of the worshippers play an important role here too, so that everyday life and the sacred form a unity in a completely Reformation tradition.

In mainly Catholic Austria, the Evangelical Church of the Augsburg Confession faces the challenge of offering children in secondary school – i. e. when Catholic children are confirmed – a comparable and yet typically Protestant ritual. The Mystery Celebration is an initiative of Margit Geley in Salzburg. Children have the opportunity to come closer to the mysteries of faith and to discover them. That happens through talks and rituals during, and outside, the service. The learning process takes a whole school year and is concluded with an act of blessing.

An initiative of the Protestant Church in Vaden has the aim of creating more awareness for bell-ringing. Martin Kares presents a brochure he has compiled with information and guidance on prayer in harmony with the bells. The project also has a digital part, with young people collecting bell sounds all over Germany and saving their recordings in a digital database. That way an old tradition can also reach and move the younger generation.

Another old tradition is presented in the second contribution by Holger Eschmann. The service of renewal of the Covenant with God is a liturgy that goes back to John Wesley and is still conducted almost unchanged in Methodist churches.

The essay by Duncan McLaren and Susan Mansfield illustrates a successful example of ecumenical interaction in Scotland. Refugio is a contemplative form of the Lord's Supper, characterised by Ignatian spirituality and the Protestant practice of this sacrament. The format is based on the premise that the Lord's Supper is not the property of individual denominations, but rather a common asset of the whole Church.

The book concludes with three good practices from the Federation of Swiss Protestant Churches. Susanna Meyer, a theological co-worker in Canton Bern-Jura-Solothurn, presents a service model from Bern that was inspired by the stations of the Thomas Mass and is especially attractive to the 40 to 60 age group.

The service described by Lisbeth Zogg Hohn engages twice with the topic of generations. The liturgy is deliberately designed to appeal to young and old, and all age groups can speak up in the proclamation part. Telling a story plays a major role besides the biblical text. It stems from a children's book and takes up the common quest of two generations for light and joy. In an age in which the church often strives to differentiate its offerings, this article is a successful example of an inter-generational service.

The final service offers an insight into the CPCE Liturgy Consultation in Vienna in 2016. Here the participants took part in the Emmaus liturgy from Switzerland. This service model shows that besides the words of institution, other forms of table fellowship can be inspiring when designing a celebration of Holy Communion. At this service, too, the church space was an important component of the event: the worshippers wandered around the crypt, nave and altar table, symbolising the disciples' walk to Emmaus with Jesus.

Finally, we must mention the question of the languages used in this publication. In the first, more theoretical part of the book we opted to print the texts only in English, the lingua franca of our time. Accordingly some of the articles have been translated from Estonian, French or German. In the second part with the good practice examples, it seemed important to keep the original language of the contributions, and if it was not English, we supplied an English translation next to it. A translation always involves the risk of losing important connotations – perhaps all the more so with worship texts that are often poetic and emotional. Some of the models operate with texts from literature or newspapers, and parts of the liturgy are almost modern works of art. Many thanks to the translators Dorothea Beck, Elaine Griffiths, Rosemary Selle and Julia Teschner! Another problem for translation was the hymns in the model services. There is not much point in translating the names of hymns into English. So we decided to just leave the information that a hymn was sung at this or that point. When adopting and adapting the ideas in their own context – and this would delight the editors – the readers can, and should, find a suitable hymn from their own church tradition and in their own language.

We wish you a good trip through the European worship landscape, and hope you enjoy discovering hidden and sometimes surprising treasures. As with any journey, this one is also meant to provide new inspiration and motivation in your daily life on returning home.

I
Fundamental reflexions/ Grundsätzliche Überlegungen

Jochen Arnold

Protestant Identity Today

Reflections on an evangelical Lutheran theology of worship in an ecumenical context

In times when the way to church on a Sunday for worship and sermon seems no longer plausible in many places, there are some theological questions that need to be asked again. What makes church church? What gives our life stability and security? This contribution begins with a personal approach and deals with the issue of evangelical identity formation in worship services. Based on this, I will then develop baselines of an ecumenical and specifically Lutheran theology of service for the current discussion.

1. What is identity, and where does it come from?

1.1 »I am I«?

»Nothing is more obvious than the identity of one's self during all metamorphoses of life«, Gerhard Ebeling tells us in his dogmatics.[1] Is that true? The (now dissolved) pop group Wise Guys disagrees, singing: »*It isn't always easy being me …*«

The self-evidence postulated by Ebeling does not seem plausible to everybody anymore. So the next question arises: When am I identical? To what do I attach my identity? – My memory, my conscious mind or external factors? I will try to give preliminary answers to these questions. For example:

»I am I« and nobody else. There is only one person within me, not two. »I am Jochen Arnold.« This name, together with place and date of

---

[1] Gerhard Ebeling, Dogmatik des christlichen Glaubens III, § 38, Tübingen 1979, 414.

my birth and the names of my parents enable an exact identification of my person.

I can also be described with the help of *personal characteristics or talents*, so others may recognize me; maybe like this: »I am slim, have no talent for technology, but I'm more or less musical.« This can also be done with social categories, which may stay consistent over my whole life, e. g.: »I have four children,« etc. A valuated characteristic in a social category is also possible if others attribute it to me: »You are a *loving* father.«

I can set myself apart from all the other Jochen Arnolds in German-speaking countries by emphasizing my *social role or my occupation*: »I am a pastor and a church musician.« A life motto could also give me some identity: »I do what I like,« or, to be less hedonistic and more in line with Kant: »I fulfil my duty.« Or: »I serve my church.«

In our late modern society, any definite statement on identity seems rather problematic. We prefer perspectives of several options. A late modern identity could thus be characterized by the inability to be fixed; instead, it must happen in every situation in the diversity of life and its choices.

Applying these thoughts to a possible *Christian* or even *evangelical* identity, I could say: I am a Christian. In a multicultural society, I confess my faith in the Triune God. That I am an evangelical (even more precise: Evangelical Lutheran) Christian can be seen from my baptism. It took place on 10/03/1968 in a simple Sunday service … On top, there is my ordination: I am an Evangelical Lutheran pastor, a lasting attribute.

My personal and professional identity – or let's say: its key data – has *significantly* changed several times. I am not only a son to my parents, but also a husband and father of four children, etc. So is the question about identity in fact about a process, about becoming instead of being something?

1.2 I become »one with …«

A sociological definition of identity is: »Personal identity is the subjective processing of biographical continuity or discontinuity and ecological consistency or inconsistency by a person against the background of their self-expectations and social expectations«.[2]

To be identical would then mean to process personal history in its respective continuity or discontinuity, in the highs and lows of one's life. This perspective brings me to a first conclusion in the form of questions:

Am I *at peace with myself* based on my life's history (including its low points), am I *at peace with others*, am I in a good relationship, am I a good boss, an honest friend, etc.? Do I live *in accordance with the world based on my own values*, do I assume social responsibility? On top of the social dimensions, there is also the religious dimension: Am I at peace with God, in light of my sin and my failures, my happiness and my hope?

Faced with such big questions, identity probably exists only partially or in fragments. But where does the continuously renewed identity come from? In which places of life does it happen?

2. PLACES OF IDENTITY FORMATION

2.1. IDENTITY FORMATION IN EVERYDAY LIFE

If somebody tells me: »Well done! That was a good seminar/a nice sermon/a touching concert,« I know that I have met social expectations or even standards of professional performance. I receive some degree of affirmation of parts of my identity, namely those connected with action, by way of recognition. The same applies to group experiences. When I put down my baton after the last note of a concert, the first thing I do is look at the faces of the musicians. Often we experience the good feeling that we have achieved something together, that we have reached a goal. Gratitude, relief and sometimes even a bit of pride.

A lot of people draw their identity from certain external attributes: A certain brand of clothing, the newest smartphone, a specific car or just their hairdo. They usually symbolize a certain attitude to life, they are meant to tell us: I belong (to a group; or: this is how to identify me).

Identity formation also happens in sports. Our national football team comes into the stadium, we hear the national anthem. The hearts of millions of people in front of the TV are beating faster. They are in solidarity

---

[2] KARL HAUSSER, Identität, in: GÜNTER ENDRUWEIT / GISELA TROMMSDORFF (eds.), Wörterbuch der Soziologie, Stuttgart 1989, 279.

with their team. In my view, national identity is partly formed by sports events. Success stabilises or increases identity. Sometimes you can hear »You never walk alone« after a defeat. Sometimes a defeat can even increase solidarity.

If my wife tells me: »I love you, I will accompany you wherever you go,« this is not based on success. I can wish for this sentence, but not demand it. It is always a gift. It is more than recognition, more than success, it is part of the basis of my existence as a man and a father, even as a human being, as a person.

But what happens if everything is lost, when there is no professional success, when the job is lost, when a relationship breaks up, when identity is at stake? Let's continue our questions. What carries us beyond these places and moments?

2.2 Identity formation on a Sunday

2.2.1 Elementary passivity: The examples of baptism and communion

Where can we find an ultimate reassurance of identity apart from our profession, image cultivation in social media, outside of romantic relationships or family?

Identity happens where I am unequivocally told: *You are accepted. I will always be at your side.* Christoph Schwöbel writes: »The Christian service as proclamation of the word and celebration of communion is the place where the identity-giving relationship to Christ, the permanent life communion with the risen Lord becomes manifest: ›Jesus Christ is the same yesterday and today and forever‹ (Hebrews 13:8).«[3]

How does that sound? »*Do not fear, for I have redeemed you,*« somebody in a cassock tells us. He is standing at a baptismal font and invokes the name of the Triune God. His competence does not stem from himself. He is called, empowered and therefore competent. A second name is mentioned: The name of the baptizand is connected with the holy name of the Triune God. This is complemented by the sign of the cross with water

[3] Christoph Schwöbel, Was ist ein Gottesdienst? Theologische Kriterien zur Angemessenheit der gottesdienstlichen Feiern, in: Hans-Joachim Eckstein / Ulrich Heckel / Birgit Weyel (eds.), Kompendium Gottesdienst, Tübingen 2011, 145f.

on the forehead: as a reminder of Jesus' death, a sign of blessing for an entire life. (In my opinion this is still valid when people end their membership in a church.)

But not every service includes a baptism, and I can't even remember my own baptism. So we ask: Where else can we experience this identity-giving power? Let's have a look at the second sacrament.

»This is my body which is given for you.« In a wonderful way, these words of the Lord at his last supper correspond to the baptismal *You are mine*: a word of power which opens the heavens for us. *Through the sensual experience of the gifts, these words effect an important act of identity formation.* I know this gift is for me, it is meant for me, not just for my neighbour. This is why Eilert Herms speaks of the »certainty of your own body«.[4]

But that's not all. At the same time, a social event is happening. The church as fellowship of sinners partakes in the holy. *It is healed by participating in Christ's reconciliation.* Pars pro toto, the church takes the whole world into a sphere of sanctification and renewal. Creation is coming home.

At another time in the service we are told that we are provided for, even more, that we are forgiven: in the confession of sin, or rather in absolution. Something nearly all other world religions consider as unusual or even blasphemous happens in church, for example with the following words: »What was shall no longer burden you. What will be shall not frighten you. God's mercy is the joy and power of your life.«[5] Such a complete acquittal can only be received as a gift. You cannot earn it or even buy it. For me, this makes it clear: *A person is not what s/he does, but what s/he receives through God's creative and forgiving love.*

All examples given so far illuminate identity formation as a *passive* event. It happens through a mandate and a promise from the highest authority.

But we can also ask: Are there any forms of *active* identity formation in a service?

---

4 EILERT HERMS, Glaube, in IDEM: Offenbarung und Glaube, Tübingen 1992, 464.

5 See Gottesdienstbuch für die Evangelische Landeskirche in Württemberg, Stuttgart 2004, 353.

2.2.2 The resonance space of faith

First of all, congregational singing comes to mind. With a simple song like *Fürchte dich nicht, gefangen in deiner Angst* (*Don't be afraid, caught up in you fear*; EG Niedersachsen 595), the members of the congregation encourage each other (see Colossians 3:16). It is the same encouragement they were given in baptism. They don't just carry this assurance in their own hearts, but share it with others. An individual and common assurance becomes a *(sung) message of encouragement.*

Speaking the words of the Lord's Prayer, Psalm 23 or similar well-known texts, another dimension of a common identity comes to mind: Speaking the words »The Lord is my shepherd« together is not only a confession of trust that transcends denominations, it also means: We are provided for. Whatever happens: Our existence does not depend solely on ourselves. The Lord is my shepherd/helper/protection/my fortress, etc.

The same is true for the creed. Before God, the world and ourselves we account for our faith. We disclose ourselves as a community belonging to Jesus Christ.[6] Since the Third Reich, this creed is spoken by the whole congregation, not only by the pastor. Such an identity creates a sense of belonging and gives resilience in dark times.

Last but not least there is the song of praise, exemplified in the Gloria or Sanctus: Here, the identity formation is four-fold. I am totally with me, with God and those who are singing with me, in heaven and on earth. Usually this is complemented by joy. Neurologists would say we are completely present, experience physical and mental presence, are a person (from Latin *personare*). This also applies to joint singing. A group identity is formed through the common breathing, metre, melody, rhythm. We do not make music in a vacuum, however, but always in the world, in specific places, maybe together with other creatures. This makes us the resonance space of the Triune God's fantasy. We partake in his richness of relationships, and in the sound become open for the

---

[6] See also Hans-Joachim Eckstein, Gottesdienst im Neuen Testament, loc. cit. (see footnote 3), 31: »The most concise summary of the creed and confession that constitute Christian identity may be found in the connection of faith and resurrection in Romans 10:9.«

connection of heaven and earth in an entanglement of times, e.g. by singing what was already sung more than 2500 years ago in the temple of Jerusalem. Where, if not here, is identity formed and even celebrated in an uplifting way?

My basic hypothesis is therefore: *If there is any theologically justified identity or identity formation at all, we can expect it to happen in our worship service. In a Christian service, identity formation and renewal happens both in elementary passivity through proclamation (also in the form of music) and sacrament and in common activity through prayer, confession and praise.*

The next question is therefore: What connects a »Protestant service« with other denominations? What was or is the specifically evangelical or Lutheran charisma in terms of service or a theology of service?

3. Journeying together – the theological understanding of service in Una sancta

3.1. Alternating address and response in dialogue – communication between God and human being

Let us begin with a simple statement. Martin Luther mentioned it at the occasion of the consecration of Torgau's Schlosskirche nearly in passing: »that our Lord may speak to us in his holy word … and we in turn speak to him in prayer and song of praise.«[7]

This wording means that a service cannot be reduced to action between human beings, but that it contains an exchange of words and sounds without analogy, in which the living God himself speaks and listens. At the same time, the gathered congregation is granted an audience with God, is allowed to be in his presence. The Second Vatican Council writes in its Constitution on the Sacred Liturgy: »In liturgy, God speaks to his people. Christ proclaims the gospel. The people then answers with songs and prayer.«[8]

---

7 WA 49,588.

8 SC 33, DH 4033: »In Liturgia enim Deus ad populum suum loquitur; Christus adhuc Evangelium annuntiat. Populus vero Deo respondet tum cantibus tum oratione.«

This also contains a Christological emphasis, which is quite appropriate for us Protestants. Particularly the meaning of the *word* for our service is clearly stated. This also applies to Orthodox churches: »The Divine Liturgy is both God's service rendered in Jesus Christ to us in public and our service in Jesus Christ before God.«[9] »The Lord is the one who is the real actor and giver, and the material church answers him with prayer and thanksgiving.«[10]

Karl Barth writes in his lecture on the Reformed Scottish Confession (1938): »*Here too, vere Deus has to come first and define everything that needs to be said about vere homo. Church service is first of all, primarily, substantially and originally divine - it becomes human action only in a secondary, derived, accidental way.* [...] For this service to become service to God, human action isn't enough, only God can make it so.«[11]

We can conclude: A liturgical event without God's word (at least read, usually also interpreted) or without prayer or song by the congregation does not deserve to be called a service. The alternation of word and response, which is now called katabasis and anabasis in liturgics, was already described by Luther in his key document *De captivitate*:

»These two should not be confused: Mass (communion) and prayer, sacrament and action, Testament and sacrifice, for one comes from God to us through the service of the priest and aims at faith, the other comes from our faith through the priest to God and aims at being answered. One goes down, the other goes up.«[12]

Despite frequent criticism of a »forced separation« of pieces of liturgy in one or the other, this differentiation of speech acts in service seems

---

[9] Orthodoxes Glaubensbuch, Frage 99, 124. What's remarkable in this dialogic definition is the double emphasis of Jesus Christ as mediator (see 1 Timothy 2:5 and Galatians 2:20) and the public confession aspect of the service for the world.

[10] Heinz Dietrich Döpmann, Gottesdienst im orthodoxen Kontext, in: Hans-Christoph Schmidt-Lauber / Karl-Heinrich Bieritz (eds.), Handbuch der Liturgik, Göttingen/Leipzig 1995, 128–138, nearly identical with Luther's wording in Torgau (see footnote 8).

[11] Karl Barth, Gotteserkenntnis und Gottesdienst nach reformierter Lehre. Zwanzig Vorlesungen (Gifford Lectures) über das Schottische Bekenntnis (1937/38), Zollikon-Zürich 1938, 191.

[12] Martin Luther, De captivitate, WA 6,526.

quite vital to me. For it does matter whether we talk and pray to God, or if we let him talk to us. The art of theologically responsible enactment of the service depends greatly on the interaction between receiving and giving.

3.2 Appreciation of the comprehensible word: The congregation celebrates the service

Comprehension is a precondition for a lively dialogue. This was one of the main concerns of Reformation. Since the 16th century, service and congregational singing have mainly been performed in the language of the people. 400 years after the Reformation, the Catholic church has taken up this idea: The celebration happens in an active participation *(participatio actuosa) of the people of God.* Among Protestants, this aspect has developed into the *primary criterion* of a service; the Evangelische Gottesdienstbuch (Protestant service book) of 1999/2000 puts it like this: »The service is celebrated in participation and responsibility of the whole congregation.«[13]

Recent studies in the field of confirmation groups and service indicate that this criterion is also of some relevance for youth today.[14] Youth like to come to church if they are taken seriously, if they have developed a relationship to those in charge and if they are involved in the planning and celebration of the service.

3.3 The service as a public gathering and origin of the church

Another fundamental aspect is the link between service and church. Time and again, the Second Vatican Council emphasized the celebration of mass, or of the Eucharist, as *culmen et fons ecclesiae*, as source and

---

[13] Evangelisches Gottesdienstbuch. Agende für die Evangelische Kirche der Union und für die Vereinigte Evangelisch-Lutherische Kirche Deutschlands (hg. von der Kirchenleitung der VELKD und im Auftrag des Rates von der Kirchenkanzlei der EKU), Berlin Hannover/Bielefeld 2000, 15 (EGb).

[14] www.landeskirche-hannovers.de/evlka-de/wir-fuer-sie/jugendliche/konfirmandenzeit/gottesdienste (accessed 22.12.2017): »There is a strong connection between the experience of youth services, the involvement of confirmands in service and the satisfaction of youth with the service. Youth services and the involvement in services result in a positive assessment by confirmands.«.

culminating point of the church.[15] *This means: The church comes from service and moves in this direction.*[16] More exactly: The church is constituted in service and is acknowledged as church in service. This is at least the view of the Augsburg Confession (1530). In article 7 (1530) it says that the church can be found where (in service) the word is taught in its pure form and the sacraments are distributed correctly, i. e. according to the gospel.[17] A bit later, Martin Luther mentioned seven holy things in his writing *Von Konziliis und Kirchen* which denote the church in the world: Word, baptism, communion, key, song, prayer, cross.[18]

This is linked to the fact that the service is *public*. It is expressed in the clear criteria for the mandate to officiate in a service (*publice docere*) of an evangelical church.[19] They have evolved over time, e. g. regarding the involvement of lectors and predicants.

The high dignity of a public service results in the selection of a specific space for its celebration in all big churches, but also in most free churches. Churches face east as a manifestation of the returning Christ and as orientation for the congregation. Lutheran churches are also consecrated, i. e. blessed for use and taken into service.

But how can we recognize a (Protestant) church today? Its beautiful building? This is comprehensible for most people. Or the people who live a Christian lifestyle? Are the visible fruits of the loving deed the *notae ecclesiae* of today?[20] Is a church service really the place where questions about suffering, sin and salvation of the world, but also about a successful

---

15 See SC 10, Denzinger-Hünermann, 4010: »Attamen Liturgia es culmen ad quod actio Ecclesiae tendit et simul fons unde omnis eius virtus emanat.«

16 Similarly regarding the mutual relationship of theology and service: Oswald Bayer, Theologie (HST 1), Gütersloh 1994, 403.

17 See BSLK 61.

18 See WA 50, 639 ff.

19 See also AC XIV with its »rite vocatus«.

20 Various church constitutions now not only refer to the Augsburg Confession, but also to the Barmen Theological Declaration, which expressly mentions obedience of the church, which witnesses »with its message and its order« that it is »the property of Christ« and »lives and wants to live on his comfort and his direction in the expectation of his epiphany« (Die Barmer Theologische Erklärung, ed. Alfred Burgsmüller / Rudolf Weth, Neukirchen 1984, 36).

coexistence of people, justice and care of creation are raised and brought before God in prayer?

3.4 Communion: Self-representation of the crucified and risen Lord

While communion was at the centre of dispute in the time of the Reformation, this discussion seems to have calmed down in recent years … Are we already in agreement? In my opinion, we have come a long way in terms of the *presence of Jesus Christ* from the discussions of the 16th or even the middle of the 20th century. From an evangelical perspective, we can look back in gratitude on 60 years of theological achievements: Among Protestant churches: The Arnoldshain Theses[21] and the Leuenberg Agreement[22]; on an ecumenical level the documents *Herrenmahl*[23], the Lima document[24] and *Lehrverurteilungen - kirchentrennend?*[25]. To me

[21] See Arnoldshain Theses of 1957, Thesis 4: »The words spoken by our Lord Jesus Christ when giving the bread and the cup tell us what he himself gives to all who come: He, the *crucified and risen Lord*, lets himself be *taken by us* in his body given for all and in his blood shed for all through his promising word in bread and wine, and *takes us* into the victory of his kingdom through the power of the Holy Spirit, so that we may believe in his promise, forgiveness of sin, life and salvation.«

[22] »In the Lord's Supper the risen Jesus Christ imparts himself in his body and blood, given up for all, through his word of promise with bread and wine. He thereby grants us forgiveness of sins and sets us free for a new life of faith. He enables us to experience anew that we are members of his body. He strengthens us for service to humankind. When we celebrate the Lord's Supper, we proclaim the death of Christ, through which God has reconciled the world to God's self. We confess the presence of the risen Lord in our midst. Rejoicing that the Lord has come to us, we await his future coming in glory« (15/16).

[23] Das Herrenmahl, Gemeinsame römisch-katholische/evangelisch-lutherische Kommission, Paderborn/Frankfurt a. M. 1979.

[24] Lima 1982: Baptism, Eucharist and Ministry. Faith and Order Paper of the World Council of Churches, 1982.

[25] Lehrverurteilungen - kirchentrennend?, Bd. I: Rechtfertigung, Sakramente und Amt im Zeitalter der Reformation und heute, ed. Karl Lehmann / Wolfhart Pannenberg (Dialog der Kirchen 4), Freiburg i. Br. / Göttingen 1986; and Lehrverurteil-

it seems we do not have to continue our dispute in this regard. Christ is present as the crucified and risen brother and Lord. Lutherans can identify with the concept of »personal presence«, connected with the biblical figure of representation (as work of Christ). Together with others, they trust in the salvific presence of Christ[26] in communion and consider it a gift. With the idea of synecdoche (*»in, with and under«*)[27], Luther has made a significant contribution. Even more important than this idea is the basic statement that it is *God who acts* in communion, not human beings. The *verba testamenti* are »words of deed«, not »words of interpretation«, they do and give what they promise, are performative, creative words of Christ.[28]

In contrast, it is worthwhile continuing the discussion about the role of the sacrifice in communion, if only for reasons of justification theology.

3.5 Mass as an ecumenical form of service – development of other forms

With regard to the liturgical format, Luther, Bugenhagen and many others continued on the path of the mass and its more than 1000 years of history. However, they also made significant corrections to the *canon missae.* For this reason, Lutherans in the whole world still celebrate mass; not together, but in a similar form like their Roman-Catholic and Orthodox brothers and sisters. Because of its clear biblical references and its poetic beauty, mass is a pearl of faith and continues to inspire music for service. The German-speaking Reformed Church has now also turned towards mass in the form of service order B.[29] On the other hand, the preaching

---

ungen – kirchentrennend?, Bd. IV: Rechtfertigung, Sakramente und Amt im Zeitalter der Reformation und heute, ed. Karl Lehmann/ Wolfhart Pannenberg (Dialog der Kirchen 4), Freiburg i. Br./ Göttingen 1994.

26 We should however distance ourselves from the difficult doctrine of *manducatio impiorum* and its link between meal and judgment. Following recent exegetic insights, it is not in line with what Paul intended in 1 Corinthians 11.

27 See Martin Luther, Vom Abendmahl Christi (1526), WA 26,444.

28 See Vom Abendmahl Christi (1528), WA 26, 287 ff.

29 See Reformierte Liturgie. Gebete und Ordnungen für die unter dem Wort versammelte Gemeinde, ed. Peter Bukowski et al., Wuppertal/Neukirchen-Vluyn 1999, third order, 45–47, and for communion, order B, 359–370.

service is another form which has made it into the service books of the United Evangelical Lutheran Church of Germany and the Union of Evangelical Churches; it is not that far away from the reformed or free church format. I consider this a positive development.

At this point we can conclude: Identity in respect of our service does not mean distinction against the (evil) world or other religions or denominations: Rather, Protestant Christians come before God, together with other people and as creatures and sinners; together with other Christians they let him speak to them, they celebrate his love and invite other people to celebrate their faith. *Communication, relationships, comprehensible language, the hospitality of Christ are the general principles of a Protestant service in the 21st century.*

This leads to the following questions and wishes: How much »recognizability« is needed today in the diversity of traditional and free forms? In my view, our current task is to continually rediscover the richness of mass and its possibilities! Kyrie and Gloria can be further unfolded, also in connection with a psalm; between Kyrie and Gloria you can insert the Grace (following the custom of the United Church). The musical colours of the ordinary must be further developed. We need a contemporary form and several »musical languages« (e.g. with a pop music ordinary) for our liturgy. Let's take up the musical impulse from the global ecumenical movement (e.g. from Latin America, Africa, gospel music)!

4. Key moments of an Evangelical Lutheran theology of service

4.1 God's service as gracious descendence and address on an equal footing

In contrast to other European languages, the German word for the gathering of the Christian congregation is *Gottesdienst* – literally, »God's service«. Martin Luther used it widely in his writings and often spelled it in two words instead of one (*Gottis Dienst* or *Gottes Dienst*). By no means is this term limited to his liturgical writings of the years 1523 to 1526, but appears throughout his whole work, particularly in his interpretations of the psalms. His ethics, the doctrine of the three realms, is based on the idea that *politia*, *oeconomia* and *ecclesia* each perform a service for each other and before God. The particular charisma of the German word is due to its double meaning: *God serves us* in proclamation, sacraments and blessing, and *we serve God* in prayer and song of praise.

Additionally, the term also contains a theological programme: »God's service« refers to God as a *serving God*. His nature is to love, to give himself. This can be observed in the service of Jesus Christ in the manger and on the cross (see Mark 10:45). »God's glowing oven full of love«[30] can best be observed in the lowliness of *Christus incarnatus et crucifixus*.[31] This service is complemented by the descendence of the Holy Spirit, who entrusts us weak human beings with his word in liturgy and sermon: »For God has humbled himself and descended to put his holy word into the mouth of the human being, so that he shall not doubt that he himself says it.«[32]

Thus, we are dealing with a God who shows himself to be human, who not only becomes human in Christ, but who also speaks to people and transforms them through his spirit in his grace.

What does that mean for our liturgical practice? I believe it is not our foremost duty to stage our service as something totally foreign or other, but to give room to the approachable God[33]. The whole God, Father, Son and Holy Spirit, whose innermost nature is love[34], shall be experienced in our service.

To put it bluntly: The service is about the practice of hospitality in the here and now, not about celebrating a »liturgical museum«. This does not exclude the cross, but it definitely leaves behind a cool form of churchliness.

---

30 See Luthers 7th Invocavit sermon for Reminiscere Sunday (1522), WA 10/III, 55.

31 See OSWALD BAYER, Theologie Luthers, 2004, 192: »Only through Christ can we look into the heart of God the Father in the Holy Spirit. Only this way can we perceive him as love.«

32 WA 12, 493.

33 See MARKUS ROTH, Die Zuwendung Gottes feiern, Leipzig 2016.

34 See also the important distinction between opus proprium and opus alienum Christi according to FC V (BSLK 955, 27f), which does not state that God is only love, but that time and again he proves to be of a loving nature in Christ.

4.2 Kyrie – lament – confession of sin

Does this result in an exclusion of dark experiences and feelings from the service? Are biblical statements about judgement banned from liturgy and sermon? No. They can and should be included, in particular in the sense of our original question about identity. But we must work with them. Especially in times of crisis and difficult transitions in life we feel: We cannot get rid of ourselves, we always carry us, our individual and collective history, our questions and our failures with us to service. We also encounter God in his holiness and with his mysteries! *It is part of the proper of an Evangelical Lutheran service that we have room for this.* Unfortunately, this room tends to recede, e. g. because speaking of sin seems offensive to many.[35] But what a relief it is to lay our burden at God's feet in the *Confiteor*. In the *Kyrie*, we reach for the mercy of God (see Mark 10:48). In the psalm of lament (see Psalms 13, 22, 69), we lament the suffering of the world, sigh together before God and await his answer with Christ (see Hebrews 5:7).

4.3 The mode: Word and faith

But this alone would be too little. We are not left alone with our questions and failures. Our service is not just a celebration of repentance and prayer. In his key writing *De captivitate*, Luther writes: »Never has God acted differently with humans than through a word of promise. And never could we act differently with God than through faith in the word of promise.«[36]

With this statement, Luther claims that in the sacrament of communion, God gives us the *forgiveness of sins and new life through the word of promise*. This assurance stands *pars pro toto* for the sacramental character of the whole service. It finds resonance in faith. Only then follows the answer of the sacrifice of praise.[37] We give God glory.

---

35 This is especially true for the confession of sin, which in some congregations is only spoken in the framework of a specific order of communion on Good Friday or the Day of Repentance.

36 WA 6,516, see WA 6,364: »Now I believe […] that mass is nothing else but a testament and sacrament, in which God gives us a promise and gives us his grace and mercy.«

37 See Apologie der CA XXIV, BSLK 354: »Sacramentum est ceremonia vel opus,

I would like to formulate a couple of *practical concerns* based on the above mentioned reflections (4.2 and 4.3): Do we allow enough room for forms of lament and confession of sin at the beginning of service? Can we really be present with our feelings and our failures? Don't we rush through the opening liturgy? We need to slow down and go deeper emotionally, also in terms of liturgy.

We need room for silence, particularly in prayer. But also the acts of promise need to be taken into account and emphasized in our service as little gems. The *Do not be afraid* in baptism, the words of institution and formula of administration, but also musical forms of the promise (*Taste and see*, etc.), and of course the sermon. We should pay extreme attention to the endings and the difficult modal verbs: Instead of »*May* God help/bless you«: *God helps/blesses you.*

However, there is another issue in Lutheran liturgy: After the classical *Confiteor* (preparatory prayer), *absolution* is missing. Where does it actually still exist in the Lutheran mass in German-speaking areas? In contrast, the *general confession* has a clear assurance similar to the grace in the opening liturgy of the United Church.[38]

4.4 Proclamation of the word and sacrament – two summits?

A good balance between word and sacrament is part of the charisma of a Lutheran service.[39] On the one hand, this is implied with the appreciation of the word: »The word has to be in swing.«[40] On the other hand, there is also an appreciation of the sacraments, which are more than »mere signs«

in quo Deus nobis exhibet hoc, quod offert annexa ceremoniae promissio, ut baptismus est opus, non quod nos Deo offerimus, sed in quo Deus nos baptizat […] et exhibet Deus remissionem peccatorum etc., iuxta promissionem: Qui crediderit et baptizatus fuerit, salvus erit. Econtra sacrificium est ceremonia vel opus, quod nos Deo reddimus, ut eum honore afficiamus.«
See also loc. cit., 356, on *sacrificium laudis* in contrast to the one-time *sacrificium propitiatorium* of Christ.

38 See as examples EGb 70 or 506.

39 See as an example Edmund Schlink, Ökumenische Dogmatik, Göttingen 1993, 514–518.

40 See Martin Luther, Von Ordnung Gottesdiensts in der Gemeinde (1523), WA 12,37.

and point to the essentials. As Lutherans, we are looking for a theological and liturgical middle ground between a mere church of the word and a church as a sacramental institution, which considers itself the original sacrament.

A rather convincing argument says: Both elements must be celebrated regularly, if possible, in combination. Karl Barth wrote in 1938:

»Would the sermon not be held and heard completely differently and would also receive more thanks in our services if all of this came visibly from baptism and moved towards communion? [...] I mention this in this context because in this hearing of the word of God, which signifies the essential church action, everything depends on it happening in the centre that is defined by the two sacraments.«[41]

But there is another argument. There is a mutual penetration and liturgical interconnection: a sacramental dimension of the word and a proclaiming dimension of the sacraments, the sacrament as *verbum visibile*, the word as *sacramentum audibile*.[42] Both forms contain the whole God, both bring salvation, only in different forms. This means: Celebrate your service with variations! It is a good thing to concentrate on one of the two, and next time on the other. Also, to omit the sermon altogether is no fundamental fault, as long as the word is read and the sacrament is celebrated.

4.5 Reference or event?

Let us now come to another theological question that was the object of a heated debate between Lutherans and Reformed Christians. Do sermon and sacraments point towards salvation, just like the index finger of John the Baptist at the Isenheim Altarpiece, or Luther on the predella of the altar in Wittenberg's Stadtkirche? Or do they give salvation? Does the assurance »given for you« provide eternal life and salvation, or does it only *inform*[43] us about this salvation and leaves the rest to us?

---

41 Loc. cit., 199.

42 See SCHLINK, Ökumenische Dogmatik, loc. cit 518, and in contrast, WOLFHART PANNENBERG (ed.), Systematische Theologie Bd. III, 373–404 or EBELING, loc. cit., § 35.

43 See BARTH, loc. cit., 191. He differs quite substantially from the framous statement by Bullinger: »Praedicatio verbi dei est verbum dei«, in: Confessio Helvetica

Luther writes in the Large Catechism: »For being baptized in God's name is not being baptized by human beings, but by God himself, so even if it is done by the hand of man, it is still God's own work.«[44] Luther's description aims at God's action in the here and now.

Against this background, it is worthwhile thinking again about what happens on a spiritual level in a service, of which the sermon is an essential part: Is it just about information, about finding a sense in life? I believe (with Luther, and in contrast to Barth): It is more, namely assignment, administration. Service is a spiritual event, which aims at our faith, and thus also at an existential transformation.

4.6 God's action and man's action – the so-called pneumatological reserve

Does God's spirit only act if we admit it? Or if those in charge prepare well enough? Does it maybe only act in some instances, similar to the blowing of the wind (see John 3:8)? I find this position at least worrying, if not heretical. It is often formulated based on modesty, sometimes grounded in theological scepticism with the addition: We don't want to stand in the way of the Holy Spirit.

A look at article V of the Augsburg Confession resolves the matter. The difference between external and internal action of the Spirit (analogue to the *verbum externum and internum*) helps in this regard.

God's Spirit is given to us through the »external« (physical-material) means of word and sacrament.[45] In, with and under church action it operates independently of the disposition of the ordained person. This may

Posterior (1562/66), see Paul Jacobs (ed.), Reformierte Bekenntnisschriften und Kirchenordnungen in deutscher Übersetzung, Neukirchen-Vluyn 1949, 175–245, here: 178.

[44] Large Catechism on baptism, BSLK 692, see also Large Catechism on the 3rd article, 654. See Otfried Hofius, Glaube und Taufe nach dem Zeugnis des Neuen Testaments, in: idem, Neutestamentliche Studien, Tübingen 2000, 271: »There is only *one* baptism, which is the one instituted by Jesus Christ, which *he himself* gives and performs.«

[45] See CA V, BSLK 58: »… *tamquam per verbum et sacramenta donatur spiritus sanctus*«.

sound »Catholic« to some, but it expresses a high degree of respect for the physical and the ministry of proclamation. God's Spirit lets Christ be present in the mouth of the preachers. »It is a great thing that each righteous pastor's and preacher's mouth is the mouth of Christ and that his word and forgiveness is Christ's word and forgiveness.«[46]

At the same time, proclamation through the ministry of preaching sets a *normative* standard (as shown in AC VII) that is fundamental to a Protestant understanding of church and service. It is about »*pure* docere« and »*recte* administrare«. As *external signs of the church*, word and sacrament do not only depend on the authority and sovereignty of the Holy Spirit, but also on a specific *apostolic doctrine*, which is defined by canonical gospel.

In order to prevent the misunderstanding of a supposedly automatic procedure or even a magical *opus operatum* and to highlight the *sovereignty of the divine Spirit*, AC V also includes the important supplement »*ubi et quando visum est Deo*«, which has often been called the »pneumatological reserve«. It makes it clear: It is completely and utterly God's decision to lay the truth of the gospel into an individual's heart and to open it up to them.

By and large, both movements, *verbum externum* and *internum*, belong together.

What are the consequences of this? I see a *pastoral-theological encouragement and relief*: We are *instruments of God*, what could be better and more beautiful? Still, we are only *instruments*, to quote Luther: »Conduits and tools« … A separation of divine and human action in the *verbum externum* is impossible.

4.7 »Institutum est« – the question of the ministry of proclamation and the interaction of different ministries

The administration of word and sacrament is linked to the *public ministry of preaching* in AC V. The divine institution of the *ministerium verbi*[47] as-

46 WA 52, 269.

47 See Schlink, Theologie, 330: »The public ministry of preaching is not a creation of the congregation necessitated by their principles of order, but directly instituted by God through the mandate and promise of Jesus Christ. The confessional writings

sures that what is said and given does not depend on human disposition, but is *independent of the faith of both the giver and the receivers.*[48]

However, it is also about an *obedient* orientation of the *munus propheticum Christi*[49]. Only in this way is the orientation of Jesus Christ to his church preserved. Still, this ministry of proclamation is located at the very centre of the congregation, for »what has come out of baptism is worthy to be called a priest, a bishop and a pope«[50].

This relates to the link between ministry and service, which is always present, particularly in the Roman-Catholic and the Orthodox churches in the debate on the apostolic or episcopal succession and the ensuing dignity of the ministry. Is there a plausible alternative in the sense of a common approach to a full communion of churches? I am afraid I cannot see one at present.

But Lutheran churches should also accept the question asked by other Protestant churches: Is the focus on the ministry of the pastor as the central ministry of proclamation a decision that must be continued in this form forever? Are there no other options, e.g. based on the Reformed doctrine of the four ministries (see Ephesians 4)?[51]

4.8 »Singing and speaking« – music as proclamation?!

A specific understanding of music is part of the Lutheran understanding of service. »The gospel is a good shout etc. of which one sings, speaks and is joyful«, as Luther wrote already in 1522 in his preface to the New Testament – a context that did not refer to music at all. So the good news

---

do not allow an opposition of the general priesthood as a divine institution and the public ministry of preaching as a human institution«.

48 See Bayer, LW, 59.

49 Also see KD I/1, 97, where Barth uses the term of the »vicariate of Christ« for the ministry of preaching. Luther put it like this in a sermon: »It is a great thing that each righteous pastor's and preacher's mouth is the mouth of Christ and that his word and forgiveness is Christ's word and forgiveness« (WA 52, 269).

50 WA 6, 407.

51 See Peter Bubmann, Der gemeinsame Dienst und die vielen Ämter, in: DtPfbl 106 (2006), 59–81, here: 60, and Gotthard Fermor, Cantus Firmus und Polyphonie – der eine Dienst und die vielen Ämter. Zur Theologie kirchlicher Berufe, PastTh 101 (2012), 324–340.

has to be sung in the first place, otherwise something essential is missing! Luther's translation of Colossians 3:16 (1534) highlights this kerygmatic understanding of music:

Lasset das Wort Christi unter euch reichlich wohnen. (Let the word of Christ dwell in you richly.)

In aller Weisheit lehrt und ermahnt euch selbst mit Psalmen und Lobgesängen und geistlichen, lieblichen (das ist tröstlichen, holdseligen, gnadenreichen) Liedern. (In all wisdom teach and admonish one another with psalms and songs of praise and spiritual, lovely [that is comforting, blissful and gracious] songs.)

Und singt Gott dankbar in euren Herzen. (And sing to God in your hearts with gratitude.)[52]

In principle, the musical proclamation of the word of Christ is a task for all Christians. Christ becomes a body of sound amidst the congregation. *The congregation does not only sing about Christ, he himself communicates with the congregation through the music.* Accordingly, Luther once stated in a dinner speech: »This way God preaches the gospel also through music.«[53]

A rich tradition of Evangelical-Lutheran church music is well aware of this *proclaiming dimension*. Among Luther's church hymns, let me

---

[52] Punctuation between the two subordinate clauses is grammatically unclear. Luther refers to the parallel text in Ephesians 5:19 and understands singing as an external as well as internal event, which contains elements of proclamation as well as praise. In contrast, more recent translations (e.g. Einheitsübersetzung) separate the clauses differently: *Das Wort Christi wohne mit seinem ganzen Reichtum bei euch.* (May the word of Christ live with you in all its richness.) *Belehrt und ermahnt einander in aller Weisheit!* (Teach and admonish each other in all wisdom!) *Singt Gott in eurem Herzen Psalmen, Hymnen und Lieder, wie sie der Geist eingibt, denn ihr seid in Gottes Gnade.* (Sing psalms, hymns and songs to God in your heart, how the Spirit moves you, for you are in God's grace.) In this case, music is »only« a response, not also a form of proclamation (see the Torgau formula).

[53] WA TR I, 1258.

just mention the examples of *Vom Himmel hoch* for Christmas, *Christ lag in Todesbanden* for Easter, and of course the key Reformation hymn *Nun freut euch, lieben Christen g'mein*.

In Luther's musical-theological legacy, his preface to the Babstsches Gesangbuch (1545), the christological-soteriological justification for singing is expressed once more: »Sing a new song unto the Lord … For God has filled our heart and spirit with *joy* through his dear son, which he has given for us to *deliver us from sin, death and devil.* All who truly believe this cannot help it but have to sing and speak about it joyfully and with pleasure, so others may hear it too and come.«[54]

What are the consequences?

First of all, we need to think about the relation between the different ministries working for proclamation. Is the ministry of church music perceived as a ministry of proclamation, and adequately appreciated by the ordained? Do we really take the chance to reach people with music seriously? Do we admit any feelings that might be stirred by music?

In addition, there are questions of a practical nature: Where is the place of the organ within the church, and where does the choir sing in service? As a proclaiming counterpart (from the front) or (from the balcony) as a sung prayer? This reflection results in the desire to rediscover the variety of functions of music in the context of our service from a liturgical and didactical standpoint.

4.9 The Lord's Supper or Eucharist?

In view of the above mentioned distinction of speech acts in communion, the question of possible consequences arises. Are the words of institution spoken as a prayer, facing the altar, or as an assurance towards the congregation? The Evangelische Gottesdienstbuch (service book) is quite clear in this regard: »In our Protestant understanding, they [the words of institution] are the proclamation of the gospel and of the valid presence of what they say.« »In occidental churches, they are considered to have consecrative powers. For this reason, they are given special emphasis in the context of the communion prayers.«[55]

---

54 WA 35, 477.

55 EGb, 27.

Is this the Lutheran proper in comparison to the two other world churches? Possibly so. However, the Lutheran tradition also knows about the Eucharistic or doxological moment. Luther writes: »If this faith is now correct, the heart must become joyful because of the Testament, and warm and melt in God's love. Praise and thanks will follow with a sweet heart, which is why mass is called *eucharistia* in Greek, which means *thanksgiving, so we may praise and thank* God for this comforting, rich, blessed Testament, just like somebody gives thanks and praise and is joyful who has been given a thousand guilders or more by a good friend.«[56]

So both must be taught and celebrated: The assurance/promise and the gratitude/praise. They are both preconditions for communion (in the Lutheran understanding), however not of an equal standing. In my opinion, there is no simultaneous existence of praise and assurance (like in the Roman liturgy, where the priest recites the words of institution in a long prayer, the simultaneous practice however aims at the moment of transubstantiation, which is a lot more than a prayer).

So the Lutheran voice could say today on the issue of communion: Be careful with your liturgy regarding the different speech acts. Don't speak the words of institution facing the altar, but towards the congregation – even risking the danger of forgetting your words![57] And don't forget the thanksgiving at the end. Thanksgiving is also essential for the celebration of the miracle.

4.10 The unclear mention of sacrifice

In Apol 24, Melanchthon makes a difference between *sacrificium propitiatorium* und *sacrificium eucharisticon (laudis)*.[58] He considered it of importance that mass is not a sacrifice offered by the church to God. Luther

---

56 WA 6,231, Sermon von den guten Werken (1520). See similarly Luther in his Vermahnung zum Sakrament WA 30/II, 614, and other writings from 1530.

57 See also the encouragement of the former pope in: Joseph Ratzinger, Theologie der Liturgie, 468: »I am always amazed that our Protestant brothers, when they transformed the medieval forms, have found a good balance between the pastor and the congregation turning towards each other on the one hand, and the common orientation towards the cross on the other hand […]«.

58 See BSLK, 354–356.

implemented this idea into liturgy and purged the canon of mass already in 1523, because it was so central to him. A (bloodless) offering of the sacrifice of mass was vehemently rejected. By now, this issue seems to have been dealt with in ecumenical discussions. But is this true? Even the Catholic church – based on an analysis of the Mass book of 1970 and its prayers – sees Luther's criticism of the sacrifice of mass as a justified concern. Reinhard Meßner writes:

> »In these statements on the offering, which separate the church offering the sacrifice (offering of body and blood of Christ) from the act of re-presentation of the sacrifice of the cross (consecration), the danger of a harmful misunderstanding of an additionally necessary reconciliatory sacrifice of the church is all too likely. […] Christ's action, which alone effects reconciliation, and the action of the church, which receives it in gratitude, are not clearly distinguished. This results in the theologically impossible thought that the church was offering the sacrifice of reconciliation.«[59]

I believe we should go even further. Of course we can speak of the sacrifice of Christ, who has given himself for us, in a theologically sound way. But we need to be careful when we deal with sacrifice in the framework of liturgy. Because the following questions are always looming: Who is the subject, who is the receiver, and what exactly is being sacrificed? So instead, I would suggest to speak of the dedication of Christ instead of a sacrifice, and never speak of a sacrifice made to God … We can express what we mean with the terms of thanksgiving and dedication.

4.11 The blessing as a word of command of the Triune God at the threshold

In his interpretation of Genesis 27:28 et seq. (Isaac's blessing for Jacob), Martin Luther states: The blessing is not a plea, it is an »indicative, constitutive act«, which »unfolds and administers what it says«.[60] This takes us back to the challenge of defining the speech acts of the blessing: Can

---

[59] Reinhard Messner, Die Meßreform Martin Luthers und die Eucharistie der Alten Kirche. Ein Beitrag zu einer systematischen Liturgiewissenschaft, Innsbruck/Wien 1989 (IthS 25), here: 211.

[60] See Luther, WA 43,525.

it be described as a »mixture of intercession and assurance«[61], as we read in a lot of textbooks?

In the Aaronic blessing (Numbers 6:24–27), the Hebrew original contains the curious grammatical form of jussive (of Latin *iubere* = to command). Its intention becomes clear in the best known biblical parallel text. In Genesis 1:3, we read: *Then God said, »Let there be light«;* (jussive) *and there was light.*

This means: It is a potent act by God, which starts with the speaking. This way, the blessing acts into the near future, based on the divine word of authority it sets something in motion, it administers an outstanding gift. God is trusted to grant wellbeing and salvation, in whatever form. So we see that the hypothesis of intercession and assurance in one is untenable.

In Luther's translation (2017) of Psalm 121, he chooses three different grammatical forms, even though there is only one used in Hebrew: Future tense, indicative and optative mood.

Er wird deinen Fuß nicht gleiten lassen, und der dich behütet, schläft nicht […] (He *will* not let your foot be moved; he who keeps you *will* not slumber.)
Der Herr behütet dich; der Herr ist ein Schatten über deiner rechten Hand. (The Lord *is* your keeper; the Lord *is* your shade at your right hand.)
[…]
Der Herr behüte dich vor allem Übel, er behüte deine Seele. (*May* the Lord keep you from all evil; *may* he keep your life.)
Der Herr behüte deinen Ausgang und Eingang, von nun an bis in Ewigkeit. (*May* the Lord keep your going out and your coming in from this time on and forevermore.)

The proper of a Lutheran theology of blessing would thus be the search of a wording for the blessing which makes its dynamics clear. In any case, the introduction: »We ask for the Lord's blessing« right before the

61 See Berthold W. Köber, Die Elemente des Gottesdienstes – Wort Gottes, Gebet, Lied, Segen, in: H. C. Schmidt-Lauber / K. H. Bieritz (eds.): Handbuch der Liturgik, Göttingen/Leipzig 1995, 689–714, here: 690.

assurance of the blessing does not make any sense. It would be different if the introduction was followed by a plea for blessing, which could be adequate for a short prayer service.

A blessing opens up the future. A blessing is an intersection of the present and the future, it is God's word of command at the threshold of tomorrow.

Another important element is Luther's comment on the aspect of Trinity. Regarding the Aaronic blessing he writes:

> »For the work of creation is attributed to the Father [...]: The Lord bless you and keep you; that means, he shall give you body and life graciously, and everything connected to it. The work of salvation is attributed to the Son [...]: The Lord make his face to shine upon you etc.; that means, he shall help you overcome your sins and be gracious to you and give you his Spirit. And the work of daily sanctification, comfort and strength against the devil and finally the resurrection from death is attributed to the Holy Spirit [...]: The Lord lift up his countenance upon you etc., that means, he shall give you strength, comfort and finally victory«[62].

In this, Luther expresses an indispensable insight which acknowledges the historical development of a theology of blessing within the Bible as a whole: The blessing contains *both* material and spiritual goods, it comes from the *Triune God* and cannot be limited to natural things in the scope of the first article. The gift of the blessing is given a new depth regarding its soteriological and eschatological contents, e.g. based on Ephesians 1:3–14. This means, e.g. for the blessing in occasional services, that it is far more than just a promise of protection and closeness: It brings us to Christ and his kingdom!

4.12 Free form – focus on the centre – orientation towards the people

A Protestant or Evangelical-Lutheran identity in a worship service does not mean to perform a specific liturgical order, which has been around

---

[62] Luther, WA 30 III, 581f.

[63] This is achieved by the doctrine of ceremonies as adiaphora, as can be found in AC VII (»Nec necesse est«) and in AC XV.

for nearly 500 years. In my view, that would be totally un-evangelic.[63] Let us preserve our Protestant freedom in our service and not be discouraged by any accusations, such as the »heresy of formlessness« (Martin Mosebach). This reproach distracts from what's essential.

What's truly essential is to maintain our orientation towards the centre. To keep going back to this centre is at the core of every Protestant church.

It is quite clearly marked by the four solae: *Solus Christus, sola gratia, solo verbo/sola scriptura and sola fide.* The hermeneutic rule of »What promotes Christ« should thus also be applied to our worship service. This makes it our standard and criterion for the understanding and shape of our service. However, a missionary orientation is also essential. We want to show others what we love. We want to win people for and through God's love. This implies a constant need to transcend borders: of our own social background, and sometimes also of the narrow confines of liturgical tradition and custom.

Thus, we need to be close to God's promise and close to the people. This is a distinctly Protestant quality, also in the worship service of the 21th century.

Holger Eschmann

Worship Service and Holy Communion in Evangelical-Methodist Perspective

The following reflections[1] on worship service and Holy Communion from the perspective of the EmK[2] (United Methodist Church in the German-language areas) open with a number of historical and denominational observations. Then the understanding of worship service and Holy Communion in the EmK is outlined, followed by a discussion of the liturgical reform process currently under way in the EmK in Europe.

1. Historical and denominational orientation

What is now known as the United Methodist Church (UMC) originated in English-speaking areas in the 18th century. It combines a number of strongly contrasting church traditions. The UMC services contain both high church, free church and regional elements.

a) First, there is the high-church Anglican legacy of the Methodists. The founders of the Methodist movement, the brothers John and Charles Wesley, were Anglican clergymen and had no intention of founding a new church. The first written Methodist service formula, known as the »Sunday Service«, was a slight revision of the Anglican Book of Common Prayer. John Wesley sent this Sunday Service to the first North American Methodist emigrants, providing them with a pattern for worship. His accompanying letter read: »I have prepared a liturgy

---

1 The revised version of a lecture given on 07. 12. 2017 at the Faculty of Protestant Theology, Tübingen University.

2 Evangelisch-methodistische Kirche.

little differing from that of the Church of England (I think, the best constituted national church in the world). Which I advise all the travelling-preachers to use, on the Lord's day, in all their congregations [...] I also advise the elders to administer the supper of the Lord on every Lord's day.«[3] This Anglican legacy, dominant in the early years, was received quite cautiously in the German-speaking EmK. In recent decades however it has seen renewed emphasis. An example of this trend can be found in the current EmK services book for Germany, Austria and Switzerland, where a detailed high-church Communion liturgy occurs in first place. Similarly, more and more EmK pastors wear a clerical collar and a cassock or an alb and stole for various church services. A further aspect of the high-church heritage is that in world Methodism – unlike in most other German-language free churches – ordination is required for presiding at communion.

b) As well as its Anglican roots, the EmK has a free-church heritage arising from the revivalist movement, with its emphasis on proclamation of the word and diaconal action. Methodism was not a movement for liturgical renewal. Rather, the spiritual and social poverty of their era drove the Wesley brothers to work for reform. The first worship meetings of the Methodists in 18th-century England and 19th-century Germany focused theologically on missionary preaching that called the listeners to faith, and on diaconal sanctification of the human being. In the early years, people continued to attend the service on Sunday morning in Anglican churches in England, and in the regional Protestant churches in Germany. Baptism and Communion took place there too. At that time the Methodists were as a rule not permitted to build their own churches and hold their Sunday services. The quite informal gatherings took place – similarly to the Pietist meetings for mutual edification – in the afternoon or evening, often in the side-room of a village tavern or in a living room.

c) We come now to the third line of tradition – alongside the high church and free church elements – that contributes to understanding the EmK

---

3 John Wesley's Sunday Service of the Methodists in North America with an Introduction by James F. White, Quarterly Review Methodist Bicentennial Commemorative Reprint, Nashville 1984, ii.

service in the German-speaking area: the Southern German service of the word or »preaching service«. Most Methodists settled in the southwest area of Germany. As a result of more liberal legislation in Wurttemberg from 1872, they were permitted to hold their own services on Sunday mornings. In doing so, they modelled their liturgy closely on their church surroundings in Germany and Switzerland. The Southern German preaching service in the style of Wurttemberg proved highly influential for the German-speaking Methodists.

An understanding of Methodist theology and worship practice will need to keep these various traditions in mind. Over time they have moved into or away from the foreground. There was a quite lengthy phase during which the free-church heritage was emphasised in Germany, forming a contrast to the regional Protestant churches, from which the Methodists distanced themselves in the interests of identity-building. For some 30 to 40 years now there has been – at least in the official documents of the Methodist Church – a renewed emphasis on the Anglican and sacramental tradition.

2. The theology of the worship service and Holy Communion in the UMC

In Methodism, the worship service and communion are known as »means of grace«, a term also used in the Church of England. In Wesleyan understanding, means of grace are »outward signs, words, or actions, ordained of God, and appointed for this end, to be the ordinary channels whereby he might convey to men preventing, justifying or sanctifying grace«.[4]

As well as the service and communion, further means of grace according to Wesley are the preoccupation with God's word in the service and at home, personal and common prayer, and fasting. Wesley did not create a specific order or hierarchy for the means of grace, although his

[4] John Wesley, Sermon 16 »The Means of Grace«, http://wesley.nnu.edu/john-wesley/the-sermons-of-john-wesley-1872-edition/sermon-16-the-means-of-grace/ (accessed on 21. 02. 2018).

writings make it clear that communion was close to his heart. He himself received communion several times a week, at a time when the Anglican custom was to do so once a quarter. As noted above, Wesley called on the preachers of the Methodist movement to celebrate communion every Sunday. This, together with his recommendation of regular use of the other means of grace, caused critical contemporaries to accuse him of sacramentalism.

God's grace is expressed in the service and communion, as well as through the other means of grace – as prevenient grace, as justifying grace and as sanctifying grace (see the quote from Wesley above). This has far-reaching consequences for the way in which the service and communion are celebrated, so that at this point we will examine the Trinitarian theological understanding of grace.

a) In contrast to the theological trend in the Age of Enlightenment, John Wesley adhered to the doctrine of human sinfulness. The human being was not able to find God of his or her own accord. But Wesley sees God's spirit already and always at work in God's creatures with prevenient grace, even in those who do not yet believe. With the help of the human conscience and the longing for meaning, fulfilment and salvation, the Holy Spirit moves people to God.
b) Like the Reformers of the 16th century, John Wesley preached justification by grace and faith alone. Faith in God and salvation in Jesus Christ are not to be seen as human achievements but as God's gift alone. Hence human beings need justifying grace. Wesley emphasised however, in contrast to some of the Lutheran traditions he encountered, that justification is not only to be understood juridically. The crucified Christ was not only doing something *for* human beings, so that God sees them as righteous, but he is also doing something *in* people through the Holy Spirit. He liberates from guilt and from the power of sin, and gives the sure gift of salvation.
c) Finally, God gives sanctifying grace through his Spirit. According to Methodist doctrine, this forms Christian men and women in Jesus' image and leads them to a life of service for God and neighbour. This sanctification too comes from grace and faith alone and is not earned by the human being. It does however call the whole person to service of heart, mouth and hands. The aim of the work of the Spirit

was, in Wesley's eyes, a change in the individual, the community and society.

Based on the threefold working of God's grace, Methodists see themselves ecclesiologically as a »community of seekers and believers«.[5] God's prevenient grace is at work among the seekers too, and this gives rise to an understanding of what is known as open communion. In the EmK, all are invited to communion, whether children or adults, baptised or unbaptised, believers or seekers. The only condition is the desire of the moment to encounter God's grace and love in Holy Communion. This openness of admission to communion, unusual among the free churches, is grounded in John Wesley's threefold understanding of prevenient, justifying and sanctifying grace. It means »that through participation in the celebration of communion, God's Spirit may both lead people to faith or establish them in faith and in certainty; the Spirit may renew their devotion to Christ and to their fellow human beings as well as responsibility in every area of their lives.«[6] This open approach to communion applies only to participation, however. In Methodism, as noted above, presiding at communion has required ordination from the earliest days. A certain tension might well be noticeable here.

Let us turn back at this point to the German context. Full Methodist appreciation of Holy Communion was at first hesitant within the German-speaking regions, probably due partly to the model of the Southern German preaching service. It became customary to celebrate Holy Communion only once a quarter, above all before or on the main festivals. Moreover, some Methodists in Germany, influenced by pietist tendencies, developed fastidious rules for receiving communion. In some congregations in earlier times, non-members were obliged to apply personally to the pastor if they wished to receive. The custom of admitting children and young people only after confirmation and reception survived up to the 1980s in many EmK churches. German-language Methodism

---

5 Cf. Berufen – Beschenkt – Beauftragt. Das evangelisch-methodistische Verständnis von Kirche, ed. Theologische Kommission des Europäischen Rates der EmK, Stuttgart/Zürich 1991, 13.

6 Walter Klaiber/Manfred Marquardt, Gelebte Gnade, Stuttgart 1993, 334.

was more than a century behind the openness at communion described above.

The late 1970s, however, brought a fundamentally new approach to the understanding and practice of communion. From a world perspective, it was the WCC's Faith and Order dialogue leading to the Lima document on Baptism, Eucharist and Ministry which caused Methodists to reflect on their own understanding and practice of Holy Communion with greater precision and a self-critical approach. This reflection was challenged by the negotiations on pulpit and table fellowship with the United Evangelical Lutheran Church of Germany. The fresh approach to the significance of Holy Communion, which was in fact for the most part a return to the legacy of early Methodism set out above, is documented in the changed wording of the church Orders. The EmK Order of 1977 reads: »The frequency of celebrations of Holy Communion is dependent on the needs of the congregations. It should be celebrated not less than four times a year«. In 1993 the same section reads: »Holy Communion should be celebrated as frequently as possible.« According to a survey, EmK congregations in Germany currently hold Holy Communion every four to five weeks, with a tendency for this to become more frequent.

International Methodism has already progressed further. In the British Methodist Church, for example, the basic form of service is Holy Communion. The UMC worldwide (to which the German UMC belongs) has a Book of Worship which no longer provides the full text for a preaching service without communion. Of course such services are still held, but in liturgical terms they are the exception. This development has resulted in fresh reflection and reforms in the EmK services in Germany, as will be set out in part 3.

3. Current reforms of the service in German-language Methodism

In most churches there is a substantial and welcome interest in questions relating to the service. Sociological church analyses indicate that attractive worship services are important for church development. The growing interest in services has produced a whole range of forms, in the EmK as well as elsewhere.

A services survey in the EmK in 2014 showed that, especially in the western part of Germany, many churches no longer structured their services according to the basic form 1A which was valid at the time. This was basically a service of the word, shaped in its structure by the worldwide union of two Methodist churches in 1968, the Methodist Episcopal Church and the Evangelical Association.[7] The new EmK resulting from this union was faced with the problem of developing, from the existing orders of service of the two churches, a common liturgy taking account of both traditions. Although the new order of service of 1973, compiled by the services commission, may be regarded as successful in its uniting of the two church strands, from today's perspective it does not come across as an organic and natural unit, but rather as a compromise. »The Gloria Patri and the Halleluja come from the Evangelical Association. The hymn of praise after the first prayer is from the Methodists, the announcements are before the sermon as in the Methodist tradition, and the Lord's Prayer comes after it as in the Evangelical Association.«[8]

Both traditions were meant to be at home in the new order of service, and for some three decades this was in fact the case. Over the last twenty years, however, there has been a growing dissatisfaction in many of our congregations with this basic form of service. Hence some fifteen years ago a specialist group responsible for services and the book of worship[9] in the German EmK started work on a new basic form of service. A sizeable conference on worship services was held, and reflections on service reforms were discussed in various bodies of the church. The reforms were to take account of theological, liturgical and anthropological aspects as well as denominational history. The United Methodist Book of Worship (1992) of the worldwide UMC, which had undergone a similar process, provided useful ideas and models.

---

7 Originally founded in the USA as a German-speaking Methodist church called Evangelische Gemeinschaft, it used this name later in the 19th century when starting up in Europe.

8 W. Klaiber, Building Up the House of God, in: K. B. Westerfied Tucker (ed.), The Sunday Service of the Methodists, Nashville, 1996, 292.

9 Fachgruppe für Gottesdienst und Agende.

Here are some of the criteria governing the work of the specialist group for services. The list is not complete, and is at some points redundant. To enable a better understanding of the group's concerns, the material is divided into the three fields »EmK heritage«, »considerations from liturgical studies« and »anthropological aspects«.

a) EmK heritage
- Taking up our tradition, the focus is especially on Holy Communion and the use of Scripture in the service (means of grace). Celebrating Holy Communion is to be »the normal case«.
- Drawing on God's threefold means of grace, the aspect of forgiveness of sins (justifying grace) in service and communion is to be accompanied by the dimensions of missional (prevenient) grace and diaconal (sanctifying) grace.
- Active participation of the whole congregation is desired (responsible grace) – in the spirit of the priesthood of all believers, and awareness of the significance of the human response to God's prevenient grace.
- Liturgical materials for personal and social topics are to be provided; innovations and spontaneous contributions are to be anchored in the liturgy (»time of concerns«).
- Bridges are to be built between different devotional styles, milieus, cultures and churches (from traditional to Fresh Expressions). Services should have their place within their own tradition (EmK Connexion) but also be ecumenically open (World Council of Churches, the Council of Christian Churches in Germany, CPCE, the Protestant Free Church Association,[10] pulpit and table fellowship).

b) Considerations from liturgical studies
- The service should offer a familiar structure which brings people together and is also flexible and open to connecting with local and church seasonal occasions.
- Liturgical materials for a wide variety of forms of service are to be produced, taking account of recent insights in this field e. g. from theatre and performance studies research, intercultural studies, etc.

---

10 Vereinigung evangelischer Freikirchen.

- The dialogic and communicative dimension of the service, the encounter between God and human being, and the congregation with each other, is to be more actively considered.
- Attention should be given to activity which is self-revelatory. Reflection should arise from the experience of the service, avoiding »homiletic« explanations of the liturgy and the talkativeness associated with this.
- The roots of the church in Judaism and the realisation of God's activity in the history of salvation should be more strongly emphasised.

c) Anthropological aspects

- The service focuses on basic theological and anthropological elements, with »listening«, »praying«, »eating and drinking« as elementary categories.
- As a celebration of life, the service should embrace elementary manifestations such as joy and grief, abundance and lack, guilt and forgiveness, praise and complaint. There should be space for renewal and transformation.
- The current desire for experience should be accommodated, along with a stronger culture of presence, contrasting with and complementing the culture of meaning and interpretation that still prevails in our church services. For this reason, more experience-oriented, physical and sensory forms of worship should be provided, offering greater interaction with the media and spaces available.

At the Central Conference of the EmK in spring 2017, the specialist group for services and the book of worship presented, after some ten years work, a new basic model for services. This model was developed in close cooperation with the UMC in Central and Southern Europe. Both Central Conferences approved the new basic structure and recommended it for use in worship in the European congregations. The model corresponds to the form of service in the Book of Worship of the worldwide United Methodist Church. And by the way, service reform in the EmK has many parallels with the history of the »renewed service book«[11] (pre-

[11] Erneuerte Agende.

sented for experimentation in 1990) and the book of services[12] subsequently adopted by VELKD and most other Protestant regional churches in Germany in 1999.

The new Methodist services model for congregations in Europe describes four parts or stations of the service, which may take different forms. The two main parts are Listening, the proclamation of the word, and Sharing, the communion. These two main parts are framed by the opening Gathering and the closing Going Forth (sending out and benediction). In its elementary simplicity, this four-part structure helps to provide a common base in our worship services. At the same time, congregations are free to shape the service appropriately according to local needs.

Visualised as a diagram, this is how the new basic structure looks:

Gathering - God calls us together
Opening, praise and prayer

Listening – God speaks to us
Reading(s) from the Bible, sermon/message

Sharing - God unites us with each other
Communion, collection of gifts, thanksgiving, announcements and responses, intercessions, The Lord's Prayer

Going Forth - God blesses us
Sending out and benediction

There may be plenty of variety in how each part is shaped: speech, music, performance, observing. The order of the elements within each part may vary. If there is no communion, other elements of the Sharing section come to the fore.

In contrast with the previous basic structure 1A, the opening prayer now precedes the Scripture readings. The time for community sharing now follows the sermon/message. And overall, Holy Communion plays a more important part, as it did for the early Christians, for John and Charles Wesley and in the worship books of the United Methodist Church and the Methodist Church in Britain.

---

[12] Evangelisches Gottesdienstbuch.

As well as accepting the new basic structure, the Central Conference of the EmK initiated a liturgical learning process. A group of trained communicators, both men and women, are ready to help local churches shape their service in accordance with the liturgical and theological foundations of the reform. The specialist group working on services and the book of worship will develop materials (liturgical formulae and examples of best practice) and make these available, so that the reform can take lasting effect on a broad basis.

I close with a brief programmatic text from the Book of Worship of the United Methodist Church: Our worship

> »is an encounter with the living God through the risen Christ in the power of the Holy Spirit. When the people of God gather, the Spirit is free to move them to worship in diverse ways, according to their needs [...] the Spirit is also the source of unity and truth. The teachings of Scripture give our worship a basic pattern that has proved itself over the centuries, that gives the United Methodist Church its sense of identity and links us to the Universal Church.«[13]

[13] The United Methodist Book of Worship, Nashville, 1992, 13.

Folkert Fendler

Quality in Worship Services

1. What is quality?

Most people love quality. If something looks good, tastes wonderful, is well made, keeps for a long time – then they can thoroughly enjoy it. Many people love church services – their music, the sermons, the atmosphere, being together. But if these two objects of love are connected it may happen that the love disappears, or at least is put off. Quality in worship? Do these two things go together? Is that the right expression to answer the question about what makes a good service?

The Council of the Evangelical Church in Germany (EKD) replied in the affirmative when, in 2009, it founded the EKD Center for Quality Development in Worship Services. The term quality development, however, awakened other associations than those of good quality, an attractive appearance and wonderful taste. Instead, it reminded people of technocratic processes: documentation, pressure to optimize, efficiency, certification. The need to clarify what was meant by »quality« rapidly became clear.

Quality has three meanings that can also be usefully applied to church services. First, the term »quality« describes the nature, or essence, of a thing. This is its original meaning, as understood by philosophers and theologians over the centuries. Then there is the colloquial usage, which simply uses »quality« as an adjective to indicate that something is good. And third, the concept is understood in quality management (QM) as the degree of fulfilling requirements, i. e. good or poor quality depend on whether the agreed criteria have been fulfilled or not.

2. Quality in worship services as a gift of God: worship services in »3C«

Working on quality in the case of a service starts with the quality of the *essence*, which can only be determined theologically. What is the essence of a service of worship? Luther is often quoted on this point, and rightly so. He says that its essence can be discovered in God speaking to the people, promising God's salvation, and the people responding in turn with praise and thanksgiving. But this minimum consensus about the essence of the service as Word and response can certainly be unpacked. If we look back over recent history regarding the theology of worship, we can distil three profiles. Services allow us to experience the *certainty of God's love*; they help us to shape the *community of hope*, and they *celebrate the mystery of faith.* Services of worship are always devised and conducted in 3C.

Certainty/community/celebrating mystery – love/hope/faith – experience/shape/celebrate: if these trios play a role in a service we are already tracing its essence. But aspects may be accentuated, in fact they always are. The question is whether that happens consciously? That is where working on the quality of the service starts: being clear about your own preliminary theological decisions. What do I myself really want to experience in the service? And – if I am someone with responsibility for planning worship – what do I want people to experience in my services? Is my prime aim to arouse or strengthen the worshippers' individual faith? Is my prime concern the relationships in the congregation, its cohesion and responsibility for the world? Is the service, in my eyes, a celebration of an ultimately unfathomable mystery, towards which we can only grope our way?

3. Quality in worship services calls for planning

While the quality of a worship service is founded in the theological assurance of its essence, it does not end there. After all, worship is also a human activity, in which many of the structures, processes and forms may be like this, but also like that. The leading question in this next step is then: Does the way I plan the service in practical terms really serve to enable what I have recognised as the essence of the service and would like to see come about? Or does it more serve as a hindrance? This opens up the great area of human preparation and decision – ranging from the seating arrangements, the culture of welcome, the choice of hymns, the texts of prayers, the relevance and rhetoric of the sermon … to the type of Holy Communion and liturgical presence at the benediction.

This is the area in which the service and its planners can really benefit from ideas borrowed from quality management. QM's logic of demand and fulfilment can also be transferred to worship. For example, if the service would basically like to strengthen the mystery of faith, phases of silence will be necessary and a constant stream of words more of a barrier. All planning decisions will be measured by this goal.

QM makes available instruments and thought patterns that help to distinguish different levels of quality and to find quality assessment criteria. The EKD Center for Quality Development in Worship Services has taken up some of these instruments and adapted them to worship services. Precisely because these are often unusual approaches to a service, they contain fresh potential, enabling us to see present-day forms of worship in a new light and to gain new ideas. Or they can help to clarify misunderstandings and overcome disagreements as we go about devising the liturgy.

4. The Kano Model

This approach was originally developed by a Japanese professor called Noriaki Kano. It comes from the services sector and distinguishes between three different levels of expectation among customers. Kano defined basic expectations, expectations regarding performance and enthusiasm factors. The basic expectations mostly relate to the general conditions and are *unconscious*. For example, at the theatre we normally expect there to be a cloakroom, that we will see the stage from our seat and that the actors will know their parts. Then we have *conscious* expectations about the performance on our night out: that the production will be interesting, that the play will be relevant to the present day, and that it will be good entertainment. Performance-related expectations may differ from person to person. Finally, enthusiasm factors exceed our expectations: the play carries us away, actors cope admirably with slip-ups, and there are free drinks in the interval.

If we play through these distinctions at a pastors' conference or in our own church council, we will rapidly arrive at the very basic issues concerning the service. We will not only learn how to distinguish between people's secret or open priorities but will find ourselves in the middle of discussions about the purpose and form of the service. Something that is otherwise addressed in vague terms (»I didn't know the hymns«, »I really enjoyed the sermon«) becomes more telling and clear by being classified in a three-stage model. And yet, with respect to worship, the Kano Model should not be left at the level of expectations. The basic and performance expectations and enthusiasm factors should be expanded in theological terms. What has to be harmonious at the service, what is essential and what is inspiring? Many who have already worked with this model have found that it is frequently the basic expectations/requirements that indicate the need to take action, and – although they are mostly superficial matters – they have a high potential for distracting attention.

5. The example of »Effects of worship services«

The EKD Center for Quality Development in Worship Services has developed criteria for the content of a good service, after evaluating recent studies on worship. They are shown in the model of the four effects (*Wirkfelder*) of worship services.

By effects we mean potential features of the service that include many of the things people expect of it and also correspond to defining its theological essence. Worship is always supposed to be about interpreting our own life in the light of the Christian message (1st effect: *interpreting meaning* in the tension between autonomy and »eternal truth«). A worship service has the potential to give people ideas for action and assistance in making decisions (2nd effect: *orienting action* in the tension between taking care of oneself and loving the neighbour). The service is meant to reach people emotionally in the depths of their existence (3rd effect: *experiencing profound emotions* in the tension between joy in life and deadly seriousness). Finally, the element of relations plays a key role in a worship service. However, this is not only in the sense of warm fellowship but also in a nuanced and phased way (4th effect: *experiencing relations* in the tension between closeness and distance, feeling at home and »in another world«).

Each of these four effects should be considered in a service and consciously planned. Naturally, they can and must be broken down into many different criteria. Traditional criteria are often lost in the organisational details (the role of music, good presentation, an understandable accent in the respective language, etc.), that are important but rarely cover the centre of the service. The *effects* start from its essence, its theological core – somewhat in the spirit of the service in »3C« – and may be spelled out differently. It is only from there that they move on to the details.

6. How do I tell my pastor?

This and other approaches to the topic of »quality in worship« will remain largely ineffective if it is not possible to establish a regular culture of discussion about the church service within the congregations. After defining the essence and finding criteria, this is the next step to be taken in a process of developing quality in worship. An open, appreciative culture of discussion is called for among ministerial colleagues and between the members of the congregation and those responsible for worship. It is one thing to reflect on the essence and shape of the service, and another to check on the outcomes. Did what was wanted correspond to what was intended? Was faith strengthened? Did the sermon come across? What feedback can the members of the congregation give, or would they like to give?

Proceeding sensitively and systematically, discreetly and yet fruitfully, is an art that still needs to be developed, and certainly cannot be left to questionnaires. Here too it is worth taking a look across the fence of the church scene to the sphere of QM, where quality is always understood as a cycle of agreements and verification of achievement. Positive experiences have already been gained with newly conceived post-worship discussions (not only talking about the sermon!) and conversational models of ministers and pastors sitting in on each other's services and giving feedback as colleagues.

A key question remains: Who are the actors in this triple process, in this worship event? Does quality development put the Holy Spirit out of a job? I would like to phrase it this way: the spirit of the worship service is the spirit of something over which we have no power of decision. The spirit of quality management is the spirit of what is manageable and what we can do. *Opus dei* and *opera hominum* in happy alternation. That is quality development in worship.

References

Gewissheit. Gemeinschaft. Geheimnis. Qualitäten des Gottesdienstes, edited by Folkert Fendler and Christian Binder, Leipzig, 2016.

Qualität im Gottesdienst, Was stimmen muss. Was wesentlich ist. Was begeistern kann, edited for the Liturgy Conferenz by Folkert Fendler, Gütersloh, 2015.

Brochures (in German) produced by the EKD Center for Quality Development in Worship Services may be downloaded at www.michaeliskloster.de/qualitaets-entwicklung/material.
- feedback
- areas of impact regarding the worship service

Olivier Favrod

Faithfulness to the Reformed Tradition and Contemporary Relevance

A brief survey of the worship landscape in the French-speaking Evangelical Reformed Church (EERV) of Canton Vaud, Switzerland

In the following paper I would like to share a few observations linked to my work in the EERV's department of Worship and Congregational Life, along with some thoughts on theological and sociological approaches to worship services.[1] It will be more an annotated snapshot and an outline of the tensions than an exhaustive analysis. This rapid sketch of the worship scene in the EERV today will describe what we do, where we are experimenting and what questions arise.

I will thus touch on my own practical experience, the EERV's regulations and liturgical documents, and list a number of studies in the bibliography.

1. A little bit of recent history

Historians agree that, in French-speaking Switzerland, the word *culte* came into common usage in the 19th century to refer to *public prayers and orisons*, other *holy assemblies* of the kind dear to Calvin, or Zwinglian »eucharists«. Its etymology[2] reveals that the *culte* mainly expresses the

---

1 These are updated notes of a talk I gave in 2013 during a liturgy conference (Assises Romandes de Liturgie) at Yverdon.

2 *Culte* comes from the Latin *cultus*, and is directly derived from *colere*, a term borrowed from the agricultural world meaning: inhabit, cultivate, honour, practice: a set of actions and rites. This quasi generic term was originally used in different religions to speak of a religious celebration (e. g. the cult of Apollo).

human role in the religious act. The word does not have the richness of the German *Gottesdienst*, a composite which expresses both God's work and the service of the people. A brief look back over five decades shows how things have changed. The norm used to be a service of worship (*culte*) conducted by a pastor following an »order of service« and reading texts drawn from a liturgy (a bound collection) adopted by Synod (republished at the end of 1966, for the last time as a single volume). Now we have a service conducted by a minister (*ministre*) and a few lay people: this has been the case since 2011 in conformity with instructions issued by the Synod Council on worship, Christian festivals, sacraments and other rites within the EERV.[3] In compliance with articles 242 ff of the Ecclesiastical Regulations (2007), the Council has made a collection of worship resources freely available in electronic form.

In his work on the liturgical movement in the Vaud region (see bibliography, A. Bardet) published in 1988, Pastor André Bardet expressed appreciation of the liturgical standards adopted by Synod in March 1984: they opened up a »space of freedom« in the service of worship. Accordingly, the EERV adopted the »Liturgie à l'usage des Eglises romandes«. This liturgy for French-speaking churches had developed out of the liturgical revival promoted by the »church and liturgy« movement (of which Pastor Richard Paquier was one of the founders), by a few French Reformed publications and also by a group concerned with pastoral and congregational life,[4] which in the 1980s set out to produce liturgical texts in contemporary language. This »space of freedom« expanded even more, prompting André Bardet (1913–2004) to express some apprehension: »When crafting ›their‹ liturgy, those officiating sometimes forget the basic elements of the service.« Yet he still took a relatively positive view of the way church services had developed since the end of the 19th century. To quote Bardet again: »Today, the service flows more easily […] It can be made more lively and dynamic when the congregation plays an active role, saying psalms together and voicing responses.« In spite of the changes mentioned by Bardet, the service remains very clergy-centred.

[3] Directive du Conseil synodal sur les cultes, fêtes chrétiennes, sacrements et autres rites au sein de l'EERV.

[4] Groupe »Pastorale et communauté«.

The congregations primarily count on the minister to plan and lead worship.

Until 1960, parish organisation focused on the Sunday service; the pastor had to be able to provide reasonable coverage of the preaching places in the parish. Several places of worship were built in the 1960s in order to bring services closer to where people lived. The »Church to Come« campaign (1998–2002), and the subsequent restructuring, shifted the focus of attention away from how to organise services.

2. The legal framework of worship in the EERV

The following articles from the EERV regulations[5] were revised in 2016 and provide the legal framework for our church services.

Art. 242 General points

The service draws the community of believers together around the Lord Jesus Christ.
The service is structured around the proclamation of the Word and the celebration of the sacraments.
Through the service, the community of believers expresses the various dimensions of Christian faith: witness, communion, service and worship.
The service is embedded in the liturgical year; it takes account of current events.

Art. 243 Liturgical elements

The main parts of the service liturgy are the following:
- salutation and invocation
- praise
- repentance and forgiveness
- Bible reading and preaching
- confession of faith, intercession, offering, Lord's Prayer

[5] Règlement Ecclésiastique (RE).

- baptism, holy communion
- announcements, sending out and benediction.

The person officiating may adapt the order to the circumstances and the congregation.

Art. 244 Liturgy

The EERV's liturgy aspires to unity in the service, the sacraments and the other rites, while leaving room for creativity.

In order to show its own internal unity, its fellowship with the other Reformed churches and the great tradition of the universal church, the EERV shall:

- publish the documents that the Synod Council has expressly prescribed for use
- publish other documents as additional resources for congregations and officiants.

Art. 245 Frequency

At least one service shall be held every Sunday in every parish, likewise on Christian festivals, unless an exemption has been granted by the regional council. This service is public.
It may be replaced occasionally by a regional or cantonal service.
The other places of worship may organise services.
Special arrangements shall be made for German-speaking parishes.

Art. 248 Places and times

In a framework defined by the regional council, the parish council shall fix the places and times of parish services.
The regional council shall fix the places and times of regional services.
The chaplaincy council shall fix the places and times of chaplaincy services.
The Synod Council shall fix the places and times of cantonal services.

Art. 250 Conducting the service

The service shall be conducted by a pastor or by a person delegated by the pastor.

The pastor shall conduct the service wearing a black gown with white bands. Wearing a white gown is subject to authorisation by the council responsible for the respective place of worship.
Some additional information:
- The use of liturgical colours is not prescribed.
- No lectionary is prescribed.
- The offering is an integral part of the order of service; it is duly announced, then taken up during the service, followed by an act of thanksgiving.

3. The environment and situation of the EERV[6]

In order to reflect on the contemporary relevance of public worship, it seems important to me to take account of megatrends in today's society. They reveal changes in mentality and affect a large part of society. While the churches are obliged to take account of these trends, they have little capacity to influence them.

We are witnessing a progressive separation of previously connected societal sub-systems, such as politics, religion, education, health, sciences/humanities and law. This is clearly reflected in more distant relations between church and state. Today people live their lives as individuals and no longer feel linked by their origin to a particular social class, profession, faith, predefined social role or place of residence. As individualisation destroys their family loyalties (social class, traditional milieu of shared values or territorial community), individuals are forming new social groups called »lifestyle milieus«. The abandoning of traditional values (discipline, obedience, faithfulness, renunciation, Sunday observance) makes it easier for people to distance themselves and lessens the moral influence of churches on their members. Today individuals live in a huge »supermarket« covering all aspects of life. The special offers of churches, including their services of worship, have to compete with other,

6 According to the report of the Council of the Federation of Swiss Protestant Churches (SEK-FEPS) on revising the SEK-FEPS constitution (annual meeting of 8–9 November 2010).

similar activities on offer. The growth in the number of people of no faith could lead us to question the public service role played by our official churches. The amount of information available is growing exponentially, communicated through a spiralling number of media. The churches must take this into account.

4. The EERV landscape

In the EERV, these major social trends are impacting on different areas of church life (parishes and elsewhere). Generally speaking, the number of those declared themselves to be Reformed has been falling regularly since 1950. In 2010 they constituted 29% of the population of Canton Vaud. In our church, the number of deaths clearly exceeds the number of births. Only 10% of Reformed parishioners, of whom almost half are aged between 61 and 75, attend a church activity at least twice a month. Only 3% go to church every Sunday and 60% of them are over 60. We have been wondering whether attending worship is linked to age. That would mean that the youth of today would take over from their elders when they reached retiring age. However, studies show that religiosity mainly stems from religious socialisation and training received during childhood and adolescence.

Christian culture is being lost. Christian references are becoming rarer and rarer among the younger generations. The transmission of Christian culture is on the decline. Standards are changing. Today we cannot claim to offer a quality event without engaging various professionals and enlightened enthusiasts.

EERV's areas of visibility are shifting. Questioned about the role of the church in society, people mention, in this order, support for the most dispossessed, the transmission of Christian values to children, the celebration of rituals at important times in life and only then the service of worship.

The fact that currently many pastoral positions are vacant, or not covered, does not affect the number of services as substitutes are available. However, this situation means that reflecting about the service ahead of time (organisation, preparation, implementation) suffers, since the substitutes are neither legitimised nor motivated to become more involved in this field. The shortage of ministers announced for the 2020s will complicate matters. EERV's financial situation is comfortable, but precarious. That reinforces the importance of fundraising, of which the service remains one of the main opportunities (offerings).

The changes imposed on parishes and regions by the current restructuring affect the service at two levels:

They have upset practices and customs with often negative consequences on church attendance.

They necessitate major investments in time and energy on the part of local actors, to the detriment of other activities, including the service of worship.

5. Taking stock

EERV has no statistics on the number of services held, nor on attendance (or even trends in this respect). So far, the proposals to make a systematic count for documentary purposes have encountered widespread, determined resistance, probably for the following reasons:

- With respect to worship, many agree in saying that it is not the number of participants that matters.
- Such an undertaking is an obligation and causes administrative expense.
- It is not possible to discover and publish figures without revealing that fluctuation is possibly related to the ministers concerned.

6. Between tradition and contemporary relevance

With respect to organising and conducting the service, the following points of tension are apparent:

The liturgical language of the usual Sunday service is really meant for an »in-group« or calls for initiation, which takes place less and less in the family or in catechism classes. In the EERV, work on language is done by a handful of people without real stimulation or coordination. It is hard to measure the gap between liturgical language and the ordinary citizen.

People have a different attitude to books now. The amount of written text is diminishing. The Reformed status attributed to »the Word« (contained in »the Book of Books«) can no longer be taken for granted.

Liturgy and hymnology are among the weak points in the current training of ministers and organists. Along with a shortage of ministers, a shortage of organists is looming, increasing the difficulty of keeping up the status quo in the long term. There is practically no investment in encouraging or training other church musicians, or enabling a production of specifically Reformed hymns.

Individuals keen to learn can nowadays discover lots of interesting and reliable information on TV, the radio and the internet. If they come to church it is mainly to share with others in a community event that nurtures their faith, questions their ideas and stimulates their behaviour.

One of the prime ways of trying to maintain, even increase, attendance is by diversifying the form of worship and seeking innovation, sometimes to suit specific target audiences. Here or there we have got carried away and some are now starting to say that every service is a special service. There is a real risk of entering into a problematic spiral. The church has long lost its monopoly on the arts and culture. The development of technologies in all fields means that our contemporaries are used to high quality events. It is getting more and more difficult to keep up this standard with the means available to the EERV.

The official EERV line is that – theologically and ecclesiologically – the service of worship is at the centre of church and congregational life. This position is subject to discussion and difficult to put into practice. There are very few parishes in which the congregation really gathers for worship. In some respects, the service seems to be only one of multiples activities offered by a parish. Moreover, the territorial principle that prevailed up into the 1960s is no longer the only model. Increasingly, the members are choosing their parish on the basis of other criteria than their place of residence; they are prepared to travel to attend the kind of service they enjoy.

If we compare the small share of a minister's working week devoted to planning and conducting a service with the central role theoretically attributed to it we find a considerable disparity. The same applies to the place of worship services in basic ministerial training, or the investment allowed for music and new means of communication.

The changes that have taken place in the last decade, notably the diminution of ministerial posts, are forcing parishes to revise their way of organising worship. Consequently, what logic should we follow to organise services? That of a strict, regular coverage of the different preaching places in a parish by the number of ministers available, which too often means that many services are only attended by the faithful few? That of a gathering aiming to attract a larger and thus more dynamic congregation, when services are held regularly in the same place? At the beginning of the 3rd millennium, the EERV is finding it difficult to discern, let alone boldly adopt, a new way forward. This is doubtless because, when trying to solve a problem of organisation and appropriateness, it does not concentrate sufficiently on the central question: why and how should we in the Reformed tradition worship God today?

The search for practicable responses to this question must, in my opinion, be an open, pluridisciplinary approach. It could lead to the emergence of a third logic for holding worship services, beyond covering preaching places and centralised gatherings – and devise a project with other parameters than those of the traditional parish, such as target audiences.

It so happens that the EERV must currently manage the gap between the number of services necessary to the life of a parish today, the number of services corresponding to the endowment of ministerial positions and the effective number of preaching places. We have no documented studies on what happens to the image of the church and Reformed faith when places of worship are turned into housing or neighbourhood centres, or abandoned altogether.[7] The approach to this issue remains very emotional.

The weight of Vaudois Reformed tradition, shaped by an insidious clericalism, hardly favours an open reflection on the question of the role and respective place of lay people and ministers in worship. Most of the

---

[7] It would be interesting to analyse the circumstances and impact of the change of purpose of several places of worship belonging to the former Église Libre after it merged with the Église nationale évangélique in 1966 to form the EERV.

people who attend prefer and expect the service to be conducted by a minister (pastor or deacon) who is trained and paid to do just that. This position could be interpreted as indicating a real lack of commitment, a form of delegation of the priesthood of all believers.

The way of thinking and experiencing the service also has an effect on the development of ecumenical relations. I will only mention this in passing, without going into the matter.

EERV has no statistics on the number of services held, or on attendance (and trends in that respect). For questions of credibility, of respect for the use of public funds and coherence in witness, EERV can no longer, in my view, escape the question of the effective cost of a service. On what conditions can a service be regarded as ecclesiologically and financially legitimate? The ecological cost of holding a service is also becoming an issue (see www.oeku.ch).

Parishes know that it is not enough to advertise a service (in newspapers, on websites) for people to come. There has to be advertising since the service is public. However, it does not lead to any great increase in attendance. To achieve that, it would be necessary to invite people to attend. That raises at least three problems:

- Extending a personal invitation is not a usual practice. The average Vaudois is shy in this field and still very marked by mainline Protestantism.
- If you invite someone to an event you have to be able to guarantee that it will turn out to be what you are proposing.
- In our open society, inviting someone to one service rather than another means opening up the dynamic of competition, which is not appreciated in the church.[8]

8 See the effect of the »newsletters« published by the EERV's main institutions along with some invitations spread via Facebook.

7. Some ways forward

In the present circumstances, I will cautiously sketch out the following lines to follow regarding public worship in the EERV:

- Maintaining and improving the quality of the traditional service. There is still progress to be made in the area of liturgical coherence, mastering communication tools and preaching.
- Welcoming and facilitating, alongside the traditional service, the emergence of new forms of worship by, and with, the defined target audience. Experience[9] has shown that it is pointless to try to organise services *for* people and that it would be wiser to rediscover the relevance of worship today *with* those interested.
- Trying to find ways in which, in the church, the possible emergence of new opportunities and forms of worship can be understood as complementary to traditional forms and not as competition. The problem is particularly complex. Conducting different services (sometimes linked to »fresh expressions«) in the framework of the same local entity soon raises questions about theology, belonging, image and different ways of responding to a common mission. It is then a matter of defining *with* whom to try and develop the new forms of worship.

In short, it is about continuing to work on

- ways of analysing and taking into account the needs and expectations of defined groups (target audiences)
- ways of proclaiming, or passing on, the Word (preaching and other forms of sharing the gospel)
- different languages (verbal, gestural, symbolic, etc.)
- the place of music, and what kind(s)
- the intergenerational dimension, or the place of children and families
- greater active participation of lay people.

[9] Of the Reformed Church of Canton St Gall, for example.

Taking this line, the partners concerned run into the following main difficulties: the current church situation (lack of time, heavy atmosphere, structural problems, clinging to tradition) is not very favourable to new ideas and experimentation and choosing priorities remains a difficult exercise at all levels of the EERV.

Working on the gap between the church and the world of today means investing major resources in many fields: theology, sociology and communication, in particular. In the field of worship (as in others) the EERV still understands itself too much as a mainline church that people have to join and not enough as a missional church called to share the life of its contemporaries and to help raise up new forms of worship and congregational life.

References

BARDET, A., Un combat pour l'Eglise, un siècle de mouvement liturgique en Pays de Vaud, Bibliothèque historique vaudoise, Lausanne, 1988.

BAUER, O., Le protestantisme et ses cultes désertés, Editions Labor et Fides, coll. Protestantismes, Genève, 2008.

BOUSQUET, I., Des cultes autrement, Olivétan, Lyon, 2007.

BÜRKI, B./ERENSPERGER, A./NEESER, D./STRÜBIN, E., La liturgie à vivre, Editions Gotthelfverlag, Zurich, 1993 [also exists in German: Gottesdienst feiern].

GENRE, E., Le culte chrétien, une perspective protestante, Editions Labor et Fides, coll. Pratique N° 23, Genève, 2008.

GISEL, P./KAENNEL, L., Encyclopédie du protestantisme, Editions Labor et Fides, Genève, 2006.

GOUNELLE, A., Le culte selon la tradition réformée, Information-Evangélisation, 1988/1.

NOUÏS, A., Le sens du culte, Editions Olivétan, Lyon, 2010.

REYMOND, B., Liturgies en chantier, Edit. Belle Rivière, Lausanne, 1984.

STOLZ, J./BAILLIF, E., L'avenir des Réformés, les Eglises face aux changements sociaux, Editions Labor et Fides, coll. Protestantismes, Genève, 2011.

Ulrike Beichert / Monika Hautzinger

Regional Worship Landscapes in the Protestant Church in Baden[1]

An empirical report

1. Why regional worship landscapes?

In several of the 20 regional member churches (*Landeskirchen*) of the Evangelical Church in Germany (EKD) we are witnessing a growth at the »middle« or »church district« level, which is located between the local parish level and the central church administration. In Baden, for example, the church district level is now being granted powers and funds that used to belong to the »top level«, i. e. the central church administration (e. g. regarding church-related staffing). Conversely, church districts are also having to coordinate decisions that are a matter for individual parishes (e. g. about church buildings). There are several reasons for this double strengthening of the »middle level«:

- With resources growing scarcer, they need to be used in a targeted and effective way. The intention is to avoid separate parishes working in parallel processes instead of together. At the same time, wrong decisions are thought to be less likely if decision-makers are close to the area concerned.
- Developments in society have led to greater differentiation in people's life situations and customs, including those of church members, who, along with everyone else, have also become more mobile. The Sinus Milieu Study for Baden-Württemberg highlighted the diversity of these life worlds (milieus), to which church members also belong. The realisation that only very few of these milieus are represented at worship has raised the question of how to devise »milieu-sensitive« services.

---

1 Die Evangelische Landeskirche in Baden.

- The idea of the one service being the central and gathering point of the parish no longer matches the empirical situation in many places. Worship life has become fragmented; Taizé services, services of praise, Thomas masses, youth services, gospel-music services are only some of the formats that have supplemented the standard service of worship. The service times have also begun to vary: besides Sunday mornings there are now services on Saturday evenings, Sunday evenings and during the week (»after-work services«).
- No parish can develop forms of worship specifically for each and every target group and milieu represented in its territory. That would overstretch its capacities and lead to fragmented groups. At the same time, the idea of one service as a gathering point for all is increasingly becoming an illusion.
- Similar differentiations arise in the other areas of church life too. That is making the fields of activity of pastors and other church workers (employees and volunteers) more numerous and complex.

For these reasons, the frame of reference for worship life is increasingly extending beyond the geographical parish. It may be the church district (in particular where it corresponds to the area of a town or city). It may also be several regions within a district (as in large country districts). This frame of reference also matches people's area of mobility better than the traditional parish.

In a working paper on challenges and prospects for worship life,[2] the Liturgy Commission of the Protestant Church in Baden therefore proposes the development of regional approaches to holding worship services.[3] They include the ability and need to distinguish between the ser-

---

2 »Leben aus der Quelle. Herausforderungen und Perspektiven für das gottesdienstliche Leben der Evangelischen Landeskirche in Baden«.

3 After defining its location (»Why do we hold services of worship?«), the working paper contains a quantitative stocktaking of worship life in the Protestant Church in Baden, a description of societal changes and their impacts on worship services, as well as strategic goals on how to deal with them; it further contains a chapter on the quality of worship services and 12 steps to implement the strategic goals. One of these steps is that of developing regional worship models. After a two-year

vices held by the various congregations in a given region (or district). For a »worship landscape« to arise, the acts of worship in the individual congregations must complement each other. Making this happen calls for discussion leading to a shared approach, which then needs to be publicised.

2. Developing a regional approach to worship services in Pforzheim

Even if many agree that regional worship plans make sense, getting there is a complicated route, full of dead-ends – particularly in an EKD member church like that of Baden, where important parts of *ius liturgicum* (liturgical law) lie with the local church leadership (i. e. the presbytery/church council).[4] That means that it is not possible to adopt and »decree« regional worship plans at the regional or district level; instead, all the congregations involved need to be won over to the idea and engage voluntarily in devising and implementing a common approach. If it is to be based on complementarity (i. e. certain worship forms and times in a parish are offered on behalf of the whole region), this may mean saying goodbye to the previous worship traditions in individual parishes. This is up to the church council to decide. If the plan is to comprise complementary elements, all congregations need to be extensively involved in a transparent and confidence-building process. It may prove helpful to bring in an advisor from outside, e. g. from the central church administration.

The Pforzheim church district has gained experience with such a process with outside support. Over a period of two years, a working group made up of six pastors from the church district (accompanied by the two authors of this paper) drew up guidelines for a regional

work process, the Liturgy Commission presented the paper to the Baden synod in October 2015, which referred it to the church districts and parishes for discussion. Feedback from the church districts came in to the central church administration until summer 2017, which formed the basis of concrete proposals to synod in October 2017.

4 *Grundordnung* (constitution), Art. 16: Responsibility for teaching, order and building up the congregation, particularly for the number and times of worship services.

worship plan, which were adopted in July 2017 by the church district synod.

The group's work comprised nine meetings and a three-day tour and documentation of all 24 church buildings in the church district. In addition, they presented their work once to a clergy conference, once to the City Church council and twice to the city synod. Besides, it planned a launch event and invited church elders from all congregations, but this did not take place. The two persons accompanying the process from the central church administration facilitated and documented the meetings. Apart from that, they devised a tool to classify all the services currently held according to certain categories, wrote an illustrated report of the church-building tour, and drafted the working group's first worship plan.

The Pforzheim district synod adopted the guidelines in July 2017. The question of how they are to be implemented is still open. This reflects the slight uncertainty that has accompanied the work from the start:

- The district working group, made up of six pastors, was formed on the basis of experience shared at a clergy conference and received its mandate from the district only afterwards. The exact nature of its mandate was not clear at first.
- The (subsequently worded) mandate to the group comprised the drafting of guidelines on worship services for the church district. Whether, or how, they were to be implemented remained an open question.
- At the same time as the working group worked on the district worship plan another three groups in the church district were studying questions of staffing, church buildings and public relations. No answer was given to the question of how the four groups related to each other.

These problems were subsequently not resolved and at two points led to difficulties in the process. Early on, the working group recognised that a high degree of mutual trust would be necessary to implement a common approach to worship services for the parishes. Consequently, one of its first actions was to plan an introductory event to get to know the bodies responsible and the worship life of the »others«. The fact that this event did not take place due to a lack of support at the local level shows that the process was not seen as binding. It is then hardly surprising that uncertainty arose again at the end of the process: the reception given the guidelines made it clear that individual congregations were ambivalent about two questions: 1. How much change is acceptable in worship life? 2. To what extent can they accept a loss of their autonomy in organising worship services?

However, after some delay, the guidelines for an approach to worship services[5] for the Pforzheim church district were finally adopted in July 2017, on the basis of the results of the working group. They still have to be illustrated and put into practice. Already, however, the guidelines are developing a certain momentum with individual regions beginning to use them as a basis for their own worship plans. Hence the worship landscape in the Pforzheim church district is coming into view with individual »gardens« growing closer together.

3. Aspects of regionalisation

For some time there have been forms of voluntary cooperation between neighbouring parishes, e. g. in the field of preparation for confirmation. Experience has also been gained at the local and regional level with cooperation in holding faith courses. Here it became clear that not every faith course can be offered in every congregation, either with respect to the people the courses are meant to reach, or to the pastors leading or involved in them.

Regional cooperation does happen in the area of service organisation – e. g. running sermon series on specific topics, swapping pulpits or holding joint services on Boxing Day, Easter Monday or the Monday after Pentecost. In many places, however, the opportunities offered by the binding cooperation in planning worship at the regional level are yet to be (further) discovered.

What is the prime aim of a regional worship service plan? Is it mainly about reducing the burden on those playing an active part in the services (which is justified and necessary), or strengthening the region in the sense of intensifying communication between the parishes? Are we looking for new ways of continuing to meet expectations or is the goal to

---

5 »Leitlinien für ein Gottesdienstkonzept«.

reach more people with differentiated offerings and thereby raise attendance at public worship?

Clarifying these questions is necessary in order to set realistic goals and not to arouse any excessive expectations. It will also enable us to pull together and deal with any anxieties, in particular in view of the downsizing of congregations and church staff. The object of our hopes must be(come) clear.

As with any cooperation it also holds true for a regional worship plan: cooperation must be wanted, and where it is suggested, or even imposed, top-down, due to structural changes, it needs at least an insight into the necessity. That is why it is necessary to describe the aim of the cooperation process as clearly as possible.

4. Steps on the way

Cooperation does not appear out of nowhere, it needs people to journey together.

The Pforzheim example shows how important it is for the church district to establish a working group with a specific mandate. That also applies to the drafting of a worship plan for a smaller region. The first thing is to check whether the extra work entailed by the process is manageable, and whether there are enough people interested in participating.

The working group plans the process, clarifies the duration, procedure and steps (What has to happen, and when?). This »masterplan« must be adopted by the church district.

Any planning starts with taking note of the existing worship landscape with its local and regional strengths and weaknesses. Compiling a tabular overview is helpful here, showing what takes place when, where and at what time. But it can also show where profiles have already developed and what target groups are currently particularly well catered for. Another question to be seriously addressed is: Where, and when, do many/few people attend? The analysis also relates to the worship space and the staffing situation of the local or regional church. This can clearly show the worship locations that can/should cooperate, and/or regarding which services/times.

Another important step is working out criteria for a regional worship plan (by the working group, or by the district as guidelines for the working group). That concerns ascertaining the aim of cooperation, and the vision of what the worship landscape will look like in x number of years. Other important questions are, for example: What do people need? If there is more cooperation, what will have to change?

Other local and regional church leaders should be drawn into the process early on. That means both, staff and volunteers. After all, the local congregations and church-goers are going to have to live with and accept the changes. Therefore it is important to reflect on what can be done so that they can move from a more passive role to become agents of change.

Psychological factors always play a considerable role in processes of change. We have to be aware of the shared history of neighbouring parishes, the kind of relations existing among pastoral colleagues, what resistance may be expected and how it can be countered. We frequently plan our changes in terms of »hard« factors such as finance, the number of posts, buildings and structures. The »soft« factors such as trust, creativity, openness, patience and relations do not come up automatically. For this reason, confidence-building measures are central to the planning. So that relations can be marked by appreciation, empathy and consideration in mutual dealings, we need gatherings enabling people to get to know each other, exchange information and establish links. These encounters between several congregations in a region have to be organised, wanted, planned, carried out and built on. Frequently that proves very complicated, but it is worth investing trust in one another and creating a fund of common experience.

It may be very helpful if the process is guided by a moderator (facilitator) from outside the region. The Protestant Church in Baden has trained a number of pastors as worship advisors who are available for referral by the central administration's Worship Unit. Moderators can help to structure the path, stay on the ball and possibly keep an eye on the necessary stopovers and feedback loops. Experience shows that their view from outside makes the process more objective and down-to-earth.

An important part of a regional worship plan, including its crafting process, is public relations. As of a certain stage, it is essential that no one feels left out or is surprised by decisions. A regional worship plan also calls for regional public relations (e.g. a shared parish newsletter). If parallel processes continue in a district/region the flow of information between them must be guaranteed.

Finally we can say: developing a regional worship plan is, in most cases, a complex process, that takes time and needs to be supported, sometimes even protected. After all, creating something new, or developing what already exists, does not happen without trying things out, taking risks and getting it wrong. But we are convinced: together we can accomplish more!

Stephan Goldschmidt

»O sing to the Lord a new song; sing to the Lord, all the earth« (Psalm 96:1)

On creating and introducing new spiritual songs

1. The importance of hymns

Hymns are of inestimable importance in Protestant services. They are far more than a welcome interruption between bits of liturgy and the spoken word. A hymn has its own weight and significance in worship. First, it is a way of praising God, by which the congregation responds to the promise of God's Word. But at the same time, a hymn is proclamation; sometimes it is also a prayer, in a deeper sense. The whole person prays – singing with their hearts, their mouths and their minds. The Hebrew term for soul (*nephesh*) covers a broad range of meaning and may describe the organ that produces sounds and tones: the throat. When we sing, the two meanings come together: the song produced by our throat has an effect on our insides. That is why it is worth doing our best to cultivate congregational singing, where it has become uninspired, and to brighten it up.

According to a double study published by the Liturgy Conference of the Evangelical Church in Germany (EKD), congregational singing is in much better shape than the widespread stereotype lament – that hardly anyone sings any more.[1] The first study, conducted in 2010, produced a surprising result: 68.4% of interviewees said they always join in the singing at church. 24.4% said that they mostly do.[2] Yet there are reasons

1 Klaus Danzeglocke / Andreas Heye / Stephan A. Reinke / Harald Schroeter-Wittke, Singen im Gottesdienst. Ergebnisse und Deutungen einer empirischen Untersuchung in evangelischen Gemeinden, Gütersloh 2011; Liturgie und Kultur 1/2014: Singen im Gottesdienst II.

2 See article in op. cit. by Heye / Gembris / Schroeter-Wittke, Singen im Gottesdienst. Eine empirische Untersuchung, 17–57, here: 41.

why singing may not be easy. The people surveyed in the two studies (2010 and 2012) named the following as the most important obstacles:

- I don't know the hymn.
- I don't like the hymn.
- Too few other people are singing.[3]

2. Why do services again and again need new hymns?

Since the most important reason given for not singing in church was that the interviewees did not know the hymn, our first question may be whether we should stick to the familiar hymns or chorales (traditionally Lutheran hymns with simple tunes sung in unison or harmony). Such a conclusion would, however, disregard the second surprise that came out of the 2010 study: »new spiritual songs« are just as popular as chorales for congregational singing. 77% of those questioned said they enjoyed singing both kinds of hymn.[4]

Anyone wishing to encourage singing in services of worship will therefore do well to mix new and traditional hymns and not to go for either one or the other. By analogy with the third criterion[5] of the *Evangelisches Gottesdienstbuch* (Protestant service book), we could say regarding hymns: familiar hymns with a long tradition and new hymns with contemporary texts and tunes should be given equal status in Protestant services.[6]

---

3 K. Danzeglocke et al., ibid., 44; likewise Liturgie und Kultur 1/2014, 16.

4 Heye/Gembris/Schroeter-Wittke, op. cit., 46. The results were similar in the second study, conducted in 2012 mainly in eastern Germany.

5 Evangelisches Gottesdienstbuch. Agende für die Ev. Kirche der Union und für die Vereinigte Ev.-Luth. Kirche Deutschlands, Berlin 1999, 15: »Familiar texts from tradition and new texts from contemporary congregational life should be given the same status.«

6 Compare also the most recent EKD investigation of church membership: Heinrich Bedford-Strohm/Volker Jung (eds.), Vernetzte Vielfalt. Kirche angesichts von Individualisierung und Säkularisierung, Gütersloh, 2015, 480. Asked what

New hymns link up more with present listening customs, which have long since been shaped by pop music – and that does not only apply to young people. For those who were born since 1950, those who grew up with the Rolling Stones and the Beatles, pop music has advanced to become a kind of defining culture.[7] If we do not include this in services, embracing it alongside other types of music, we will unintentionally exclude whole groups of people and their way of listening. By contrast, anyone concerned to plan an inviting service will ensure that there is a varied selection of hymn styles and inevitably try out new hymns. This mix of hymns from different epochs and with different styles can be compared to those areas of life in which it is normal to have a variety of different styles side by side. In architecture or in a church building, for example, it makes sense that each age has to develop its own style.

3. The quality issue

New hymns are often viewed with suspicion and assumed not to be up to the standard of the old, familiar chorales. Anyone who makes Paul Gerhardt the benchmark for a hymn will find very few hymns to compare with his. It is my observation, however, that there are hardly any clear-cut criteria for judging the quality of hymns. Nor do experts always agree on whether a song or hymn meets quality standards. Perhaps it remains a matter of taste whether a hymn is rated good or less good. Hymns that seem to perfectly reflect the lives of some, strike others as theologically shallow. The assessment of different styles is frequently subjective as well, and depends on our own preferences.

In addition, hymns are able to concentrate emotions and later release them. A hymn evokes experiences bound up with it and singing it can

they want to experience at a Sunday service they give what might at first sight appear to be contradictory answers. Ultimately, however, these replies show that people would like different styles of music in services: 70.3% wish for mainly traditional church music and 61.3% prefer modern hymns.

7 Harald Schroeter-Wittke, Singen im Gottesdienst II: Kommentar aus theologischer Sicht, Liturgie und Kultur 1/2014, 42–45.

bring back memories, e.g. of a wedding, a funeral, our confirmation, a Kirchentag or a certain period in our lives. And here new hymns have a structural disadvantage over the familiar ones (also including some from the second half of the 20th century). They still need to prove themselves and be accepted in the everyday life of congregations and individuals.

Yet this step also has something to do with quality: what qualities (including physical properties) must a song have for the congregation to enjoy singing it? At this point, different quality criteria start to compete. The conventional ideas of quality such as innovation and complexity conflict with the criterion of easy access and singability. The latter both suggest a lower degree of complexity or even borrowings from well-known pop and rock pieces. Furthermore, studies of church membership suggest that – from the angle of the congregation – a happy, confident mood is important at a service, and that can also become a quality criterion for hymns.[8]

The fact that modern spiritual songs seem not to wear well after a few years is not a sign that old chorales are of higher quality. After all, they too went through a long selection process with only a few standing the test of time. The new songs will not be spared this fate. Even if only a few dozen of the songs written around the turn of the millennium finally survive, they will have been worth writing.

4. How do new spiritual songs come about?

The late 1960s saw the emergence of a new type of musician, the singer-songwriter. They wrote both the lyrics and the tune and sang their own songs. They also accompanied themselves, generally with an acoustic guitar. Singer-songwriters spread rapidly in the Christian music scene too, and their songs were included in worship services. To this day many of the new spiritual songs stem from such singer-songwriters, who have popularised their songs in concerts, on records and lately also on web

[8] On this question, see Wolfgang Huber/Johannes Friedrich/Peter Steinacker (eds.), Kirche in der Vielfalt ihrer Lebensbezüge. Die vierte EKD-Erhebung über Kirchenmitgliedschaft, Gütersloh, 2006, 454.

platforms. Not all of them also interpret their songs, however. Many remain in the background, writing and/or composing songs for others to sing; they publish their songs in song-books or (if they were commissioned) in official hymn-books.

Another source of new songs and hymns is holding competitions. In 1960 the Tutzing Protestant Academy advertised that it was looking for hymns with tunes matching »the musical resonance capacity of young people, formed by jazz and light music«[9]. The winner was »Danke für diesen guten Morgen« (»Thank you for giving me the morning«) by Gotthard Martin Schneider; it was one of the first of the new genre »new spiritual song«. In 1962 it topped the German charts, the only hymn ever to have become a hit, and it is probably one of the most well-known recent Christian songs. However, in 1993 it was almost omitted from the *Evangelisches Gesangbuch* (the hymnbook of the Protestant churches in Germany, Austria and Alsace-Lorraine) due to the set ideas about conventional quality mentioned above.

Other successful hymn competitions were more focused. Since 2010 there have been several contests, seeking e. g. hymns for Passiontide, baptisms or weddings. They included the Reformation hymn-writing competitions run by CPCE, or jointly by the EKD and German Protestant Kirchentag for the 500th anniversary of the Reformation. Frequently several hundred people have taken part in such hymn contests (e. g. on the Passiontide and Reformation themes), written the verses and then, in a second step, arranged the texts selected. Independently of the hymns chosen at the end, the high participation was a value in itself – with hundreds of people reflecting on how a contemporary hymn can, for example, express the Passion of Jesus or Christian faith. Moreover, some hymns from the contest have been included in official song-books and have since established themselves in congregations. For good reasons, two winning songs have been included in the weekly hymn plan starting in 2018, one from the Passiontide contest (»In einer fernen Zeit« by Othmar Schulz and Andreas Brunion) and one from a baptismal hymn contest (»Ich sage ja« by Okko Herlyn).

---

9 Quoted from https://www.cantus.org/wissen/wissen-popular.php (accessed on 09. 11. 2017).

Many new spiritual songs are also created during the workshops that the Kirchentag has held over the last fifteen years, before compiling the Kirchentag songbook. About 40 people with a gift for writing and arranging lyrics work together for several days, along with singer-songwriters. They produce new songs around the respective Kirchentag theme and on the biblical texts selected for its worship services and Bible studies. Participants work in a process of friendly consultation in bigger or smaller groups. The results of the song workshop are later critically screened by the project planning group responsible for compiling the Kirchentag songbook. The new songs are spread by the Kirchentag participants using the songbooks, and are often accepted in their congregations. This trend is intensified by the fact that many of the regional churches hosting the Kirchentag make the songbooks an official supplement to their Protestant hymn book, as happened with »*Wort*Laute« (Hanover, 2005) or »*Lebens*Weisen« (Cologne, 2007).

We should not forget the songs from the churches the world over that are translated into German. First it was primarily hymns from European countries or North America, but meanwhile they also come from other regions of the world. The Kirchentag song books always include such hymns, but the songbook »*frei*Töne« – jointly compiled and published by the Evangelical Church in Germany and the Kirchentag for the Reformation anniversary and the 2017 Kirchentag – marked a quantum leap. It includes numerous hymns from all over the world, mostly with the original text and the German translation. Selecting new hymns from European countries is also an emphasis of the Interdisciplinary Ecumenical Hymn Seminar, which has been held annually since the 1990s.[10] The documentation of the seminars includes songs originating from the Netherlands, Scandinavia, the United Kingdom or other European countrie, that have been translated into German. Among the regular speakers was Jürgen Henkys (died in 2015), whose song broadcasts developed enormous popularity and are widely known to this day.[11]

---

[10] Christa Reich, Interdisziplinäres ökumenisches Seminar zum Kirchenlied im Koster Kirchberg, in: Liturgie und Kultur 3/2017, 115–117.

[11] His poetic adaptations of hymns in other languages are found in: Stimme, die Stein zerbricht. Geistliche Lieder aus benachbarten Sprachen, München 2003; Du

5. Teaching new spiritual songs

Having good quality new songs is one thing, but getting people to sing them is quite another. That is not just a question of their quality but also involves communication. Since even the finest songs are ineffective if they are not sung in services and in congregations, creating new songs must be supplemented by the educational process of teaching them.

The 2017 Kirchentag songbook »*frei*Töne«, in which 42 songs and hymns appear for the very first time, illustrates how to promote the learning of new songs. First of all, companion volumes were issued for accompaniment by a stringed instrument or a brass band. In »*frei*Töne« many songs were only reproduced with the melody line, so an additional choir book was edited with harmony arrangements. Some Centres for worship services and church music also deal with new songs. Workshop/Course participants have become multipliers who can practise them with their own choirs and brass ensembles. Formats of community singing, which often happen during the Kirchentag, make people want to sing the new songs. By the end of the Kirchentag in Berlin and Wittenberg participants knew some of the songs written for 2017 very well, and took them home to their congregations afterwards.

But on top of this, more efforts are needed to make the new hymns known. After the publication of their new hymnbook *Gotteslob* in 2013, Catholic dioceses adopted the format of »songs of the month« in order to teach congregations twelve new hymns in the course of a year. In the 1950s the Protestant church took up an idea from the 1930s of »songs of the week«, which were intended to broaden the congregational repertoire over the years. Back then, the songs of the week were mostly 16th century chorales but now they also include new spiritual songs. The weekly hymn plan starting from the first Sunday in Advent in 2018 proposes two hymns for each Sunday and religious festival (and the week following it), of which one is usually a new spiritual hymn. So that the about thirty hymns going beyond the core part of the Protestant hymnbook can also be sung, the Liturgical Conference is also working on a database with

---

hebst die Erde an das Licht. Lieder aus anderen Ländern. Jürgen Henkys Nachdichtungen, München 2016.

accompaniments, tips for performance, ideas for hymn sermons and other materials.

The internet with its forums and platforms offers countless ways of making new hymns known. Some musicians upload new songs as video clips. Frequently new songs are found online with their tunes and texts, which is often against copyright. According to their own account, copyright risks involved in spreading songs on the internet was one of the reasons leading to the founding of the American platform Christian Copyright Licensing, Inc. (CCLI). This commercial platform disseminates the latest songs of praise in a professional manner. Meanwhile there is also a German version of CCLI.

6. New hymns and the revision of the Protestant hymnbook (EG)

A study conducted by the EKD's Liturgical Conference and the Theological Faculty of Leipzig University suggests that the time is now ripe for a new hymnbook.[12] There is apparently an increased demand for contemporary hymns, while a number of hymns seem dispensable: they are simply no longer sung. The study shows that a clear majority of the over 2600 people surveyed from all EKD member churches favour at least a moderate revision of the hymnbook (72% of the congregational members and 90% of those working professionally with the hymnbook). The decision has now been taken to start revising the hymnbook in 2018.

Seen from today, the revised hymnbook is expected to

- be both an analog book and an app or e-book; Other digital formats should also be considered as well; we must seize all available options in the digital age to ensure that hymns, both old and new, are easy to learn for those not used to them and enjoyable to sing;

[12] Yvonne Jaeckel/Gerd Pickel, Das Evangelische Gesangbuch. Nutzungsgewohnheiten und Einschätzungen. Ergebnisse einer empirischen Studie zum Evangelischen Gesangbuch, in: Liturgie und Kultur 2/2016, 6–32. See also Stephan Goldschmidt, Ist die Zeit reif? Brauchen wir ein neues Evangelisches Gesangbuch? Ibid., 53–63.

- be a congregational *role book* and enable the community to participate in the service, and at the same time be a »house book« to deepen personal spirituality;
- offer appropriate space to time-honoured hymns and traditional texts, along with hymns and texts corresponding to the faith and life of people today and to their listening habits;
- take account of changed church and theological insights and, in particular, provide a greater choice of hymns in response to the growing importance of new occasional offices, besides the traditional ones (baptisms, weddings, etc.);
- cater for different needs in terms of its variety of styles, different singing and listening customs of all generations, and different forms of spirituality;
- contain hymns and texts from the ecumenical movement in different languages, including multilingual versions, and keep up lively relations with other churches in the world. In particular, the new hymnbook is to consider the versions of the interdenominational working party for ecumenical hymns (*Arbeitsgemeinschaft für ökumenisches Liedgut*).

7. Conclusion

New songs have arisen in the church throughout all the ages. The plea of the psalmist to always sing new songs to God (Psalm 96:1), has been fulfilled over the centuries. These songs are primarily ways of praising God. But we should not forget that they are also of inestimable worth to the people who sing them. They foster faith, arouse deep emotions and are, in a holistic sense, an expression of Christian hope.

William Jourdan[1]

Multilingual Services

Between challenges and richness of experience

1. The context

It is nothing new: for many years even in Europe many Protestant congregations have been experiencing the presence of people coming from other countries. The policy of the churches in dealing with this issue has always been and still is varied, up to the present day. In some countries the choice was made to create specific ministries for people of other languages; in other churches, the idea has been to give space within the existing congregation to those coming from another country, in trying to worship together in spite of spiritual, theological and linguistic differences.

Being a minister in the Waldensian Church in Italy, I have had the privilege during the last seven years of serving in two congregations in the North-East of Italy, where the presence of people coming from African countries constitute most of the congregation. The members of these two congregations – both in the Methodist tradition[2] – are mainly Italian and

1 I express my thanks to Ms Marianne Wade for investing some of her time in correcting my written English in this essay. She has been one of the witnesses to the attempts to shape a service in which people from diverse cultural backgrounds could find a common spiritual home.

2 Since 1975 the Waldensian Church in Italy has consisted of the union of the previous Italian Methodist Church and the Waldensian Church: the two churches merged in one common body, keeping the particular and original identity of the local congregations. This is the reason why, at local level, the congregations keep the original identification – Methodist or Waldensian – though they all belong to the *Chiesa Evangelica Valdese – Unione delle chiese metodiste e valdesi* (Evangelical Waldensian Church – Union of Methodist and Waldensian Churches).

Ghanaian people, with some other individuals coming from diverse cultural or national backgrounds. The larger congregation in a medium-sized town called Vicenza has quite a long history: it was founded in 1869 by an English missionary whose name was Henry James Piggott. He was responsible for the Wesleyan Mission in Italy and spent most of his ministry in Italy. After a first period of strong ostracism in town against the presence of the Protestants,[3] the congregation was accepted and is today well-represented in cultural and ecumenical circles.

During the last 25 years, due to the economic development of the region, the presence of immigrant workers has gradually increased. Many of these people first came alone and later brought their families; many of those who came, especially from Ghana, belonged to Methodist and Presbyterian congregations back home, and a good proportion looked around to find »their« church in Italy[4]. More than 20 years ago, the first Ghanaian members of the congregation started to approach the church, at first just a few people and gradually more and more. Of course, it was a joy – but also somehow a shock for the Italians – to recognize that the congregation was changing: the service visitors were no longer a few Italians and a few Ghanaians, but a lot of Ghanaians (up to 100!) and a few Italians (around 15).

It would take too long to describe the various aspects of this process, which brought about a profound change in the life of this and many other congregations.[5] I would rather just share two important considerations,

---

3 This is well proven by the witness of local journals, attesting the obstacles created to the first pastors in town. One of the Italian main novelists of the period, born in Vicenza, Antonio Fogazzaro, recognized the presence of these »strange Protestants« describing in one of his novels the figure of a preacher, whose name was Antonio Dalla Fontana, linked to the local Methodist Church. For further information, see Giorgio Spini, »Relazione introduttiva su A. Fogazzaro, E. Cecchi, R. Bacchelli, D Giuliotti, G. Papini«, Il protestante come personaggio nella letteratura italiana del Novecento, Arenzano: Caroggio, 2005, 11–16.

4 Most people coming from Ghana and living in the neighbourhood of Vicenza worship in other Pentecostal and Evangelical Churches. Though the economical crisis of recent years led many people to emigrate again, the presence of these ethnic churches is still high: almost 20 around Vicenza.

5 For a general overview, see Paolo Naso / Alessia Passarelli / Tamara Pispisa,

and then concentrate on the dimension of multilingual services. Firstly, what happened in Vicenza is to be understood under the caption »Being Church Together«, i. e. the attempt to create congregations in which people from different cultural backgrounds can worship and live their faith together. This project has a clear view, I would say, but lacks clearly-defined steps for proceeding. In some congregations the integration has taken place quickly, in other congregations more slowly. Secondly, this project thrives because of different experiences: there is no single correct model which is good or even perfect, while everything else wrong. This consideration is very important with respect to the question: how should (or can) we shape a multilingual service? What I'm going to describe has been an attempt, it can't be considered a general pattern.

2. Together but in different languages: is it really integration?

We may ask whether a worship service held in more than one language can really convey the message of the gospel or may rather just create confusion. I must say that before my experience in Vicenza, I never raised this question. It was not necessary for me: I'd been worshipping in congregations where the language was either English or German (both not my mother language), but I could understand each. What happens when people from another country, not really (or not yet) skilled in the language of that country attend a church service where they can't really understand what is going on? Would it be appropriate to translate everything? Is translation enough to make you feel at home in the church? Questions like these and many others should always accompany the reflections on this topic. Throughout the years of my service in Vicenza, with the help of brothers and sisters asking themselves similar questions, I've come across them again and again: the final answer was always marked by a provisional nature. Because of this I'm convinced that with regard to people coming from other countries, living now in Europe (in

Fratelli e sorelle di Jerry Masslo – L'immigrazione evangelica in Italia, Torino, Claudiana, 2014.

my case, in Italy), it is important to respect the fact that their faith is rooted in another language, but, at the same time, to encourage them to find new roots for their faith in the language of the country where they live. To explain this aspect, I've always tried to show the parents that this effort can help the younger generations in their journey of faith. Every teenager belonging to a protestant church in Italy is aware that he or she belongs to a minority; if the language of your faith – »the language of the church« – is one of the dialect of a West African country, how would it be possible for you to explain your faith identity if somebody is asking about it?

It was not always a convincing argument, I must admit, but together with the consideration that the service was held not only for people from Ghana, it was possible to find a middle way. What does this mean, precisely, a middle way? I will try to describe it pointing out three aspects on which it was important to reflect: the order of service, the hymns, and the sermon.

3. THE ORDER OF SERVICE

An order of service or liturgical order is not just a way of putting together the various parts of a service; it is also a way of expressing our theological and spiritual understanding of things. When people from different theological backgrounds come together to worship, it is important to recognize what is important for them. The point is not mainly: what do you like in your order of service? The question is: what is essential for you to recognize a service as *your* service, in which you find yourself at home from a spiritual point of view? I will give one example to make this clearer. In the liturgical tradition of the Methodist Church in Ghana, as in many other churches in Africa, the collection of the offerings is a time of praise and thanksgiving. It is not just about sharing a part of your goods for the work of the church, it is about recognizing that the Lord has been good to his people also in granting them the possibility of this gesture of giving. If in a Waldensian and Methodist church in Italy the offerings are usually collected sitting at your place and putting it in a bag going through the pews, in congregations with many Ghanaians the offerings are collected bringing it to the front of the church and ... dancing! To integrate this liturgical element in the order of service has not been as difficult as one might imagine: it took more time to understand that it was not merely dancing, but a way of expressing praise to God. Similar examples could be made in the other direction: there are elements of the Italian order of service, which needed to be kept in the new shape given to the service. Not everything has been completely changed, it was not necessary, and it would not have been helpful: the new pattern of order of service aimed to make people feel comfortable at home, even if we had to make some changes in positions of furniture.

In the small experience of the Vicenza congregation a key role was played by the booklet with the order of service for every Sunday: it was bilingual (Italian/English) and displayed the various steps of the service. If a prayer was said loud in Italian, the English version was printed on the paper and vice versa. The hymns were mainly in two languages and the Bible readings were both in Italian and in English. Of course, it is important to keep concentration taking part in such a service and especially at the beginning it was a bit heavy, but over time it became more natural.

4. The hymns

As in every protestant church, the role of music and hymns in the service is very important in our Italian churches. Another question was, how to solve the problem of hymns in a multilingual service?

As I said before, it is not only a short time since Italian protestant Churches started experiencing the project »Being Church Together«. The question »how can we sing together?« already came up many years ago. The standard hymn-book of the Methodist and Waldensian Churches in Italy is the so-called *Innario Cristiano*[6]. It is a collection of 354 hymns belonging to different traditions (Reformed, Lutheran, Methodist): some of the texts are translations of foreign hymns, other are originally from Italy. The standard hymn book of the Methodist Church in Ghana is the *Methodist Hymn-Book* used also by the Methodist Church in the UK. Some

[6] Torino, Claudiana, 2000.

texts are translated into Italian, other texts have the same melody as hymns in the Italian Hymn-book. In 2007, a study group belonging to the Northern District of the Waldensian Church in Italy published a small hymn-book[7], made up of 93 hymns to be used in public service. Most of them are bilingual (Italian/English) but some texts are also in Twi (one of the Ghanaian languages spoken by most of our Ghanaian church members). It is an important instrument to sing together: the liturgical problem is that many of these hymns are for Advent, Christmas and Easter time, so it is not always possible to use them.

It was then necessary to find resources to help widen the range of hymns. With the help of some websites[8], it was possible to find many English texts fitting Italian melodies. In this way, the Italian congregation members could sing their hymns and the Ghanaians could sing with them the English text. Also vice-versa, translating some hymns from the Methodist Hymn-Book, it was an occasion for Italian protestants to learn new melodies and new words to sing their faith.

I am not a musician and I cannot give any kind of technical judgement on this experience. My general impression is that, despite some difficulties, it was possible nevertheless to sing in two different languages with joy and passion; sometimes it was quite clear that the two languages were interfering with each other, but on other occasions it was possible to perceive that the difference was not an obstacle, on the contrary, it was a sign of the richness that the diversity in church can bring. I will always gratefully remember the impression left in me on those occasions in which Italian and Ghanaian Protestants were singing together joyfully in English and in Italian a hymn written by Johann Crüger in the XVII century: is this not also an image of the church that we will experience tomorrow?

---

7 Cantiamo Insieme – Let's Sing Together (Innario bilingue inglese/italiano – English/Italian Bilingual Hymnal).

8 I refer especially to www.hymnary.org offering a comprehensive index of hymns and hymnals in English and in other languages.

5. The sermon

I don't want to discuss at this point what type of implications the multicultural context[9] may have for homiletics. I just would like to emphasise, from my own experience, that preaching in a multicultural context drove me to look, Sunday after Sunday, for ways of expression marked by clarity of concepts and simplicity of words. I am sure I was not able to fulfil this goal, but that was the aim! When I talk about simplicity I do not mean that the message of the gospel should be delivered in a trite way, but that the words and the concepts we use should consider the fact that we are talking with people whose mother language is another one and whose cultural background is different. We help people to grow in the new cultural context only if, also in the sermon, we can start from the point where they are. Simple words or simple examples are not less effective in preaching especially in a context where a translation should follow.

To preach in Italian and to offer a translation in the dialect spoken by the Ghanaian members of the congregation was the most effective solution. First of all because not all of the Ghanaians can speak fluent English; secondly because it gives the parents an opportunity to recognize that their children are not completely lost in the »new« culture, but they are a true bridge among cultures; thirdly, it offers the opportunity to learn new words recognizing them in the translation. Of course, also in this case, both Italians and Ghanaians need to accept with patience that there will be a time in which a foreign language is spoken: that can create at times a bit of dissatisfaction.

6. Final Remarks

As I said from the very beginning, my attempt has not been to offer a general pattern that can be applied in every situation. I think that the context of Italian Protestant congregations, where most of local churches

---

9 The bibliography is wide, just to have an idea I suggest the interesting paper of Daniel L. Wong, An Intercultural Homiletic: Preaching Amidst Cultures (consulted under www.academia.edu).

are pretty small (in comparison to big protestant congregations in Germany or Switzerland, for example) grant the opportunity to elaborate some proposals that in other contexts would not be helpful or even reasonable. At the same time, the experience accumulated through the years by different congregations can offer a basis for further reflections in other places.

Our churches in Italy are aware that the process that has brought us to the point where we are now is not simply something that happened by chance. More or less a quarter of our churches in Italy are involved in the project »Being Church Together«. The presence of people from African, Asian or South American countries is probably no longer increasing as it was fifteen years ago, but we are trying to find a balance. We see the richness and, at the same time, the deep challenge that the encounter of people from different cultural backgrounds is displaying.

One of the areas where this two-sided dimension (richness and challenge) can be experienced is the service. Sometimes it seems that, though we recognize from a theological perspective that we are one in Christ, we are not able to celebrate this unity in the service to God. Sometimes it seems that both sides perceive the difficulty of this enterprise without recognizing the joy of the encounter. It is rather like walking on a mountain path where the strenuous effort prevents us from seeing how far we actually are. It is necessary to stop and look back down to the valley. We should apply this point of view also to the life of those churches experiencing a multicultural dimension. They have been changing through the years and also the faith of members of the congregation has been changing through the years. Of course, there are new challenges to face, but also a new richness to experience.

Katrin Kusmierz

Celebrating the Lord's Supper in German-speaking Reformed Switzerland

Some recent liturgical developments

Over the past hundred years the liturgy of the Lord's Supper has changed considerably in Swiss Reformed German-speaking churches. The following article traces these changes, taking a 1911 liturgy from Basel as a starting point[1] and comparing it to the recent proposals of the *Deutschweizerische Liturgiekommission,* the Liturgical Commission of German-speaking Reformed Switzerland (hereafter Liturgical Commission).

The Liturgical Commission, a standing commission of the Conference for Liturgy and Hymnology of the Reformed Churches in German-speaking Switzerland[2] was mandated to produce liturgical texts and materials. The Conference for Liturgy, a body consisting of delegates from all Cantonal Churches in German-speaking Switzerland, is also responsible for the publication of the hymn books.[3] Recently, the standing Liturgical Commission was replaced by a coordinating committee that now strategically plans the liturgical tasks ahead; the actual writing of materials is then delegated to subcommittees with varying members depending on the respective topic to be worked on.

So far five volumes with liturgies have been published: for Sunday worship (1972), for worships on festive days within the ecclesiastical

---

1 Kirchenbuch für die evangelisch-reformierten Gemeinden der Kantone Basel-Stadt und Basel-Landschaft, Basel 1911, 276–282 (in the following called Church Book for Basel).

2 Liturgie- und Gesangbuchkonferenz der Reformierten Kirchen in der deutschsprachigen Schweiz.

3 The »Gesangbuch der Evangelisch-reformierten Kirchen der deutschsprachigen Schweiz«, Basel and Zurich 1998 and the ecumenical »Rise up Plus – das Liederbuch«, Lucerne/Zurich/Basel 2015.

year (*Festtagsgottesdienst*, 1974), for the Lord's Supper (1983), for baptism (1992) and for funerals (2000). In addition to these comprehensive volumes, four liturgical structures (*Gerüste*) have been included in the hymn book of 1998: for the regular worship (*Predigtgottesdienst*, no. 150), for a worship service with baptism (no. 151), a service with an act of confession (no. 152) and a service with a celebration of the Lord's Supper (no. 153). 2011 saw the publication of a small pocket-edition (*Taschenausgabe Liturgie*) comprising examples of liturgies for various occasions, including three liturgies for the Lord's Supper.[4] Additional materials can also be found on the website of the Liturgical Conference.[5]

We will now compare the first of the 1911 liturgies assembled in the Church Book for the Reformed Congregations in the Cantons of Basel-City and Basel-Landschaft (environs) with the structure or order in the hymnbook (no. 153), as well as with the first of the liturgies in the *Taschenausgabe Liturgie.* This comparison should help us to see how the liturgy of the Lord's Supper has evolved over the past 100 years and bring out the main characteristics on which liturgy no. 153 is based.[6]

1. LOOKING BACK

Some hundred years ago, the Church Book for Basel offered the following liturgical structure for the Lord's Supper: A prolonged *exhortation* was followed by a *confession of sins* including the assurance of pardon, the *words of institution*, a *prayer* before communion and the *communion* proper. A *prayer of thanksgiving* concluded the Lord's Supper.

In the early 20th century every cantonal church had its own liturgy, primarily based on its respective Reformation heritage. From the 1950s,

4 Liturgie- und Gesangbuchkonferenz der evangelisch-reformierten Kirchen der deutschsprachigen Schweiz, Liturgie Taschenausgabe, Zürich 2011.

5 See www.gottesdienst-ref.ch, especially the subheading »Liturgie«.

6 See also ANDREAS MARTI, Agendenfreier Gottesdienst als wissenschaftliche und praktische Aufgabe. Entwicklungen im Bereich der evangelisch reformierten Kirchen der deutschsprachigen Schweiz, in: Jahrbuch für Liturgik und Hymnologie 56/2017, 29–48.

the German-speaking churches in Switzerland strove for greater liturgical unity by establishing the joint Conference for Liturgy. In 1983 it published a volume on the Lord's Supper[7] comprising a collection of 14 liturgies (in addition to liturgies for the various festive Sundays in the ecclesiastical year): it ranged from liturgies modelled on the eucharistic form, with those from Calvin, Oecolampadius or Zwingli, to more contemporary liturgies, including a liturgy for celebrating the Lord's Supper with children. The basic, plain liturgical structure followed at the time, and still widely used today, consists of the following elements, which are not much different from the above-mentioned order: a more or less prolonged introduction (*Abendmahlsbesinnung*), the words of institution, the Lord's Prayer, the communion proper and a prayer of thanksgiving. This type of liturgy is more narrative in character (see below).

It was not the intention of the Liturgical Commission to propose one common, »binding« liturgy, since it would most probably have been rejected by the congregations.[8] The commission thought it more appropriate to offer a broad variety that would better reflect present-day liturgical praxis, which is still not only marked by regional differences but also by a pronounced liturgical autonomy of congregations and pastors. Due to this variety the volume became a work of reference, but did not have the effect of creating a liturgical consensus.

By accepting the common hymn book in 1998, the cantonal churches also approved the above-mentioned set of liturgical structures, which form a common liturgical ground to build on. The intention of these structures was to offer a framework which would guarantee a certain order and establish a minimal commonality. But at the same time it would allow pastors to prepare worship services in a way which can also be responsive to the context and situation of the congregation.

This idea of a liturgical framework to be filled out was originally proposed by the Reformed Church in the Canton of Zurich. In 1969 it published an order of worship that in many ways pioneered a change in the perception of the liturgy, which later on became influential in the whole

---

7 Liturgiekonferenz der evangelisch-reformierten Kirchen in der deutschsprachigen Schweiz, Liturgie. Band III. Abendmahl, Bern 1983.

8 Ibid., 8.

of German-speaking Switzerland. Up to then the service had been very much centred on the sermon, which was framed by prayers and hymns.[9] The rest of the service (apart from the sermon) was not regarded as an end in itself. The 1911 Church Book for Basel, for example, does not offer a fixed liturgical order for regular Sundays laying out the whole of the service, but only a collection of prayers.

For regular Sunday worship Zurich proposed a basic structure consisting of five phases (*Wegschritte*), which was taken up in the hymn book of 1998 (no. 150): the collect (*Sammlung*), adoration (*Anbetung*), proclamation (*Verkündigung*, including the readings and the sermon), intercession and blessing. The five phases lay out a path the congregation would walk from beginning to end, from arriving, gathering together, giving praise, listening to the proclamation of the word, to the intercessions and the moment when everyone is sent out into everyday life again. Each of the five phases has its own characteristic function within the narrative of the liturgy. According to the Zurich liturgical commission, a deep knowledge of these functions should enable pastors to prepare for the worship service responsibly. All in all, there has been a growing awareness of the fact that the liturgy unfolds its own ›drama‹ and follows its own logic.

The liturgy for the Lord's Supper proper as published in the hymn book of 1998 (no. 153) is based on this liturgical approach and shows a significantly different structure compared to that of 1911:

Setting the table (*Zurüstung des Tisches*)
Praises (*Lob*)
Words of institution (called *Abendmahlsbericht – account of the Lord's Supper*)
Prayer (*Abendmahlsgebet*, including an epiclesis, anamnesis, the Lord's Prayer and a sharing of peace)
Communion
Prayer of thanksgiving

[9] There is a special term in Swiss German reflecting the central importance of the sermon: If somebody expresses their intention of attending a church service, they say: »Ich gang z'Predig«, meaning »I am going to the sermon«.

The Lord's Supper follows after the collect, a confession of sins, the readings, the sermon and the intercessory prayer. After communion, the service is rounded off with the blessing. The phase of *adoration* is transferred from the beginning of the service (see the hymn book, no. 150) to the liturgy of the Lord's Supper proper. Instead, the confession of sins is included at the beginning of the service (see below).

2. What has changed? Comparing the Liturgies of 1911 and 1998 (2011)

2.1 Changes in meaning

From the middle of the 20th century, the Lord's Supper became an issue of debate not only among pastors and theologians, but also among active church members, for example on the occasion of the Swiss Evangelical Synod from 1982 to 1987[10]. The synod assembled delegates from cantonal churches across Switzerland and debated pressing issues for the church, among others the state of worship in general, but also more specifically the Lord's Supper. The reason for this renewed interest was a great dissatisfaction and discomfort with the way the Lord's Supper was celebrated. Church-goers were hesitant to participate in the Lord's Supper for various reasons. Alfred Ehrensperger, one of the most profound experts in liturgical studies in Switzerland, observed that »endless admonitions«, and a strong emphasis on guilt and repentance, have resulted in a kind of »fatigue« with regard to the celebration of the Lord's Supper.[11] It was not celebrated as a feast of joy, but in a severe, heavy, al-

---

[10] Schweizerische Evangelische Synode, Schlussdokumente Heft 3: Lebendige Gemeinden – Erneuerung des Gottesdienstes, o. O. 1987. In addition to the Swiss Evangelical Synod, a similar process took place in Zurich, i. e. the *Zürcher Disputation* from 1984: Evangelisch-reformierte Landeskirche des Kantons Zürich (Hrsg.), Zürcher Disputation 84: Ergebnisse. Beiträge zur Standortbestimmung und Erneuerung unserer Kirche, Zürich 1987.

[11] Alfred Ehrensperger, Der evangelisch-reformierte Abendmahlsgottesdienst in den Kirchen der deutschsprachigen Schweiz. Sein Charakter, sein Aufbau und seine Vorbereitung, in: Jahrbuch für Liturgik und Hymnologie, 44/2005, 9–41, 14. See also Ralph Kunz, Eucharistie neu entdeckt – Zur Wirkungsgeschichte der re-

most fearful atmosphere. The Liturgical Commission's 1983 volume on the Lord's Supper criticised this development.[12] It stressed that an Easter atmosphere of thanksgiving and joy would be much more appropriate.[13] In the meantime, the theological understanding of the Lord's Supper had also changed, or rather had been widened. Issues of confession of guilt and forgiveness have long been central to its theology and liturgy. But other aspects had come to the fore: the Lord's Supper as celebration of the communion between the participants, and also between participants and God[14], on the one hand, and as a liturgical praxis which strengthens participants in their life and faith, on the other. In addition, the aspect of communion as an act of sharing together bread and wine as God's gifts was gaining in importance, an act which recalls God's care for creation. These new theological approaches refer to a broader biblical witness going beyond the »original« scene of the Last Supper and reaching out to other accounts of Jesus eating with people on different occasions. Recent theological approaches were also much more mindful of the Lord's Supper's inherent link to Pessach.[15]

These changes in meaning were to be reflected in the new structure as proposed in no. 153 in the hymn book and taken further in the *Taschenausgabe Liturgie*, according to the Liturgical Commission. Its intention was to free the liturgy from the »dust of admonition and moralis-

---

formierten Abendmahlstheologie, in: Der neue Gottesdienst. Ein Plädoyer für den liturgischen Wildwuchs, Zürich 2006, 60.

12 Liturgiekonferenz der evangelisch-reformierten Kirchen in der deutschsprachigen Schweiz (Hrsg.), Liturgie. Band III. Abendmahl, Bern 1983, 20.

13 Ibid., 21.

14 Interestingly enough, the focus on communion and community can already be found in the third liturgy in the *Church Book for Basel*, 287–294.

15 »Das apostolische Herrenmahl ist weder einseitig eine Erinnerungsfeier an Jesu Mahl mit vorwiegend sündenvergebender Wirkung, noch einfach eine Fortsetzung der Mahlzeiten des Auferstandenen mit seinen Jüngern, bei der sich die Gemeinde in besonderer Weise seiner dauernden Gegenwart bewusst wird. Es ist vielmehr, von den Urkunden her gesehen, beides in einem. Hinzu kommt noch die Beziehung zum Passamahl.«, Liturgiekonferenz der evangelisch reformierten Kirchen in der deutschsprachigen Schweiz (Hrsg.), Liturgie. Band III. Abendmahl, Bern 1983, 14.

ing« und to redefine it as a feast of thanksgiving, praise, joy and community.[16]

In most places and up to the middle of the 20th century, communion was only celebrated four times a year, a fact which also contributed to the above-mentioned estrangement of both worshippers and pastors from the Lord's Supper. To counterbalance this development, the Swiss Evangelical Synod suggested that the Lord's Supper should be celebrated more frequently, roughly once a month. Indeed, this has been the case in many congregations to this day.

2.2 The Lord's Supper as an integral part of the service

In no. 153 the Lord's Supper is understood as an integral part of the worship, i. e. it is not just added at the end of the ›normal‹ service as was the case in earlier liturgies. Those members of the congregation who did not want to partake in communion were dismissed after the blessing. This had the effect that for many members of the congregation the Lord's Supper became something exclusive, the prerogative of only a few. This was compounded by the admonition that only those who were worthy of it should take communion (1Cor 11:27–29).

Most congregations in Switzerland have adopted this new order and now there is hardly any service to be found with an official dismissal before the Lord's Supper. This full integration of the Lord's Supper had already been recommended and introduced in the volume published by the Liturgical Commission in 1983.[17] But for the Liturgical Commission that designed the liturgy in the *Taschenausgabe Liturgie* it was important not only to integrate communion into the whole of the service, but to underline the close connection between the Lord's Supper and the rest of the service with regard to theme and content. Both parts of the liturgy were to focus on one specific theological aspect and unfold it in the sermon as well as in the liturgy of the Lord's Supper proper.[18] In doing so,

[16] Liturgiekommission der evangelisch-reformierten Kirchen in der deutschsprachigen Schweiz, Protokoll der 363. Sitzung, 15. 11. 1992, 2074.

[17] Liturgiekonferenz der evangelisch-reformierten Kirchen in der deutschsprachigen Schweiz (Hrsg.), Liturgie. Band III. Abendmahl, Bern 1983, 19f. and 40.

[18] Liturgie- und Gesangbuchkonferenz der evangelisch-reformierten Kirchen der

it was to take account of the broadened theological and biblical horizon. The first liturgy proposed in the *Taschenausgabe Liturgie* spells out what this could mean[19], focusing on the Lord's Supper as an act enabling a new beginning, which strengthens and nourishes the faith of people who hunger for life in fullness. However, the intention of closely intertwining the celebration of the Lord's Supper proper with the first part of the service has had little resonance within liturgical praxis, probably because it is very laborious to implement.

2.3 Confession of sins

As I have mentioned, one reason for the uneasiness with celebrating the Lord's Supper among congregation was the strong emphasis on the sinfulness of human beings and their need for salvation. A look at the first of the 1911 liturgies in the Church Book for Basel confirms this. Sin and repentance are dominant motifs. There is, of course, a confession and an assurance of forgiveness and, in addition, a prayer of sanctification right after the words of institution. This is followed by the admonition that those who want to enjoy communion should have proved themselves worthy of it.

In the Liturgical Commission's view, repentance and forgiveness of sins are still important elements in a service which includes a celebration of the Lord's Supper. But the commission strongly recommended separating a confession of sins from the act of communion proper and inserting it at the beginning of the service. This separation is intended to avoid communion being seen »unilaterally as a visible expression of absolution«[20].

---

deutschsprachigen Schweiz, Taschenausgabe Liturgie, Zürich 2011, 37. See also Andreas Marti, Agendenfreier Gottesdienst als wissenschaftliche und praktische Aufgabe. Entwicklungen im Bereich der evangelisch-reformierten Kirchen der deutschsprachigen Schweiz, in: Jahrbuch für Liturgik und Hymnologie 56/2017, 41.

[19] Liturgie- und Gesangbuchkonferenz der evangelisch-reformierten Kirchen der deutschsprachigen Schweiz, Taschenausgabe Liturgie, Zürich 2011, 37.

[20] Liturgiekonferenz der evangelisch-reformierten Kirchen der deutschsprachigen Schweiz, Liturgie. Band III Abendmahl, 22; see also 36.

2.4 The »Abendmahlsgebet« (prayer)

The structure of the service in the hymn book (no. 153) introduces a new element: a prayer sequence (*Abendmahlsgebet*) that consists of an epiclesis, an anamnesis recalling God's salutary deeds towards his people, the Lord's Prayer and a sharing of peace.[21] The insertion of such a prayer is quite striking in comparison to the liturgical forms published in 1911 and later on. In doing so, no. 153 cautiously takes up elements from the eucharistic form.

Inserting a longer prayer sequence slightly changes the character of the liturgy. As mentioned before, earlier liturgies were more narrative, e. g. recounting one aspect of the meaning of the Lord's Supper or the reason why it is celebrated. Here communication is predominantly horizontal between the pastor and the congregation. This narrative character of the liturgy became even more pronounced in the 1980s and 1990s – among other reasons as a consequence of the endeavour to promote and to communicate new theological interpretations of the Lord's Supper. In no. 153, or more specifically in the *Taschenausgabe Liturgie*, the congregation/the pastor more often addresses God in prayer, thereby changing the direction of communication. In some ways this also reduces the cognitive elements in favour of the ritual aspects, even if the above-mentioned intention of strongly linking the first part of the service to the Lord's Supper slightly balances this out.

The introduction of an anamnesis[22] and an epiclesis resonates well with a Reformed theology of the Lord's Supper. To remember and to recount God's deeds of salvation is, for example, central for Zwingli's perception of the Lord's Supper. Through remembering, salvation is renewed

---

[21] Cf. Peter Bukowski et al., Reformierte Liturgie. Gebete und Ordnungen für die unter dem Wort versammelte Gemeinde, Neukirchen ³2010, 341.

[22] Cf. Hans-Christoph Schmidt-Lauber, Die Eucharistie, in: Hans-Christoph Schmidt-Lauber/ Michael Meyer-Blanck/ Karl-Heinrich Bieritz, Handbuch der Liturgik und Praxis der Kirche, Göttingen 2003, 227ff. as well as Alfred Ehrensperger, Überlegungen zum Anamnesecharakter und zur liturgischen Einheit des reformierten Abendmahlsgottesdienstes in der deutschen Schweiz, in: Alfred Ehrensperger, Lebendiger Gottesdienst. Beiträge zur Liturgik (hrsg. von Ralph Kunz und Hans-Jürg Stefan), Zürich 2003.

and actualised in the lives of those present.[23] In a Reformed perspective it is the Holy Spirit who brings this about, as expressed in the prayer for the Holy Spirit's presence in the liturgy.

Alfred Ehrensperger has stressed the fact that the act of anamnesis not only relates to salvation from sin through the death and resurrection of Christ, but should refer to the whole life of Jesus and everything he did, from the incarnation to the parousia.[24] Moreover, it recalls God's actions in creation, the covenant with Israel and the acts of liberation in its history.[25] The corresponding broadening of the understanding of salvation is clearly noticeable in many of the liturgies currently used in congregations.

2.5 From the *Words of Institution* to an *Account of the Lord's Supper*[26]

In no. 153 in the hymn book and and the frst liturgy in the *Taschenausgabe Liturgie,* the term *words of institution* (*Einsetzungsworte*) is changed to *Abendmahlsbericht*, a notion that could be translated as *account of the Lord's Supper*. The intention is to stress the fact that these words are not essential in the sense that they accomplish something. It is not the words, but the whole of the ceremony, celebrated in communion with each other, and the work of the Holy Spirit that together contribute to the way the Lord's Supper can become a salutary experience for those participating. The *words of institution* are seen as a narration, or a Scripture reading

---

23 Hans-Christoph Schmidt-Lauber, Die Eucharistie, in: Hans-Christoph Schmidt-Lauber/ Michael Meyer-Blanck/ Karl-Heinrich Bieritz, Handbuch der Liturgik und Praxis der Kirche, Göttingen 2003, 227f.

24 Alfred Ehrensperger, Überlegungen zum Anamnesecharakter und zur liturgischen Einheit des reformierten Abendmahlsgottesdienstes in der deutschen Schweiz, in: Alfred Ehrensperger, Lebendiger Gottesdienst. Beiträge zur Liturgik (hrsg. von Ralph Kunz und Hans-Jürg Stefan), Zürich 2003, 61.

25 Ibid. 62.

26 Andreas Marti, Agendenfreier Gottesdienst als wissenschaftliche und praktische Aufgabe. Entwicklungen im Bereich der evangelisch-reformierten Kirchen der deutschsprachigen Schweiz, in: Jahrbuch für Liturgik und Hymnologie 56/2017, 43.

with the effect of creating a link between the present celebration with the original scene of the Last Supper. This account legitimises and justifies the ritual itself. The *Taschenausgabe Liturgie* follows this path by offering the *words of institution* in a new and alternative wording. This is to be understood as part of the endeavour to render these central words more intelligible for men and women of today and to allow for new theological insights to be taken up.

2.6 Exchanging a sign of peace

To shake hands with fellow worshippers and to exchange words of peace is still – to this day – a rather unfamiliar element for Swiss Reformed Christians, except for congregations where it has since been carefully introduced. But even so, many participants do not feel comfortable with it, because for them it is too intimate and personal. However, this liturgical element gives expression to two important motifs: it signifies the communion between those present, who long for peace and who are in the need of peace. It is an act of symbolic reconciliation before all come together at the table. And second, offering one another a sign of peace brings to mind that reality is still marked by strife and conflict and that the world, too, is in need of salvation.

3. Conclusion

As we have seen, the liturgical structure offered in the hymn book introduces some new elements into the liturgy of the Lord's Supper: an act of praise, an anamnetic part, the prayer for the presence of the Holy Spirit and the exchange of peace. Significant is also the separation of the Lord's Supper from the act of repentance and the confession of sins as well as the fact that it is no longer treated as an appendix to the service, but integrated into the whole of the liturgical narrative.

Both no. 153 and the first liturgy in the *Taschenausgabe Liturgie* choose a path midway between liturgy as anamnetic narrative and liturgy as prayer. It takes up some eucharistic elements, but interprets them anew from a Reformed perspective. Still, this is a sign of the growing ecumenical convergence and understanding after Vatican II. In Reformed liturgical tradition in Switzerland, too, the eucharist has constantly been a point of reference for the liturgical conception of the Lord's Supper over the last 100 years. The 1983 publication by the Liturgical Commission lists one liturgy that is crafted on the basis of the eucharistic form. It even suggested liturgical dialogues (rather unfamiliar in Reformed circles) for which a special booklet had been published, intended for the use in congregations. Yet it did not make a substantial impact. In the French-speaking part of Switzerland, a liturgical renewal (»renouveau liturgique«) in the early 20th century had the effect of orienting the liturgy of the Lord's Supper much more towards the eucharist. The recently published liturgy of the Reformed Church in the Canton of Aargau[27] follows this lead, decidedly linking itself to the liturgical traditions of the Early Church. Such a strong orientation towards »catholic« (in the broad sense) forms has been, and is still, debated and contested[28] – raising the question of what is characteristic for a Reformed tradition of the Lord's Supper and how much it should or can absorb other liturgical traditions. However, the Aargau liturgy produced for the 2017 Reformation quincentenary has sparked a new debate on the Lord's Supper.

The fact that the hymn book with no. 153 primarily offers a *structure* for celebrating the Lord's Supper is programmatic and typical of the liturgical context of German-speaking Reformed Switzerland: a structure that can be filled and allows for different theological and liturgical emphases and a constant process of contextualisation. This liturgical freedom is an important asset and a substantial factor for the liturgical identity of the Reformed Church in Switzerland and its clergy. But it also presents a great challenge to those who (re-)write and form these liturgies

---

27 Sabine Brändlin/Gottfried W. Locher/Dieter Wagner, Reformierter Abendmahlsgottesdienst. Liturgieheft, Zürich 2017. In addition to the liturgy itself, four compositions have been commissioned: a classic version, a »pop-version«, a version with traditional Swiss folk music and a nativity play. Swiss television broadcasted four services with these compositions (22. 1./16. 4./10. 9. and 24. 12. 2017) which are available at https://www.srf.ch/sendungen/gottesdienst/ (accessed on 30. 1. 2018).

28 For a critical review, see Andreas Marti, Agendenfreier Gottesdienst als wissenschaftliche und praktische Aufgabe. Entwicklungen im Bereich der evangelisch-reformierten Kirchen der deutschsprachigen Schweiz, in: Jahrbuch für Liturgik und Hymnologie 56/2017, 44–48.

for use in congregations on a regular basis. In addition, it is leading to a variety of forms and wordings, which some also see as problematic in the sense that church-goers cannot get used to, or own, one fixed form. A certain fixed order in the liturgy and/or some recurrent words would relieve those responsible for worship, and might facilitate participation of the worshippers, on the other. Therefore, a more constant and regular use of relatively fixed liturgies in the congregations would be helpful. But all these issues are to be debated.

Indeed, it seems that the time is ripe for a renewed discussion and reflection on the Lord's Supper and its liturgical form. The hope is that it could also provide some fresh inspiration for both pastors and congregations. In many cases, the Lord's Supper is still not an essential and integral part of congregation's liturgical life. Therefore, the Coordinating Committee of the Conference of Liturgy and Hymnology of the Reformed Churches in Switzerland, for example, plans to embark on a process that, on the one hand, provides new materials for the above-mentioned, rather new elements of the liturgy and, on the other hand, tries to inspire the liturgical culture in a way that the Lord's Supper can become an important spiritual source for individuals, congregations and for the church as a whole. While producing liturgical materials is probably less difficult, the latter task might prove more challenging.

Phill Mellstrom

Participative Worship

Good practices in the Church of Scotland

In this article we will explore some basic concepts of participation in worship and explore its theological, social and cultural contexts. We will read six examples of models of participation and how they are created for and implemented in a localised setting.

The word liturgy is derived from the Greek: λειτουργία or leitourgia, which literally means »work of the people«. By its very nature, therefore, worship should be participatory. The phrase itself »participatory worship« is somewhat tautologous. The idea of worship being something that we are not actively involved in, either consciously or physically, let alone spiritually, is problematic and raises the question »How can it be the work of the people if the people are not involved?«

1. »How can it be the work of the people if the people are not involved?«

Worship practice has taken many forms throughout the centuries, with many different movements responsible for influencing the practice of some denominations and awakenings in others. Recent history reflects the shift in certain church cultures that defines a worshipping style that attracts worshippers of a certain type. Some churches will dedicate long periods to preaching, with the congregation participating in a few hymns. Others will feature a weekly Eucharist with a short homily and a mix of congregational responses in reciting the creeds, saying set prayers and physically moving between standing, kneeling, sitting, shaking hands or sharing peace, or perhaps making the sign of the cross. In some Pentecostal traditions the sermon is just as participatory as the singing, with call and response throughout and a tendency to call to the front for prayer. So then, when we consider all the elements within our worship and who gets to make the decisions concerning them, what might this tell us about how participative our worship really is?

2. The Scottish context

The typical experience of a worshipper in the Church of Scotland includes elements of traditional liturgy with various prayers of approach, supplication and confession, hymn singing and reading and preaching of the word. In recent years there have been more requests for different ways of gathering, and different or alternative styles of worship. Often various elements of contrasting styles of worship will be blended with a more traditional style, or elements of modern worship or band-led music, creating a fusion of styles. At best this is a way of blending a service that will allow for different ages and stages to connect with preferred styles of worship, but it can – and often does – end with a sense of busyness and lack of cohesion, resulting in ineffective liturgy and unsatisfied or disconnected worshippers. There has been a growing attraction toward traditional, participative and so called »Celtic« styles of worship, with many pilgrims from around the globe visiting historic sites such as Iona to feed on the rich heritage of worship that developed in such places. The Church of Scotland, and indeed the Church in Scotland, are fortunate to have a relationship with the Iona Community, with many people becoming members or associates, who take elements of the theology and worship practice back to their local church settings. The Wild Goose Resource Group has been hugely influential not only in the hymnody of the Church, but in the renewal of the practices and theology of worship. A renewed interest in monastic rhythms and a trend toward ancient-modern has highlighted the need for quality of participative liturgy, a deeper sense of prayer and a desire to see these practices being linked with the renewal and transformation of society to create a more just and hopeful future for all.

The backdrop to all of this is a declining membership and an ageing church population, although not all denominations are experiencing this, with many independent city churches seeing growth in attendance, predominantly in the student age range. This has been the case for at least a decade, with a younger audience being drawn to modern band-led worship in larger churches in particular urban settings. However, in more recent times there has been a growing awareness of the need for worship practice that not only allows for a more authentic experience of church, but also that the values of the faith that people are aligning themselves to are visible in the churches' expression of worship and mission. Further questions are being asked, not only of the values that we display in our worship and missional behaviour, but of the experience that we have in our gathered times of worship.

Is there a trend within worship that sees singing as the main (and often only) participation within corporate worship?

- Are we employing faulty liturgy?
- Are we designing poor spaces that do not allow for connection, rooting or wonder?
- Are we providing fewer opportunities, not only for people to participate, but to develop leadership roles; highlighting a power struggle between professional and non-professional? Is there an unhealthy dependence on worship bands to provide an emotional element to the way a worship service is delivered and experienced?

This is not something that is confined to a particular expression of church or style of worship, but more broadly there seems to be a deficiency in creating and leading services/liturgies that invite or require the engagement of the congregation.

3. Key issues to consider

Passivity in gathered worship, where it is done to us or for us, can breed apathy and rather than equipping people with the tools they need for living out their faith, we are spoon-feeding them and acting as »gatekeepers« who hold the key to the secrets of worship. If the praying and reading/interpreting of scripture is purely the preserve of professionals, how can an ordinary person in the pew possibly have the skills to correctly do these things for themselves at home, with their families or in any context that does not have a professional worship leader present?

In many progressive evangelical churches the word *worship* refers directly to music. The use of »modern« music (which is still several years behind the creative curve) is defined as »contemporary« worship. This terminology is surely questionable, as something that is truly contemporary needs to be more than in step with the zeitgeist, but must connect with the present on a social, political or cultural level. What we would call »contemporary worship« is an element of the sung worship which is, for now, similar to the current or recent trend in music found in secular or everyday society and culture. A more accurate, nuanced and sophisticated definition can surely only describe an experience that had all its worship practice rooted in how we are engaging with politics, science and technology, culture and the arts and the political, economic and ecological spheres of world events; rather than something that looks or sounds »current«. When we have worship practice that does not purposefully exclude these areas, but truly allows people to root their prayer in all that is happening around us and within us, that allows our reading of scripture and our theology to both dig into the biblical root and find its appropriate lens and application through experience and paradigm. When our songs are not just expressions of adoration, but protest at the injustices we see, which express the lament we feel yet often do not share in community; if that is our experience of worship, then and only then can we call it »contemporary«. Any worship practice or model that continually lifts people away from their reality in an attempt to be transcendent yet never truly roots itself in the realities of our lives, communities and world, cannot be effective and is theologically unbalanced. If we continually avoid painful and difficult subjects like the #metoo movement, migrant crisis, toxic masculinity, abuse of power in business and politics and scandals such as the Panama Papers, how do we empower people to recognise God in the midst of these things? How do we enable them to pray? How do we enable them to apply and interpret scripture and to feel the wind of the Spirit as we seek to recognise or be prophets in this time?

4. Generational and cultural trends

Many churches and worshipping communities comprise members of different generations, including people who are directly responsible for the creation and delivery of worship and those who are taking part in the liturgy as members of the congregation. Of course the converse is also true (especially in the Church of Scotland), where many congregations are made up of only the older generations. Each generation has its own characteristics and behavioural habits. These not only affect how their world view is shaped and perhaps how that would affect their perspective on mission, but also their learning styles and the ways they might choose to express themselves. It is necessary to consider how these character traits affect creativity and willingness to make appropriate and strategically relevant change; and how welcoming and accessible these gatherings will be to visitors from different generations or worshipping styles.

The »Traditionalists« or »Silent Generation«, who were born around 1945, would generally value loyalty, economic stability, hard work and diligence. They often do not like change and display a more conservative and risk-averse approach. Often citing duty before pleasure, they can often be more reticent in expressing emotion.

»Baby Boomers« or those born around 1946 to 1964 were born into a time of vision and experimentation. They would often be idealistic and actively challenge the establishment; not to topple the system, but to take control and impose their values on it. Often described as the »me« generation, they have a tendency to be domineering, individualistic and were the first generation to display a habit of consumerism.

»Generation X«, born around 1965 to the late 1970's, were children born into crisis. Living in a time when divorce rates soared and capitalism and consumerism were rife, they tend to love change whilst seeking balance, be drawn to visual stimulae (they are often called the MTV generation) and are less interested in something being true, but more concerned about whether it works. More introspective than the Baby Boomer and often associated with more emotional or intimate worship content (predominantly musical in nature).

»Millennials« are those born from the late 1970's or early 1980's. This is a generation that has been targeted by marketing their whole life. The often cited trait of seeking authenticity is linked to this desire to see past the hook or gimmick and connect with something real. There is a desire to connect and be rooted; experience and encounter are part of their preference for ritual, sacrament and participation in worship.

We can see from the traits associated with each generation and with the experience of marketing, MTV and various other significant events within each lifetime, that there will be noticeable differences and idiosyncrasies in the way people from different generations learn or express themselves. This can be seen in their preferred worship style; ranging from how they pray, how they read or question scripture, which musical preferences are evident and which elements of worship practice will be given priority as their main theological influence. As people »church shop« they may once have looked to the quality of the teaching and preaching, whereas throughout the late 1980's, 90's and early 2000's, there was a steady increase in the appeal of churches with the best worship band. What we see now in movements towards »hipster church« or »un-cool church«, is another attempt to deal with the packaging, rather than the deeper, more theologically nuanced issues.

In recent years there has been a marked shift in how people respond to society and culture and in particular, Millennials have seen the move towards questioning the validity of the institutions that were once considered the hallmark of our societies. Banks, broadcasters and Church have all come under scrutiny, with various scandals and issues that have led to a questioning of values and therefore an eye to how much influence these institutions should be allowed. The tendency of a Millennial to want to understand what you stand for, what your values are and what your story is, lies in this sense of experience. It is not enough to know that something is »true«; there has to be a sense of something »felt«. There needs to be more than a cerebral response or an assent to a proposition; there needs to be an emotional response and beyond that a practical response driven by a sense of activism, all rooted in a requirement to be authentic.

Millennials are not the only ones asking if rooting themselves in a more traditional feel of church, with a paced liturgy, allows them to feel more in touch with the moment and to disassociate themselves from the hustle and bustle of life without disconnecting from reality. Many people are moving away from assenting to a proposition and instead are looking for the mystery contained within the sacraments. A desire for experience is perhaps a common generational trait of the past 20–30 years and its different expressions during this period may mark the style of church that has emerged.

The greater the impact of seeking authenticity, the more we question the idea of performance-led worship experiences[1]. This is perhaps a felt need that has been evident for a while. The growing dissatisfaction that has been written about in evangelical worship in the USA has been noticed in the UK. The engagement in »Fresh Expressions« and the early 2000's »Emerging Church« movements that seek to grow culturally relevant and organic expressions of church, rather than the church planting model of establishing a particular style of church/worship, has gained momentum over the past decade or so. Churches that have a main service with a particular style or model of worship (generally modern or band-led) are re-orientating the style and pattern of their weekly worship to create different services for different people. This may be in response to a growing interest in more traditional practices, monastic habits and the idea of rhythm within the whole of life.

5. PREFERENCE IN WORSHIP

In his book, »Sacred Pathways«[2], Gary Thomas explores the impact of learning style and expressive style on our encounters with God. As with personality types or learning styles, we tend to favour certain ways of expressing ourselves; for example, we may hear a lot about people encountering God in nature, or when they are engaged in acts of social justice. As we each reflect on the times where we have felt most connected to God, we can find, as Thomas did, that the traditional »Quiet Time« or

[1] http://www.patheos.com/blogs/ponderanew/2015/09/04/3-reasons-contemporary-worship-is-declining-and-5-things-we-can-do-to-help-the-church-move-on/
http://www.patheos.com/blogs/ponderanew/2015/10/19/8-reasons-the-worship-industry-is-killing-worship/
http://www.internetmonk.com/archive/50453
https://sharperiron.org/article/how-worship-format-destroying-evangelical-church.

[2] GARY THOMAS, Sacred Pathways, Zondervan, 2010.

mode of worship of a particular church may in fact inhibit how aware we are of God and may become a barrier to our engaging with God in worship and in everyday life.

Dave Csinos has further developed this idea and Suzi Farrant, the Young People and Young Adult's Development Worker for the Church of Scotland, discusses this in her web article:[3]

> Worship is an integral part of faith formation; it is as we encounter God that our faith forms and develops. But creating worship that everyone is able to engage with can be a real challenge as we all appear to like different things. This has led some to consider if there are any patterns to how adults worship; Gary Thomas in his book Sacred Pathways suggests that there are nine spiritual temperaments. As leaders it is worth exploring these ideas, as it helps us to understand how our own preferences in worship affect the worship opportunities we prepare for others.
>
> More recently Dave Csinos has extended this line of thinking to how children worship and having conducted a piece of research with children from different congregations in Canada he concluded that there are four different spiritual styles – word, emotion, symbol and action – and children have a marked preference for one of them. He goes on to suggest that when children disengage from worship it is most likely because what is being offered is not enabling them to encounter God as it doesn't fit their spiritual style, rather than being because they are not interested in God.
>
> Young people and adults also have preferences that are contained in these same spiritual styles, although as we get older, developing cognitively and have more experiences of worship our preferences broaden so that we can become more adept at encountering God through more than one of the different styles.
>
> Over recent years times of all age worship have been known to instil fear in those preparing and those attending as by trying to reach people of all different ages at the same time they don't really work for anyone. If we change our focus from being all age worship to being all styles worship we have the potential to unlock these times and create worship experiences that enable all to encounter God together.

---

3 http://www.churchofscotland.org.uk/resources/children_and_youth/leaders/faith_formation/spiritual_styls – this material is adapted from Roots all age and age related material.

Word

Those that have a preference for the word style, know God when they know about God. For them, the spoken and written words used in worship are important; they encounter God through well-read Scripture readings, through the words of hymns, through the words of prayers, through the exposition of the Word through sermons. Knowledge about God is important so enabling people to understand how the different stories in the Bible fit into a whole is a worthwhile activity. When praying, people with a preference for the word style are likely to feel uncomfortable with extemporary prayer as they would struggle to muster the right words to use on the spot. For them taking time to craft prayers, selecting what they consider to be the right words in the right order, enables them to encounter God.

Emotion

Those that have a preference for the emotion style, know God when they can feel God, especially when they're with others. For them a sense of personal renewal and getting in touch with their feelings as they worship are important; they encounter God through music, drama, dance, being with and sharing with one another. Jesus is most often perceived in relational terms, as divine friend so emphasising the personhood of God through the different bible stories is a worthwhile activity. Personal relationships are treasured by people with a preference for the emotion style, so enabling them time within worship to cultivate them is important, as is the sharing of personal testimonies. Conversely long periods of silent reflection or not being able to actively participate in worship makes them uncomfortable and doesn't enable them to encounter God.

Symbol

Those that have a preference for the symbol style, know God through mystery, symbols and images. They value abstract symbols and metaphors as they find that words can't describe the transcendent adequately. They sense God through beauty, awe and wonder, and in the natural world so God can be felt in the mountains or in a stained glass window. For them meditation and chants can be really worthwhile activities and they value times for silent reflection as they like being alone to wonder about God. They are more likely to be uncomfortable participating in group activities too often or being asked to pray out loud.

Action

Those with a preference for the action style, know God when they are doing the work of God. Spirituality for them is very much something to be lived so they have an unquenchable thirst for justice, seeing God in the cry of the poor. They really like welcoming people as they come into church, writing letters, signing petitions and raising money for charity campaigns. Their zeal for such activity can sometimes be isolating for them, and they get really uncomfortable when no one shows enthusiasm for such things. For them being part of groups filled with only bible stories and craft activities is uncomfortable and doesn't enable them to develop their faith.

6. Creating worship for all

»The Christian community should be an artistic community. For human beings were made in the image of the creator, and are therefore intrinsically creative. When we are creative, we testify, wittingly or unwittingly, to the existence, beauty and diversity-loving nature of the creator. So when that image is renewed (Colossians 3:10), our creativity will be renewed too. And while creativity can be displayed anywhere, in the office, in the home, in the garden, in the park, on the football pitch – for we must not divide the ›sacred‹ off from the ›secular‹ – we would also expect it to adorn our life together in the Christian community. Art and crafts and designs and fabrics and music and drama and poetry and dance all beautified the liturgy of the temple, and they should beautify our praise of God and our life together today«[4].

As we take note of how society is shifting and communities gather around communal activities, in coffee shops and places of architectural or artistic interest, we see the desire for connection with others on a deeper level and the expectation of an experience or encounter. People want to feel connected with something beyond themselves and many are seeking out divine encounters beyond the recognised sacred spaces within society and engaging in ritual in these places of meeting. »Imitations of God's truth can penetrate us, even transform us, as we open ourselves to the creative endeavours of painters and poets, musicians and moviemakers. We begin to see new things that speak to us of the truth of a God who is freedom, love and grace … and a God who knows and un-

---

[4] Michael Lloyd, Café Theology, Alpha Publishing, 2005.

derstands the realities of the human condition. So, as pain, suffering, doubt, fear, love, joy and despair are played out in images before us, so we discover the truth about ourselves«[5]. As we look to the practices of the art world and acknowledge the power of symbol and image in encountering God, we see spaces framed with thresholds moving us toward specific pieces of art that invite the viewer to move through stages of liminality,[6] allowing for a deeper encounter with the art work. If the theology of our worshipping community is undermined by the theology of its building, layout and the practices undertaken in the space, how effective can any liturgy be? Do we have practices and rituals that support cultural and common memory, or do they in fact hinder our approach to God and disempower openness, honesty and vulnerability with each other?

What are the lessons we need to learn from how we engage with the arts that can be applied to our worship practice? As we acknowledge the power of the arts to critique culture, to offer protest and call out injustice, to hold a mirror up to ourselves and to society, what then is lacking in our ritual and liturgy within the church context that would allow us to engage fully in these issues and root our worship in a healthy ecclesiology and eschatology? Is it reasonable to expect a single part of the liturgy such as a sermon or a bank of songs to be effective in allowing people to fully engage with God in an honest way? Is it reasonable to expect a rounded and rooted worship experience if we limit peoples' participation to a few songs or a creed?

As we reflect on this we need to move beyond a shallow critique when we compare our ineffective gatherings to the ones criticised by the Minor Prophets like Amos. When we condemn our practice and its lack of consideration for social justice, but only seek change to attract younger people, or fix what we see as a deficiency in our community, then we are perhaps missing the point. In Luke 7, Jesus quotes Aesop's fables: »To what then will I compare the people of this generation, and what are they like? They are like children sitting in the market-place and calling

---

5 GRAHAM BUXTON, Celebrating Life: Beyond the sacred – Secular Divide, London: Authentic Media, 2007.

6 ARNOLD VAN GENNEP, Rites of Passage, Psychology Press, 1960.

to one another, ›We played the flute for you, and you did not dance; we wailed, and you did not weep.‹«

This parable of dancing children is used to level criticism at the Pharisees, Scribes and Jewish theocrats, who are voicing the »spirit of the age« in their oral laws or Mishnah, but jealousy and envy is driving their challenge to John the Baptist and Jesus. They are concerned and angry that Jesus and John (and the crowds who follow them) are not dancing to their tune. It is perhaps ironic that those churches that seek to attract large numbers or certain demographics with their »flutes and dirges«, do not truly understand the »spirit of the age«. As in the original fable, when the piper tries to catch fish and realises his efforts are somewhat misguided, perhaps we need to reconsider the deeper theological and spiritual needs of the people seeking authentic churches that will allow them to »dance or weep« in tune with God's leading.

The demographic within our congregations and in our communities has changed and keeps changing. We need to listen to these voices as we shape our worship and as we assess the validity of our ways of gathering, the shape of our ritual, liturgy and the expression of our missional behaviour. The habits and practices of people in art galleries and public spaces and their interaction with space need to be considered when we are creating the spaces for worship and liturgies for worship. As we allow room for the individual appropriation of worship and encounter with God that is not prescribed by a worship leader who has to navigate the wide spectrum of the congregation's needs and preferences – while at the same time being attuned to the Holy Spirit – it is worth considering the concept of curating the worship space, rather than presiding over the liturgy. Originally a term used in the art world, the concept of worship curation affords worshippers the space to have encounter and epiphany in tune with their connections between their own lives and stories and God.

Seth Godin[7] suggests that »Art isn't only a painting. Art is anything that's creative, passionate, and personal. And great art resonates with the viewer, not only with the creator. Art is a personal act of courage, something one human does that creates change in another.« This may be

---

7 Seth Godin, Linchpin: Are You Indispensable? Portfolio, 2010.

one approach to creating and leading worship, whether that means opening a space, as in the idea of worship curation, or within the various acts written and created for liturgy. As we invite others to participate, the acts begin to take on new and different meanings that create different ways of becoming more aware of God; by encountering others, encountering the space and activity or ritual within, or encountering oneself as the time for reflection contemplation is offered. In her Theology Masters Essay, Pam Mellstrom expands on Seth Godin's thought of art as an act that one *does* and considers the impact of a community's involvement in the creative process.

> »Creativity does not truly come from the popularised notion of the tormented artist, struggling with the muse. True creativity, is born in community as men and women of God listen to each other (and to him), as we seek to understand each other's woundedness and strengths[8].
> Songwriter Michael Card alludes to the value of the arts and how they offer an opportunity for individuals to come together to collaborate or respond to something, to sing his or her song«[9]. The collaborative process creates a space where individuals can share ideas, offer something of themselves and build connections with those involved in the work. This is something that is recognised by Jeremy Begbies »Theology through the arts«[10] projects and will resonate with those involved in the rehearing and refining process such as music ensembles or casts of drama productions. The journey toward the completed work can bring moments of insight and depth, but also doubt and frustration and times of »not knowing«. These are valuable, essential even, for the work to find its completion, as Lorraine Cavanagh suggests »... the creative process in order to be truthful involves struggle ...«.[11] Creative gatherings, acts and spaces require that we bring our history and experience to the creative process for it to have integrity. Our arts should not necessarily attempt to 'make pretty or perfect' difficult subject matter. Nadia Bolz-Weber

---

8 MICHAEL CARD, Scribbling in The Sand-Live DVD, World Entertainment, 2002.

9 HELTZEL, Resurrection City, 2.

10 EDIT JEREMY BEGBIE, Sounding The Depths: Theology Through the Arts, London, SCM Press, 2002.

11 LORRAINE CAVANAGH/EDIT JEREMY BEGBIE, Sounding The Depths, SCM Press, 2012, 107.

> asks the question, »Is spirituality an attempt to smooth out our rough edges? But do our rough edges not keep us connected to God and give our lives texture«[12]. The church could learn from the arts how to hold the tension between our raw and honest reality and that for which we hope; moving past shallow ritual and ineffective liturgy to a more open, creative space that allows honest voices of doubt, fear, confusion, anger, joy and hope, to blend as communities move together between light and shade, consonance and dissonance.

Creators and leaders of worship approach the creative act in many different ways. The formalised leading of worship in traditional liturgy would be criticised by those who feel a freer, more open style of worship is appropriate. However, those who prefer freedom in their worship are even more locked into a way of acting (or »ordo«) than they would care to admit. Both of these polarised styles would benefit from a more improvisational element to their creation and delivery. This in turn may allow for the more entrepreneurial among the worshippers to explore the space within the liturgical form and allow participants to appropriate the elements of worship practice in ways that allow them to fully encounter God in ways that are real and relevant for them.

This resonates with the different disciplines in jazz music; the basic form of the piece is the framework which holds the space for improvisation. Each of the musicians weaves in and out of roles from soloist, to accompanist. Their virtuosity and interplay heightens the collective imagination, in turn creating art that is more than just the sum of its parts and continually challenges and expands the paradigm within which it is created.

In her essay, Pam Mellstrom continues:

> The individual and collective imaginations particularly of adults, has in part been eroded and consumed by our physical reality so that for many, our space to dream is limited to the resources we have available and can lack divine vision. We, through conscientious decision making, apparent lack of options or through risk aversion have subdued our imaginings to the realm

[12] NADIA BOLZ-WEBER, Accidental Saints: Finding God in All the Wrong People, London, Canterbury Press, 2015.

of »that which is achievable« rather than truly letting our imagination take flight. In contrast the artistic community rely on their imagination as currency for their work, they harness their skills and fuel their projects with their creative imaginings and this drives what they do. What would our churches and communities look like if we took our imaginative capacities seriously, what if we considered our imagination to be a »... a fragment of the mind of God that offers treasures, mysteries and gifts«[13] would this not transform the very core of spiritual rituals and activities.

7. CONSUMERISM IN WORSHIP

There is always a need for balance between creating accessible opportunity to encounter God and giving people what they think they want. As we explore the idea of how we most naturally meet with God, we must not allow the idea of style over substance to dominate and remain as the driving factor of how we create and deliver times of worship, as this can lead us to the consumerist scenario that Kierkegaard's dialogue below invites us to critique.

> »What goes on between the speaker and the hearer in a genuine edifying discourse? It is so on the stage, as you know well enough, that someone sits and prompts by whispers; [he is hidden;] he is the inconspicuous one; he is and wishes to be overlooked. But then there is another, he strides out prominently, he draws every eye to himself. For that reason he has been given his name, that is: actor. He impersonates a distinct individual. In the skilful sense of this illusionary art, each word becomes true when embodied in him, true through him – and yet he is told what he shall say by the hidden one that sits and whispers. No one is so foolish as to regard the prompter as more important than the actor.
> Now forget this light talk about art. Alas, in regard to things spiritual, the foolishness of many is this, that they in the secular sense look upon the speaker as an actor, and the listeners as theatregoers who are to pass judgment upon the artist. But the speaker is not the actor – not in the remotest

13 NIGEL FORD / EDIT JEREMY BEGBIE, Sounding The Depths: Theology Through the Arts, London, SCM Press, 2002, 69.

sense. No, the speaker is the prompter. There are no mere theatregoers present, for each listener will be looking into his own heart. The stage is eternity, and the listener, if he is the true listener (and if he is not, he is at fault) stands before God during the talk. The prompter whispers to the actor what he is to say, but the actor's repetition of it is the main concern – is the solemn charm of the art. The speaker whispers the word to the listeners. But the main concern is earnestness: that the listeners by themselves, with themselves, and to themselves, in the silence before God, may speak with the help of this address.
The address is not given for the speaker's sake, in order that men may praise or blame him. The listener's repetition of it is what is aimed at. If the speaker has the responsibility for what he whispers, then the listener has an equally great responsibility not to fall short in his task. In the theatre, the play is staged before an audience who are called theatregoers; but at the devotional address, God himself is present. In the most earnest sense, God is the critical theatregoer, who looks on to see how the lines are spoken and how they are listened to: hence here the customary audience is wanting. The speaker is then the prompter, and the listener stands openly before God. The listener … is the actor, who in all truth acts before God.«[14]

In this discourse, Kierkegaard raises some interesting issues. As we look at our experience of worship, how does it measure in terms of who the audience is in your experience?

There are principles within our worship practice that can empower or disempower response. The balance of liturgy can often be towards a passivity rather than participation. Are we seeing the most notable area of participation within our worship as being the congregational singing?

Passivity in worship can often be overlooked in the context of sung worship. If the aim of an extended time of singing is to create space for freedom and room for the Holy Spirit to prompt and lead, then how does this fit in line with Kierkegaard's synopsis? The dependency on the worship band and worship leader to tell us where we are going theologically, either through the specific theology of a song or through the theme used as the narrative arc for this part of the liturgy, can breed a passivity in

[14] Søren Kierkegaard, Purity of Heart, 180–181 (SV XI114–15); reprinted in Parables of Kierkegaard, Thomas C. Oden, ed.

the congregations curiosity and also be confusing depending on the theological arc of the teaching or sermon. Further problems arise when considering recent trends in modern worship music that have led to inaccessible music (perhaps dependent on your age and taste) with vocal ranges within the melodies that are unsingable for large groups of people within the congregation/audience and a marked trend in the same themes tackled by different songs.

The Contemporary Christian Music Industry, which makes its money from selling music to the masses, has a bigger influence on what music is being used in our churches than we would care to admit. Large numbers of congregations all over the world will repeatedly use the songs of the most popular artists, at the expense of lesser known artists or material, regardless of quality. The question needs to be asked, whether the theology of these songs is compatible with that of the community and the experiences of those gathered, if the musical style is appropriate and whether the importing of worship material written out of context rather than material written by the community is more appropriate? How culturally relevant are the most popular worship songs of today? How in tune are they with various issues facing our societies?

When we have songs that do not connect with our lived experience, then our sung worship becomes disconnected from our reality. If the »worship« of your church revolves around singing, then this issue of disconnection becomes so acute, that not only is there a theology divorced from key issues of justice, equality or any other felt need within the community, but there is more danger of relegating the congregation to the state of audience. This is further compounded by a consumer-driven market place being the primary driver of material for this style of worship rather than an honest exploration of the needs of the community and the adequate worship vocabulary to move beyond praise, to being able to articulate openly and honestly, concerns of injustice, voicing lament, crying out in anger against oppression, honestly speaking of doubt and speaking and singing our stories mixed with the bigger story of God.

There have been different movements and trends throughout the liturgy and worship of the Church since the Church came into being. There is constant reference to how a church may be focusing on becoming a more biblical version of church, but in fact the evidence and outline of how a church gathered within the bible is limited and does not give sufficient insight into the formality or informality of the gathering. We do not get the sense of transition from community gathering to intentionally becoming a worship gathering. We have some writing from the early Church that shows us process of catechism, outlines areas of worship practice and sacramental worship, but we do not get a blow by blow account of all the elements that are included in our liturgies.

In her book, Ruth C Duck[15] writes,

> »With the Second Vatican Council came an awakening in worship that radically transformed Catholic worship and influenced worship in many other Christian communions. At the heart of this awakening, sometimes called the liturgical renewal movement, was the recovery of an active role for the laity in worship, or, to paraphrase the Constitution on the Sacred Liturgy, their ›full, conscious, and active participation.‹ Before this era of renewal blossomed, many congregations regarded clergy as either their primary worshippers whom the congregation observed or perhaps as entertainers who inspired and entertained the laity. But a new ecclesiology was emerging, emphasising a vision of the church as the body of Christ living out a vibrant faith expressed in worship and lived out in the world. In this understanding, worship was the work of the Laos, the whole people of God, lay and ordained, male and female, adults and children. The worship assembly shared a common baptismal vocation and a corporate priestly role. Preachers, priests, presiders, musicians, and other leaders were coming to be understood as enliveners of the congregation's worship, not entertainers or primary worshippers.«

Is the norm for the content, delivery from the front or platform or elevated pulpit and all propositions that requires ascent rather than reflection or response?

Are the prayers said *with* rather than *by* the people attending?

Are we designing and delivering liturgy that promotes passivity, or are we creating environment and opportunity for people to engage with God and with each other in community?

Who is in control of the parameters of what is considered liturgically acceptable?

---

15 RUTH C. DUCK, Worship for the Whole People of God, Westminster John Knox Press, 2013.

Who gets to decide how the room, church or space for worship is arranged?

These questions start to point towards where the power lies. If there is a dominant figure who controls the parameters for decision making, for what rituals and elements are appropriate for the liturgy, then the worship is ultimately not participative. If this is the case then how can we model a more egalitarian expression of worship that allows us to consider a more egalitarian sense of community?

8. Experiencing the power of participation

Different forms of participative worship can allow for a more nuanced encounter with God, whether through reflective and contemplative practice, questioning the text as we gather around the scriptures or imprinting deeply the experience of teaching and prayer through movement, touch and other sensory experiences. Jo Love tells the story of encounters with God through such forms of worship.[16]

> Participative Liturgy
>
> At the age of 19, one of my colleagues had a conversion experience. Brought up in a typical Presbyterian church, and knowing little of other traditions, curiosity prompted him to attend an Episcopalian evening liturgy on Maundy Thursday. Almost fifty years later, the memory is retold in vivid detail. The descending darkness. The reciting of Psalm 22. People lifting tables and chairs and processing them out of the sanctuary. The altar being stripped naked of all its usual furnishings. More lights going out. The silence but for the footsteps of the deliberately hurried and wordless exit en masse. »I had never experienced anything like it. It was an overpowering feeling of *being* one of the disciples, participating in the denial, abandoning Jesus … nothing that might have been preached could have drawn me into the story quite so palpably.«

---

[16] Jo Love is Development Worker for Wild Goose Resource Group, a semi-autonomous project of the Iona Community. https://www.wildgoose.scot – Wild Goose Resource Group website.

Another colleague recounts a worship service exploring the relationship between faith and wealth. The liturgy included a contemporary and intentionally comedic dialogue between two churchgoing »gentlemanly bankers« daring to break the money taboo and compare their bank statements, sharing details of investments, savings, financial advisers and deals, all the while oblivious to the slow approach of an elderly woman and the chink-chink of her small coins dropping into the plate beside them, before she shuffled off unnoticed.

Following this drama, there was a meditation about money, our use of it, and the good it can do. People were invited to hold a small value coin in their hand, turning it over and over with their fingers as they listened. »The feel of the penny coin, the feel of it warming with the heat of my hand, connected to me … the weight of it, the sensation of its metal … and then after the meditation, to take that coin to the plate at the front and drop it in, hearing the sound of it hitting the plate … it's hard to explain, but it gave me a much more visceral connection with the story and that whole question of the place of money in my life and faith …«

One of my own lasting memories of being moved and changed by a particular liturgy was in an ecumenical gathering exploring the Lord's Prayer. Each phrase of the prayer was given creative expression in a »station« around the sanctuary, and for a given time, people were free to move around and engage with the stations as they wished, in any order.

I came to the »Our Father« station last of all, set out on the communion table – three large candles on tall candlesticks, an icon depicting each Person of the Trinity, and a starkly simple set of about twelve large cards laid around the table top, each bearing the name of God in a different language. *Our* Father. *All* of us, *everywhere,* the entire 7.6 billion family of humanity. I had known and prayed this prayer how many times over how many years? It was in those moments, as I came near that table and stood alongside others, my eyes taking in what was there, my mind reacting to the symbolism, that my unconscious and unexamined image of God as *my* Father, melted away forever. This shift did not happen in a logical stream of thought. I am sure that no reasoned, spoken argument making the same point, could have hit home with such impact. *Our, our, our* Father.

We ought to find it a very strange thing that our churches have so much non-participative liturgy! How can we hope to be drawn towards God, to make a worthy offering of ourselves to God, to be fully engaged in an act of worship together, if our bodies and senses and emotions are largely inactive?

How valuable, and transforming, and memorable, when worshippers are not »done to« or »done for« or »done at« – »as if we're an audience« – but given room to choose and make an authentic, appropriate and individual response to God and God's Word. The action may be what others are also doing, but we are making our own meaning – as one friend put it »we are all choosing to light a candle, but as we do so, we are having our own thoughts inside, knowing that others are having their own thoughts too«.

We would do well to open up some thoughtful conversation about the legacy of the Reformation which elevated the pulpit and set the learned person on high above the presumed illiteracy of the people. How might we redress the balance where our patterns of worship have erred too far towards control, reserved power in one person or place, encouraged a suspicion of our bodies and emotions as »unholy«, or viewed congregations as empty vessels lacking wisdom and insight despite years of human existence, experience and encounter? The danger inherent in too much passivity is that worshippers get the message that »we have nothing to offer«. Another quote from a colleague – »When worship allows me to explore and express my own understandings, rather than being told what to think or believe or how I ›should‹ act upon what has been preached, then it roots my spirituality in my actual lived life. It's not abstract. I do feel the need for space to respond differently from what I might be ›told‹ from the front!«

So I am reminded, too, of the process of devising and co-leading »SoS«, more a liturgical installation than a service of worship. As the title suggests, this was an hour-long encounter with the Song of Songs, not seeking to explain or expound the text, but offering an immersion in its material. The air was scented by incense and spices; there were bowls of fruit to eat; there were hanging white fabrics which could be meditatively painted with honey, wine or oil. There were artworks inspired by the text and love songs to sing or listen to. People were free to move between these elements of the installation and involve themselves as they chose. In the middle third of the hour, the full book was passionately read aloud by a man and a woman and the friends. And for many of those present, most evocative of all were the two beds draped with sumptuous red satin.

How often do spontaneous conversations arise after hearing a sermon? Time and again, when people have had the chance to *engage* more of themselves and in more creative ways, then talking about it afterwards happens much more readily. And we become aware of a huge variety of associations and reflections. The beautifully draped bed caused one worshipper to reflect, »I was shocked by the bed. But then I loved the way it was showing that the delights of the home are holy.« Another said, »It was wonderful to have so much sensory stimulation, and I just thought, wow, desire is alright!« A third made this connection – »My bed is where my children crawl in for a cuddle. To see that in a place of worship was like God honouring me as a mum – I've never felt that before.« To hear and share these stories of what has been precious and important for us, how we have met with God, in a time of worshipping together, deepens relationships and broadens our awareness of how God is among us.

The spoken word is not the only channel through which God speaks! God uses many ways. Jesus in his intriguing parables used many visual illustrations from nature and took the most familiar of everyday items, such as food and money, to paint pictures about what matters to God and what God's dreams look like. If, in our worship, all we are doing is listening, our minds tend to wander. When worship involves having things to see, or do, to touch, smell, or taste, then there is a greater openness for everybody to be caught up in this time and place where we are in God's presence together, in the glorious exchange of giving our love and concerns to God and hearing God's love and concerns expressed to us.

None of this is an argument to dispense with sermons and the spoken word. But again, there is so much scope to expand our repertoire for the ways that talking has a place in liturgy. In our regular midweek liturgy, we often follow the scripture reading with a time of conversation, initiated by one question such as, »Of all the stories God could have inspired to be in the Bible, why do you think this one made it?« Or, »If this story was the only story we had about God interacting with people, what would you make of God? What would you think God is like?« Or, »If this text is a call to action, what is it we should do to be faithful to its call?« Or simply, »What strikes you about this text?« Such conversations draw out the wisdom and insight and life experience mentioned earlier. There is nothing prescriptive about how it unfolds; no right or wrong answers; no intellectual prowess required to participate. And how rich these conversations are!

God had the imagination to bring into being an incredible cosmos in all its beauty and colour, its variety and surprise. It is a small way to honour that imagination in return, that our worship be crafted and curated in creative ways that make room for participation, opening us up to God, each other and ourselves.

9. The move to participatory forms in worship in a local setting

The past few decades of educational development has created a paradigm shift in which educations role has progressed from »filling empty vessels«, through »planting seeds and nurturing« to more of a greater sense of »pilgrimage« where the teachers and learners are *fellow pilgrims*. This has implications for our worship gatherings, raising questions of the use of sermon or the tone and delivery of material for children and young people and whether indeed there should be a more multi-generational approach without peer distinctions.

Darren Philip (who has explored this paradigm shift) writes about his experience of working within a team, creating worship that meets the diverse needs of a worshipping community that is an amalgamation of several denominations with a mix of worship preferences and experience.[17]

> Livingston United Parish Church
>
> Until four years ago, Livingston United Parish Church had six places of worship on a Sunday morning, each offering a very similar style of service. As in most Reformed churches in Scotland, these were led by a single voice (usually a member of clergy), followed a well-established pattern and were largely passive for members of the congregation, whose only involvement was the singing of hymns and, for some members, the occasional reading. (One church member often joked that the only interactive part of the worship was uplifting an offering.)
>
> When the Parish took the decision to bring the six worship centres together into one single place, they decided to offer an alternative alongside the inherited form of worship and find a way of enabling the worshipping community itself to create and lead an interactive time of worship which all ages and abilities could participate in.
>
> Twelve people from the congregation, from a variety of backgrounds and experiences, offered to become part of three teams of four which would plan these weekly all-age services. Each team had at least one musician in its number and would be supported by a member of the church's ministry team.

---

17 Darren Philip is Development Worker at Livingston United Parish Church.

Working on a rotational basis, teams began to plan and lead worship in blocks of four weeks at a time.

Teams meet, generally in one of their members' homes, to discuss ideas and create a liturgy, a process often involving the consumption of much food and drink. They take as their source each week's gospel reading in the lectionary and begin by discussing what the reading says to each of them and what it might say to the church or the wider world. These ideas are then distilled into a single theme around which the liturgy is structured.

When it comes to the content of worship, the teams are encouraged to be as creative as possible and there is no set order or formula that is used. The only guideline is that the worship must be interactive, offering all who are present the opportunity to participate.

As the process of planning worship together has developed, the teams have started to follow a simple four-part order to aid their planning and thinking:

1. **Gather** – something to mark the intentional gathering of the people in this unique space and time to worship God. This has taken many forms, including singing, a spoken call-and-response, the invitation to uplift an object or symbol, a phrase to say together in British Sign Language, the lighting of a candle and the sharing of some simple food.
2. **Engage** – present the lectionary reading and enable people to think about it. This has often involved drama, song, discussion, putting actions along to a reading, a video prepared in advance by members of the congregation, interviewing a character from the story or involving the whole congregation in creating a piece of artwork depicting the scripture passage.
3. **Respond** – creating space for people to make an individual or corporate response to the Word of God. This has involved personal acts, such as lighting a candle, writing or drawing a prayer, blowing bubbles, cutting out articles from a newspaper, placing a stone on a cairn, walking a labyrinth, planting a seed, shredding a confession or reflecting on a piece of music; as well as communal acts, such as weaving a net together, washing one another's feet, dancing or movement, group discussion, creating a collage, moving round different prayer stations or making cards to send prisoners of conscience.
4. **Send out** – marking the end of the formal act of worship and taking that out into the world. This typically involves something to take away or think about during the week, but has also involved a sung or said-together blessing, the joining of hands, a procession out of the church and a time of silence.

These elements are held together by using a variety of styles of music, with an appropriate song bridging the gap from one part of the worship to the next. One important aspect the teams consider is how the worship space is prepared to contribute to the overall feel and theme of the worship. Lighting, colour, visual centrepieces and even layout of seats have been used to enhance the worship experience. For example, one Trinity Sunday, seats were arranged in a triquetra, a Celtic symbol of trinity. On another occasion, all furniture and seating was removed from the sanctuary as the worship considered those who had fled their homes and were left with nothing. Worship has also taken place outside or in other parts of the church (even, once, in the kitchen) if that was felt to create the right environment for the theme.

One of the challenges of leading this style of worship is holding everything together and ensuring that things flow together well. Teams have found it useful to appoint an individual to be responsible for »overseeing« each act of worship and communicating throughout with musicians and those leading to ensure things run smoothly.

After four years, the congregation has grown in number and involvement, with many new worshippers (including some who had long-ago disengaged from church) joining. More of the congregation are involved in the planning stage, and the ministry team have reduced their involvement to a minimum. Each planning team has appointed from its own number a coordinator who takes responsibility for pulling the liturgy together and involving others in the congregation. There is a feeling of ownership and belonging as the congregation is increasingly involved in the planning, delivery and participation in worship.

(Some photographs can be seen at http://www.lupc.org.uk/aaw/.)

National Youth Assembly

Another place where interactive worship is planned in a collaborative way is the Church of Scotland's National Youth Assembly. This weekend gathering of young adults typically involves a wide variety of worship styles.

A worship team is gathered, composed of staff members (themselves former NYA delegates) along with young people who will be attending the event. They meet to discuss the themes of that year's event, and share ideas of scripture passages which may be relevant. Once a passage has been chosen for each time of worship, they split into smaller teams to plan each act of worship, drawing other young people into their planning.

Each act of worship at the event follows a distinctly different style – some loud and upbeat, others quiet and reflective – but all try to create a space where the whole worshipping people is involved. This could be through inviting people to participate in symbolic action (such as anointing with oil or moulding a piece of clay), discussion in small groups or imaginative contemplation. An object or symbol from the act of worship is often carried into the day's other events, and the programme has allowed for ›worship de-construction‹ workshops where delegates can reflect on why particular aspects of liturgy were used and what enabled them to feel close to God.

Again, the use of space, including visuals, lighting, sound and room layout is used to emphasize a theme and immerse people in an experience. On one occasion, a floor-to-ceiling wall was constructed down the middle of the worship space, segregating worshippers as they reflected on the situation in Israel/Palestine, and each person helped de-construct the wall with each prayer offered. Often, the worship is not restricted to one place, and has taken the form of a pilgrimage around the area, with the liturgy taking place at different locations along the route.

(An example of a liturgy created at the NYA can be found at https://www.resourcingmission.org.uk/worship/starters-for-sunday/day-pentecost-2013-additional-materials.)

Common to both examples is the way liturgy is planned collaboratively, the freedom from set structures or orders, the inclusion of interactive elements (which usually involve people getting out of their seats and moving around) and the deliberate use of space to enhance the worship experience. By bringing together people from different backgrounds, experiences and theological perspectives and giving them the space and permission to bounce around ideas of what worship could be like, rich and engaging liturgy has been created, liturgy over which the whole people can claim ownership.

10. A specific example of a participatory form of worship

Paulo Freire, in his »Pedagogy of the Oppressed«[18], challenges a paradigm of education that seems more like indoctrination into an oppressive system driven by commerce than the drawing out of knowledge and creativity from within the learner. We have to ask questions of the ethics of

---

[18] Paulo Freire, Pedagogy of the Oppressed, Bloomsbury Academic, 2000.

education within our worship gatherings and ensure that this leads to freedom and creativity rather than ensuring capitulation to the current practices and norms. There should be room for what can be categorised as »play«. This concept of play concerns ideas and activities which are not work or ordered and structured. Ritual comes into this category of play and this provides a context where something valuable can happen that would not be seen as valuable in the context of the oppressive paradigm, but is in fact an essential part of our human activity which allows us to connect with and tend to our deeper selves or souls.

»Ritual is a culturally constructed system of symbolic communication. It is constituted by patterned and ordered sequences of words and acts, often expressed in multiple media, whose content and arrangement are characterised in varying degree by formality (conventionality), stereotypy (rigidity), condensation (fusion) and redundancy (repetition).«[19]

Exploring this notion of »play«, Michelle Brown from the organisation, Godly Play[20], writes about how they create space for people (primarily children) to wonder, create and experiment in the context of worship.

Worship through Godly Play

Towards the start of Sunday worship at Portobello and Joppa Parish Church our minister welcomes the children to leave for the halls for our children's ministry. There are those in the congregation who may view this as the »childcare time« or crafting and bible story time, however the minister and I view this time as continued worship in the halls. Everything we do in the halls is a further opportunity for the children and young people to grow closer to God and praise Him through exploring the Bible stories in various ways. During the summer at PJPC, our worship time in the halls takes on an even more liturgical format as we share Godly Play sessions.

Godly Play is an engaging way of exploring childhood spirituality through discovering our Christian faith and heritage. It is not about learning lessons, keeping children entertained or telling them what they need to know. It is about experiencing and exploring the sacred stories of God's people, of knowing Jesus through his life and his parables, and understanding the way in

19 Stanley J. Tambiah.

20 Godly Play website.

which we approach God through liturgical action and silence. A full Godly Play session mirrors the liturgical set up of worship in church.

We begin with the welcome. This welcome is first at the door. Each child is greeted by a person standing there. The person says hello and welcomes each child individually, getting down to their level to chat with them eye-to-eye. When the child is ready, they make their way into the room and find a cushion in the circle by the storyteller. This marks the second part of their welcome. The storyteller then says hello and chats with the child as they get settled. When everyone has arrived, the door person finds a seat by the door, ready to welcome any late arrivals. Meanwhile, the storyteller will continue to build the circle, perhaps with a prayer, some silence, with a song or game, or just finishing the group conversation.

In a Godly Play room, the children are surrounded by all of the stories. There are the Sacred Stories (the history of God's people), the Parables, and the Liturgical Lessons (including Advent, Christmas, Lent, Easter, Baptism, Communion, the Holy Family and the Circle of the Church Year). When everyone has arrived and we are »all ready«, then the storyteller gets the materials for the story.

The children are reminded from the beginning that these stories belong to them and to pay close attention to where the story comes from as then they can always take it out and work with it later. As the story is told, silence is kept as we experience the story by seeing the materials laid out before us and hearing the storyteller slowly and quietly explain what is happening. Amazingly, this focused form of storytelling really works with children and adults of all energy levels. After the story is told, the storyteller looks up and engages the participants in a time of wondering which gives space to reflect on the story. This question time is a safe place for people to express their thoughts out loud or silently. All answers are equally valued.

Once the wondering is finished, participants are invited to a time of response through art, reading, writing or play. With the help of the door person in the room, some children choose to draw, paint, glue, work with clay or create anything they can imagine with the multitude of art materials at hand. There are also finger labyrinths, building blocks, books and other response materials available. Other children stay with the storyteller and explore the story further for themselves with the materials or they can choose to get another story from the room and tell that one. Each story in the room is crafted with care so that they are easy for the children to work with and through telling the stories, the storyteller models for the children how to work with the materials so that later the children can work with the materials on their own. This method of sharing the stories comes from the Montessori tradition.

When the response time comes to a close, the children are welcomed back to the circle to share in a feast. Usually this feast is something simple like a bit of fruit and some crackers or a biscuit. Some water or juice is served as well. A couple of children help the door person to pass out the feast around the circle. We wait until everyone has received their food and drink and then a blessing is said or sung. Then we share in conversation as we enjoy our feast. As we finish the feast, the napkins and cups are tidied away and the door person returns to the door to meet parents and carers there. The storyteller says a goodbye to each child individually, offering them a blessing until we meet again in the circle for another Godly Play. The door person also says goodbye with a blessing as we reunite the children with their families.

This routine of welcome, blessing, story, wondering, response time, feast, prayer, and blessing as we say goodbye is kept each Godly Play session. It mirrors the church service. The welcome we receive at the church doors and from the minister at the start of worship echoes our welcome at Godly Play. Our blessing as the circle is built mirrors the call to worship and silence in church. The telling of the story, is equal to the readings in church. We are told in church where to find this story in the Bible if we would like to read along or look at it later. Similarly, the children have the Bible all around them through the stories in the room and they are told where to find them if they ever want to explore the story themselves. The wondering after the story in Godly Play mirrors the sermon. This is the time to unpack the story we just heard and to reflect on it. In our response time, we echo the response to the readings and sermon that the congregation is doing through singing, praying and responding with offering. At Godly Play, we are offering God our praise through art creations, further reflection or engaging further with the stories. This time of response is our response to God and His word, just as the offering plate is often seen as the response to God's word and His works in the church. When we gather for our feast in Godly Play, we are gathering around to share a meal and we model what they will hopefully experience when they share communion in church. We offer prayer in thanks for the feast, just as in church we pray in thanks for the communion we are about to receive. When the children are sent out with a blessing, it is also as we are sent out of the church with a benediction and a final hymn.

This time in the hall is so much more than people often expect. A full Godly Play is participative liturgy. It gives meaning to religious language for children. It gives space for them to explore their spirituality and for the children and adults involved to be a mutual blessing to each other as we explore these wonderful stories and liturgical action lessons.

A great example of this participative liturgy in practice is at Cramond Kirk, where the first Godly Play room was set up in 2009 by Alex Mackenzie. She has been telling Godly Play there for 8 years. The children at the church really responded to this new way to explore their faith and the Bible, so much so that Alex needed to get more people trained in Godly Play at her church and add a second Godly Play room to accommodate all the children taking part. The second room replaced a projector room in the church. When the pre-teens and teenagers came into the room on the first Sunday it was open, they felt the space needed something more before they could begin sharing Godly Play there. The young people had been through the spiral curriculum of stories with Alex for eight years now and were seasoned Godly Players. Before they could share Godly Play in this new space, they wanted the room to be sanctified.

Though Alex had another story in mind to share, the young people chose the Holy Family story. This story sits in every Godly Play space at the centre of the focal shelf, directly behind the storyteller. Without ever being told, the young people had picked up on the unspoken lesson that this story is the most central and important story to share. When Alex came to the wondering part of the session, she asked the circle »If there was anything they could leave out of the story, but still have all that they needed.« The circle decided that they only needed the Christ Child and the Risen Christ. This was all that matters. Alex sat back in amazement, seeing the depth of wondering and engagement these young people had with this story and have had over the eight years of Godly Play at Cramond.

Alex and I recently reflected on the impact of Godly Play in our work and the way this ministry has grown since it first came to Scotland in 2003. It was then that Carrie Applegath and Fiona Fidgeon first went down to England to be trained to be storytellers by Godly Play UK and then brought it back to Edinburgh. It started off in just the Scottish Episcopal Church and the Church of Scotland and has since been shared in several other denominations. It moved from just Edinburgh to all over Scotland. In 2010, Margaret Grant and Alex Mackenzie started Godly Play Scotland, to further the work of Godly Play here. Alex became the first Godly Play Trainer for Scotland in 2010 and this year she has been joined by two new trainers, Richard Knott and myself, Michelle Brown. It is a growing time for this ministry.

II. CREATING RESOURCES FOR PARTICIPATIVE WORSHIP

The ›Spill The Beans‹ writing collective have been involved in writing liturgies that encourage active participation in multi-generational worship for a number of years. The following article from Peter Johnston explores their ethos and how they respond to felt needs within communities that they work with[21].

Participative Worship and Spill the Beans

Introduction

What is worship if it is not participative? For many practitioners who lead acts of worship, whether ordained or non-ordained, there will inevitably be a tension between the desire to encourage participation in a communal act of worship and the time and creative energies required to do so.
Within our tradition, participation was for many generations limited to congregational singing. This remains important, of course, but increasingly is expected only to be the most obvious sign of participation.
The urge to encourage and help congregations embrace liturgy that is more participative has been a core part of the effort to create the Spill the Beans Worship Resource[22].

Spill the Beans Worship Resources
In 2009 a few Church of Scotland ministers started a conversation about pooling our creative resources. Each of us were frequently writing liturgy, developing creative forms of worship expression, and preparing materials that would allow all ages of worshippers to engage with the themes of a worship service. At the time we began this conversation we were mostly based in the Revised Common Lectionary.
That conversation developed over the course of two years of experimentation in our own congregations and the team grew to embrace ordained and non-ordained members from a variety of denominations.
Always at the heart of our thinking was the desire to engage people of all ages in scripture's story. Through story we feel the blood of faith pumping through our lives, through story we can engage people in deeper truths and

[21] Peter Johnston is Parish Minister (Aberdeen: Ferryhill) and Editor of Spill the Beans.
[22] http://spillbeans.org.uk/.

bring an honesty to our worship that allows space for uncertainty, mystery and questions.

It has never been the intention of the Spill the Beans to prepare »ready-made« resources. What has always been at the heart of our thinking is that we are writing and devising ideas that we would use in our own congregations and then making those resources available to others to facilitate their own creativity.

Sometimes that has led to some difficult discussions as a team when, for instance, we completed a three year cycle of resources for the Revised Common Lectionary in 2014 and decided to embrace a four year cycle of the relatively new Narrative Lectionary[23]. Some of those who were using the resources we create wanted us to stick with the RCL. We knew in our own hearts that we wanted to explore different scriptural ground, different stories, to that we had so often ploughed with the RCL and so we made the decision that fit with what would best energise and enthuse us as a creative team.

While we do add some spit and polish to the contributions that come to us for the final published quarterly books, the hope is that the elements contained within each issue will act as inspiration for local congregations and leaders to use these as a spring board for their own worship and creativity.

Participation at Multiple Levels

The Spill the Beans Resource Team would see participation taking place at a variety of different stages and levels within the planning process and act of worship. It begins with the regular meetings of members of the Spill the Beans Resource Team to plan the next issue, usually covering three months of worship. These collaborative days allow us time to look at the scriptural texts and share ideas both about the texts and how we might engage congregations. On their own, these are extremely valuable ways to participate with other worship leaders to gain from each other's insights into the scriptural stories.

The resource ideas we then contribute range widely in form. Partly that depends on who the particular contributors have been for those elements. This helps to give a variety to the resources and allow different congregations to find something to inspire their own style of worship.

The range of ideas that encourage participation range from the simple to the more involved. For instance, we usually provide an idea or perhaps some questions to stimulate conversation amongst worshippers as they gather for worship or perhaps as part of a »welcome time«. In a relaxed way this engages

23 https://www.workingpreacher.org/narrative_faqs.aspx.

people that they are going to be more involved in worship and that this is a communal act done together. We set the tone that this is not an actor/audience dynamic.

We also try to provide a visual cue that helps engage worshippers in the theme, drawing connections between each week.

As examples, in a recent issue we suggested a sign post to which were added direction signs each week, a member of the congregation adding each one[24]. It was a delight to see varied examples of these sign posts shared on our Facebook page[25] from congregations across the world.

For Advent 2017 in my own congregation we have created a large 4 m x 3 m artwork that hangs at the front of the church. We utilised the gifts of a German art student who is part of our worshipping community while studying to help facilitate this piece of community art. She created the backdrop utilising the stories we will focus on during Advent. Members of the congregation at an evening event at the start of Advent were invited to engage with those stories, led by reflective questions, and to create elements for the final art work which will be added week by week as the large image is unfurled.[26] This involved participation from the congregation's Worship Team, our resident art student who relished the opportunity to work on such a large scale (and thereby adding to her portfolio) and gave the whole congregation an opportunity to be involved in the creation of that artwork. The young girls from our local Girl Guides meeting on that same night all became involved in this creative process too, abandoning what the Guiders had planned in order to take part: a great example of intergenerational participative worship based around Scripture's story.

The Spill the Beans Resource Team have always provided forms of story retelling that engages with the Bible story in different ways: from placement in a modern cultural setting, to dramatic form utilising a range of voices, to humorous, to poetry and song. Finding ways for the story to live and for worshippers to find a hook into the story is vitally important.

---

[24] https://scontent-lht6-1.xx.fbcdn.net/v/t31.0-8/21457636_2021758198044513_6656123473212609919_o.jpg?oh=8fa67878f84e6d449ea47274d21b8182&oe=5AD5383D.

[25] https://www.facebook.com/spillbeansresources.

[26] https://scontent-lht6-1.xx.fbcdn.net/v/t1.0-9/24174193_2059718254248507_917240935526535982_n.jpg?oh=4aeacd89112aac06b9c5820be6bf9922&oe=5A9587D1.

The resources for age groups, from age 3 upwards to teenagers, also keep a strong tie to the themes that emanate from the Scriptural story. These provide craft ideas, games, activities and discussion materials. This is very challenging to do consistently. It is easier with some Bible passages than others: Romans is not without its challenges for those trying to create craft ideas for children. We deploy a range of ideas in each issue and having seen the age group leaders of my own church work with the material, the buffet-style we have adopted works well in stimulating them to adapt and make their own the ideas offered knowing the children for whom they are planning and what works best for them to participate.

As part of my editing process, I have recently found the value of meeting with members of my own congregation's Worship Team to read through some of the reflections and dramatic readings for the upcoming issue and getting feedback thereby on what works and what needs more development. This also gives our Worship Team members a helpful advance look at what is coming up.

The Spill the Beans Resource Team also provide some ideas for worshippers to take away with them after the act of worship so that they can continue to reflect on the themes of the previous service during the week. Some congregations print these ideas into their Order of Service or provide them on a card for people to take away.

Creating a Crowd-Sourced Lectionary

As we approach the end of a complete four year journey with the Narrative Lectionary (summer 2018) we thought long and hard about what to do. We felt that we would be completing our four year partnership with the Narrative Lectionary for the time being but knew that we would need to wait another year to return to the RCL in 2019 at the start of Year A. This provided us with an opportunity to do something different and so we embarked at the beginning of 2017 in an exercise of engaging with worship leaders and worshippers in churches who had been using Spill the Beans in congregations predominantly from the UK, USA, Australia and New Zealand. We sought information from them about both their favourite stories and, of primary importance to us, which Bible stories they felt they rarely heard during worship.

Taking this feedback we embarked upon the task of creating our own lectionary to cover the period from August 2018 to November 2019 when we will quite deliberately engage with stories that are not covered by either the RCL or Narrative Lectionary. This is a very exciting prospect for the team and has been made possible by the participation of many congregations in sharing with us which stories they long to hear in a worship context. One might call it a crowd-sourced lectionary. It is another experiment for the team, but one that fits well with our ethos of experimentation and engagement with the scriptures in an honest manner: not just the familiar well-lit spaces but also the more dimly lit corners of the scriptures.

Online Participation

An area of worship participation that is proving both challenging and exciting is the development of an online congregation who join our congregation for worship each Sunday morning via our live video streaming service. This has the great benefit of enabling people to participate in the communal act of worship even when they are unable to be present. This is a real boon for a congregation which, like many others, has many elderly members some of whom find it difficult or impossible to come to the church itself any longer. It has also proved helpful for church members who have had to take work away from home and find themselves living in different countries but want to keep a connection to home. They are able to join, in real time (or later), the act of worship and still feel a connection to the congregational worship. This has also proven very helpful on some important occasions such as funerals or weddings when family members or friends have not been able to be present in person but can still participate from a distance.

There is great scope for this to be two-way participation via the adoption of online chat windows or twitter. This is an area we are still exploring.

12. Developing authentic worship

The Church of Scotland's Resourcing Worship Group began to explore the idea of worship development in authentic and organic ways. As a result they engaged in conversations that were hugely informative in shaping the next steps towards national development of worship. A series of conversations with academics, ministers, worship leaders, community leaders, writers, practitioners and others was framed by the question ›Where do you see worship touching the heights and depths of our human experience?‹ This developed into the writing of the »Conversations in Worship« resource. An article written for The Guild of Healing and St. Raphael considers the ethos of the resource and explores how it has the capacity not only for developing worship, but for healing communities.

Healing stories and worship development
In this article, Phill Mellstrom reflects on the process of creating a new church resource. Initially, it was aimed at getting members of a church to talk about worship, but the initiative led them to discover that getting people who see each other Sunday by Sunday to talk at a deeper level, leads into a place of deep healing and encounter.

Conversations in Worship has been the culmination of a series of concurrent conversations happening within several areas of development for the Church of Scotland. As many people within the church look to new ways of developing areas/aspects of church life, they can fooled into thinking that there is an elixir – a formula or program that can fix all ills, solve all problems and be all things to all people. This is not and cannot be the case. Each congregation is unique. It has a unique set of relationships between many different individuals and although there may be at times similar themes or patterns emerging in behaviour or issues faced, there is not a one-size-fits-all resource that can make every church function perfectly.

There are resources produced that once contextualised, can deliver results that will aid the development of a particular area of church life. How though, do you as an average congregation map out the complex social, economic, political and spiritual landscape within which you find yourself? Understanding that these worshipping communities are made up of complex layers of relationships between individuals who each have their own stories allows us to see something important. As we share our stories, with the opportunity to hear and be heard, we begin to grow community. If we can foster the values of listening without judging, engaging in generative dialogue that encourages self-reflection, mutual understanding and creative response; then we can begin to see a way forward in building new narratives shaped by shared stories and nurture communities of common memory.

When hearing the story of another, we could make the mistake of assuming that the place they have found themselves in on their journey is somehow more valuable than where you find yourself. This notion of understanding your »here«, perhaps allows us to look deeper at the origins of the »Conversations in Worship« methodology.

In 2014 a conversation began, framed by the question »What does it look like when worship touches both height and depth of our lives?« This was our attempt to understand where our »here« was. To help us map out the landscape, we asked people to use this question as a springboard to share their stories and allow us to hear real experiences and collect data about worship within the Church of Scotland.

In the past there had been attempts to capture data about worship in various audits. Instead of creating a tool to measure how effective the existing resources and models were in equipping and empowering people in worship, the idea was to move towards hearing stories of how people encountered God. The root idea of worship is how we experience and encounter God and in some way respond or find space for transformation. Whether that is through prayer, song, hearing and interpreting scripture or through rituals such as communion, stories of encounter in this way would allow us to hear what was happening on a personal level for the individual and understand what elements within the worship life of churches were providing the environment and opportunity for these encounters to happen.
As we continued our dialogue with theologians, liturgists, ministers, worship leaders and everyday people from the pews, we began to hear a common thread – »If you want people to get excited about worship and look towards developing worship … get them talking about it«. This lead to the development of a simple methodology and a series of questions that could frame conversations around the idea of encounter and worship. A series of pilots were set up to test the questions and observe the conversations that they unlocked. In each of the pilot sessions we took care to create an environment of sharing and listening without judging. This led to many conversations that saw participants become increasingly more vulnerable in their sharing. We often found that by simply holding a safe space to share, people would immediately respond by sharing deeply personal stories straight away.
We heard stories not only of height and depth, but stories that were profoundly personal and deep rooted. Stories that were releasing the pain of old wounds; stories that were celebrating the joy of faith; stories that expressed grief over broken relationships; stories that told of the richness of human experience; stories of encounter; stories about who we are as individuals. In the telling of the stories, and in the act of listening, healing was sensed not only on a personal level but also within the community.
In crafting the questions to frame these conversations, we considered what this would look like as a development tool. There was a fine balance to strike between opening up people to the idea of developing worship and simply valuing and honouring a space that would allow honest, open sharing without any other agenda. This informed our approach to creating our methodology and toward crafting the questions that would allow people to have open conversations that would encourage generative dialogue through self-reflection and understanding of another's point of view.
To reflect the idea of both height and depth within our worship, we wanted not only to ask people to share what would be a predominantly positive ex-

perience about an encounter with God; but to also allow for sharing and reflection on times of worship that were »less than what we longed for«.

Much of the feedback from the early pilots talked about more than just a sense of catharsis from sharing deeply personal stories of healing, but also a real sense of being valued and learning about others in the room whilst strengthening, deepening or beginning a relationship.

The act of sharing and asking people to be vulnerable was at first thought to be entirely counter cultural. While the predominant culture within many churches can be to remain guarded and not share deeply, we have found not only an appetite for sharing, but also a clear need for people to be heard, for relationships to be deepened and at times healed.

Many groups that we gathered to have conversations were part of existing communities, but we at times also gathered several groups of people together who did not know each other and found that through the use of our methodology and questions, people moved to a deeper sense of sharing and valued the time spent hearing other stories that encouraged and affirmed their own stories.

We continue to explore new conversations that can be started and to roll out this process in other areas of church life, to support and encourage worship and discipleship in the creation of celebrating, healing and open communities.

To find out more about the »Conversations in worship« resource, go to http://www.churchofscotland.org.uk/worship[27].

This article is used with permission from The Raphael Institute[28].

13. Conclusion

If an elite few has sole responsibility for the creation and delivery of worship that engages and inspires; that educates and releases the imagination; that provides space for wonder and healing; that breeds connection and community; that connects and roots our theology in the places that we live out our lives; how will they be able to speak to each person

27 http://www.churchofscotland.org.uk/worship/conversations_in_worship.

28 https://raphael.gohealth.org.uk/.

who is involved in the worshipping community, or ever break out from the confines of the church?

Simon Chan[29] writes:

> »Understanding the liturgy [...] is a necessary step for ecclesial formation. But effective formation is more than understanding; it also presupposes some degree of engagement with the liturgy. One of the key phrases in the Constitution of the Sacred Liturgy of Vatican II is ›active participation‹. This phrase contains many rich ramifications, but if it is to be properly understood, it needs to be set within the broader context of liturgical spirituality.
> Liturgical spirituality has to do with the relationship between liturgy and Christian living. How does the liturgy form us into the body of Christ?«

What would we conclude if we regarded Chan's question as a serious critique of the effectiveness of our worship practices and ways of gathering people? Do they provide an opportunity for people to use their gifts to create and deliver a liturgy that allows us all to feel something more than just a sense of community, but rather, a vital and valued part of the Missio Dei?

Are we engaging with Luther's principle of the priesthood of all believers rather than reinforcing the societal norms of worship that is led from the front by people of a particular age, gender and sexual orientation?

Is there a more egalitarian approach that can provide a balanced professional/non-professional leadership that will gather communities who truly worship (in spirit and truth), or are we creating a group of people who are merely witnesses to primary worshippers, who have worship done to or for them?

Do the oppressive systems and structures of politics, governance and austerity perpetuate a deficit of imagination in the church, repressing imagination and fomenting reductionism?

Are we in danger of being complicit in propping up the status quo or being unable to tap into an alternative consciousness that gives space to

---

[29] Simon Chan, Liturgical Theology – The Church as Worshipping Community, InterVarsity Press, 2006.

the prophetic creativity that is so often seen in what might be called the secular realm?

If the worship of the church is to be truly participative and is to avoid the pitfall of passivity within worship, which in turn breeds the habit of passivity within our faith, then not only must it be something actively *done by* our congregations, but we must ask how *all* in our communities can contribute to the worship, learning, praying, singing, gathering and sending out that forms our liturgies. We can learn from the processes of producing and curating public art, from architecture that encourages participation and community and from educational environments that tease out the knowledge within us and heighten our creativity and curiosity.

Detweiler and Taylor[30] write: »The search for understanding and healing can be found on canvases or on pews. But a case can be made that the art world offers a more open environment for expressing pain and suffering than the church does«.

If the people are not involved, then liturgy is, by definition, missing a vital component of what makes it effective, relevant and life giving. If the people are involved, then we are all the more likely to see liturgy achieve its purpose of empowering us all to better love God and love one another.

30 Barry Taylor/Craig Detweiler, A Matrix of Meanings: Finding God in Pop Culture, Baker Academic, 2003.

Sam Richards / Simon Peters

The United Reformed Church (URC) and Liturgy

Worshipping and serving together in diversity

1. Serving together in unique ways

> *»The United Reformed Church, believing that it is through the freedom of the Spirit that Jesus Christ holds his people in the fellowship of the one Body, shall uphold the rights of personal conviction. It shall be for the church, in safeguarding the substance of the faith and maintaining the unity of the fellowship, to determine when these rights are asserted to the injury of its unity and peace.«* (URC Basis of Union)

Since its inception in 1972, the United Reformed Church has viewed diversity as one of the greatest gifts with which God has blessed us. In bringing the Presbyterian Church in England together with the Congregational Church in England, in Wales and later the Churches of Christ in 1988 with the Congregational Union of Scotland joining in 2000, the URC has shown huge levels of commitment to the idea that all people and groups are called to be part of the Body of Christ, each believing, worshipping and serving in the unique ways which God calls them to.

45 years later, the URC remains every bit as committed to that vision, ever seeking new and innovative ways to encourage and equip all people to listen for the call of the Holy Spirit and to respond, looking to each other for support, insight and challenge when needed, making sure that we are not abusing the principle of diversity to do whatever we please, but rather seeing it as an opportunity for everyone to reach their full potential in God.

This view is reflected very much in the URC's approach to liturgy and the production of liturgical materials, most visibly perhaps in the denomination's Book of Worship, which, since the first edition in 1980 has contained the words of John Huxtable who says, »The orders found here are not prescribed. It is not expected that they will be used in our churches to the exclusion of others. Yet we believe most of these services reflect the ethos of our Church and of its inherited traditions«.

In line with this open approach, the only liturgical elements required to be practiced by local churches are contained with the services for Baptism and Marriage, the conventions for the practice of Holy Communion and the promises made by people entering membership, ministry of word and sacraments, eldership or service as a Church Related Community Worker (CRCW). Put simply, the URC limits prescribed liturgy to very precise moments in the lives of individuals, groups and the Church in order that these most special occasions may be conducted in full, visible unity with the whole URC, using words and practices which are shared across the denomination. Everything else with regards to worship, including within the very services where these words and practices are used, should be arranged on a case-by-case basis in order to help people in the specific context, place and time where worship is taking place to connect with and respond to God.

In some ways, this may seem quite inconvenient for those trying to catch a glimpse of the URC's identity and theology, not least as liturgy is often seen as a sure and certain way of maintaining good order and structure in a denomination's life. However, the URC's commitment to diversity as a core identifying principle should not be seen as a weakness. In fact, much of its strength and effectiveness in terms of encouraging and equipping people of all ages, status and backgrounds in growing in their relationship with God, comes from this very conviction.

Perhaps the best way to explore this is through some of the non-prescribed, yet well thought out liturgical materials and focusses which the denomination produces and supports. It will not be possible, sadly, to explore all of these here, but looking at two aspects, namely the denomination's work across generations and across the Body of Christ, should offer a reasonable insight into the United Reformed Church's approach to liturgy.

2. Working across generations

> *»Children are equal partners with adults in the life of the church [...] The full diet of Christian worship is for children as well as adults [...] As a church community we must learn to do only those things in separate age groups which we cannot in all conscience do together.«* (URC Charter for Children in the Church)

Today's church could have as many as seven generations potentially spanning more than ten decades: infants, children, young people, emerging adults, young adults, middle-aged adults, older adults. Church is one of the few places in society that remains multigenerational – a characteristic we seek to treasure in the URC. For most of the rest of life (home, school, work, social life) people are segregated into groups of predominately one or two generations. But there is a fundamental difference between multigenerational and intergenerational. Churches can cater for these generations separately (with programmes, services and activities aimed at different groups) and be multigenerational. Our churches can cater for these generations together, intentionally creating communities that bring people of all ages together in worship, discipleship, service, mission and ministry: intergenerational. The latter is potentially more challenging but reflects the biblical theme of God establishing human community to be intergenerational family, and making his promises »from generation to generation« (see Genesis onwards).

Not every individual URC congregation will have all (or even many) of the generations represented every time they gather – but every congregation is part of the wider United Reformed Church that does contain all ages. The URC's »more than welcome« programme at Greenbelt (annual festival of faith and arts in the UK) last summer provided an excellent example of how generations can connect and be a mutual blessing. Remote and elderly congregations created a banquet of knitted food that children, young people and adults at the festival enjoyed collecting in a picnic treasure hunt exploring the fruits of the spirit, whilst considering who is invited to the Lamb's heavenly banquet. Gifts were appreciatively shared, and life received through being part of something bigger.

Jesus reminded his adult disciples of their need to learn from children and their need to learn how to be like children (Matt 18:1–7). Jesus reminds the chief priests and teachers of the law that God has called worship from children – liturgy that they need to engage with if they are to understand the new revelation of God in their midst (Matt 21:16).

The most important principle in carrying out any type of intergenerational work is to ensure that it caters, authentically and relevantly, for people of all ages. It is not about involving children and young people in the activities of adults or vice-versa. It is about finding ways of involving everyone in ways which will enrich and enthuse all participants. That happens most naturally when people know each other – they then have grace for the differing tastes, needs, and attention spans of the generations. All give and take, serve and are served.

2.1 Messy Church

Messy Church is a form of intergenerational church which encourages everyone to have fun while exploring the Bible, faith and spirituality. It has developed from the work of Lucy Moore, Martyn Payne and others, and is now supported by BRF (Bible Reading Fellowship) with publications, events and regional coordinators. It has grown into an international movement, which many URC churches have embraced precisely because it offers a flexible and adaptable way to engage all ages in worship.

Every church will run Messy Church sessions differently but the most common pattern begins with a warm welcome. After the welcome, all ages are invited to enjoy different activities, games and a number of crafts which explore elements of a Bible story or theme in various ways, with questions that stimulate conversations between the generations about God, faith and living the Christian life today. Then comes an opportunity to experience and reflect on the theme together during a time of gathered celebration with songs, Bible storytelling and prayer (often incorporating some of the craft produced earlier) before sharing a simple meal. The DNA of all Messy Churches is found in its five key values of Christ-centredness, hospitality, creativity, celebration and being an intergenerational expression of church.

Check out the Messy Church website for more ideas.[1]

---

[1] https://www.messychurch.org.uk/.

2.2 Pilots

Pilots is an ecumenical, non-uniformed organisation open to all children and young people aged 5–18, offered by the URC to our own churches and others. It is founded on a core belief that every child and young person matters. Consequently, Pilots aims to meet the needs of each community in which it functions, offering children and young people safe and caring environments to flourish in the knowledge and love of Jesus Christ. Pilots companies, based in local churches around the UK, usually meet on a weekday night, providing different activities, games and challenges to suit all ages and abilities, spending some time in age-specific groups, and some time altogether. Pilots also encourages children and young people to develop their leadership skills and hopefully, in time, take more and more of a role in planning and delivering the programme for their company. Again the emphasis is on adapting a very flexible model to serve the local context – very URC!

To support the work of local companies, the URC through the Pilots Management Committee, Pilots Publications Board and the Pilots Desk provide a number of resources and services. In addition to »The Compass«, the main manual of Pilots, full of information, guidance, games, activities and suggestions, there is a magazine for members and leaders, organised UK-wide events and training. In particular the annual Worship Materials are designed to encourage and enable Pilots (children and young people) to lead worship and create a service for their local church. This resource is also given to the whole URC church to encourage other children and young people in creating liturgy, and churches to give them the opportunity. The annual Overseas Voyage materials to help Pilots learn more about a different country each year and widen their engagement with mission and the worldwide church. Pilots also offers the whole URC intergenerational events such as »The Big Day Out« which include worshipping together along with many other activities.

3. Working across the body of Christ

> *»You did not choose me, but I chose you and appointed you so that you might go and bear fruit – fruit that will last – and so that whatever you ask in my name the Father will give you.«* (John 15:16 – New International Version)

Walking the Way: Living the life of Jesus today is the umbrella term for the United Reformed Church's focus on lifelong Christian Discipleship and Mission. It explores what it means to actively follow and learn from, eventually being transformed by, Christ. It's for all ages and stages of the Christian journey, whoever you are, whatever your existing relationship with Jesus Christ and the Church is, regardless of your personal circumstances. It's for you whether you have been following Jesus for five days or five decades.

The purpose of Walking the Way is to support everyone in recognising and living out their call to God's Mission in all aspects of life, both within and outside the Church. Whoever we are, we are each created by God with unique gifts and talents to help build God's Kingdom of joy, justice, peace and love for all. Whether we work in a factory or an office block, whether we volunteer at our local foodbank, sing in a choir, enjoy playing sports or knitting, we are all called to participate in God's Mission where we are, making the world a better place, for ourselves and others, as we follow Jesus faithfully. This is what Missional Discipleship is all about!

Walking the Way is also about asking what the Church, its systems, structures, ministries and activities need to look like, locally, regionally, nationally and globally, to make this a reality. This involves uncertainty, risk and change, but Walking the Way is about making sure everyone is equipped to face the challenges which we all face.

Part of this involves the production and promotion of resources, including materials to equip people in exploring Missional Discipleship through worship, not simply as a corporate or formal activity, but a fundamental thread running through our entire lives, solidifying everything in our relationship with Jesus.

To this end, in addition to liturgies and suggestions for advent[2] and lent which we have already released[3], we are also producing some unique resources which offer people a chance to explore Walking the Way in their own contexts, including some short films[4] to help people consider the concept of Missional Discipleship, some popular movies to watch and ask questions[5] about, discussions people can enjoy over some drinks at the bar[6] and some suggestions for reaping the benefits of exploring discipleship in intergenerational[7] ways, to name but a few.

In order to assist people in finding the materials most suitable to them in an efficient and interactive way, Walking the Way will also launch an innovative online library system with a Venn diagram at its heart, allowing users to instantly find resources about Walking the Way on their own, walking with a few, walking with many or anything in between, depending on what they need.

To support local congregations and individuals in a more structured way, Holy Habits[8] by Andrew Roberts, as well as accompanying study booklets[9], come highly recommended. In bringing the ten habits mentioned in Acts 2:42–47 (Worship, Eating Together, Breaking Bread, Prayer, Fellowship, Serving, Gladness and Generosity, Sharing Resources and Making More Disciples) together with other biblical and real life examples and questions, Roberts encourages readers to consider their own lives, both within and outside the Church, seeking God's presence in everything they are, have and do, and shaping their response accordingly.

In line with the URC's commitment to diversity, all of these are written, produced or promoted in a purposefully non-prescriptive form

---

2 https://urc.org.uk/liturgies-from-advent-to-epiphany.

3 https://urc.org.uk/images/WalkingtheWay/documents/Walking_the_Way_in_Lent_310118.pdf.

4 https://urc.org.uk/wtw/films.html.

5 https://urc.org.uk/images/WalkingtheWay/documents/WtW-watching-the-screen-leaflet-310118.pdf.

6 https://urc.org.uk/images/WalkingtheWay/documents/WtW-pub-discussion-leaflet-310118.pdf.

7 https://urc.org.uk/images/WalkingtheWay/documents/Intergenerational_activities.pdf.

8 http://www.holyhabits.co.uk/.

9 https://urcshop.co.uk/index.php?route=product/product&product_id=257.

with applicable content for users from a range of theological perspectives whilst, at the same time, seeking to offer enough of a challenge to encourage everyone to grapple seriously with questions of how worship, faith and life interact in the development of Missional Discipleship.

To this end, Walking the Way is also working closely with the London Institute for Contemporary Christianity (LICC) to devise a suitable accompaniment programme to support local churches in translating their explorations in Missional Discipleship into words, actions, plans and strategies which help them to build communities which share God's love in ways which empower people to live out their God-given call, rather than simply keep the »machine«, which Church so often becomes, running. This short video[10] from the LICC explains the aim of Missional Discipleship in a clear, concise and accessible way.

This expanded view of Missional Discipleship, looking beyond Church settings (the Church gathered) to encompass faith in all aspects of life (the Church scattered), as well as seeking to build the relationships needed to ensure this can happen for all God's people, reaches to the heart of what liturgy is all about, living out our faith in ways which allow our relationship with God, our worship of God and our response to God's call for our lives to work together in harmonious praxis, with worship encompassing all aspects of life in order to fuel and enable this process.

With this insight, however, comes the realisation that resources, although very useful, cannot in and of themselves build a Church with Missional Discipleship radiating throughout it. If that were the case, there would be no need for Walking the Way, given the amount of resources which the United Reformed Church and partners around the globe have produced around Discipleship and Mission over the years! As such, the main focus of Walking the Way is not simply to produce resources, offer suggestions or devise strategies for the short term, but rather to ask the questions, encourage the encounters and offer the challenges needed to build and maintain strong connections and relationships between everyone, across all areas of Church and societal life, in the long term. Through this, people will be able to better recognise and sup-

---

10 https://www.youtube.com/watch?v=TVKbvE-HQeI.

port each other in their unique, yet united, calls to Discipleship and Mission, knowing their personal and collective value in the eyes of God, seeking to build lives, communities, churches, nations and, ultimately, a world which is prepared to respond to God's will.

Kaido Soom

Development of Liturgy in Estonian Evangelical Lutheran Church

1524 can be regarded as the beginning of the Lutheran church in Estonia as this is the year when Tallinn town council decided to support the Reformation. By 1526 all of Estonian towns had turned to Lutheranism.[1] With that began the development of the Lutheran liturgy in Estonia. This process can be divided into four phases. In order to understand the modern day developments concerning the liturgy in the Estonian Lutheran Church it is necessary to understand how it has developed in the past. The history of the liturgy in the Estonian Lutheran Church has been analysed by Marko Tiitus[2] in his recently published textbook[3], the following overview of liturgical history is based on his work.

1. Johann Briesmann's post-reformation service

In 1527 Dr Johann Briesmann was invited from Königsberg to Riga where he became a preacher at the cathedral and began working on and implementing a new order for church services based on Martin Luther's *Formula Missae*. Briesmann's liturgical handbook was published in print in Riga in 1530. In 1533 the Livonian Diet in Valmiera decided that the ceremonies and ecclesiastical order in Riga, Tallinn and Tartu must be uniform. It is likely that manuscriptual translations of Briesmann's handbook were in circulation.

---

1 Seppo Zetterberg, Viron historia, Helsinki, 2007, 148–151.

2 Marko Tiitus, Usupuhastus ja sellele järgnev liturgiline areng luterlikus kirikus – in a collection of articles by Kaido Soom, Liturgika, Tartu Ülikool 2015, 116–138.

3 Kaido Soom, Liturgika, Tartu Ülikool 2015.

In the foreword to his handbook Briesmann explains that church ceremonies are nothing but an external expression of faith and the Gospel. A pastor does not sin even if he wears an alb, a surplice or a chasuble and sings a psalm in Latin. Briesmann has not attempted to create a brand new order for service, but rather to remove from the Roman rite the kinds of elements that could not be accepted according to evangelical teachings. From his handbook an impression can be derived that the Livonian lutherans preferred a solemn traditional service as opposed to the unruly meetings of enthusiasts. The Divine Service is held mainly in German with some traditional Latin parts and the *Kyrie* in Greek.

The order of Briesmann's Divine Service is as follows: *Introitus* (in Latin) - *Kyrie* (in Greek, Latin and German) - *Gloria* (Latin or German) - *Salutatio* and collect (in German) - epistle (half a chapter or less from Pauline Epistles or Acts of the Apostles) - *Alleluia* (afterwards Ps 117, another psalm or Luther's litany can be sung) - gospel (following the principle of *lectio continua*) - creed (Luther's *Wir glauben all an einen Gott*) - sermon - preface (in German) - a small bell is rung as a sign of consecration - words of consecration - *Sanctus* (in German and Latin) - Our Father (in German) - *Agnus Dei* (in Latin and German) - *Pax Domini* (seen as an evangelical absolution) - Eucharist (*Jesus Christus unser Heiland* is sung by the choir) - collect (in German) - benediction (sung alternately by the priest and the congregation or choir)[4]

2. Swedish church handbook of 1699

Northern Estonia belonged to the Kingdom of Sweden from 1561, Livonia from 1621 and Saaremaa from 1645. During the reign of Gustav II Adolf the question of central church government became the main church-political problem. Adopting a unified liturgical order was seen as a part of the same issue. In 1686 a new church law was created in Sweden. It came into effect as an ecclesiastical constitution for all the provinces of the kingdom and was printed in Swedish and German the following year.

4 Marko Tiitus, op. cit., 130-131.

In 1693 a new church handbook was published in Uppsala, its Estonian version was printed in Tallinn in 1699.

Order for Sunday service in the Swedish 1699 handbook: Preparatory service: morning song, *Te Deum laudamus* or a song for calling the Holy Spirit – *Laudes* and Our Father – sermon on a chapter from the catechism – collect (prayer for God's mercy and blessing so the service would be fruitful) – exhortation to confess – *Confiteor* – absolution (optative) – *Kyrie* – *Gloria* and *Laudamus* – *Salutatio* and collect – epistle (read or sung) – a song according to the church calendar – singing the gospel (during consecration) – Luther's paraphrase of the Nicene creed, on great holidays the Nicene Creed – a song according to the church calendar – sermon – penitential rite – priest's exhortation to pray and give thanks – litany or prayer of the church – intercession for the sick or departed, thanksgiving prayers for those who have been healed – engagement announcements – intercession for those that will take part in the Eucharist – Our Father – announcements – song or a verse from a song – preface (dialog and *Vere dignum* that contains the words of consecration) – *Sanctus* and *Benedictus* (read or sung) – Our Father (sung by the priest) – exhortation to receive the sacrament – *Pax Domini* (evangelical absolution) – sharing the bread and the chalice (*Agnus Dei* or other communion songs are sung) – *Salutatio* and collect – *Salutatio, Benedicamus* and Aaron's blessing that are concluded with the Trinitarian formula – a verse for the king and other power holders. If there is no one to take part in the Eucharist, then the sermon is followed by singing and blessings. In the 1699 handbook all parts of the divine service are in Estonian. The Swedish liturgy that had been translated into Estonian, Latvian and German became the standard for Estonia and Livonia and remained in use until the beginning of the 19th century.[5]

---

[5] MARKO TIITUS, Usupuhastus ja sellele järgnev liturgiline areng luterlikus kirikus – in a collection of articles by Kaido Soom, Liturgika, Tartu Ülikool 2015, 132–134.

3. The 1834 handbook

In 1827 Emperor Nicholas I decided to reform the Lutheran church within the entire Russian empire. The new church law was intended to meet the general principles that had been in effect so far, but also set the balance of powers between the state and church. To reach this goal a committee was called together and started its work in 1829. Their work was based on the Swedish 1686 church law and 1693 church handbook alongside with the Prussian union church handbook of 1829. The new handbook in Estonian was published in 1834.

Order for the divine service according to the 1834 handbook: song by the congregation - *Gloria Patri* or Trinitarian preface - exhortation to confess - *Confiteor* - *Kyrie* - absolution (optative) - *Gloria*, on great holidays *Laudamus* was read by the priest - congregation sings *Au, kiitus olgu igavest* (*Soli Deo gloria* in Estonian) - *Salutatio* and collect - gospel or epistle - *Alleluia* - Apostle's creed or on great holidays the Nicene creed - song by the congregation - sermon - prayer of the church - announcing engagements, intercessions, thanksgiving prayers, Our Father, blessings from the Scripture - song after the sermon - *Issanda nimi olgu kiidetud ja austatud* (*Praised and honored be the name of our Lord*) - collect - Aaron's blessing.

If Eucharist is part of the service then the service continues after the song following the sermon has been sung in the following manner: dialog and preface - *Sanctus* and *Benedicta* - Our Father - words of consecration - *Pax Domini* - sharing the bread and the chalice (*Agnus Dei* is sung) - *Benedicamus* - collect - Aaron's blessing.

Influence of the Prussian union handbook can be observed mainly in placing the *Kyrie* in between the *Confiteor* and absolution and in placing the words of consecration after Sanctus, Benedictus and Our Father's prayer.

Attempts at liturgical reform by the Livonian liturgical committee that was led by Theodosius Harnack resulted in a revised church handbook that was approved by the Livonian Synod in 1883 and printed in Estonian in 1889. In the Livonian handbook the order for church services has been renewed and new liturgical details have been added. The more significant changes made in the handbook to the orders of Sunday service and divine service compared to the handbook from 1834 are: adoption of

Introitus after the opening song; extensive exhortation to confess; replacing *Gloria* with the verse from Revelations 5:12 *Worthy is the lamb ...* to which the congregation answers by singing the third verse from *Au, kiitus olgu igawest* (*Soli Deo gloria*); reciting the prayer of the church from the altar after service from the pulpit has ended; leaving off the *Benedictus* (though it was not prohibited); a prayer to receive the Eucharist before and Our Father after the words of consecration. The liturgical bases for the divine services of the church calendar were significantly enriched and new pericopes were taken into use. The Livonian handbook became the basis for liturgical reform in the entire Russian Empire.

The liturgical reform of the XIX. century reached its completion in Estonia and Livonia with the adoption of the imperial church handbook on 19 March 1897 that was published in Estonian in 1902. The 1902 handbook or rather a revised and corrected version published by the exile church (*Eesti Evangeeliumi Luteriusu Kirik* or Estonian Evangelical Lutheran Church continued its work in exile after 1944 due to the Soviet occupation in Estonia) in Stockholm in 1951 (reprinted in 1979 and 1994) is still in use in many Estonian Lutheran churches to this day. It mainly follows the order for divine service set in the 1834 handbook while adopting some changes made in the 1889 handbook.[6]

4. Modern-day liturgical reforms and the 2009 handbook

After the 1902 Agenda was published and the Estonian Lutheran Church had become independent, talks began regarding the need to put together a new church handbook. In 1936 a trial version was published and work with that continued at conferences of religious scholars. In 1939 the situation changed both politically and for the church, the planned reform was never carried out. New memberships of handbook committees continued their work during the Soviet period, but the political climate of the time made their endeavours unsuccessful.[7]

6 Marko Tiitus, op. cit., 134–137.

The year 1991 was revolutionary for both the republic of Estonia and the Estonian Lutheran Church. Estonian independence was restored on 20 August 1991[8] and the process of regaining independence that preceded it undoubtedly had a strong effect on the church as well. A songbook committee that had worked parallel to the handbook committee had by that time concluded its work and in 1991 a new church song and prayer book was printed and taken into use on the First Sunday of Advent in 1991. This was possible thanks to the Estonian Church abroad. Also in 1991, a new liturgical committee was founded, which decided to write a new handbook and put together liturgical auxiliary materials for the already existing handbook.[9] In society the role of the church had grown, since during the Soviet era the church was the only institution not under complete government control. After Estonian independence was restored the church became significantly more active while the limitations set by the previous government were lifted and the people turned to churches *en masse*. This activation of church work was also expressed in reforming the liturgy.

In 1991 a liturgical committee was called together and Tiit Salumäe (then a provost and priest at the congregation of Haapsalu, currently bishop) was elected to lead it and pastor Peeter Paenurm appointed as secretary. The committee worked in several memberships, its members were selected from the members of the General Synod. In putting together the committee the preparedness, personal interest and competence of candidates was taken into account. From outside the circle of members of the General Synod it was possible to include people as experts.[10]

The limitedness of the Estonian committee's options for their own research forced them to be more open to the research and experiences of other churches. The Estonian liturgical committee cooperated strongly with the handbook committee of the Finnish Lutheran church, where

7 Peeter Paenurm, EELK liturgilise komisjoni tegevus aastatel 1991–2005. Usuteaduslik ajakiri 1/2005, 39–40.

8 Seppo Zetterberg, Viron historia. Helsinki 2007, 717.

9 Peeter Paenurm, op. cit., 39–40.

10 Ibid, 42.

the handbook was being renewed at the same time. The goal of the liturgical committee was to put together a new one, but they had to deal with several topical issues as well. For example, in the beginning the question of vestments was under scrutiny and the use of an alb was allowed parallel to a preaching robe (*talaris*). Attention was also given to consecration and blessing ceremonies. Additionally, the committee worked on preparations for various general worship services. All that hindered the speed at which the preparations for the new handbook could move forward. In order to better inform new clergymen who had joined the church, intermediary instructions for church services were published in 1996.[11]

In its work the liturgical committee used the handbooks of churches similar to the Estonian – Finnish and German – a lot. Some freshness and ecumenicity were provided by materials from Anglican and American Lutheran traditions. The reform of church services in the Catholic Church was also observed. An important publication by the committee were the materials for renewing church services bublished in 1999.[12]

The liturgical committee finished the new handbook in 2007. At the time there was a thorough and heated discussion over its contents. The Episcopal Council presented a draft for the new handbook for approval to the Clerical Conference (of which clergymen of the Estonian Evangelical Lutheran Church are members) in 2008. At the vote that took place during the conference, 82 eligible clergymen could express their position. To approve the draft support from 2/3 or 55 clergymen was needed. Since 47 votes were counted in favour and 35 against the draft, the new handbook was not approved.[13]

Dr. theol. Aarne Hiob was critical of the new handbook:

> »The handbook is connected to a certain concept and has tipped the liturgy as close to Catholicism as possible while still barely fitting into a Lutheran framework. The [proposed] general impression would be quite different from that which we are accustomed to. The texts have become more cut-and-dry,

---

11 Ibid, 45–47.

12 Ibid, 47–56.

13 Newspaper Eesti Kirik, http://www.eestikirik.ee/eesti-kirik-kusib-20/ (accessed 21. 11. 2017).

reality of revelations is emphasized. Some Early Christian and Medieval elements have been brought up, which in itself is good, but in this case results in creating a system that in my opinion does not contribute to the relationship between church and society but rather hinders it. Why even have liturgies then? One of the most important reasons for reforming the liturgical order is to improve the relationship with modern people, not to complicate it further by introducing a liturgical order that is more complex and in my opinion stuck in the old times.«[14]

Chairman of the liturgical committee Tiit Salumäe said after the vote:

»It is a pleasure that the draft found such wide support and what has been said of it being the project of a small clique has been proven untrue. As far as I know, no one holds services precisely according to the old handbook. The book of ceremonies found in the new handbook is widely used. I believe even more so, than the book of services, though for example the new order for the children's service is prevalent. I am happy over the general developments in the field of liturgy: the rise of importance of the Eucharist as a part of the service - communion on every Sunday has become commonplace rather than an exception. When we take a look at how the congregation nowadays takes part in the service, then we see that enormous progress has been made: people read along to Our Father's prayer, the creed and *Confiteor*. Many clergymen have taken to saying farewell to people after the service. When I began my service in 1975 the congregation would not read any of these texts aloud. The congregation was a passive side that only took part by singing along. The ice has started to melt. I am certain that the liturgical reform cannot be stopped.«[15]

After the decision made at the Clerical Conference, the Estonian Lutheran Church was faced with an odd situation. While more than half of the clergymen had voted in favour of the new handbook, it was no possible to officially adopt it, since it had not gathered the support of two thirds of the clergymen. The issue was solved by the next Episcopal Council that was held in February 2008. There it was decided to establish as valid liturgical order in the Estonian Evangelical Lutheran Church both

14 Ibid.

15 Ibid.

the handbook published in Uppsala in 1951 (and reprinted in 1979 and 1994) and the new handbook that was drafted in 2007.[16] Therefore, in the Estonian Lutheran Church two handbooks and two orders of service remained in effect. The new handbook was printed in 2009. It is comprised of four books: handbook of services, handbook of readings, handbook of ceremonies, and handbook of blessings and consecrations. It is a voluminous work with 1700 pages[17] of text. In comparison, the old agenda only had 300 pages.[18]

The new handbook on ceremonies gives the clergymen an opportunity to make their own choices from various alternative texts and prayers and therefore make the ceremonies more contextual for the participants. While in the old handbook the volume of church ceremonies directed at the congregation was 54 pages[19], in the new handbook the subject is handled on 220 pages[20]. The new handbook offers texts in more modern Estonian and a new translation of the Bible from 1997 is used. For these reasons the new handbook is used by many congregations including several of those where the order of the service is based on the old handbook.

In terms of order of the service the new handbook also offers several alternatives for putting together the service. Almost half of the handbook of services is the chapter on exchangeable parts of the service or *proprium*. It has abundant sources on the church calendar and different subjects of church life. As such, this chapter concerning the *proprium* is the largest and most diverse out of those in previous Estonian Lutheran handbooks. In the chapter on services five main orders are presented: divine service, service of the word, divine service for workdays, divine service for families, children's service, and additionally prayer meetings and source materials for services on church holidays. New liturgical music has been created both for the divine service and other services. The Finnish Lutheran church helped in this regard both by giving example, advice and material support. [21] The Finnish and Estonian handbooks are

---

16 Decision of the EELC Episcopal Council 19. 2. 2008 nr 2.

17 Jumalateenistuste käsiraamat. Tallinn, 2009.

18 Eesti Evangeeliumi Luteri Usu Kiriku Agenda 1951.

19 Ibid.

20 Talituste käsiraamat, Tallinn 2009.

very similar by construction. This is a sign of good cooperation between these two churches. For example, the pericope system in the Estonian handbook is based on the Finnish Lutheran Church's Book of Gospel (*Suomen evankelis-luterilaisen kirkon kirkkokäsikirja II. Evankeliumikirja. 1999*). The selection of readings for smaller holidays and on other subjects has been put together by the EELC liturgical committee.[22]

In comparison between the 1951 and 2009 handbooks it stands out that the new handbook gives several alternatives for holding a service. In reality the picture is even more colourful in the Estonian Lutheran Church than the orders in the handbooks give reason to believe. Namely, several congregations and their clergymen have created their own combinations based on the 1951 and 2009 handbooks. Therefore it can be claimed that the church services in Estonia are vibrant in variation. While there were many disputes over the adoption of the new handbook these have now settled and everyone follows the order and model that they see to fit best.

The 2009 handbook's main aim is to make the congregation a more active participant in the proceeding of a service by providing them with specific parts in which they can serve along:

> »Secular workers of the congregation can actively participate and serve by reading texts from the bible, holding the prayer of the church, collecting alms, greeting people when they arrive at the church, decorating the church, and also as cantors or members of the choir. During Eucharist a secular assistant may help pass the chalice if they have received appropriate preparation and the priest of that congregation so wishes.«[23]

Compared to the 1951 handbook the following notable changes have been made to the order of worship services in the new 2009 handbook:

- *Salutatio* now follows after the song in the beginning of service.
- *Kyrie* now follows after absolution.
- The creed is said after the sermon.

---

21 http://www.eelk.ee/intranet/liturgiakasiraamatu_esitlus.html (accessed 22. 11. 2017).

22 Jumalateenistuste käsiraamat, Tallinn 2009, 15.

23 Ibid, 21.

- Eucharistic prayer has become more sizable. In addition to traditional words of consecration it also contains *postsanctus*, epiclesis of the consecration, acclamation, anamnesis, epiclesis of the communion, and doxology.
- An opportunity to bring the Lord's peace to other churchgoers by exchanging a handshake has been introduced into the divine service.
- Announcements and *dismissio* are in the end part of the service.[24]

In conclusion it can be said that the Estonian Lutheran Church throughout its history has been a developing church in constant process of liturgical renewal and these positive processes can be observed in modern-day Estonia as well.

---

[24] Jumalateenistuste käsiraamat, Tallinn 2009, 340–366.

Hannelore Reiner

»For we are not the ones who could maintain the Church …«

A stroll through the history of the Protestant Church A.&H.C. in Austria and how this has affected the structure of the Church and its forms of worship

1. Preface

The history of the Protestant Church A. & H.C. in Austria began not with the Reformation, but reaches back over 1,000 years of Christian confession on the territory of current-day Austria. This is evident in some of the buildings used as Protestant churches for decades on end, which date back to the pre-Reformation era.[1]

2. The Protestant century 1523–1626

Reformation thought also infiltrated the monasteries, towns and villages in the Habsburg hereditary lands astonishingly early. Celebration of the Eucharist »in dual form«[2], preaching in German and the marriage of priests or appointments of preachers became clear signs that a congregation had turned Protestant. However, worship was still celebrated in the existing churches and chapels. This was completely in line with Reformer Martin Luther's thinking that the church building itself was less of a concern for worship than simply finding a meeting room for those being preached to and celebrating the Lord's Supper.[3] This explains why

---

1 This includes, for example, the now Protestant St. Martin's Church in Attersee, which was first mentioned way back in the Carolingian era.

2 Bread and wine; cf. G. Reingrabner, Protestanten in Österreich, 1981, 41f.

3 Martin Luther's sermon at the church consecration in Torgau on 5 October 1544.

traces of Protestant life can also still be found in the Roman Catholic Churches that then existed again after the Counter-Reformation. The diverse epitaphs and gravestones alone – such as in the city church of Eferding in Upper Austria, the Renaissance font in the city church of Steyr in Upper Austria, but also in the chancel of St. Jacob's Church in Villach in Carinthia and the Protestant winged altar of Schladming in Styria – with their Biblical motifs and verses from the Lutheran translation of the Bible attest to the Protestant confession of those who worshipped and were buried here. But besides these, the Protestant guilds also erected new Renaissance-style churches, such as what is now Klagenfurt's cathedral. Chapels were also installed in the Protestant estate schools of Graz and Linz that were built by the guilds. In some places, the division of pastoral activities worked well between the (still) Catholic ministers and the Protestant preaching beneficiaries, with the effect that »concurrent churches« were established in many houses of worship, such as can still be seen today in the construction design of the Roman Catholic town church in Vöcklamarkt, Upper Austria.

3. Clandestine Protestant faith 1627–1781

The onset of the Counter-Reformation made it increasingly difficult to celebrate Protestant worship in the native language and with German chorales in previously Catholic churches. Noblemen, citizens and peasants alike all faced the same choice – to either revert to Roman Catholicism or go into exile. For Austrian Protestantism, this heralded the era of the home church and clandestine worship and prayers. In these cases, the »hoamliche G'läut«[4] (Secret Bell) summoned the literate to read prayers, sermons and the prayer books that had been smuggled mainly from Nuremberg and Swabia into Austria.[5] Holy Communion could only

[4] A ringing of bells that both called the clandestine Protestants to worship, but also served as a kind of *battle bell* for the peasants' uprising in Upper Austria in 1526.

[5] The book of sermons by Johann Spangenberg, with a foreword by Martin Luther himself, was particularly popular, although Habermann's prayer book and Johann Arndt's »Real Christianity« were also widespread.

be held if a Protestant pastor from Germany dispensed it, which was seldom the case. These services of worship were conducted at secret locations, which frequently lay in very isolated places, such as in the Seekar Church, a cave in the rocks on the Black Peak above Gosau, Upper Austria, or at the »Dog Church«, a steep rock face in the Kreuzen valley in Carinthia, whose engravings - some in mirror writing - still attest to those acts of worship forbidden under the Habsburgs. Thus the secretly Protestant Austrians were only able to worship publicly by visiting the Protestant county of Ortenburg near Passau. It wasn't only the clandestine Protestants from Upper Austria who went there, but also those from Styria and Carinthia. This was made possible under the pretence of making a pilgrimage to Altötting in Bavaria, but then heading to the Protestant church in Ortenburg instead. To the outside world, they appeared to be not overly devout Catholics, but attended confession at Easter, partook in the Eucharist and had their baptisms, marriages and funerals performed by the local priest. This special situation - a church with neither congregation nor priest, an underground church - endured for over 160 years. The hallmarks from this era are still apparent in many Carinthian congregations, but also around the Dachstein region in Upper Austria and Styria, to this day. Non-ordained men and women lead home prayers and feel responsible for continuing and handing down the faith in Protestant tradition. A certain rejection of lengthy liturgies in worship has also endured since this time.

4. The Patent of Toleration issued by Joseph II in 1781 and its repercussions

Just one year after assuming the business of government from his mother Maria Theresa, Joseph II started to introduce many reforms in the Habsburg Empire. For instance, he issued the Patent of Toleration on 13 October 1781 for those subjects disposed toward the Lutheran or Reformed confessions. The Patent defined them as non-Catholics and permitted them henceforth to found parishes wherever 100 families or 500 individuals declared themselves Protestant, also to build prayer houses and appoint a pastor. It is scarcely imaginable today how delighted and grateful the Protestants of that era were to the Emperor. And yet this tolerance also included many restrictions. For instance, the prayer houses were not to be identifiable as a church from the outside, which meant no towers or bells and not even arched windows. The main entrance could not face the street. The fees for ceremonies still had to be paid to the Roman Catholic pastor, even if they had been performed by his Protestant counterpart. The great effort and time that could be involved in completing a prayer house is exemplified by the construction of that on the main road to and from Linz. The plan to build it was already made in 1826. However, the authorities delayed work from starting for 18 years. Permission was finally granted in 1841; only for work to be halted the following year. It required the intervention of the eminent Protestant confectioner Johann Konrad Vogel from Linz for the prayer house's eventual completion in 1844.[6]

It was possible to circumvent the prohibition of towers and arched windows at times. Political circumstances, such as during the Napoleonic era at the start of the 19th century, when parts of Carinthia and Upper Austria no longer stood under Habsburg rule, opened up new possibilities. The prayer houses in the Carinthian parishes of Zlan, Trebesing and Eisentratten, for example, were built with arched windows, which identified them as special buildings from the outside. The Lutheran lumberjack and inventor Georg Hubmer also secured permission for the round windows in the prayer house in Nasswald, Upper Austria, by petitioning the Emperor.[7] The Roman Catholic St Martin's Church in Attersee, Upper Austria, became Protestant in 1812 by means of an exchange.[8] This furnished the Attersee parish with a church complete with tower and bells, which was not to be revoked even after the return to Habsburg Austria. Despite all the obstacles and difficulties, the newly established parishes set to work with great fervour. Besides parsonages and schools, they built prayer houses and cemeteries. The funds for construction were

---

6 See: Vom Bethaus zur neuen Martin-Luther-Kirche, issued by Evang. Pfarrgemeinde Linz, 1997, 10f.

7 See: O. Janetschek, Der Raxkönig, 1972, 177ff., and W. Pusch, Familiengeschichten aus St. Aegyd, 2003, 15.

8 H. Reiner, Wasser des Lebens-umsonst, 200 Jahre evangelische Pfarrgemeinde A. B. Attersee, 2013, 6.

mainly donated by Protestant citizens and peasants, along with the timber required, but above all people's personal labour. A great deal of time, manpower and money was invested in the first prayer houses of the »tolerance congregations« by those who would meet there for worship upon their completion. Without the support and help of wealthy individuals, mainly from Germany, building such prayer houses would have been inconceivable for many of the tolerance congregations. For instance, the merchant Johann Tobias Kiessling from Nuremberg donated a crucifix for the prayer house in Hallstatt in Upper Austria, which was completed in 1785. The baroque winged altar, which nowadays stands in the prayer house in Obertraun, Upper Austria, was probably also a gift from Kiessling.[9]

As the number of publicly confessing Protestants quickly grew, the converts were encumbered with yet another obstacle. Anyone who wanted to be Protestant had to absolve »conversion lessons« from the local Roman Catholic priest, whose purpose was of course to dissuade them from their intention.

As there were no trained theologians in Austria at the start of the tolerance era, pastors were drafted in from the neighbouring churches in Württemberg and Bavaria, but also from Transylvania and Silesia. Congregations had to pay the pastors themselves,[10] which was a particularly

[9] »Hallstatt, along with its Protestant citizens, had made friends around the world […]« in the words of E. G. Goetze to mark the prayer house's 200th anniversary in 1985. He could never have imagined that 30 years later the church in Hallstatt would be attended daily by crowds of visitors from the Far East, which has also led to Sunday services of worship including elements delivered in English. After the Protestant Church A. & H.C. in Austria recently started providing pastoral care for tourists, the extremely popular tourist destination of Hallstatt has now become a key location in this respect. A pressing need now seems to have arisen to tailor the nature of the parish's services even further towards the hordes of visitors, but without neglecting pastoral care for local congregation members. See: Die Christuskirche im Fokus des Tourismus, in: Gesichter, Geschichten, Konturen, 2015, 126ff.

[10] It was only with the Patent of Toleration in 1861 that pastors in Austria were allowed to use the professional designation of *pastor*, which at least put their title on a par with Roman Catholic office holders.

heavy burden for some poor congregations and might also explain why some pastors switched parishes so many times. It is easy to understand why each of these clerics also brought along the liturgy and agenda he was familiar with and introduced these into the new congregation. The hymn books were a particular problem. The hymn book recommended by the Vienna Consistory at the end of the 18th century was rejected across the board by the Upper Austrian and Upper Styrian tolerance congregations because of its rationalist tendency and the omission of popular songs from clandestine years. For this reason, in 1856 Jakob Ernst Koch, a pastor in Wallern, Upper Austria, published a new book that augmented a Bavarian hymn book with the familiar songs. Despite initially being rejected by the Consistory, it caught on far and wide.[11]

When Franz Joseph I permitted Protestants to build towers in the mid-19th century, many Protestant congregations began restructuring or extending their prayer houses. Some built a new church with a tower and bells beside the old prayer house, others even replaced the original building entirely. Square windows were replaced by arched forms and stained glass. Only the Patent of Toleration in 1861 allowed for direct access from the street, which provided the Protestant Christians with a new public presence.[12] The interior design of the earliest Protestant churches in modern-day Austria was characterised by plainness and simplicity. The altar in the apse usually had a large altarpiece with a scene from the New Testament, or it was carved by local artists, as in the Protestant church in Gosau, Upper Austria. A communion rail surrounded the altar, at which the kneeling participants received the elements of the Lord's Supper. The chancel above the altar that is found in most Protestant churches in Burgenland did not catch on in Upper Austria or amongst

---

[11] While studying in Rostock, in 1858 Jakob Ernst Koch III wrote enthusiastically to his mother in Wallern: »[…] that 12,000 copies of the Upper Austrian Hymn Book have already been sold and, because four congregations in Bohemia are introducing the same, 800 have been sent Prague and 300 to Heřmanovy Sejfy«. Worte der Erinnerung an J. E. Koch, issued by Presbyterium der Evangelischen Pfarrgemeinde Wallern, 1908; cf. L. Temmel, Evangelisch in Oberösterreich, 1982, 79.

[12] See: K. Schwarz, Von der Toleranz zur Religionsfreiheit, aus: Jahrbuch des o. ö. Musealvereines 156, 2011, 189.

the Carinthian tolerance congregations. It is usually situated to the left, but sometimes to the right of the church's chamber, or entered from the vestry. The font stands in a central position between the chancel and the altar.

5. Away from Rome – towards the Gospel 1890–1914

The call »Away from Rome« stems from a speech given by the physician Theodor Rakus in 1897 in the Sofiensaal in Vienna, in which he called for withdrawal from the Roman Catholic Church on the basis of what he called its »ultramontane policies«.[13] Without any conscious action of its own, the Protestant Church in Austria was drawn into the storm of the Great German and anti-Catholic movement. The numerous conversions – around 5,000 people per year between 1898 and 1903[14] – led to the foundation of new parishes, mainly in Styria, but also in Lower Austria. The construction of places of worship for the newly formed congregations reflected the new spirit. The freshly formed Protestant congregation in Mürzzuschlag, Styria, benefited from substantial support from the Roman Catholic regional poet Peter Rosegger for the church that it was to construct and readily complied with his wish for an image of Maria inside. Nor were the few Protestants in Zwettl, Lower Austria, perturbed by the inscription of Bismarck's words that the Germans »feared God, but nothing else«[15] over the entrance to the small newly built church. However, it was a different matter with the diaspora churches designed by the German architect Otto Bartning. As the grandson of a Protestant prelate, Bartning, who came from Karlsruhe, had a lifelong special interest in theological issues, particularly in worship. He was still an architecture student when he designed the Protestant Peace Church in Peggau, Styria. A further 17 churches were to follow suit around the Danube Monarchy until 1914. Helmut Pommer, the first pastor of the congregation in Krems, Lower Austria, which arose from the Away from Rome movement in 1905,

---

13 See: G. Reingrabner, ibid., 238.

14 Ibid.

15 G. Reingrabner, ibid., 241.

had studied together with Bartning and persuaded him to build the church in Krems in 1912. Instead of the neo-gothic style common to Protestant churches built in Austria at that time, Bartning designed a central structure with an octagonal interior for Krems. The congregation was supposed to gather around the altar and chancel. The church's chamber was designed to be conducive to worship without overshadowing it, as Bartning explained in the article »New church buildings«, which he published in 1919.[16] One hundred years on, the congregation members sitting on the rows of benches are still actively involved in the act of worship in Krems, thus adhering to the intent of the famous church architect. The church of the parish in Dornbirn, Voralberg, one of Austria's current-day nine congregations of the Protestant Church H.C., was also designed by Bartning.

A speciality amongst the congregations and churches that emerged around the turn of the 20th century has to be St. Aegyd, Lower Austria. Protestant lumberjacks from Salzkammergut also worked in the huge forests here, owned by Lilienfeld Abbey and the county of Hoyos. At the end of the 19th century, the few Protestant families celebrated worship in private homes. But already in 1902 it was decided to build a church for the small preaching station that belonged to the Protestant parish of St. Pölten. The lumberjack families could never have managed this on their own, not even with the aid of the middle-class Protestant families from St. Pölten and Vienna who spent their summer holidays in St. Aegyd. It was a great stroke of luck that the major industrialist Karl Wittgenstein, the father of the famous philosopher Ludwig Wittgenstein, came to settle there. Karl's father had already converted to Protestantism from Judaism. Wittgenstein donated the plot for the church, financed the majority of its construction and commissioned the Jugendstil architect Josef Hoffmann from Vienna to design the Woodland Church, as it is still known to this day. It was to remain Hoffmann's only sacred building. Astonishingly, despite the enduring enthusiasm for Jugendstil and the works of the »Vienna workshops«, this prime example of a Jugendstil church in St. Aegyd has become largely forgotten. This might also have something to do with its remote location. However, the current congregation members of

16 See: entry for Otto Bartning in Wikipedia (accessed 07. 10. 2017).

St. Aegyd am Neuwald value their church as a haven of security and enjoy the beauty of its white and blue decoration.[17]

Even if the motives of the new Protestants at the turn of the 20th century are open to question, the numerous new congregations and church buildings are clear evidence of a turn »towards the Gospel«. The following years spanning World War I, the inter-war period in the corporative state, and most certainly the period under National Socialism, presented a trial of faith and steadfastness for the members of the fledgling Protestant Church A.&H.C. in Austria.

6. Growth of the Church 1944–1970

No one in the Protestant Church in Austria could have imagined what would happen in 1944/45. Entire populations of villages in the German settlements throughout south-eastern Europe, mainly in northern Transylvania, were evacuated westwards as the Russian soldiers advanced. After weeks on the road, some came to rest in the North of Vienna or Lower Austria. But thousands were accommodated on farms and in earth huts in Upper Austria and in the Salzburg Flachgau. Most travelled onwards to Germany – some even as far as the United States or Canada – after the end of the war. However, a considerable number had found work in Austria and remained here. The neighbourly aid that Transylvanians were accustomed to practising also helped them get through the difficult post-war years. The Protestant churches were filled with Lutheran Saxons from Transylvania. And so the Vöcklabruck Peace Church, for instance, held three services of worship on Sundays. The old Hospital Church in Schwanenstadt, Upper Austria, also quickly ran out of room. A struggle broke out over the reserved seats paid for by the local members of the congregation. To provide pastoral care for the many new congregation members, the pastors and teachers amongst the newcomers were taken on by the Protestant Church. In all, 81 churches and 58 parish halls were built by 1961. This number of new builds was repeated during the fol-

[17] See: W. Pusch, ibid., 155ff.

lowing decade.[18] Once again, generous aid from the Gustav Adolf Association, donations from abroad and above all countless hours of voluntary work by congregation members made these many new church buildings possible. Working alongside one another brought the Austrian locals and new arrivals closer together. After the Transylvanians had originally stuck to the familiar hymn books from home that they had brought with them, from 1960 on, the Austrian *Protestant Church Hymn Book* gradually caught on. This also contained an *Order of Worship* that the Synod A. C. had passed together with the hymn book. The new diversity in the congregations was also reflected in Confirmation celebrations, with girls and boys from Transylvanian families wearing their traditional Saxon costume, while their Austrian counterparts continued to opt for dark festive clothing. The robes worn by the pastors also differed. Whereas the Austrian and German officiants wore the customary ruffs, the displaced pastors donned finely pleated robes with clips.

The Upper Austrian pastor's son Hubert Taferner designed the architecture of many of the new churches that needed building. He carefully considered each congregation's particular wishes. For instance, Transylvanian touches are clearly evident in the Church of Mercy in Rosenau-Seewalchen in Upper Austria, such as its sturdy fortified tower that is so reminiscent of the fortress churches in Transylvania. The existing mother congregations also substantially helped with the building of churches in the newly established parishes.[19]

The first tentative steps towards establishing a new relationship between the Christian confessions post-1945 were reinforced by the resolutions of the Vaticanum II. It became possible for Protestant congregations to buy or lease disused Roman Catholic churches, as was the case with St. John's Church in Timelkam and the Church on the Rock in Schärding, both in Upper Austria.

---

18 G. Reingrabner, ibid., 287.

19 For instance, the tolerance congregation in Rutzenmoos, Upper Austria, collected a sum of 24,000 Schillings for its former sub-congregation in Schwanenstadt and donated 45 cubic metres of timber to build its church. See: B. Folberth, Das Werden der evang. Pfarrgemeinde A. B. Schwanenstadt, 1987, 32.

7. Instead of closing churches – opening new ones

The membership of the Protestant Church A. & H.C. began shrinking year on year from 1970 on. There are many reasons for this. Of all couples getting married, 80 percent are inter-confessional. With regard to christening children, the majority confession is chosen in many cases. The proverbial »diaspora resilience« of which generations of Protestants had been so proud no longer applies to the same degree. The congregations are getting older, even if the pastors attend closely to young people in religious and Confirmation classes. In many congregations, »alternative worship« has been offered for decades that differs – with regard to either the timing of services, style of music, or form – from the ongoing main Sunday morning services based on the EKD's 1999 liturgy book, as passed by the synod A.C. Besides special children's and infants' services, multi-generational worship is also offered in an attempt to appeal to all age groups in an all-embracing parish service. Despite all these efforts, there is no halting the general trend towards private practice of worship and secularisation. This also means that preaching stations and sub-congregations are being abandoned and parishes merged into wider associations.

Nonetheless, this hasn't stopped some congregations from very recently still taking the plunge to build new churches, above all in the diocese of Lower Austria.[20] This could well be a sign of the old resilience of Austrian Protestantism, which pays more heed to preaching and celebrating the Gospel than to counting its numbers. It also provides hope for the future, »for we are not the ones who could maintain the Church; nor was it our forefathers; nor will it be our descendants. But rather it was, still is, and will be in the future He who says » ›I am with you always, unto the end of the word‹ …«.[21]

[20] In Klosterneuburg, Waidhofen/Thaya and Hainburg, eminent architects designed houses of worship to meet both the needs of the diaspora congregations and the style of the dawning 20st century.

[21] M. Luther, Wider die Antinomer, 1539, WA 50, 476f.

II
Examples of good practice / Beispiele guter Praxis

Signe Malene Berg

The Church of Our Lady and the Churchnight[1]

1. In brief

1.1 The Night Church phenomenon

When darkness descends on the land, a number of churches remain open in the larger towns. The Night Churches provide a space for calm and reflection and a different kind of experience in the city's night life.

The Night Churches experiment with form and content. The atmosphere is often informal and relaxed, and what takes place in the Night Churches varies from church to church. The church is often lit up by candles, and evocative music is played. In many churches there is a short service or concert during the evening.

1.2 Drop in

The Night Churches are often open for many hours. You can come and go as it suits you and you can sit in peace and quiet as long as you wish or you can join in activities in different parts of the church.

In the Night Church you can also have a confidential talk. The priests and other staff in the Night Churches are experienced in conversations on existential subjects, and like all priests in the established church they have a duty of confidentiality.

1.3 Who comes to the Night Church?

People of all ages and with widely different backgrounds use the Night Churches. You are not required to be familiar with the church's rituals

[1] The Church of Our Lady and the Nightchurch. Text: Signe Malene Berg© Translation: John Kendal Published by the Council of the Church of Our Lady, Copenhagen 2015. Used with permission of the author.

and language. In particular, the Night Churches are visited by people »out on the town«, who drop in for a while before moving on into the night.

1.4 The first Night Church

The first Night Church opened in Copenhagen Cathedral in 1999 and offered evenings with subdued lighting, quiet and candlelight. Since then it has developed into a Night Church with talk groups, an amateur choir, concerts, events, visits by artists and services. There are candlelit globes and tables with candles where one can write a prayer and light a candle. On the floor there is a cross made of candles surrounded by shards of glass and one can scratch one's name on a mirror altar. There are ChillOut Nights with dreamy electronic music and reworked versions of biblical stories, a gospel workshop and much more.

2. Prayer

Quiet and prayer

Ever since the Night Church's beginning its visitors have been able to write their own prayers on small slips of paper. The prayers written during the evening are read aloud in connection with the concluding midnight service. Some of the prayers have been collected in the book »Kære Jesus Kistus« (Dear Jesus Christ) and together give a fascinating picture of the questing spiritual life of a modern metropolis at night. A picture of many very different people who use the church: young people on their way to a discotheque, restless souls wandering through the night, the homeless, couples in love and the desperately lonely. And the book gives those who would like to pray but don't know how, ideas as to how freely a prayer can be formulated.

3. Music – atmosphere

3.1 The music of the night

Music and singing have been part of religious acts since man thought of striking two pieces of wood together to create a rhythm. Who can imagine a church service without hymns and organ music? But actually such church services do exist, and are called quiet meditation services to indicate that here something unusual is at stake.

Music and singing are quite basic elements in the Night Church's services. They can open doors when we wish to focus our thoughts or surrender ourselves. Music and singing in their unique forms are indisputably among the phenomena that most readily affect our feelings and most readily give form to the feelings we cannot express in words.

Music can bring us beyond the limits and borders set by words and our reason, and bring us into a state in which borderlines dissolve and in which it is possible to have experiences in which words and concepts cease to suffice.

Like the Divine, music is a universal phenomenon that transcends all language barriers and with its border crossing property gets the Divine to break forth everywhere, when it wishes to, spontaneously and in many forms.

3.2 Liturgical laboratory

As a liturgical laboratory the Night Church has in the course of the years sought out and experimented with music as a way of propagating the Gospel. Today the Night Church's music profile ranges from the soprano voice singing hymns alone in the dark over acoustic music to electronic music and DJs, who bring their sound pictures into the space of the church. On the face of it very different kinds of music, but fundamentally tailored to the same pattern. The music is intended to evoke calm, focus, security, intimacy and love. In interaction with the setting and lighting the music is intended to launch the churchgoer and the community on a journey towards the infinite, towards God.

3.3 God Goes Deep

One Night Church arrangement in particular, *God Goes Deep*, uses the setting and the music as tools to set the churchgoer free from words and concepts. *God Goes Deep* can best be described as an open church space in which music from selected DJs and powerful lighting form a backdrop for deep reflection and spellbound fascination. Interacting with C. F. Hansen's architecture and Thorvaldsen's apostles and Christ, light and sound become bearing elements that create a little fairy tale and a sense of enchantment inspired by the church's interior as a whole. The magic of a moment and a story that you can freely enter and leave, where the history of the space, the apostles along the walls and Christ at the altar almost become living and palpable.

4. Art

Art visits the Night Church

The Night Church seeks to function as a liturgical laboratory in the tension field between art and church. Artists are invited to be responsible for a given Night Church evening in an innovative collaboration between church and culture. The idea is to explore new and relevant ways in which the Gospel can be communicated, ways that make use of the forms of expression available to modern art. The meeting nearly always takes place in a creative and experimental collaboration in which the artist as well as we in the Night Church work to establish a shared spiritual space, a third space. The artist is given an opportunity to create an artistic frame in the church for an evening. This freedom to fill in a frame is unique to the Night Church, and in its work here it moves away from a traditional understanding of the church based on organisations and structures, to replace it with a more network based view. Church has become a verb instead of a noun, i. e. we »church« together, and move together out into unknown waters. The Night Church is thus a concrete expression of what in theology – inspired by the Polish sociologist Zygmunt Bauman's concept of *liquid modernity* – we have called *liquid church.* A flowing church in a flowing modernity, i. e. a quite new, untraditional way of thinking, dreaming and imagining church. Typical of this is the Night Church's use of art installations to involve viewers actively and through this aesthetic interaction to propagate the Christian universe.

One of the key words in this collaboration is interactivity. The art is not aesthetic but applied art, which means that the art comes in as an element that is the space and the evening, an element with which one can interact. The art thus becomes liturgical. We have the permanent installations: *The Cross of Light* by Ingemar Thalin, *Job's Corner* by Mette Fredholm and finally *The Mirror Altar* by Peter Callesen.

The art in the church is there to mediate the Gospel. Of course. The church is not a neutral space or the artist's own stage. And the good artist takes this into account and is humble in the face of the task. The space and its story bind the art to something specific and given beforehand.

We have had musicians in the church who assumed that they could just play their usual concert repertoire, but who once they were in the situation, discovered that they couldn't. For some there is a severity of context and a service that are too stringent for them to be there with their art, and they say »No, thank you« to participating. Others take it as a challenge, a journey of exploration.

When art moves into the church, it is quite natural that it should be harnessed in the service of the church, and for the same reason it is the church's task and responsibility to think about art in a theological perspective, to reflect on its meaning. This is an excellent idea, but not necessarily in a creative collaboration with the artist herself. There is plenty of space within the church, more space than in any other institution, for theology and the preaching of the Gospel are relevant almost everywhere. It is when the church dares to set art free and fully unleash its arsenal that it can make a significant contribution to society, to its consciousness and understanding of reality.

5. The installations

5.1 The Cross of Light

The Cross of Light, in which one lights a candle on a cross based on the four elements, was created by the Swedish priest and artist Ingemar Thalin. Here is what he says about the thinking behind the work:

> »My goal has been to make an aesthetically formed artwork but which in itself can also contain the dark and painful aspects of life. Oppositions are one of the mysteries of life.
> The form is that of a cross with its centre, along with the areas that are represented around the cross and which give the cross its form.
> The rectangles that the installation consists of are formed in such a way that they can be filled with content. They are formed as trays. The content, message of the cross depends on what is placed in these trays.
> The cross contains mirrors and broken glass. The mirrors make it possible for us to see ourselves as we are through the crushed and splintered glass.

The glass is dangerous and if we pick it up, we risk hurting ourselves and blood will be spilt.
The crushed glass may remind us of anger and grief that something has been broken, the crushed glass may remind us of Krystalnacht or of the bottles we smashed in despair that nothing could end my alcohol abuse, etc.
God shares our lives with all that involves of insufficiency and vulnerability to the attacks of evil.
The earth bears us and also receives our bodies when we die. The earth is thin shit that God has used to feed us humans ever since the morning of the Creation. The earth has to do with life and reminds us that our time is limited. In the earth we can hide our treasures and we can sow our seeds. The earth creates nearness to our creator.
The centre of the cross. The shells that rest on a bed of sand. Mussels are something delicate, beautiful that open themselves to us. In them we find water. Water which is both dangerous and life-giving. The Bible's relationship to water has many facets. Water brought the message of life. The presence of the spirit is manifest. From death to life is illuminated in its symbolic value.
To light a candle in this installation we have to kneel down within the cross, a liturgical act that supports faith.
Fire, water, earth, air. The four elements are present to show God's all-embracing care.«

5.2 Job's Corner

Job's Corner, where one writes a prayer of complaint to God and impales it on a cross, was produced in collaboration with the artist Mette Fredholm. It derived from conversations with visitors to the Night Church in which it transpired that they didn't know about the aspect of faith that has to do with being able to complain to God, to scold Him, the almighty creator of heaven and earth.

Mette Fredholm writes:

»One day in my sitting-room my eyes fell on my grandmother's washboard: It's old and pretty worn, and I could see her hands rubbing and scrubbing on the washboard with a lot of thoughts running through her head. If she had been in a heavy mood, she would probably have been rubbing extra hard, and the washboard gave me the association: water running and dripping from grief and anger. The washboard's colour is bluish and the complementary colour to blue is orange, and all of a sudden there appeared in my imagination a big rousty sheet of iron, whose orgies of orange could be joined to the blue hues of the washboard in a sharp complementary contrast of colour. When the washboard with its clearly marked grooves was mounted on the rusty sheet of iron a Wailing Wall appeared.

The idea is to use this symbolic Wailing Wall – not for humble, quiet weeping but for complaints and shouting. Concretely by having a sponge in a stone vessel containing water stand nearby so that one can press water over the grooves on the washboard. In this concrete act one does not turn one's back on God. It is – like Job – complaints and cries directly to God. An open dialogue. To turn one's back on God is equal to being filled with bitter rage that is directed towards others in order to give vent to one's feelings.

Job and God were in a dialogue. In our day God is revealed together with a further dimension – Jesus – God's son.

A cross is mounted with nails on the Wailing Wall in Job's corner. It is a symbol of the cross on which Jesus hung, and in his weakness cried his complaint to God: My God, my God, why hast thou forsaken me? Jesus did not get a direct answer – only after three days did God reveal himself in Jesus' resurrection from the dead, and the whole world was given hope that God hears us and acts. This cross is conceived as an outstretched hand from God to us through Jesus. Here one can lay one's griefs by writing a prayer on a slip of paper and spiking it on the nails of the cross. And on the Wailing Wall next to the cross Jesus' words from 1Peter 5:7 – meant as a direct touch – »Casting all your care upon him; for he careth for you«.

5.3 THE MIRROR ALTAR

The Mirror Altar was made for the Night Church in 2006 by the artist Peter Callesen. One scratches one's name on a mirror fragment and fixes in to a wall – and if one kneels, one will in the fragment be able to see one's reflection in the face from a concealed icon of Christ.

Peter Callesen writes:

»1 Corinthians 13:12 For now we see through a glass, darkly; but then face to face; now I know in part; but then I shall know as also I am known.

I have always found the above text from the Bible beautiful and interesting. It contains a mysticism, a chink into the divine – and it is probably the case that what we can only sense, guess at, is more exciting than what we can clearly see – perhaps because the mysterious leaves room for us to form our own pictures of the divine.

But what I find most interesting in the text is the comfort it contains. For me the words in part contain a recognition and understanding – by God – of the fact that life is rarerly experienced as something whole, but on the contrary often as something that contains splits and is incoherent, indeed as something that is broken.

It is, then, not only about my being allowed to sense God, but just as much about God seeing and knowing me as I am; he cognises and re-cognises me in the midst of my fragmentation. And it therefore seems more credible and comforting when we are told that we shall at some time see clearly and feel whole.

I also came to think of the words of the Blessing, Lord, let thy countenance shine upon you, when I had sketched out the Mirror Wall. That is in fact what happens when the light from the candles shines on the icon, which is reflected in the small mirror fragments, which in turn shine on the persons sitting in front of the Mirror Wall.

The intention is that the wall should contain an interactive element. I believe it is important that the church should offer the seeker various ritual practices, in which he has the possibility of setting a personal imprint on the ritual. The idea is therefore that the visitor to the Night Church should bring along a small mirror and attach it to the stand (with the help of wire fixed to the back). It may be a picture of our submission to God: that we come to God broken or incomplete. At the same time we are also contributing to creating a larger picture of God, or one might say that God can use the broken, the divided. We are all branches on the trunk.

Another possibility is to scratch or write one's name on the mirror as a recognition and reminder of the fact that God sees our names, that we are inscribed in his book or the book of life.«

References

Berg, Signe / Morten Wassmer (eds.), Kære Jesus Kistus, Jeg tror sgu ik' på dig. Kun lidt. Copenhagen, 2011.

Berg, Signe Malene, Møder i mørket. En andagtbog fra Natkirken. Copenhagen 2009.

Ward, Pete, Liquid church, 2002.

www.tnatkirken.dk.

Christiane Dohrn

Geburtstagsfest als Gottesdienst – Gottesdienst als Geburtstagsfest

Ein Fest-Gottesdienst-Projekt aus Anlass der 350-Jahrfeier der St.-Jakobi-Kirche Stollberg[1]

1. Ausgangspunkt und Idee

Die Festwoche zum 350. Kirchweihjubiläum wurde geplant. Alle Veranstaltungen bewegten sich im traditionellen Rahmen: Die Gemeinde sitzt in den Kirchenbänken und vorne wird etwas aufgeführt, Musik, Gespräch, Theater.

Einen Geburtstag feiere ich anders, mit Essen und Trinken, mit festlicher Kleidung, vielleicht etwas Programm und Tanz.

Angestoßen durch ein Gespräch mit einer Kollegin entstand die Idee, die Gemeinde zu einem Fest einzuladen, das eigentlich ein Gottesdienst ist. Sie sollte die Möglichkeit haben zu erleben, dass gottesdienstliches Feiern Feiern sein kann, dass das Haus Gottes ein Festsaal ist und fröhliche Ausgelassenheit nicht nur in Liedtexten des Gesangbuches stattfindet. Kurz: Die Kirche ist ein Ort des Lebens.

2. Die Projektgruppe

Nach ersten Gesprächen mit vertrauten Gemeindegliedern und der Grobvorstellung des Projektes im Kirchenvorstand, bildete sich eine Gruppe von sieben Menschen, teils aus der sogenannten Kerngemeinde, teils kirchliche »Randsiedler«, die gemeinsam das Fest über sieben Monate sehr detailliert planten.

Bedacht wurde sehr genau Folgendes:

---

[1] Evangelisch-Lutherische Landeskirche Sachsens.

- Wer ist eingeladen?
- Wann findet das Fest statt?
- Was gibt es zu trinken und zu essen?
- Wie ist die Kirche eingeräumt?
- Wie ist die Kirche ausgeleuchtet?
- Wie sind die Tische geschmückt?
- das Festprogramm, -ablauf, inklusive Zeitplan
- Kinder auf dem Fest

3. Die Kooperationspartner

Wo Unterstützung nötig war, erhielten wir sie. Der Tischlermeister, der die Bänke vor 10 Jahren gebaut hatte, half uns beim Aus- und Wiedereinbau der Kirchenbänke. Die Stadt half beim Transport und der Zwischenlagerung der Kirchenbänke. Die Freiwillige Feuerwehr stellte uns Biertische in ausreichender Anzahl zur Verfügung. Fleischermeister und ein benachbartes Restaurant bereiteten Suppen zu. Bäckermeister stellten drei Geburtstagstorten her. Eine Catering-Firma stellte uns kostenlos Geschirr und Gläser bereit.

Die Reaktionen auf das Fest waren unterschiedlich und erstaunlich. Unterschiedlich: Von »Das war ein tolles Fest!« über vielfältigen Dank »für diesen wunderschönen Abend« bis hin zu: »Also mit dem Geburtstagsfest konnte ich nicht so viel anfangen. War es nun ein Gottesdienst oder ein Fest? Ich wusste nicht so richtig, was das sollte.«

Erstaunlich daran war, dass vor allem ältere Gemeindeglieder sehr angerührt davon waren, ihren Kirchenraum so anders und »so schön« zu sehen und zu erleben. Jugendliche und kirchliche »Randsiedler« äußerten sich rundum positiv und überrascht, dass »so etwas in der Kirche möglich ist.« Besonders gefreut hat mich die Reaktion eines emeritierten Pfarrers. Er sagte: »Das Fest hatte alles, was ein Gottesdienst braucht: Gebet, Lesung, Predigt, Gesang, Segen. Das Fest war für mich ein durch und durch inszenierter Gottesdienst.«

Die Idee, das Kirchweihfest wie ein Geburtstagsfest zu begehen und zu feiern, hat zu einer großen Resonanz auf die gesamte Festwoche in der Gemeinde und der Stadt geführt. Die Verbundenheit der Gemeinde und der Stadt mit ihrer Kirche erhielt so einen deutlichen Schub, der hoffentlich noch lange nachklingt.

Als wertvolle Bilder bleiben: Der leere Kirchenraum an den Übergängen von Aus- und Einräumen. Einmal um Säulen gehen, die sonst immer mit Bänken umstellt sind. Die Lichtinstallationen, die den Raum veränderten. Vor allem aber die Menschen, die zum Altarplatz kommen, und dort nicht eine karge Hostie in Empfang nehmen, sondern fröhlich von der üppigen Torte essen. So verschwenderisch kann das Leben sein.

4. Was ist auf andere Gemeinden übertragbar?

Den Kirchenraum für eine besondere Aktion zu verändern, erfordert Mut und Fantasie. Aber der Gewinn ist groß. Der Raum, der Ort, an dem sich die Gemeinde versammelt und Gottesdienst feiert, wird lebendiger, neu und intensiv wahrgenommen. Die Verbundenheit wird gestärkt. All das wirkt sich positiv auf die Atmosphäre in der Gemeinde und ihren Gottesdiensten aus.

Sicher ist der Reiz einer solchen Aktion in einer alten Kirche höher als in einem modernen Mehrzweckraum, aber das Besondere lässt sich überall mit liebevollen Details wie Tischschmuck o. ä. hervorheben. Insbesondere tragen Lichtinstallationen zu einer neuen Wahrnehmung bei.

5. Der Ablauf des Festes

Präludium

Eröffnung: Im Namen Gottes, des Vaters, des Sohnes und des Heiligen Geistes. Amen. Gott ist da! Wir alle sind da! Nun kann unser Fest beginnen, ein Fest für Leib und Seele.

Lied: Ein Fest für Leib und Seele[2]

Begrüßung: Herzlich willkommen zum Geburtstagfest unserer Kirche. Unser Geburtstagskind hat sich geschmückt und zeigt sich in ungewohntem Gewand. Ich hoffe, Sie haben alle einen Platz gefunden. Seit

---

2 Singt von Hoffnung 034, Neue Lieder für die Gemeinde, hrsg. von der Evangelisch-Lutherischen Landeskirche Sachsens, http://www.liederdatenbank.de/songbook/22148.

etwa 700 Jahren sind Menschen an diesen Ort gekommen, um hier zu beten, aus Sorge und Not heraus oder aus Freude und Dankbarkeit. Wir hören nun Worte, die an den Psalm 84, dem Psalm für das Kirchweihfest, angelehnt sind.

Psalm und Gebet mit drei SprecherInnen, im Raum verteilt:

1: Wie lieb sind uns Deine Wohnungen, Gott,
2: wie schön ist es, bei Dir Platz zu finden.
3: Wohl denen, die in Deiner Nähe wohnen.
1: Ach, Gott, wie sehnten wir uns danach,
wieder an diesem Ort zusammenzukommen,
zu singen und zu beten, Deinen Namen zu feiern.
2: Jetzt sind wir froh und zufrieden:
Der Vogel hat ein Haus gefunden,
die Schwalbe ein Nest für ihre Jungen –
und Deine Gemeinde, Gott, den Ort, Dein Lob zu singen.
1: Wie lieb sind uns Deine Wohnungen, Gott,
2: wie schön ist es, bei Dir Platz zu finden.
3: Wohl denen, die in Deiner Nähe wohnen.
2: Kann Gott denn wirklich bei den Menschen
eine Wohnung finden?
Ist nicht der Himmel und das ganze All zu klein,
Gott zu fassen?
Wie könnte es da dies Haus tun?
3: Wende Dich zu uns, Gott!
Wenn Menschen Deine Nähe suchen,
erhör ihr Bitten und Beten.
Lass Deine Augen offen sein über diesem Haus
bei Tag und Nacht.
1: Wende Dich zu uns Gott!
Wenn Menschen hier zusammenfinden.
sei mitten unter uns.
Lass Dein freundliches Lächeln in diesem Haus erstrahlen.
3: Wie lieb sind uns Deine Wohnungen, Gott,
2: wie schön ist es, bei Dir Platz zu finden.
1: Wohl denen, die in Deiner Nähe wohnen.
3: Großer Gott, lange haben wir uns auf diesen Abend vorbereitet. Vieles haben wir überlegt und wieder verworfen. Aber wir haben immer wie-

der gespürt, Du bist mit uns. So bitten wir Dich, lass uns heute Abend auf's Neue erfahren, dass wir bei Dir Platz haben, so wie wir sind. Stärke uns durch Deine Gegenwart.

2: Großer Gott, an so vielen Orten bin ich in dieser Woche gewesen, manches ist gelungen, anderes hat nicht geklappt, manches Gespräch hat mir gut getan, anderes hat mich geärgert. Aber jetzt bin ich in der Kirche und kann ablegen, was mich belastet. Dafür danke ich Dir.

1: Großer Gott, wie ein großer Zeigefinger ragt unser Kirchturm in den Himmel. Ein sichtbares Zeichen für Deine Gegenwart in unserer Welt. Wie ein Festsaal sieht unsere Kirche heute aus. Wenn es hier schon so schön ist, wie schön wird es dann erst in Deinem Reich. Wir wollen Dich loben mit unserem Gesang und Dich preisen mit unserem Tanz. Amen.

Gloria: Allein Gott in der Höh sei Ehr (EG 179, 1 + 2)

Gemeinsamen Tanz nach: Siegfried Macht, Gesangbuchlieder als Tänze entdecken.

Dem Tanz zu EG 179 schloss sich ein *Walzer* an.

Kindersekt wird verteilt: Wir stoßen auf die Jubilarin an. Lasst uns miteinander anstoßen auf unsere Jubilarin. Wir wollen sie pflegen und bewahren und auch weiterhin mit Leben erfüllen und uns füllen lassen.

Verkündigung: Szenen aus dem Theaterstück »Höckner's Erben«, das die Geschichte des Wiederaufbaus der St. Jakobi-Kirche erzählt.

Tanz am Platz

Festrede:

Liebes Geburtstagskind! Oder besser, denn Deinem Alter angemessener: Liebe Jubilarin!

Wir feiern Deinen Geburtstag! Den 350. Nach menschlichen Maßstäben ein stattliches Alter.

Generationen haben an Dir gebaut: angebaut und umgebaut, repariert und renoviert. Durch die Jahrhunderte hindurch haben Menschen Dich gestaltet, äußerlich und innerlich.

Du warst und bist ein besonderer Ort für unsere Stadt und für die Menschen, die hier lebten und leben. Was macht Dich zu so etwas Besonderem?

Du, liebe Jubilarin, bist ein sichtbares Zeichen für die Verbindung zwischen Himmel und Erde, zwischen Göttlichem und Menschlichem. Außen ragt Dein

Turm hoch hinauf. Wenn die Wolken tief hängen, sieht es aus, als stoße deine Spitze an den Himmel. Die dicken Mauern drinnen schirmen ab. Sie bieten uns Schutz und Sicherheit. Und zugleich ist hier in Deinem Inneren eine große Weite zu spüren. Zu allen Zeiten haben Menschen hier drinnen nach Stille und Besinnung gesucht. Abgeschirmt vom Alltagslärm, umgeben von dieser Weite fällt manches klein-klein des Alltags ab und man kann ahnen, das Leben ist mehr – mehr als Essen und Trinken, Schlafen und Arbeiten. Ein Hauch vom himmlischen Glanz wird so spürbar.

Oben auf Deiner Empore und damit dem Himmel ein Stück näher, steht die Orgel. Zu allen Zeiten wurde in Dir musiziert. Mal laut, mal leise, mal fröhlich und festlich, so wie heute, ein andermal traurig und klagend. Menschen kommen zu Dir, um Musik zu hören. Hier drinnen klingt es anders als in einem Konzertsaal. Denn hier ahnt man, die Musik dient einem Höheren. Musiker spielen nicht allein des Beifalls wegen, sondern zur Ehre Gottes. Was Worte nicht ausdrücken können, bringt die Musik vor Gott. Und zugleich bringt sie in den Menschen etwas zum Klingen und Schwingen. Ein Hauch von himmlischem Glanz wird so hörbar.

Auch die Kanzel ist erhöht. Sicher auch, weil der Prediger, die Predigerin von dort aus besser zu verstehen ist. Aber nicht nur. Zu allen Zeiten sind Menschen zu Dir gekommen, um Gottes Wort zu hören. Und Menschen haben sich bemüht, in ihrem Wort Gottes Wort hörbar zu machen. Eine Rede halten oder eine Rede hören kann ich auch draußen auf dem Marktplatz. Aber hier drinnen spricht und hört es sich anders. Auf dem Weg zwischen Sprechen und Hören ereignet sich etwas. Redende und Hörende wissen, es kommt nicht nur Menschenwort zur Sprache. Gottes Gegenwart tritt hinzu.

Liebe Jubilarin, Du bist ein sichtbares Zeichen für die Verbindung zwischen Himmel und Erde, zwischen Göttlichem und Menschlichem. Zu Deinem Geburtstag wünsche ich Dir natürlich Gesundheit: Dein Dach möge immer dicht sein, Deine Mauern fest und die Farbe an Deinen Wänden frisch. Mögen sich wie in den vergangenen Jahrhunderten so auch in Zukunft Menschen finden, die Dich hegen und pflegen und auf Dein Wohlergehen achten. Die Weisheit des Alters hast Du schon mit deinen 350 und mehr Jahren. Die muss ich Dir nicht wünschen. Aber ich wünsche Dir, dass in Dir diese Weisheit bewahrt bleibt und Du dennoch jung bleibst, und offen für Neues und Neue. Und das wichtigste zum Schluss: Ich wünsche Dir den Segen Gottes.

Wir danken Gott, dass er Dich durch Höhen und Tiefen, durch ruhige und unruhige Zeiten erhalten und bewahrt hat. Möge Gott auch weiterhin seine schützende Hand über Dir und den Deinen halten. Nun danket alle Gott! Amen.

Lied: Nun danket alle Gott (EG 321)

Geburtstagsgrüße von der katholischen Gemeinde und Baptistengemeinde

Überleitung zum gemeinsamen Essen: Nun ist es an der Zeit, dass wir uns stärken und gemeinsam essen. Wenn das Brot, das wir teilen, als Rose blüht und das Wort, das wir sprechen, als Lied erklingt, dann hat Gott unter uns schon sein Haus gebaut, dann wohnt er schon in unserer Welt.

Lied: Wenn das Brot, das wir teilen[3]

Essen

Lied: Danket dem Herrn (EG 333, 1 + 2 + 4)

Geburtstagsgrüße der Landeskirchlichen Gemeinschaft und der Methodistengemeinde

Rezitation und Liedvortrag: Was wäre ein Geburtstag ohne Überraschung? Was wäre ein Geburtstag ohne Liebe, ohne Gott und was wäre ein Geburtstag ohne die Hoffnung auf das Reich Gottes?

Tanz-Zeit

Präsentation der Geburtstagstorte: Etwas fehlt noch zu einem richtigen Geburtstagsfest.

Wissen Sie, was ich meine? Was wäre ein Geburtstagsfest ohne Geburtstagstorte?

Abschluss mit Dank an alle Mitwirkenden und Helfenden: Unser Fest neigt sich dem Ende. Ich möchte mich jetzt bei allen bedanken, die dazu beigetragen haben, dieses Fest vorzubereiten. Die Helfer und Mitplaner bekommen eine Rose zum Dank!

Lied: Ausgang und Eingang, Anfang und Ende. In einem großen Kreis lasst uns voneinander Abschied nehmen. Im Pilgerschritt haben sich alle in einen großen Kreis um den gesamten Kirchenraum begeben.

Schlussgebet und Vater unser: Am Ende dieses Festes, am Ende dieses Tages lasst uns noch einmal still werden vor Gott und beten. Herr, wir preisen dich. Du bist der Abend, du bist das Licht und die Nacht. Du bist der Anfang und das Ende der Zeit. Dir danken wir für die Schönheiten des Tages und die Heraufdämmerung deiner bergenden und behütenden Nacht. Unser Leib, unsere Seele, unsere Sorgen sind bei Dir. Schenke uns Ruhe und Geborgenheit und – wenn es soweit ist –

---

3 http://www.liederdatenbank.de/song/21561.

einen guten Schlaf in einer Zeit ohne Angst. Lege Deine Güte in unser Haus und lass Deinen Engel bei uns sein, es komme, was mag. Amen.

Abendlied

Segen: Lasst uns in diese Nacht und in die kommenden Tage gehen mit dem Segen Gottes: Gott sei vor Dir, um Dir den rechten Weg zu zeigen, Gott sei hinter Dir, um Dich zu schützen, Gott sei neben Dir, um Dich zu bewahren. So segne Dich Gott – Vater, Sohn und Heiliger Geist. Amen.

Postludium

Christiane Dohrn

A Birthday Party as a Service of Worship – A Service of Worship as a Birthday Party

A project to organise a joyful service of worship to celebrate the 350th anniversary of St. Jakobi Church in Stollberg

1. How it all started – an idea

A week of celebrations was being planned to mark the 350th anniversary of the church's consecration. All the events were of a traditional nature – the congregation sitting on the church pews with music, talks and theatre taking place up at the front.

I celebrate birthdays rather differently – with food and drink, festive clothes, and maybe some entertainment and dancing.

While chatting to a colleague, I hit upon the idea of throwing a party for the congregation in the form of a service of worship. They should have the chance to experience how worship can truly be *celebrated*, that the House of God is a festival hall and that joyful exuberance can also be found beyond the lyrics of hymn books. In other words, that the church is a place filled with *life*.

2. Project group

After first talking to close friends in the congregation and outlining the project to the church council, a group of seven was formed, including some key members of the congregation and some from the sidelines, to spend seven months planning the party meticulously.

They carefully considered the following issues:

- Who was to be invited?
- When would the party take place?
- What food and drink would there be?

- How would the church be set up?
- What lighting would be used in the church?
- Table decoration
- The programme and running order for the party, including timings
- Children as guests

3. Co-organisers

Wherever we needed support, we received it. The carpenter who crafted the pews ten years ago helped us to remove and replace them. The town authorities helped to transport and store the pews for the duration of the party. The voluntary fire brigade lent us enough trestle tables to cover our needs. Master butchers and a neighbouring restaurant cooked soups. Master bakers produced three cakes. A catering company provided us with crockery and glasses for free.

The reactions to the party were both different and astonishing. Different: From »What a great party« and many expressions of thanks »for this wonderful evening« through to: »Well, I couldn't really get my head around the idea of a birthday party. Was this a service of worship or a party? I didn't really know what to make of it.«

The astonishing thing was that the older congregation members were particularly moved to experience their church looking and feeling so different and »so beautiful«. Young people and those on the sidelines of the church revealed that they were thoroughly impressed and surprised that »something like this is possible in the church«. I was particularly pleased by the reaction of a retired pastor, who said: »The party had every key element of a service of worship – prayer, readings, a sermon, singing and blessings. For me, the party was a perfectly planned service of worship.«

The idea of marking and celebrating the anniversary of the church's consecration like a birthday party went down very well with the congregation and the town for the entire week of celebrations. This significantly strengthened the affiliation of the congregation and the town with their church, which will hopefully resonate for a long time to come.

Precious lasting images: The empty space inside the church while we were clearing and refurnishing it. The unique chance to walk around pillars that are otherwise always surrounded by pews. How much its appearance was changed by the different lighting. But above all the image of the people approaching the chancel – and instead of receiving a meagre host merrily tucking into lavish cake. That's how extravagant life can be.

4. What is transferable to other congregations?

Changing the church's interior for a special occasion calls for courage and imagination. But there is so much to be gained from the venture. The space where the congregation gathers and celebrates worship becomes livelier and is perceived with fresh eyes and intensity. The sense of affiliation is strengthened. This all generates a positive atmosphere in the congregation and its services of worship.

Certainly, the charm of an undertaking like this is greater in an old church than in a modern-day multipurpose hall, but this special effect can be created anywhere with some loving attention to detail such as table decorations and the like. Different lighting is particularly effective in creating a new perception.

5. Party programme

Prelude

Opening: In the name of God, the Father, the Son and the Holy Spirit. Amen.

God is here! We are all here! Now our party can begin, a party for body and soul.

Song

Welcome address: Welcome to our church's birthday party. The church has dressed up for the occasion and is looking very special indeed. I hope that you have all found somewhere to sit. People have been coming here for almost 700 years to pray – because they were worried or in need, or for reasons of joy and gratitude. We will now listen to words from Psalm 84, relating to church consecrations.

Psalm and prayer with three speakers dotted around the room

1: How lovely are Your dwelling places, God,

2: How wonderful it is to find a place at Your side.

3: How happy are those who live close to You.
1: Oh, God, we longed
To gather again at this place,
To sing and to pray – and to celebrate Your name.
2: Now we are happy and content:
The bird has found a house,
The swallow a nest for her young –
And Your congregation, God, a place to sing Your praise.
1: How lovely are Your dwelling places, God,
2: How wonderful it is to find a place at Your side.
3: How happy are those who live close to You.
2: Can God really find a home amongst people?
Are Heaven and the entire universe not too small to hold God?
How could this house manage it?
3: Turn to us, God!
When people want to get close to You,
Hear their pleas and prayers.
Let Your eyes watch over this house,
Both day and night.
1: Turn to us, God!
When people gather here,
Be in our midst.
Let Your friendly smile light up this house.
3: How lovely are Your dwelling places, God,
2: How wonderful it is to find a place at Your side.
1: How happy are those who live close to You.
3: Great God, we have spent a great deal of time preparing for this evening. We considered and then rejected many ideas. But we always felt Your presence amongst us. So we ask You to let us discover anew this evening that we have a place at Your side, however we are. Strengthen us with Your presence.
2: Great God, I have been to so many places this week, where some things worked out and others didn't; some conversations did me good and others perturbed me. But now I am in the church and can cast aside all my burdens. I thank You for this.
1: Great God, our church tower points up to the sky like a huge index finger. A visible sign of Your presence in our world. Our church looks

like a banquet hall today. If things are already this pretty right here, how beautiful will it then be in Your kingdom? We want to praise You with our songs and celebrate You with our dancing. Amen.

Gloria

Group dance according to Siegfried Macht, *Turning hymns into dance*

The dance to EG 179 was followed by a *waltz*.

Children's fizzy drink is handed out. We drink a toast to the birthday celebrant. Let's raise a glass together to the church. We want to maintain and care for it and continue to fill it and ourselves with life.

Proclamation: Scenes from the play »Höckner's Heirs«, which recounts the reconstruction of St. Jakobi's Church.

Dance on the square

Celebratory speech:

Happy birthday to you! Or, perhaps more appropriately, considering your grand age: Congratulations on reaching this wonderful milestone! We are here to celebrate your birthday! Your 350th anniversary. This is a ripe old age in human terms.

Generations have believed in you – built and modified you, repaired and renovated you. Over the centuries, people have shaped you both inside and out.

You have always been and remain a special place for our town and for the people who lived here in the past and do so today. What is it that makes you so special?

As you celebrate your anniversary, you are a visible sign of the connection between heaven and Earth, between the Godly and human realms. Outside, your tower reaches up high. When the clouds hang low, your spire seems to touch heaven. Your thick inner walls enclose us. They provide us with sanctuary and security. And at the same time, a vast space is created within. People have always entered this place in search of peace and reflection. Shielded from everyday noise, surrounded by this expanse, some of the trivialities of everyday life ebb away and we get to feel that there is more to life – more than eating and drinking, sleep and work. A hint of Heavenly splendour is revealed.

Up above in your gallery, and thus a little bit closer to heaven, stands the organ. Music has always resounded here in your chamber. Sometimes loud, sometimes quiet; sometimes joyful and celebratory, as today, other times sad and mournful. People come to you to listen to music. It sounds different here from in a concert hall. For here music serves a higher purpose. Musicians don't play just for applause, but rather in honour of God. Music expresses to God things that cannot be said in words. And at the same time, it causes people to join in and sway.

And so a hint of Heavenly splendour can be heard.

The chancel is also elevated. For one, because the preacher can be better understood from up high. But not only for this reason. People have always come to you in order to hear God's Word. And people have endeavoured to make God's Word audible through their own. We can also give or listen to a speech outside on the market square. But inside this church we talk and sound differently. Something takes place along the way between speaking and listening. Speakers and listeners know that it's not just human words being said. God's presence is added on top.

As you celebrate your anniversary, you are a visible sign of the connection between heaven and Earth, between the Godly and human realms.

I also wish you good health on your birthday, of course. May your roof always be watertight, your walls solid and your interior paintwork fresh. May there always be people in the future, as in centuries past, to maintain and care for you and to ensure continued well-being. At the age of 350 and beyond, you have already acquired the wisdom that comes with age. I do not need to wish you this. But I wish for this wisdom to reside within you, while you also remain young at heart and open to new ideas and people. And I have saved the most important wish until last: I wish you God's blessing.

We thank God for preserving and maintaining you throughout highs and lows, throughout peaceful and tempestuous times. May God continue to place His protective hand over you and yours. Now thank we all our God! Amen.

Song

Birthday greetings from the Catholic and Baptist congregations

Switch to shared meal: Let us fortify ourselves by eating together. When the bread that we eat unfurls like a rose and the words that we speak resonate in song, then God has built his house amongst us and already lives in our world.

Song

The meal

Song

Birthday greetings from the Regional Church and Methodist congregations

Reading and song performance

What would a birthday be without a surprise?

What would a birthday be without love, without God, and what would a birthday be without hope for the kingdom of God?

Time to dance

Presentation of the birthday cake: Something is still missing to make this a proper birthday party. Do you know what I mean? What would a birthday party be without a birthday cake?

Conclusion with thanks to all organisers and helpers

Our party is now nearing the end. I would now like to thank everyone who was involved in the preparations. The helpers and co-organisers are given a rose in thanks!

Song: »Exit and entrance, beginning and end« Let's say farewell to one another in a big circle. Everyone shuffles to form a large circle around the church's whole chamber.

Closing prayer and the Lord's Prayer: As this party and day both draw to a close, let us once more fall silent before God and pray: Lord, we celebrate You. You are the evening, You are the light and the night. You are the beginning and the end of time. We thank You for the beauties contained in the day and the twilight as Your recuperative and protective night approaches. Our bodies, our souls, our worries lie with you. Bestow us peace and security upon us and – when the time comes – sound sleep in a time without fear. Place Your benevolence in our house and let Your angel be with us, whatever might come to pass. Amen.

Evensong: Everyone stays in the circle for this.

Blessing: Let us venture into this night and the days to come with the blessing of God:

May God be before you to show you the way; may God be behind you to protect you; may God be at your side to preserve you.

God bless you – the Father, the Son and the Holy Spirit. Amen.

Postlude

Gunnar Garleff

Gottesbegegnung im Raum feiern

kreuz.weg.wandel – Gottesdienste zur liturgischen Raumerfahrung

1. Wort und Raum

Der evangelische Gottesdienst ist ein Wortgeschehen des unsichtbaren und sichtbaren, des gesagten und des gesungenen Wortes. Er ist quasi »Wortkult« (Alexander Deeg) und alles ist darauf ausgerichtet, dass Gott spricht und die Gemeinde hört, dass die Gemeinde betet und Gott erhört. Und so sind auch unsere Kirchenräume auf das Wort ausgerichtet, damit »nichts anderes darin geschehe, denn das unser lieber Herr selbst mit uns redet durch sein heiliges Wort und wir wiederum mit ihm reden durch das Gebet und Lobgesang.«[1]

Der Glaube kommt aus der Predigt (vgl. Röm 10,17); allerdings steht der evangelische Gottesdienst immer in der Gefahr, dass sein gesamtes Geschehen auf den Hörsinn eingeengt wird. Aber menschliche Wahrnehmung geschieht in der Regel über mehrere Sinne, nicht nur über den Hörsinn. Zum Hören treten Riechen, Schmecken, Tasten hinzu. Diese Sinne beziehen sich besonders auf die Raumwahrnehmung. Was ich beim Hören im Raum sehe oder rieche, wie ich sitze, liege, stehe, hat Einfluss auf das, was ich hörend wahrnehme. Aber der Raum ist nicht nur ein Wahrnehmungsraum, er ist zugleich Bewegungsraum. Menschen sind leibräumliche Wesen und alles Leben ist von Raum umgeben und findet im Raum statt.

Dies gilt entsprechend auch im Gottesdienst. Wer an einem Gottesdienst teilnimmt, bewegt sich im Gottesdienstraum: Er begeht ihn beim Eintreten, er steht und sitzt, er wandelt beim Abendmahl und ggf. bei der Taufe. Das Wortgeschehen Gottesdienst ist daher immer zugleich ein

---

1 Martin Luther, WA 49,588.

Raumgeschehen. Der Raum wirkt dabei auf die liturgische Inszenierung des Evangeliums. Seine Gestalt zeugt zugleich vom Gottesdienstverständnis seiner Zeit.

2. Die »neue Friedenskirche« von 2012

Wie sehr der Raum die liturgische Feier und die persönliche Erfahrung im Gottesdienst beeinflusst, tritt besonders deutlich hervor, wenn der gewohnte Kirchenraum verändert wird. Im Zuge einer großen Renovierung der 1910 eingeweihten Heidelberger Friedenskirche wurde ihr Innenraum 2012 neu gestaltet.

Die Friedenskirche wurde 1910 auf dem Grundriss eines griechischen Kreuzes gestaltet. Die ca. 1000 Plätze verteilten sich ursprünglich auf drei große Emporen sowie im unteren Bereich derart, dass die Plätze unter den Seitenemporen im 90°-Winkel zum Hauptschiff angeordnet waren. So war gewährleistet, dass der mächtige Kanzelaltar im relativ kleinen Altarraum von allen Plätzen gut zu sehen war. Entsprechend dem Wiesbadener Programm wurden die Orgel und die Chorempore hinter der Kanzel platziert. Alle liturgischen Orte mit Ausnahme des Taufsteins waren so in einer Sichtachse angeordnet. Rein optisch war alles auf die Predigt ausgerichtet.

Eine erste Renovierung 1960 brach diese Raumordnung auf. Kanzel, Altar und Taufstein wurden im Altarraum nebeneinander angeordnet, so dass der Altar als Ort des Gebets und des Sakraments eine eigene von der Kanzel unterschiedene Würdigung erhielt. Die Kanzel wurde im Vergleich zu 1910 näher an die Gemeinde gerückt. Der damalige Pfarrer Karlheinz Schoener begründet diese Veränderung: »Das Wort, das von dort verkündet wird, geht an die Gemeinde heran, weil es sie ›angehet‹.«[2]

Die Neugestaltung des Kirchenraums von 2012 setzt dagegen das ursprüngliche Wiesbadener Programm um, erweitert es aber zugleich. So werden erstmals konsequent Taufstein, Altar, Kanzel und Orgel in einer Sichtachse angeordnet. Die ehemals klare räumliche Trennung von Or-

[2] Karlheinz Schoener, Der neue Altar-Raum, in: 50 Jahre Friedenskirche Heidelberg-Handschuhsheim, 1960.

gel- bzw. Chorempore und Altarraum wird durch eine verbindende Stufenanlage aufgelöst, welche zugleich dazu führt, dass der Altarraum zu einer Altarinsel in der Mitte des Kirchenraumes wird. Die Stufenanlage ist dabei zugleich Chorempore und Kanzelort, wobei die Kanzel je nach liturgischem Bedarf auch entfernt werden kann. Ebenso ist der Altar beweglich. Für Konzerte kann er in vier Teilen an andere Orte des Kirchenraumes gestellt werden oder er kann zu besonderen Anlässen in seiner äußeren Form gestaltet werden.[3] Im Zuge der Neugestaltung wurden die Bänke im unteren Kirchenraum entfernt und durch Stühle ersetzt. Bis auf Orgel und Taufstein ist in dem neuen Raum der Friedenskirche alles dynamisch und fließend.

3. Kreuz.Weg.Wandel oder die etwas andere »Bauphase 9«

Wie jede Neugestaltung einer Kirche, ging auch die Renovierung der Friedenskirche mit Konflikten einher. Die einen wollten den alten Raum bewahren, die anderen die liturgischen Traditionen, wieder andere den Kichenraum auf die liturgischen und kirchlichen Herausforderungen von Gegenwart und Zukunft hin gestalten. Nach der Wiedereinweihung der renovierten Friedenskirche trat zunächst Ruhe ein. Die Gemeinde feierte im neuen Raum ihre traditionell mit qualitativ hochwertiger Kirchenmusik und theologisch anspruchsvoller Predigt gestalteten Gottesdienste. Schon bald bemerkten Gemeinde, Ältestenkreis und auch Architekten, dass ein veränderter Raum auch eine veränderte liturgische Gestaltung zur Folge hat. Nicht nur die liturgischen Wege der Liturgen sind andere, sondern auch die Raumwahrnehmung der Gemeinde.

Die Architekten machten den Vorschlag, die im Architektenvertrag vorgesehene sogenannte Bauphase 9, welche quasi die Übergabe einer Gebrauchsanleitung für die Nutzung des Raumes darstellt, umzuwandeln in eine Reihe von Workshops und Gottesdiensten, in denen der neue Raum gottesdienstlich erprobt werden sollte. Das Ziel: Die Gemeinde eig-

3 Beispiele für Raumgestaltungen im Zusammenhang von Gottesdiensten finden sich unter friedensgemeinde.wordpress.com.

net sich ihren Raum im liturgischen Vollzug an. Die Idee zur Reihe »kreuz.weg.wandel« war geboren.[4]

Der besondere Fokus der Gottesdienste dieser Reihe lag auf der Raumerfahrung. Das Ziel dieser Gottesdienste war nicht, ein »zweites Programm« zu etablieren, das dann neben die gewohnten Sonntagsgottesdienste tritt, sondern durch das besondere, den Kirchenraum in die liturgische Gestaltung bewusst mit einbeziehende Feiern, das Erleben des Raumes im »normalen« Sonntagsgottesdienst zu fördern. Es gab daher auch keine spezielle Zielgruppe, sondern alle, die gerne Gottesdienst feiern, waren eingeladen.

Zur Vorbereitung der Gottesdienste wurde ein kleines Team gebildet, das aus dem Pfarrer und der Pfarrerin, dem Kirchenmusiker, zwei Architekten, dem Künstler, der die Prinzipalstücke 2012 entworfen hatte, zwei Ältesten und einigen Gemeindegliedern bestand. Ziemlich schnell kamen wir in der Vorbereitung zur Einsicht, dass das Ziel, den Raum als Ort von Christusbegegnungen besonders erfahrbar zu machen, nur möglich wird, wenn wir den Raum je neu für den Gottesdienst gestalten und dabei zugleich auch die gewohnte Statik des Gottesdienstes (jeder sitzt auf seinem Platz) aufheben. Der Einzelne soll sich und Gott im Raum erfahren; die Gemeinde soll sich im Raum bewegen.

Zugleich war uns im Vorbereitungsteam bewusst, dass jede Regieanweisung im Gottesdienst die Erfahrung stört. Uns war wichtig, dass wir eine elementare Liturgie feiern wollten, die ohne Zwischenworte auskommt und sich allein auf das Geschehen in Raum und Wort konzentriert. Dabei sollte die Gemeinde als Mitfeiernde ernst- und wahrgenommen werden. Jeder Einzelner sollte jederzeit die Möglichkeit haben, sich selbst als am Gottesdienst beteiligter und den Gottesdienst gestaltender Akteur wahrzunehmen. Die Grenzen zwischen liturgischen Performern und Performten sollten fließend sein.

---

4 Der Titel der Reihe ist dabei von einer zeitgleichen Diskussion über die Gestalt des Kreuzes beeinflusst. Das Kreuz in der Friedenskirche ist als Kreuznegativ in den schwarzen, aus Bronze hergestellten Altar eingelassen. Viele Gemeindeglieder vermissten allerdings ein Standkreuz. Die Reihe »kreuz.weg.wandel« umfasste daher im Jahr 2015 nicht nur drei Gottesdienste, sondern auch drei Vorträge zum Thema Kreuz und Gottesdienst.

Nicht nur die Liturgie der Gottesdienste sollte von der gewohnten Sonntagsliturgie abweichen, auch die Verkündigungsform. Statt einer Predigt wurden einzelne Textfragmente nebeneinander gestellt und in den Kontext einer verbindenden biblischen Geschichte eingefügt. Die Textfragmente stammten aus der zeitgenössischen Literatur. Entsprechend dem Gesamtkonzept verzichteten wir auf einen zentralen Verkündigungsort, sondern lasen und sprachen aus verschiedenen Ecken des Raumes.

Und da der Hörsinn nicht für sich allein steht, sollten auch die anderen Sinne angesprochen werden: Mahlszenen und Tauferinnerung, gemeinsamer Wandel durch den Raum waren konstitutiv für die Gottesdienste.

Der Wandel im Raum sollte dabei sowohl in der Stille geschehen als auch durch Musik und Gesang. Bewusst haben wir Lieder ausgewählt, die möglichst kurz und schnell memorierbar sind. So hatte die Gemeinde die Hände frei und bedurfte keines Gesangbuchs. In der Friedensgemeinde haben Kirchenmusik und Chorgesang einen hohen Stellenwert. Solisten (Percussion, Geige, Querflöte) begleiteten die Gottesdienste. Insbesondere der Percussionist brachte dabei den Raum zum Klingen, in dem er auf Geländern, Bänken, ja selbst dem Altar musizierte. Bewusst haben wir bei der Planung auf den Einsatz von Chören verzichtet, da diese das Konzept des gemeinsamen Wandels durchbrechen würden.

Die Konzeption der Gesamtreihe war zeitintensiv. Dreimal drei Stunden Beratungen waren nötig, um die ersten drei Gottesdienste der Reihe »kreuz.weg.wandel« zu konzipieren. Pro Gottesdienst wurden zwei weitere Treffen angesetzt, teils auch mit praktischer Probe. Das Vorbereitungsteam bekam ein Gespür dafür, was im Raum möglich ist. So fiel die Vorbereitung der Gottesdienste in einer Nachfolgereihe im Jahr 2016/2017 wesentlich leichter.

4. Beispiel »Stehen im Kreuz – Umkehrerfahrung als Quelle gesellschaftlichen Wandels« (Buss- und Bettag 2015)

Mitwirkende: Acht Sprechende, vier »Ordner/Lichtträger«, Percussionist, Pianist

Raumgestaltung: Die Altarviertel sind bei den Evangelistentafeln aufgestellt, dabei ist das Innere des Altars sichtbar. Die Kirche ist entstuhlt, ca. sechzig Stühle sind locker verteilt im ganzen Kirchenraum mit dem Prinzip des größtmöglichen Abstandes der Stühle zueinander (= Vereinzelung), keine achsiale Ausrichtung auf Altarstufe, um den Taufstein herum wird Raum gelassen.

Im Taufstein sind ein bis vier Teelichter, die Schale schwebt etwa zwanzig Zentimeter darüber an vier Bändern in Richtung der Raumachsen.

Ablauf

1. Teil: Ankommen

Den Raum auf sich wirken lassen, Leere und Fülle. Keine Ausrichtung auf den Raum, Ausrichtung irgendwie auf sich selbst in der Suche des Zentrums. Die Menschen setzen sich (keine Instruktion erforderlich), als Beginn geht das Licht aus, nur Spot auf dem Taufbecken und die Kerze darunter. Auf den Stühlen liegt eine kleine Karte mit Liedtexten.

Musik mit Marimbafon

Sprecher 1 *(von unten)*: Es ruft die eine Stimme des Propheten Johannes:

Sprecher 2 *(von oben)*: In der Wüste bereitet dem Herrn den Weg, macht in der Steppe eine ebene Bahn unserem Gott (Jes 40,3). Darum: Seht zu, bringt rechtschaffene Frucht hervor, die eure Buße zeigt (Mt 3,8).

Vier Sprecher aus dem Off (= aus den vier Treppentürmen bei offener Tür) sprechen erst hintereinander (Pausen), dann mehr und mehr durcheinander Kernsätze der vier Evangelisten. Im Sprechen ein allmähliches Crescendo, trotzdem Secco, nicht zu theatralisch. Durch die Überlagerung der Stimmen und Worte entsteht ein Chaos, das durch die zunehmende Percussion auf den Geländern und/oder Bänken oben auf der Empore verstärkt wird. Es endet im Decrescendo.

Sprecher 3: Wenn eure Gerechtigkeit nicht besser ist als die der Schriftgelehrten und Pharisäer, so werdet ihr nicht in das Himmelreich kommen (Mt 5,20).

Sprecher 4: Die Zeit ist erfüllt und das Reich Gottes ist herbeigekommen. Tut Buße und glaubt an das Evangelium (Mk 1,15).

Sprecher 5: Der Menschensohn ist gekommen, zu suchen und selig zu machen, was verloren ist (Lk 19,10). Selig seid ihr Armen; denn das Reich Gott ist euer.

Sprecher 6: Ein neues Gebot gebe ich euch, dass ihr euch untereinander liebt, wie ich euch geliebt habe, damit auch ihr einander liebhabt.

2. Teil: Kreuzgang

Vier Lichtträger kommen mit vier Kerzen herein. Bewegen sich die Stufenanlage diagonal hinunter und zu der ersten Tafel. Alle Mitwisser erheben sich und wandeln durch den Raum zum Licht, nonverbal werden alle Teilnehmenden eingeladen mitzuziehen und sich im Raum zu bewegen.

Beim Wandel: Lied: Kehret um, kehret um und ihr werdet leben (EG 650)

1. Tafel Markus: Gemeinde stellt sich um das Altarviertel. Der erste Lichtträger stellt seine Kerze in das Altarviertel, das zu zwei Seiten offen ist und im Kerzenlicht golden leuchtet.

Sprecher 3 (Evangelist): Die Zeit ist erfüllt und das Reich Gottes ist herbeigekommen. Tut Buße und glaubt an das Evangelium (Mk 1,15).

Percussion auf dem Altarteil unterhalb der Evangelistentafel.
Stille

Sprecher 3 (Evangelist): Die Zeit ist erfüllt und das Reich Gottes ist herbeigekommen. Tut Buße und glaubt an das Evangelium (Mk 1,15).

Stille

Sprecher 1 und 2 im Wechsel:
Der nachfolgende Text ist eine Collage von Überschriften aus drei Tageszeitungen der vorangegangenen Woche.

Kein Weiter-so
    Die Zeit davor und die Zeit danach
Deutschland hält inne
    Wir wissen vergleichsweise wenig
Zahl der Organspender steigt leicht
    Steuereinnahmen steigen langsamer
An einer Welt ohne Verfolgung arbeiten
    Brücken bauen statt Mauern einreißen
Die Deutschen lieben Actioncams
    In Abrissfirma eingebrochen
Kein Weiter-so
    Ratlosigkeit statt Randale
Beim BND haben wir Kaffee getrunken und gequatscht
    Eine neue Ära der Qualitätssicherung
Effiziente Maschinenverwaltung
    Effizienzziele der Regierung unter Beschuss
Weniger Einsendungen für den Mückenatlas
    Kartellamt prüft Beschwerde
Kein Weiter-so
    Sie wünschen sich eine gute Zukunft
Lebensfreude im Visier
    Alle auf die Couch?
Zum Wahnsinn ist es nur ein kleiner Schritt
    Kein Weiter-so
Entscheidung für das Leben

Stille

Sprecher 7:

»… eine eingewurzelte angst wo

es das flüstern gibt, das flüstern gibt
das älteste und zärtlichste mitwissen der zellen

betrachte diesen markt, betrachte diesen import
export von vätern, die hälfte büttel
die hälfte gequälte soldaten betrachte

ihr stammloses letztes verschwinden, metall
gegen metall, während die menge an sich nicht angebautem mais
zunimmt und der mangel an trinkwasser zunimmt

sprich bald von milde, sprich bald vom mysterium
des salzes, sprich bald von vermittlung, menschen,
mut; erzähl mir daß man den marmor der banken
essen kann, erzähl mir daß der mond schön ist,
daß der moa ausgestorben von der grünen melone

frißt, daß die munterkeit gedeiht, es sie gibt,
daß es das moostierchen gibt, den makrelenschwarm gibt, methoden
für verzicht, für abstieg gibt,
physische verteilung wie in gedichten von unvergleichlichen erdgütern
gibt, mitleid gibt«[5]

Lichtträger setzen sich mit drei Kerzen in Bewegung zur zweiten Station. Die Gemeinde folgt dem Licht.

Lied: Kehret um, kehret um und ihr werdet leben (EG 650) *(dabei Wandel durch den Raum)*

Dieser Ablauf wiederholt sich an den drei verbleibenden Altarteilen. An ihnen wird jeweils der Satz des Evangelisten gelesen und dieser mit Percussion am jeweiligen Altarelement in Klang umgesetzt. Sprecher 1 und 2 lesen jeweils eine Collage von Überschriften der Tagespresse und Sprecher 7 ein literarisches Textfragment. Dieser Teil des Gottesdienstes schließt mit Instrumentalmusik auf Marimbafon und Flügel ab.

3. Teil: Taufe als Einheit in der Verschiedenheit und Umkehrpunkt zu einem neuen Leben

Während der Musik nehmen die Lichtträger nacheinander jeweils zwei Gemeindemitglieder an der Hand und führen sie zum Taufstein, Aufstellung als vier Blöcke in Raumrichtung (= Kreuz) außerhalb des Bodenquadrats[6], in dessen Mitte der Taufstein steht.

---

5 Inger Christensen, alfabet, 1981.

Sprecher 1 *(von unten):* Es ruft die Stimme des Propheten Johannes:
Sprecher 2 *(von unten)*: In der Wüste bereitet dem Herrn den Weg, macht in der Steppe eine ebene Bahn unserem Gott (Jes 40,3). Darum: Seht zu, bringt rechtschaffene Frucht hervor, die eure Buße zeigt (Mt 3,8).

Lied: Wasser vom Himmel (EG NEK[7] 568)

Sprecher 2: Wir sind auf dem Weg der Umkehr! Ein Weg der Erinnerung – ein Weg der Hoffnung – ein Weg des Lebens. Wir wollen das Ja zum Leben zeichenhaft spüren in der Tauferinnerung. Lasst euch das Zeichen des Kreuzes in die Hand zeichnen und den Segen des dreieinigen Gottes zu sprechen.

Vier Personen schöpfen mit kleineren Schalen aus der Taufschale und gehen dann die Reihe entlang jeweils gegenüber. Die Zeichenhandlung wird mit dem Wort abgeschlossen: Gott spricht: Ich will dich segnen und du sollst ein Segen sein (Gen 12,2).

4. Teil: Abschluss
Lied: Bleib bei uns Herr (EG 488)
Vaterunser
Lied: So sei es Herr (EG 266,5)

Die Sprecher und Lichtträger verlassen schweigend den Raum und begeben sich zum Hauptportal. Die Gemeinde folgt.

---

6 Der Boden der Friedenskirche besteht aus grauen Fliesen. Um den Taufstein herum sind diese auf einer Fläche von ca. 4 qm mit Weinblättern und Lutherrosen gemustert.

7 Regionalteil Nordelbien.

5. Weiterentwicklung der Reihe

Im Jahr 2015 haben wir drei derartige Gottesdienste gefeiert. Sie standen unter folgenden Titeln und Raumakzentuierungen:

5.1 Sonntag Invokavit: »Pflügen im Karst – Wüstenerfahrung als Quelle persönlichen Glaubens«

Biblische Geschichte: 1 Kön 19: Elia auf dem Weg zum Horeb.

Raumgestaltung: ein leerer Kirchenraum, die Stühle zu Wüstenbergen gestapelt, unter einer Empore Sitzkissen für die Speisung mit Wasser und Brot.

Bewegung im Raum: Von der oberen Mittelempore wandelt die Gemeinde singend durch die Treppenhäuser und den wüstleeren Kirchenraum, lagert sich wie Elia unter der Empore, empfängt dort Wasser und geröstetes Brot. Der neue Aufbruch führt sie die Stufenanlage hinauf, dort Lagerung und ein kurzes Bibliolog, der die Erfahrungen Elias ins Leben zieht.

5.2 Gründonnerstag: »Feiern im Zweifel – Mahlerfahrung als Quelle gemeinschaftlichen Lebens«

Biblische Geschichte: Mahlbericht nach Mk 14

Raumgestaltung: Der zentrale Raum der Friedenskirche ist als Mahlraum abgrenzt. Dazu sind die vorhandenen Stühle zu Mauern gestapelt. In der Mitte des Raumes ist eine große Tafel mit Tellern und Gläsern gedeckt. Im Eingangsbereich ist das Essen für ein Sättigungsmahl bereitgestellt.

Bewegung im Raum: Der Gottesdienst beginnt vor dem Kirchenraum. Die Gemeinde betritt gemeinsam die Kirche. Jeder nimmt am Eingang etwas für das Mahl mit, sowie dazu eine Kerze pro Platz. Gemeinsam wird die Tafel für das Mahl gedeckt. Im Anschluss sitzt die Gemeinde zu Tisch. Im Verlauf der Feier wird neben dem sakramentalen Mahl auch ein Sättigungsmahl gefeiert. Unterbrochen wird die Feier durch den ordnenden biblischen Text einerseits, sowie aus kurzen theologischen Impulsen und literarischen Fragmenten andererseits. An besonderen Schnittstellen der dramatischen Handlung des Mahls wird jeweils ein Altarelement aus dem Altar herausgerückt. Am Ende wird aus dem Altar ein schwarzes Tuch entrollt, das die Kirche und die Gemeinde durchkreuzt. Den Abschluss des Gottesdienstes bildet das Tenebrae[8], im Anschluss verlässt die Gemeinde den Raum und singt beim Verlassen der Kirche »Meine Hoffnung und meine Freude«.

5.3 Buss- und Bettag: Stehen im Kreuz – Umkehrerfahrung als Quelle gesellschaftlichen Wandels (s. o.)

Die Durchführung der Reihe »kreuz.weg.wandel« hat zu einer bewussten Wahrnehmung des Raumes als Element der liturgischen Gestaltung in der Friedenskirche geführt. Ohne dass ein eigenes neues Gottesdienstformat entstanden ist, wird Kirchenraum mehrmals im Jahr bewusst akzentuiert und damit als liturgisches Element eingesetzt. So werden bei Taufen die Stühle bewusst um den Taufstein zentriert. In der Adventszeit wird die Kirche für eine Woche komplett leergeräumt und in ihrer Mitte ein großes Labyrinth aus Tannenzweigen gelegt, dessen Ziel und Wendepunkt der Taufstein ist. Zur Tradition ist inzwischen die Taufe der Konfirmanden in diesem Labyrinth geworden. Auf dem Weg zur und von der Taufe durchwandeln die Täuflinge das gesamte Labyrinth. Der Altar wird in der Weihnachtszeit gedreht und geöffnet und beherbergt in sich die Krippe und strahlt dabei das Kreuz an. Neben diesen wiederkehrenden Ereignissen wurde im Reformationsjahr eine vierteilige Reihe zu Luthers sola-Formeln durchgeführt, in deren Gottesdienste vor allem auch die Kunst im Raum (Kirchenfenster) sichtbar gemacht wurde.

6. Gottesbegegnung im Raum feiern

Die Reihe »kreuz.weg.wandel« hat der feiernden Gemeinde den Raum der Friedenskirche neu geöffnet. Fünf besondere Faktoren für den liturgischen Gewinn der Konzeption seien abschließend genannt:

- Die Einbeziehung und jeweilige liturgische Veränderung des Raumes fördert die liturgische Beteiligung aller Mitfeiernden. Das Kommuni-

[8] Vgl. Passion und Ostern. Agende für evangelisch-lutherische Kirchen und Gemeinde Band II, Teilband 1, Hannover 2011, 60.

kationsgeschehen ist nicht mehr allein auf das Reden und Hören konzentriert, sondern schließt auch die Wahrnehmung im Raum ein.

- Die Gemeinde tritt liturgisch in Interaktion. Es ist nicht mehr allein die Interaktion zwischen Liturg und Gemeinde oder den liturgisch-sprechend beteiligten Personen, sondern alle sind miteinander im Gottesdienst unterwegs, feiern gemeinsam und kommunizieren. Christus begegnet in der kommunizierenden und feiernden Gemeinde.
- Der Gottesdienst als darstellendes Handeln ist bewegend und nimmt den Menschen als ein leibräumliches Wesen ernst. Menschen werden nicht nur seelisch-emotional bewegt, sondern auch körperlich.
- Die Einbeziehung der Dimension Raum geschieht ohne zusätzliche Worte. Sie reduziert vielmehr die häufig zu beobachtende Wortlastigkeit evangelischer Gottesdienste. Die Funktion des Gottesdienstteams ist dabei vor allem durch nonverbale Kommunikation in Bewegung zu setzen.
- Die durchgeführten Gottesdienste sind familienfreundlich. In einer Gemeinde mit vielen Kindern und Familien ermöglichen die Gottesdienste mit besonderem Raumbezug die Partizipation aller Menschen, da sie auf die einseitige Konzentration auf das Hören einer Predigt verzichtet. Es ist bemerkenswert, wie durch die Akzentuierung des Faktors Raum die Gottesdienste eine besondere spirituelle Dichte erfahren haben und die liturgische Spannung über die gesamte Dauer gehalten werden kann.

Gunnar Garleff

Encountering God in the Worship Space

kreuz.weg.wandel[1] – services focusing on experiencing liturgical space

1. Word and space

The Protestant service is a verbal event of the invisible and visible Word, where words are both spoken and sung. It is almost a »cult of the word« (Alexander Deeg) and everything is focused on God speaking and the congregation listening, and on the congregation praying and God listening. As a result, our church buildings are also focused on the Word, so that »nothing else is happening herein except that our dear Lord Jesus Christ himself speaks with us through his holy word and we in turn respond to him through prayer and the singing of praises.«[2]

»Faith comes from what is heard« (Romans 10:17) and in a Protestant service there is always a risk of the whole event being reduced to the sense of hearing. But human perception generally occurs through several senses, not just through hearing. We also see, smell, taste and feel. These senses relate particularly to our feeling for space. What I see or smell in a room, how I sit, lie or stand – all this influences what I perceive through hearing. But a space is not just for sensory perception, it is also for movement. Humans are physical beings who occupy space, and all of life is surrounded by space and takes place in spatial settings.

This also applies in worship. Anyone who attends a service moves around in the worship space: they enter it through the door, stand and sit, move back and forth at Holy Communion and, as the case may be, at a baptism. The verbal event is also always a spatial event. The space im-

---

1 Literally »cross.way.move/change« (a pun evoking the stations of the cross, moving and changing).

2 Martin Luther, WA 49.588.15 (LW 51.333).

pacts on the liturgical presentation of the gospel. At the same time, the form given to the church space testifies to the understanding of worship in the respective era.

2. The »new Friedenskirche« of 2012

The extent to which space influences the liturgical event and personal experience in the service becomes particularly clear when a familiar church space undergoes alterations. One example of this is the Friedenskirche (Peace Church) in Heidelberg, Germany. First consecrated in 1910, it underwent major renovation and remodelling of its interior in 2012.

In 1910 the church was designed in the form of a Greek cross, which has limbs of equal length. The approximately. 1000 places were originally found in the body of the church and in three large galleries, the places under the side galleries being arrayed perpendicular to the nave. Everyone had a good view of the massive »pulpit altar«, which was positioned in a relatively small chancel (altar area). In accordance with the Wiesbaden programme,[3] the organ and choir gallery were placed behind the pulpit. All liturgical locations except the font formed a straight line. In purely optical terms, all eyes were focused on the sermon.

The first renovation in 1960 broke with this spatial arrangement. The font, pulpit and altar were lined up next to each other in the chancel, so that the altar as the place of prayer and sacrament was highlighted, apart from the pulpit. Unlike in 1910, the pulpit was now moved closer to the congregation. Karlheinz Schoener, pastor at the time, justified this change: »The word proclaimed from there goes straight to the congregation because it concerns them.«[4]

---

3 From 1890 Wiesbaden pastor Emil Veesenmeyer gained support for his conviction that Reformed churches should visually express the importance of the sermon. Both the altar and the pulpit were to be in the central axis, with the organ and choir aligned behind, facing the congregation. Traditional church architecture had placed the pulpit on a side pillar and the organ and choir gallery at the back of the church.

The 2012 remodelling of the church respected the original Wiesbaden programme and went even further. For the first time, the organ was clearly lined up with the pulpit, altar and font. The former barrier, that had clearly separated the organ/choir gallery and the chancel (area around the altar), was bridged by connecting steps, which at the same time made the chancel a kind of »altar island« in the centre of the church space. The stairs now accommodate both the choir and the pulpit, although the latter may also be removed as required by the liturgy. The altar is likewise mobile. To make space for concerts, it can be taken apart and its four quarters placed elsewhere in the church. It can also be put together differently for special occasions.[5] The remodelling included removing the pews and replacing them by chairs. Except for the organ and font, everything in the new church interior is dynamic and fluid.

3. The way of the cross, or variations on Construction Phase 9

As always happens when a church is remodelled, the renovation of the »Peace Church« caused a lot of discussion and disagreement. Some wanted to preserve the old space, others the liturgical traditions, yet others wanted the church building to reflect the liturgical and church-related challenges of the present and future. After the church was reconsecrated, things first quietened down. The congregation kept attending its services with their tradition of high-quality church music and theologically challenging sermons. Yet everyone – the congregation, the parish council and the architects – soon noticed that altering the space also means changing liturgical patterns. Not only does the liturgy take new directions, people perceive the space differently.

The architects' contract provided for a Construction Phase 9, which amounted to handing over rules for use. Now, instead, they had a different

4 Karlheinz Schoener, Der neue Altar-Raum, in: 50 Jahre Friedenskirche Heidelberg-Handschuhsheim, 1960.

5 Examples of spatial design in connection with our worship services may be found at friedensgemeinde.wordpress.com.

idea – to hold a series of workshops and services in which people could try out forms of worship in the new space. The aim was for the congregation to appropriate its space in liturgical enactment. The idea of a *kreuz.weg.wandel* series was born.[6]

The special focus of services in this series lay on getting a feel for the space. The aim was not to establish an »alternative programme« alongside the usual Sunday service. It was simply to promote times of worship that deliberately brought the church space into liturgical planning, thereby enhancing the experience of space in a »normal« Sunday service. There was no special target group – everyone who wanted to attend worship was invited.

A small team was formed to plan the services, consisting of the two pastors, the church music director (organist), two architects, the artist who had designed the principal items (pulpit, altar, font) in 2012, two elders and a few members of the congregation. During the preparations we soon realised that it would only be possible to achieve our aim of making the space particularly significant as a place to encounter Christ if we redesigned it for every service and also abolished the familiar format (with everyone sitting in their own seat). Each individual was to meet themselves and God in that space, and the congregation was to move around.

At the same time, the preparatory team was aware that giving instructions disturbs the atmosphere in a service. We wanted to create an elementary liturgy that managed without explanation and concentrated solely on the event taking place in space and in words. The congregation – as co-worshippers – were to be perceived and taken seriously throughout. Every individual was to be able, at all times, to perceive themselves as an actor involved in the service, helping to shape it.

Not only was the liturgy to deviate from the usual Sunday order of service, but also from the way of preaching. Instead of a sermon, individ-

---

[6] The title of the series was influenced by a simultaneous discussion about the form of the cross. The cross in the Friedenskirche is set into the dark bronze altar in low relief. However, many church members missed an upright cross. For that reason the *kreuz.weg.wandel* series in 2015 comprised not only three services but also three talks on the topic of the cross and worship.

ual text fragments were placed next to one another and fitted into the context of a Bible story. The texts stemmed from newspapers and contemporary literature. In keeping with the overall approach, we did without a central place of proclamation; those reading and speaking stood in different corners of the church.

And since the auditory sense does not stand alone, we wanted to appeal to other senses. Scenes of meals and remembrance of baptism were woven into the services, along with moving together through the church interior.

People were meant to move around either in silence or accompanied by music and singing. We deliberately chose hymns that were short and easy to remember, so that the congregation did not need a hymnbook and had their hands free. Church music and choral singing enjoy high status in our church. Soloists (percussion, violin, flute) accompanied the services. The percussionist, in particular, set the rafters ringing by beating his rhythms on railings, pews (in the galleries), even on the altar. We deliberately did not involve choirs as they would not have fitted with the idea of moving round together.

Planning the whole *kreuz.weg.wandel* series was time-consuming. It took three three-hour sessions to conceptualise the first three services of the series. Then two more sessions were needed per service, in some cases with a rehearsal. The preparatory team got a feeling of what is possible in the space, which made planning a follow-up series of services in 2016/2017 much easier.

4. An example: »Standing in the cross – experiencing repentance as a source of social change« (Day of Penitence and Prayer,[7] 2015)

Participants: Eight speakers, four »light-bearers«, percussionist, pianist
Spatial design: The four quarters of the altar are placed below the four Evangelist panels hanging on the walls, so that we can see inside them. The rows of chairs have been cleared away; about 60 chairs are now standing untidily around the whole church. The principle is maximum distance between them (representing isolation), and they are not facing the altar stairs, in order to leave space around the font.

One or several tea-lights are placed on the font, the basin being suspended about 20 cm above it by four strings connected to the two galleries.

Part 1: Arrival
Take in the space, emptiness and fullness. At first you are disoriented in the space; somehow you focus on yourself in your quest for the centre. Everyone sits down (no instruction necessary). The light goes out to indicate the beginning; there is only a spotlight on the basin and the candle on the stone below it. A small card with hymn texts lies on the chairs.

Marimbaphon music

Speaker 1 *(from below)*: It is a voice of the prophet John:
Speaker 2 *(from above):* In the wilderness prepare the way of the Lord; make straight in the desert a highway for out God (Is 40:3). Hence: Bear fruit, worthy of repentance (Mt 3:8).

7 *Buß- und Bettag* (held shortly before the beginning of Advent) was introduced in the 19th century as a Protestant religious festival and observed as a public holiday throughout Germany. However, since 1995 only the Free State of Saxony has retained it as a work-free day, so now services are often held in the evening.

Four more speakers (standing in the four stairwells with the doors open) recite core phrases from the four Evangelists one after the other (with pauses), then closer and closer together. Their voices intermingle and rise to a crescendo, but it is still liturgical recitative, not too theatrical. The cacophony is reinforced by the increasing percussion on the railings, and/or pews up in the galleries. Then it quietens down into a decrescendo.

Speaker 3: For I tell you, unless your righteousness exceeds that of the scribes and the Pharisees, you will never enter the kingdom of heaven (Mt 5:20).
Speaker 4: The time is fulfilled, and the kingdom of God has come near; repent and believe in the good news (Mk 1:15).
Speaker 5: For the Son of Man came to seek out and to save the lost (Lk 19:10). Blessed are you who are poor, for yours is the kingdom of God (Lk 6:20).
Speaker 6: I give you a new commandment, that you love one another. Just as I have loved you, you also should love one another (John 13:34).

PART 2: WALKING THE CROSS

Four light-bearers enter (diagonally down the staircase) with four candles and move to the first Evangelist panel. All those in the know rise and walk through the room to the light. Nonverbally all participants are invited to go along and move in the space.

When moving: Hymn

1. Evangelist panel of St Mark: Congregation stands around the quarter-altar. The first light-bearer places their candle inside the quarter-altar, which is open on two sides so that the bronze shines golden in the candle-light.

Speaker 3 (Evangelist): The time is fulfilled, and the kingdom of God has come near; repent and believe in the good news (Mk 1:15).

Percussion on the quarter-altar near the Evangelist panel.
Silence

Speaker 3 (Evangelist): The time is fulfilled, and the kingdom of God has come near; repent and believe in the good news (Mk 1:15).

Silence

Speaker 1 and 2 alternately
The following text is a collage of headlines from three daily papers of the previous week.

No business as usual
The time before and the time afterwards
Germany stops for a while
We know comparatively little
Number of organ donors rises slightly
Tax income rises more slowly
Work on a world with no persecution
Build bridges instead of pulling down walls
The Germans love action cameras
Demolition company broken into
No business as usual
Perplexity instead of riots
At federal intelligence service we drank coffee and chatted
A new era of quality assurance
Efficient machine management
Efficiency goals of government under fire
Fewer contributions for the mosquito atlas
Cartel office examines complaint
No business as usual
You wish for a good future
Joy of life targeted
Everyone onto the couch?
It is only a small step to going crazy
No business as usual
Decision for life

Silence

Speaker 7:

»… an ingrown dread where

whisperings exist, whisperings exist
the cells' oldest, fondest collusion

consider this market, consider this import
and export of fathers, half bullies
half tortured soldiers, consider

their barren last vanishing, metal
to metal, as the amount of unsown maize
grows and the water shortage grows

speak now of mildness, now of the mystery
of salt; speak now of mediation, of mankind, of
courage; tell me that the marble of banks
can be eaten; tell me that the moon is lovely,
that the extinct moa eats green melon,

that merriment exists, is thriving,
that moss animals and mackerel shoals exist, that
means of giving up, of descent, exist, and

physical portioning out, as in poems, of matchless earthly goods, that pity exists«[8]

Light-bearers start moving with their three candles to the second station. The congregation follows the light.

Hymn (while moving through the room)

---

[8] INGER CHRISTENSEN, Alphabet, 1981; translated by Susanna Ried, New Direction Books, 2000, 44.

The above procedure is repeated at the three remaining quarter-altars. A verse from the Evangelists is read at each of them and turned into sound by percussion at the respective altar element. Speaker 1 and 2 each read a collage of headings from the daily press and Speaker 7 adds a short literary text. This part of the service concludes with instrumental music on the marimbaphon and grand piano.

Part 3: Baptism as unity in diversity and a point of turning towards new life

During the music the light-bearers each take two members of the congregation by the hand and lead them to the font. They form four blocks (i.e. a cross) outside of the square with the font in the centre.[9]

Speaker 1 *(from below):* The voice of the prophet John calls:
Speaker 2 *(from below)*: In the wilderness prepare the way of the Lord; make straight in the desert a highway for our God (Is 40:3). Hence: Bear fruit, worthy of repentance (Mt 3:8).

Hymn

Speaker 2: We are on the way to repentance! A path of remembrance – a path of hope – a path of life. We want to affirm life in a symbolic sense by remembering our baptism.

Let someone make the sign of the cross on your palm and promise the blessing of the triune God.

Four people scoop water into smaller dishes from the baptismal basin and go along the rows of people signing them with the cross on their hand or forehead and saying: God says: I will bless you ... so that you will be a blessing (Gen 12:2).

---

9 The church floor is paved in grey tiles. About 4 square metres around the font are patterned with vine leaves and Luther roses.

Part 4: Conclusion
Hymn
Lord's Prayer
Hymn

Speakers and light-bearers leave the space in silence and move towards the main door. The congregation follows.

5. Further development of the series

In 2015 we held a series of three such services of worship. They had the following titles and spatial accents:

5.1 Invocavit Sunday: »Ploughing the desert – wilderness experience as a source of personal faith«

Bible story: 1 Kings 19: Elijah on the way to Horeb.

Spatial arrangement: an empty church, the chairs stacked as mountains in the wilderness, cushions under one of the galleries for the meal of water and bread.

Movement in the room: From the middle gallery the congregation moves singing through the stairwells and the deserted church interior, camps like Elijah under the gallery, then receives water and toasted bread. The new start leads them up the choir stairs where they camp again and participate in a short role play (*Bibliolog*) that makes Elijah's experiences relevant to our own lives.

5.2 Maundy Thursday: »Celebrating in times of doubt – common meals as a source of life in community«

Bible story: a meal as told in Mark 14

Spatial arrangement: The central area of the church is market out as a space for the meal. The chairs available are stacked into walls. A large table, laid with plates and glasses, stands in the middle. Enough filling food is set out in the entrance area.

Movement in the space: The service starts outside the church. The congregation enters it together. At the entrance, everyone takes something for the meal and a candle for each place. Together they finish laying the table for the meal. Then the congregation sits down at the table. During the proceedings a real meal takes place alongside the sacramental supper. The ceremony is interrupted by the structuring biblical text, on the one hand, and short theological inputs and literary fragments, on the other. At special points in the dramatic action of the meal, a piece of the altar is pulled out. At the end, a black cloth is rolled out of the altar and criss-crossed through the church and the congregation. The service ends with Tenebrae prayers.[10] The congregation then leaves the space, singing as they exit the church »Meine Hoffnung und meine Freude« (»In the Lord«).

5.3 Day of Penitence and Prayer: »Standing in the cross – experiencing repentance as a source of social change« (liturgy described in full above)

Conducting the *kreuz.weg.wandel* series led to a conscious perception of space as an element of liturgical design in our church. New worship formats have not taken over entirely, but several times a year we use the church space to make deliberate points, and thereby as a liturgical element. For example, during baptisms the chairs are deliberately centred around the font. In Advent the church is completely emptied for a week and a big labyrinth of pine branches is laid in the middle, with the font as the goal and turning point. It has become a tradition to baptise confirmation candidates in this setting. On the way to and from baptism they walk through the whole labyrinth. The altar is turned around at Christmas and opened up to accommodate the crèche, with the high-relief cross in the spotlight. Besides these recurring events, in 2017 a four-part series was held on Luther's *solae*, with services particularly illuminating the artworks in the church (stained glass windows).

---

10 Tenebrae (darkness) prayers are said on Maundy Thursday, Good Friday and Holy Saturday, accompanied by the extinguishing of candles. German prayers are published in: Passion und Ostern. Agende für evangelisch-lutherische Kirchen und Gemeinde Band II, Teilband 1, Hannover, 2011, 60.

6. Encountering God in the worship space

The *kreuz.weg.wandel* series has reopened the church space to the worshipping community. To sum up, here are five specific features of the liturgical benefit gained:

1. The involvement and respective liturgical altering of the space furthers the liturgical participation of all present. The communicative event no longer concentrates solely on speaking and listening, but includes sensory perception in the spatial context.
2. The congregation interacts liturgically. Interaction is no longer solely between the liturgist and the congregation or between the people involved in speaking the liturgy. Instead everyone in the service is actively worshipping together and communicating with each other. Christ meets us in the participatory, worshipping community.
3. The service as representational action is moving and addresses the fact that humans have bodies taking up space. People are moved not only spiritually and emotionally but also physically.
4. Involving the spatial dimension takes place without a lot of extra words. Instead, it reduces the frequent wordiness of Protestant services. The chief function of the worship team is to set things in motion through nonverbal communication.
5. The services conducted are family-friendly. In a congregation with a lot of children and families, services that especially involve the surrounding space enable everyone to participate, as they forgo the one-sided concentration on listening to a sermon. It is remarkable to see how, through accentuating the space factor, services have taken on a special spiritual density and the liturgical tension can last the whole time.

Margit Geley

Geheimnisfest

Ein Modell aus Salzburg, Österreich

1. Grundsätzliches

Das Geheimnisfest ist ein Fest zur Tauferinnerung und zur Vertiefung des Abendmahlsverständnisses. Aus den beiden Sakramenten (sacramentum) ergibt sich der Name »Geheimnisfest«.

Zielgruppe sind die evangelischen Kinder der 2. Volksschulklassen (ca. 8 Jahre) am Gebiet der Pfarrgemeinde.

Ziel des Festes ist es, Kindern wesentliche Inhalte der beiden Sakramente begreifbar und fühlbar werden zu lassen. Dadurch entsteht eine Erinnerung an die eigene Taufe im alttestamentlichen Sinn, in dem *sich erinnern* bedeutet: etwas Vergangenes in die Gegenwart holen und hier relevant werden lassen. Das Abendmahl gewinnt durch das »Miteinander-Feiern« und durch das »Über-die-Bedeutung-Sprechen« an Wichtigkeit für das Leben des einzelnen Kindes. So ist es keine Erstkommunion, sondern setzt Erfahrung mit dem Abendmahl voraus und ermöglicht diese.

Im Rahmen des Festes (nicht in der Vorbereitung) werden die Kinder von ihren Familien gesegnet.

Das Geheimnisfest in der vorgestellten Form ist ein hochschwelliges Angebot, das von Kindern und deren Eltern die Bereitschaft erwartet, an einigen Familiengottesdiensten und den Vorbereitungsterminen teilzunehmen (siehe unten).

Das Geheimnisfest ist eingebettet in eine Gemeindearbeit, die viele verschiedene Angebote für Kinder und deren Familien macht und eine Brücke zur Konfirmation schlägt. Die Kinder eines Jahrganges treffen sich bei der Konfirmation wieder und erkennen sich dann unter den veränderten körperlichen Voraussetzungen dennoch in einer alten, neuen Vertrautheit und Verbindung. So soll eine Beheimatung in der Kirche (als Raum) und ein Vertraut-Werden mit der Pfarrperson entstehen. Nur über eine feste Bindung an eine Person entsteht m. E. auch Bindung an Kirche und an den Glauben. Geleitet werden Vorbereitung und Fest von der Pfarrperson – ähnlich wie bei der Konfirmation.

2. Theologie

Kinder sind Teil unserer Kirche – nicht erst in der Zukunft, wenn sie erwachsen sind, sondern im Hier und Jetzt, unabhängig von ihrem Alter. Kinder sind theologiefähig. Alle relevanten theologischen Fragen werden von Kindern gestellt und können mit Kindern besprochen werden. Es gilt eine Sprache zu finden, die verstehbar ist. Es gilt die eigene Theologie zu überprüfen und zu hinterfragen auf das, »was *ich* glaube«. Der eigene Glaube wird vehement herausgefordert und hinterfragt. So gilt es Geheimnisse des Glaubens zu finden, die für mich selbst und auch für die Kinderwelt Bedeutung haben. So gilt es, Taufe und Abendmahl als für sich selbst bedeutsam werden zu lassen, sich selbst aufs Neue die verschiedensten Dimensionen dieser Sakramente zu vergegenwärtigen und sich (wieder) neu berühren zu lassen. Es gilt die eigene Bedeutung im Herzen zu erfassen und dann diese Bedeutung für die Kinder erlebbar werden zu lassen. Wir erinnern uns an die Aussage Jesu: »Wenn ihr nicht werdet wie die Kinder …!«

Diese Geheimnisse des Glaubens erfahren die Kinder während der Vorbereitung auf das Fest.

3. Entwicklungspsychologie

Kinder mit ungefähr sieben oder acht Jahren, also in der 2. Volksschulklasse, befinden sich in der Regel an einem Umbruch. Sie haben ihre Kinderzeit mit dem für diese Jahre typischen magischen Verständnis der Welt fast hinter sich. Sie beginnen abstrakter zu denken und Glaubens- und andere Inhalte zu hinterfragen. So könnte man sagen, dass sie am Beginn einer neuen Ära stehen, die sie selbst schon ahnen, jedoch noch nicht fassen können. Am Ende der 2. Klasse sind aus den kleinen Kindern, die sie am Schulanfang noch waren, große Kinder geworden, denen die herannahende Pubertät schon langsam anzusehen ist.

Für diese Zeit muss nun eine Brücke für Glaubensfragen gefunden werden. Ich habe das Geheimnis, die Schätze, die Schatzkiste, das Exklusive, das nicht verraten werden muss (aber darf), als gute Brücke gefunden für diese Altersstufe. Es gibt eine hohe Attraktivität für Geheimnisse in diesem Alter, für das Besondere, und auch für wichtigere Fragen und Antworten, die in den Geheimnissen versteckt sind – und von den Kindern mit Leichtigkeit gesucht und gefunden werden.

4. Ablauf

Dauer: ca. ein Schuljahr
Vorbereitungstermine:

1. Im Herbst für Eltern und Kinder: allgemeine Information und basteln einer Schatzkiste (Schuhschachtel, glitzerndes Papier, Goldstaub, usw.), Erhalten eines ersten Schatzes. Dieser Abend ist ein »muss«, weil er den Bogen für das Jahr spannt.
2. Teilnehmen an mindestens vier Familiengottesdiensten, zu denen die Kinder und Familien jeweils schriftlich eingeladen werden. Die Kinder bekommen nach jedem Gottesdienst einen Schatz. Ich schreibe mir auf, wer welchen Schatz schon wann bekommen hat. Wer öfter zum Gottesdienst geht, bekommt mehr Schätze.
3. Sechs Vorbereitungstermine für die Kinder à zwei Stunden: Ein Geheimnis wird verraten, das sich an einen Schatz knüpft. Abendmahl wird gefeiert in erweiterter Form, d. h. mit Brot, Butter, Schnittlauch.
4. Für die Eltern: Ein Infoblock, eine gemeinsame Abendmahlsfeier mit den Kindern, Segnen der Kinder im Geheimnisfest.
5. Geheimnisfest (s. u.) als Gottesdienst mit Tauferinnerung, Segen und Zusage der Liebe durch die Eltern, Abendmahlsfeier.
   In diesem Gottesdienst wird das Geheimnis des Geheimnisfestes am deutlichsten für die Kinder und deren Familien. Menschen werden berührt über das Aussprechbare hinaus.

Schätze, die sich immer wieder ändern:

- Kleines Herz
- Kerze

- Glasflacon mit Gold
- Kleiner Drache
- Glitzernde Murmel
- Holzbilderrahmen - wird bemalt
- Kleiner Trinkbecher - wird bemalt und beschriftet
- Edelstein

Geheimnisse: Auch die ändern sich natürlich immer wieder, je nach Bedürfnissen der Kinder oder auch der Pfarrperson:

- »7« die heilige Zahl, ich bin am Anfang vom Jugendlich-Sein
- »durchs Teilen wird's mehr, nur Sorgen werden weniger«
- »Kinder verstehen mehr von Gott als Erwachsene«
- »Liebe ist stärker als der Tod«
- »500 x 5 Mio - Gott wollte genau mich«
- »Gott ist immer da - was geht, weil er unsichtbar ist«
- »Gott ist da, wenn wir aufeinander achten«
- »7 x 70 - so oft muss ich vergeben, so oft wird mir vergeben - Versöhnen macht froh«

Weiteres in der Vorbereitungszeit:

- Fotos, Kleidung, Taufkerzen, Geschenke von der Taufe anschauen
- Für die Eltern und Geschwister ein Mahl bereiten und dazu von den Schätzen hergeben
- Die Kirche für den Gottesdienst schmücken
- Gestalten von wunderbaren Bilderrahmen, Einladungen, evtl. Taufkerzen
- Miteinander spielen
- Abendmahl feiern und alles dazu fragen, was jede/r fragen will (warum sage ich: das ist Christi Blut, warum wird man nicht krank, wenn alle aus einem Becher trinken, wie viele Geheimnisse gibt es eigentlich, warum heißt es Abendmahl ...)

Das Geheimnisfest findet als Familiengottesdienst im Frühjahr statt. Am Altar steht für jedes Kind:

- Taufkerze
- Foto mit selbstgestaltetem Bilderrahmen
- Glasflacon mit Wasser für Kreuz
- Ein kleines Tier oder Herz

Alles wird mit den Kindern gemeinsam hergerichtet.
Jedes Kind wird von der Familie/Taufpaten gesegnet:

- Liebesbotschaft
- Wasserkreuz auf die Stirn: »Du bist getauft«
- Segen

Dazu steht die Familie vorne mit dem Kind am Altar und sagt diese drei Dinge laut vor der versammelten Gemeinde. Was gesagt wird, entscheidet jede Familie selbst und bereitet es auch eigenständig vor.

5. Informatives zum Schluss

Das Konzept habe ich in der Pfarrgemeinde Salzburg Matthäuskirche entwickelt. Zum ersten Mal wurde es dort im Mai 2002 gefeiert – seitdem jährlich. Einige andere Gemeinden haben das Konzept übernommen und für ihre Gemeinde adaptiert.

Die Kraft des Konzeptes entwickelt sich, wenn man es viele Jahre feiert, da sich die Kinder bei der Konfirmation wieder begegnen und einen viel tieferen Zugang zu ihrer Taufe und damit dann auch zum Wesen der Konfirmation finden. Das Geheimnisfest ist Teil eines Gesamtkonzeptes für die Begleitung, Seelsorge und spirituelle Entfaltung von Kindern und ihren Eltern.

Gesegnet werden ist ein sehr inniger Ausdruck der Liebe Gottes.

Zur Vorbereitung empfiehlt sich ein kleines Team.

Margit Geley

Mystery Celebration

A model from Salzburg, Austria

1. Concept

The mystery celebration is a celebration to remember baptism and to promote the understanding of communion. The name »mystery celebration« is based on the two sacraments (sacramentum).

The target group are Protestant children of the second form in the area of the parish.

With this celebration, we try to render the essential content of the two sacraments comprehensible and tangible for children. This results in a baptismal remembrance in the Old Testament sense: remembering something means bringing past events to the present and giving them relevance here. Through our common celebration and our discussion of its importance, communion gains more importance in the life of each child. It is not a First Communion but requires some experience with communion and enables it.

In the framework of this celebration (not during preparations), the children are blessed by their families.

The mystery celebration in the present form is a high-threshold offer; it is expected of the children and their parents to participate in a number of family services and preparatory meetings (see below).

The mystery celebration is part of a comprehensive congregational work which reaches out to children and their families and builds a bridge to Confirmation. Children of the same age meet again for Confirmation and remember each other despite their changed physical appearance in an old and new familiarity and connection. The celebration is also meant to make the children feel at home in the church (as a space) and build a connection to the pastor. I believe that a strong relationship to a person is needed to be able to form a deep connection to the church and the faith. Like for Confirmation, preparations and the celebration itself is led by the pastor.

2. Theology

Children are part of our church – not only in the future when they have grown up, but here and now, irrespective of their age. Children are capable of theology! All relevant theological questions are asked by children and can be discussed with children. We need to find a language that can be understood. We also need to check our own theology and challenge »what I believe«! Our own faith is strongly challenged and under scrutiny. Thus, I need to find mysteries of faith which have an importance for myself as well as for children. I have to give new meaning to baptism and communion for myself, to re-encounter the different dimensions of these sacraments and to let myself be touched again. I have to feel their meaning in my heart and then find a way to let the children experience this meaning. We remember Jesus' statement: »If you do not become like children …!«

These mysteries of faith are experienced by the children during the time of preparation.

3. Developmental psychology

At the age of 7 or 8, in second form, children undergo a transition. They have nearly left their childhood with the typical magical understanding of the world behind them. They begin to think in more abstract terms and to challenge faith and other teachings. You could say that they are at the beginning of a new era, which they already have a glimpse of but cannot yet grasp. At the end of second form, the small children that once started school have already become bigger children who are awaiting puberty.

For this period, they need a bridge for issues of faith. I have found the concept of mystery, of treasures, a treasure chest, the exclusive, which does not have to be (but can be) shared, to be a good bridge for this age group. At this age, mysteries and secrets are quite popular, as is something special, and the children have an interest in important questions and answers hidden in the mysteries – which are easily searched and found by children.

4. Course of events

Duration: about one school year
Preparatory meetings:

1. In autumn for parents and children: general information, children make a treasure chest (shoe box, glittery paper, gold dust) and receive their first item of treasure. This evening is a must because it prepares the ground for the whole year.
2. Attendance at at least four family services, with written invitations to children and their families. After each service, the children receive another treasure. I write down who has already received which treasure. Children coming to the service more frequently receive more treasures.
3. Six preparatory meetings for the children, 2 hours each: 1 mystery is told that is linked to a treasure. We celebrate communion in a wider sense, i. e. with bread, butter, chives.
4. For the parents: an information event, a celebration of communion together with the children, blessing of children in the mystery celebration.
5. Mystery celebration (see below) in the form of a service with baptismal remembrance, blessing and assurance of love by the parents, communion.
   In this service, the mystery of the mystery celebration becomes clear – for the children as well as their parents. People are touched beyond what can be put into words.

Treasures which change from time to time:

- Small heart
- Candlc
- Glass flacon with gold

- Small dragon
- Marble with glitter
- Wooden picture frame – to be painted
- Small drinking cup – to be painted and written on
- Gem

Mysteries: also changing from time to time, depending on the needs of the children or the pastor:

- 7, the holy number, I am at the beginning of being an adolescent
- Sharing increases things, only worries decrease
- Children understand more about God than adults
- Love is stronger than death
- 500 x 5 million – God wanted me exactly
- God is always there – which works because he is invisible
- God is present when we watch out for one another
- 7 x 70 – this is how often I must forgive, how often I am forgiven – forgiving makes happy

Miscellanous in the time of preparation:

- Looking at photos, clothes, candles, presents of one's baptism
- Prepare a meal for parents and siblings and give some of the treasures for this
- Decorate the church for service
- Decorate picture frames, invitations, maybe baptismal candles
- Play together
- Celebrate communion and ask all questions about it (Why do I say: This is Christ's blood, why don't we become ill when everybody uses the same cup, how many mysteries are there, why is it called communion …)

The mystery celebration is celebrated in the form of a family service in spring.
On the altar for each child:

- Baptismal candle
- Photo with self-decorated picture frame

- Glass with water for cross
- A small animal or heart

Everything is prepared together with the children.
Each child is blessed by their family/godparents:

- Message of love
- Water cross on the forehead: »You are baptized«
- Blessing

The family stands with their child in front of the altar and says these three things aloud before the congregation. Each family decide individually what they plan to say and prepare these statements independently.

5. Further information

This concept was developed in the congregation of Salzburg Matthäuskirche. We celebrated it for the first time in May 2002 and have been doing so since. A number of congregations have taken up the idea and adapted it for their congregations.

The strength of the concept develops over time, when children meet again for Confirmation and develop a much deeper connection to their baptism, and thus also to their Confirmation. The mystery celebration is part of a comprehensive concept for the accompaniment, pastoral care and spiritual development of children and their parents.

Being blessed is a very intimate expression of God's love.

A small team is recommended for preparations.

Martin Kares

Gebetsläuten im Tageslauf

Eine Initiative des ökumenischen Beratungsausschusses für das Deutsche Glockenwesen

1. Gebetsläuten im Tageslauf

Zu Beginn der Kampagne stand die Beobachtung, dass in vielen Kirchen- und Pfarrgemeinden das Wissen um Recht, Funktionen und Inhalte des Gebetsläutens im Tageslauf dramatisch verloren gegangen ist, selbst für das Läuten verantwortliche Personen nicht auskunftsfähig sind und der flächendeckenden, omnipräsenten und unüberhörbaren Aufforderung zum Gebet zumindest von christlichen Gemeinden kaum noch Folge geleistet wird.

Fragt man ortskundige Personen zu den wochentäglichen, über den Tag verteilten Läutezeiten, ist man überrascht: Die Antwort: »Um 11.00 Uhr wird geläutet, um die Bauern vom Feld zu rufen« war noch eine der häufigsten, andere Personen hatten irgendwo gehört, dass zu dieser Stunde traditionell »gegen die Türken« geläutet würde. Abgesehen davon, dass man hier sicherlich Fragen zum Realitätsbewusstsein (der Bauer hört heute in seiner schallisolierten Treckerkabine eher Heavy Metal und sicher nicht die Glocke …) und zur political correctness stellen muss, birgt diese Situation eine hohe Brisanz. Man stelle sich vor, im Rahmen eines Gerichtsverfahrens zu einem Glockenstreit wird ein bestellter Gutachter in den betreffenden Ort gesandt. Dieser befragt eine zufällige Auswahl von Menschen, die in Hörweite der Glocken leben – und auch Verantwortliche der Gemeinde. Er stellt beispielsweise folgende Fragen:

- Wissen Sie, warum wochentags außerhalb von Gottesdienstzeiten Glocken läuten und können Sie dies den Menschen in ihrem Ort erklären?
- Kennen Sie die Widmungen »ihrer« Glocken und haben diese einen Bezug zu den Läuteanlässen?

- Wissen Sie, dass das Glockenläuten gesetzlich nur zu ganz bestimmten Anlässen und Handlungen geschützt ist?

Selbst hauptamtlich Mitarbeitende der Gemeinden sind häufig nicht in der Lage, die Fragen plausibel und sachlich richtig zu beantworten. Bei Ehrenamtlichen - die zum Teil sogar die Uhr programmieren, welche die Läutezeiten steuert - sieht es großteils noch düsterer aus: »Es läutet schon immer um 11.00 Uhr«, »der Vorgänger hat mir das so gesagt«, oder »12.00 Uhr - das ist doch politisches Läuten«.

Es ist naiv zu glauben, dass ein Richter daraufhin bei solchen Läuteanlässen auf ein besonderes Recht der Kirchen in Bezug auf die »freie Religionsausübung« erkennen wird. Eine dann »nachgeschobene«, weil nachträglich beschlossene Läuteordnung hätte in einem solchen Verfahren keinen Bestand.

Mit der Initiative der Kampagne »Hörst du nicht die Glocken?« soll aber mehr erreicht werden, als dass Verantwortliche in den Gemeinden künftig besser auf kritische Fragen antworten können. Die Kampagne soll die Kraft und das Potential neu entdecken und verbreiten helfen, die wir als christliche Gemeinden mit den Kommunikationssignalen der Glocken seit Jahrhunderten haben. Sie soll neu die Chancen aufzeigen, die in einer gemeinschaftlich verabredeten, regelmäßigen Hinwendung zu Gott im Gebet liegen. Die Kampagne nutzt die sich immer stärker ausbreitende Sehnsucht nach individuell gelebter Frömmigkeit und Spiritualität, stellt diese aber in einen übergeordneten Zusammenhang und hat im Modell der »konzentrischen Kreise« das Ziel, dass sich Individualität am Ende auch wieder in Gemeinschaft finden kann.

Selbstverständlich gibt es Orte mit verdichteter, lebendiger, praktizierter Gebetstradition, in denen es eine reflektierte Selbstvergewisserung oder Neupositionierung des Läutens im gesellschaftlichen Leben (noch) nicht braucht, weil Inhalte und Anlässe auch mit Zugezogenen und Neuankömmlingen selbstverständlich kommuniziert werden oder der Anteil von nicht mit der Kirche verbundenen Menschen gering ist; aber die Zahl der Orte und Stadtteile nimmt offenkundig dramatisch zu, wo die lauten Signale christlichen Glaubenslebens nicht mehr verstanden werden und zunehmend eine Toleranzdiskussion auslösen. Dies betrifft alle Konfessionen gleichermaßen. Hoffnung machen andererseits neue Gebetskreise oder Netzwerke wie das Ökumenische Stundengebet. Hier finden sich Menschen regelmäßig zusammen, um die »Basisliturgie des Volkes Gottes« zu feiern.

Dem Beratungsausschuss für das deutsche Glockenwesen ist bewusst, dass diese Kampagne verstärkt auch Glockengegner auf den Plan rufen kann. Auf die Frage »Hörst du nicht die Glocken?« werden sie antworten: »Ja, ich höre sie – und sie nerven mich gewaltig«. Selbst aus Kirchenleitungen kam die besorgte Anfrage, ob man das Thema lieber doch nicht bearbeiten sollte. In einer ausführlichen SWOT-Analyse wurden die Stärken und Schwächen, die Chancen und Risiken der Initiative gesammelt, beraten und bewertet. Ein mit Teilnehmenden aus unterschiedlichen Arbeitsfeldern von Kirche und Gesellschaft bunt besetzter Workshoptag brachte weitere wichtige Erkenntnisse. Das Ergebnis war, die Kampagne in zwei Stufen zu planen und zu realisieren: In einem ersten Schritt werden die Gemeinden, Dekanatsleitungen und Öffentlichkeitsbeauftragten sensibilisiert und auskunftsfähig gemacht. Dazu dient ein »Leitfaden für Gemeinden, ihre Verantwortlichen und Mitglieder«. Er beginnt mit den oben bereits gestellten Glockenfragen für Verantwortliche und antwortet darauf:

> Wenn Sie alle drei Fragen mit *Ja* beantworten können: Herzlichen Glückwunsch, Sie sind auf mögliche Anfragen bestens vorbereitet! Wenn nicht, informiert Sie diese Schrift, damit Sie sich künftig noch bewusster am Klang der Glocken erfreuen oder erfahren, was so alles hinter dem Läuten steckt.

Die erste Doppelseite gibt zu Geschichte und Kultur der Glocken Auskunft:

> **5000 Jahre – und kein bisschen leise …**
> Glocken gibt es seit über 5000 Jahren, seit ungefähr 1500 Jahren werden sie im Christentum als Rufinstrumente und als Zeichen für liturgische Handlungen eingesetzt. Mit ihren weltumspannenden Klängen verbinden sie die Kulturgeschichte der Menschheit und sprechen Menschen an – gleich welcher Hautfarbe, welcher ethnischen Herkunft, welcher Nation sie auch immer sein mögen.
> Glocken rufen zum Gebet und zur Fürbitte, sie zeigen Zeit und Stunde an und erinnern an die Ewigkeit. Für den Dienst in der Kirche werden sie im

Gottesdienst eingeweiht. Die kirchenrechtliche Widmung bestimmt und begrenzt ihre Nutzung. Die Gemeinden legen die Läuteanlässe fest.
Der Gebrauch der Glocken hat sich im Laufe der Jahrhunderte in einzelnen Kulturlandschaften unterschiedlich entwickelt. Regionale Läutesitten sollen weiter mit Leben gefüllt werden. Mancherorts braucht die Läutepraxis jedoch einen neuen Impuls, um künftig im Getriebe der Welt mit ihren Botschaften positiv wahrgenommen und akzeptiert zu werden.

Das zweite Thema betrifft Begriffe und Ordnungen, da es hier häufig Unklarheiten gibt:

»... denn sie wissen, was sie tun«
Häufig wird der Uhrschlag mit dem Läuten verwechselt. Der Uhrschlag ist nur vordergründig eine Zeitansage, ist aber auch so zu verstehen, dass er an die Vergänglichkeit und das Fortschreiten der Zeit erinnern soll – »Meine Zeit steht in Deinen Händen«.
Das Läuten mehrerer Glocken als Ruf zum Gottesdienst ist als Code in der Gesellschaft noch gut verständlich. Läutet jedoch eine Einzelglocke, begleitet diese entweder eine liturgische Handlung im Gottesdienst (Segen, Gebet, Wandlung) oder sie fordert außerhalb von Gottesdienstzeiten zum Gebet auf. Der Ruf zu Gottesdiensten, liturgisches Läuten und das Gebets- oder Angelusläuten auch an Werktagen sind die einzige Legitimation einer christlichen Gemeinde, Glocken läuten zu dürfen. Die Verantwortlichen einer Gemeinde müssen daher – vor allem wenn keine Unterlagen darüber zu finden sind – Läuteanlässe und -zeiten beraten und in Form einer Läuteordnung beschließen.
Vor einem Beschluss zum Gebetsläuten besteht die Chance, sich einmal mit den eigenen Läutezeiten, -anlässen und -widmungen und denen der benachbarten Gemeinden zu beschäftigen. Die Uhrzeiten des Läutens sind an vielen Orten nicht aufeinander abgestimmt, teilweise auch noch aus altem Konkurrenzdenken der Konfessionen heraus. Dies sollte heute überwunden sein. Ebenso entspricht es nicht mehr der Lebenswirklichkeit, beispielsweise auf dem Land um 11.00 Uhr mit dem Glockenklang den Bauern vom Feld zu rufen. Ohne eine bewusst festgelegte Widmung der Läutezeiten setzen sich Gemeinden dem Vorwurf aus, die Glocke sinnentleert zu gebrauchen.

In »Alltag und Rhythmus« geht es um überlieferte und neu zu bedenkende Läutezeiten.

Puls der Zeit

Eine lange, bis in die frühen Hochkulturen zurückreichende Tradition ist es, den Tag in Dreistunden-Schritte zu unterteilen. Mönche in Klöstern übersetzten dies in Tagzeitengebete, die sie bis heute praktizieren. Auch zum Angelusläuten wird regelmäßig morgens, mittags und abends gebetet. Aktuell setzt sich wieder die Erkenntnis durch, dass einem Burnout durch Rhythmisierung des Tages vorgebeugt werden kann.

Die Läutezeiten 9.00 Uhr, 12.00 Uhr, 15.00 Uhr oder 18.00 Uhr ergeben auf dem Zifferblatt ein Kreuz. Bei der mancherorts entstehenden Diskussion über das Frühläuten wäre eine Option, es auf 9.00 Uhr zu verlegen. Dies könnte auch in Kindergärten oder Schulen (im Religionsunterricht) als Zeichen zum Mitbeten / als Segen für den Tag aufgenommen werden.

Sich neu auf das Gebetsläuten im Tageslauf zu besinnen, heißt: nicht mehr, sondern bewusster läuten. Wenn in einer Gemeinde beispielsweise das Mittagsgebet oder das Abendgebet Tradition hat, reicht dies völlig aus. Von großem Wert für das Miteinander kann sein, wenn das Läuten an vielen Orten zu einer (oder mehreren) der gennannten Uhrzeit(en) erfolgt. Es kann dann ein Gemeinschaftsgefühl aller Christinnen und Christen entstehen: Das Gebet geschieht in dem Bewusstsein, dass gleichzeitig im ganzen Land Menschen mit Gott in Zwiesprache treten.

Gemeinsame Gebete können verbinden und verändern: Sie haben sogar die Wiedervereinigung unseres Landes mit ermöglicht.

Der Abschnitt »Widmung und Botschaft« widmet sich den Gebetsanliegen, welche den Glocken beim Guss oder durch Widmung mitgegeben werden.

Heavy Metal

Die meisten Glocken haben bereits beim Guss Widmungen erhalten. Sie enthalten Bibelzitate oder sind biblischen und kirchlichen Persönlichkeiten oder Heiligen gewidmet. Manche Inschriften lassen Glocken stellvertretend für uns Botschaften verkünden, auch wenn wir gerade selbst nicht anwesend oder unaufmerksam sind: »ora pro nobis – bitt' für uns« oder »O Land, Land, Land, höre des Herrn Wort«.

Die primäre Aufgabe einer läutenden Glocke ist, zum Gottesdienst oder zum Gebet zu rufen. Sie verkündet eine Aufforderung, motiviert zum Handeln, erinnert an den Dienst Gottes an uns und an unseren Dienst an Gott. Sie unterbricht den Alltag, die Gleichgültigkeit, sie mahnt und erinnert. Glocken verkünden laute »Heavy Metal«-Botschaften. Sie sollen im Getriebe der Welt gehört werden. Direkte Anwohner werden dabei durch gesetzliche Schallpegelobergrenzen und turmakustische Maßnahmen geschützt, Läuteanlässe und -dauer sind begrenzt und begründet.

»Distanz und Nähe« beschreibt mögliche Haltungen und einen Weg der Annäherung beim Hören von Gebetsglocken.

Hin und weg

Bislang erschließt sich die Bedeutung des Tagesläutens nur einem »eingeweihten« kirchlichen Zirkel, das Läuten selbst wird aber von allen gehört. Das Läuten einer Gebetsglocke kann Erinnerungszeichen für eine Atempause, für Reflexion, für individuell gelebte Gottesbeziehung sein, aber auch einen Impuls für Begegnung und Gemeinschaft beinhalten. Je nach Situation und christlich-kirchlicher Sozialisation begleitet es einen möglichen Weg von außen nach innen – ein Modell des spirituellen Wachsens:

- Glocke hören – »Mittagsgeläut«
- Innehalten – Zäsur des Tagesablaufes im Bewusstsein, dass sich viele Menschen in diesem Moment der Welt und ihrer Bedürfnisse (z. B. Frieden, Gerechtigkeit, Bewahrung der Schöpfung) – auch stellvertretend – gedanklich annehmen.
- Gedenken – Innehalten mit dem Gedenken an persönlich verbundene Personen, z. B. »Bitte um Gesundheit«.
- Gebet – Hinwendung zu Gott als Adressat oder Begleiter für persönliche oder gemeinschaftliche Anliegen.
- Gemeinsames Beten nach einem verabredeten Ritus an gemeinsamem Ort (Tagzeitengebet).

In »Toleranz und Respekt« wird reflektiert, wie man Angehörigen anderer Religionen das Gebetsläuten nahebringen und Teilhabe anbieten kann. Muslime äußerten sich durchweg positiv über die Perspektive, dass das Tagzeitenläuten unter Christen künftig wieder stärker als Ruf zum Gebet verstanden werden soll. Öffentliche Gottesverehrung im Tageslauf sei in Deutschland ohnehin kaum erkennbar.

An die große Glocke hängen

Auch Menschen, die der Kirche und dem Christentum nicht verbunden sind, können das Läuten einer Glocke als positives Signal verstehen. Dabei hilft

es, dessen Widmungen zu vermitteln: Das Mittagsläuten als Bitte um den Frieden und das Abendläuten als Bitte um die Bewahrung der Schöpfung können vermutlich von vielen akzeptiert oder zumindest toleriert werden. Gemeinsam an das Wohl der Menschen und der Welt zu denken und entsprechend zu handeln, eint Religionen und Weltanschauungen.
Die in der breiten Gesellschaft latent vorhandene positive Grundhaltung gegenüber Glocken – sie erinnern an biografische Stationen, an zugesprochenen Segen, an den Frieden, an Heimatgefühl – ermöglicht, Glockenläuten weiterhin als selbstverständlichen Teil des Zusammenlebens wahrzunehmen.
In ländlich geprägten Gemeinden gibt es das »Totenläuten« oder »Scheideläuten«, sobald der Tod eines Menschen im Ort bekannt wird – oft unabhängig von dessen Religionszugehörigkeit: In dieser Situation sind alle gleich.
Ein begründeter Umgang mit öffentlichen, unverwechselbaren Signalen des Glaubenslebens kann überzeugen – und zur Diskussion auffordern. Fragen wie »Warum läuten tagsüber Glocken?« oder »Muss die Kirche einen solchen Lärm veranstalten?« können mit der Einladung »Wir beten zu Gott und für die Welt – vielleicht können Sie dies zumindest tolerieren oder sogar mitmachen« beantwortet werden.

Das Kapitel »Kreativität und Umsetzung« beschreibt eine Vielzahl von Aktionen und Veranstaltungen rund um das Thema Glocken, mit denen Gemeinden das Potential des Themas erschließen können.

In »Kirchenjahr und Anlässe« werden allgemeine Hinweise zum Läuten – besonders zu Gottesdiensten – gegeben.

Süßer die Glocken nie klingen

Die Wahl einer Glocke als Gebetsglocke sollte auf ihre Widmung/Inschrift abgestimmt sein. Es macht wenig Sinn, beispielsweise die Tauf- oder die Totenglocke hierfür einzusetzen.
Bis hierher haben Sie Anregungen zum Gebetsläuten mit einzelnen Glocken im Alltag erhalten. Da immer wieder danach gefragt wird, folgen hier auch noch einige grundsätzliche Regeln zum Läuten mehrerer Glocken zu Gottesdiensten:

- Bei Geläuten mit mehr als zwei Glocken darf und soll man zu den verschiedenen Anlässen und passend zum liturgischen Kalender mit unterschiedlichen Glocken läuten. Ein Organist zieht auch nicht bei allen Liedern immer alle Register.

- Die Advents- und Passionszeit sind Fastenzeiten. Dies darf sich auch beim Läuten hörbar zeigen, indem mit weniger Glocken als an »normalen« Sonntagen geläutet wird. Von Gründonnerstag bis zum Ostermorgen schweigen die Glocken, evangelische Gemeinden sollten am Karfreitag nur mit der größten oder Christus-Glocke zum Gottesdienst rufen.
- Auch bei Beerdigungen und Trauerfeiern soll das Geläute darauf hinweisen, dass etwas fehlt, dass Trauer angesagt ist, indem mit weniger Glocken oder mit einem Moll-Motiv geläutet wird.
- Die Christusfeste sind die Höhepunkte des Kirchenjahres. Hier darf und soll dann alles läuten, was Klöppel hat. Festliche Geläute darf es auch bei besonderen Ereignissen in der Gemeinde geben (Kommunion, Konfirmation, Bischofsbesuch …)

Abschließend wird in »Pflicht und Kür« zusammengefasst, was Gemeinden bedenken müssen und was sie gegebenenfalls an zusätzlichen Maßnahmen ergreifen können.

Ergänzt wird der Leitfaden durch ein Merkblatt für Kirchendiener, Küster, Mesner, Sakristane. Dort heißt es:

Das richtige Läuten von Glocken ist eine verantwortungsvolle Aufgabe. Läuten muss mit Inhalt gefüllt werden, sonst ist es »ein tönend Erz oder eine klingende Schelle«. Elektrische Läuteanlagen und Läutecomputer nehmen den mit dem Läuten betrauten Personen heute viele Aufgaben ab. Trotzdem ist es wichtig, auch diese technischen Hilfsmittel zur Ehre Gottes und mit Herz und Verstand zu bedienen.

Mit der Glocke durch das Kirchenjahr

Für Gemeinden mit drei und mehr Glocken sollte es zur Selbstverständlichkeit werden, zu Gottesdiensten je nach Kirchenjahreszeit und Anlass mit unterschiedlichen Glocken zu läuten. Der Organist zieht auch nicht immer alle Register beim Spielen. Zu den Fastenzeiten Advent und Passion darf gerne auch das Geläute »fasten«, indem eine oder mehrere Glocken schweigen. Zur Geburt und Auferstehung Christi wird die Freude dann auch durch den Glockenklang deutlich. Diese und weitere Variationsmöglichkeiten sind in einer Läuteordnung festgehalten, welche die Gemeindeleitung beschließt. Dabei muss auf die Widmung der Glocken und auf harmonische Zusammenhänge geachtet werden.

Ein- und Ausschalten der Glocken
Leider werden häufig die Glocken viel zu schnell nacheinander oder sogar fast gleichzeitig eingeschaltet. Das Einsetzen der Glocken sollte einen Weg zum Gottesdienst hin beschreiben, man rennt oder stolpert ja normalerweise auch nicht dorthin. Jede Glocke von klein zu groß läutet mindestens eine Minute und darf ihren Klang entfalten, bevor die nächste Glocke hinzutritt. Diese Einschaltverzögerung kann auch leicht in der Läuteautomatik eingestellt werden. Das Ausläuten geschieht ebenfalls von klein zu groß: Der Klang der am jeweiligen Tag größten Glocke bleibt bis zum Ende stehen.

Läutedauer
- Wie lange dauert ein Vaterunser? Langsam gebetet, vielleicht eine Minute. Das Gebetsläuten kann daher auf drei Minuten begrenzt werden und wird dann auch von anderen nicht als Störung empfunden.
- Für das »Einläuten des Sonntags« sind 5 Minuten ein guter Richtwert. Das Läuten vor dem Gottesdienst sollte keinesfalls länger als 10 Minuten dauern – gerade in größeren Orten macht sich fast niemand mehr erst beim Erklingen der Glocken auf den Weg zur Kirche.
- Begleitet Glockenläuten einen Sarg auf dem Weg zum Grab, darf die Totenglocke erst verstummen, wenn der Sarg dort angelangt ist.

Geläutepflege
Die richtige und differenzierte Verwendung der Glocken reduziert auch den Verschleiß der Läuteanlage. Die Berufsgenossenschaft schreibt die Wartung durch eine Fachfirma einmal pro Jahr vor. Es sollte selbstverständlich sein, dass Aufstieg und Glockenstube sauber gehalten werden – besonders auch in den Ecken, da sich dort sonst gerne Rost und Fäulnis einnisten und großen Schaden verursachen. Ein schadhafter Vogelschutz oder mangelnde Sicherheit beim Aufstieg zur Glockenstube können dazu führen, dass das Geläut von der Berufsgenossenschaft stillgelegt wird.

Was nützt es, wenn durch den »Leitfaden« und das »Merkblatt« letztlich aber nur die Rahmenbedingungen des Gebetsläutens in Erinnerung gerufen und geklärt werden, aber Impulse zum Neubeleben der christlichen Praxis des Tagesgebetes fehlen?

Als erster Baustein hierfür wurde in großer ökumenischer Eintracht ein Gebetsheftchen für die Hosen- und Handtasche erstellt (A7-Format), das zu persönlichen, spirituellen Auszeiten einlädt. Diese Schrift will den Anspruch einlösen, dass das Gebetsläuten künftig mehr Menschen zum Mitbeten anregt und ein Mini-Ritual für persönliche Auszeiten anbietet. Das kurze Ritual der »Gedanken im Tageslauf«, welches je nach Situation angereichert werden kann, ist hier wiedergegeben. Zunächst folgt ein kurzer, vorbereitender Text, der später überblättert werden kann:

Pausen im Alltag – Für mich und dich:
Eine Glocke läutet und macht mich aufmerksam. Ich lasse mich auf die Einladung ein, mein Tun zu unterbrechen und mir und meinen Gedanken und Gefühlen Raum zu geben. Ich komme zur Ruhe, suche einen geschützten Raum – vielleicht, indem ich einfach die Augen schließe. Oder ich entzünde eine Kerze, vertiefe mich in ein Symbol, das mir dabei hilft, meine Gedanken zu sammeln, nehme einen Gegenstand in die Hand, der mich zur Meditation anregt. Ich fühle mich mit mir selbst und anderen verbunden. Ich höre in mich hinein und öffne mich für eine Begegnung mit Gott, der alles, auch mich, durchdringt.
Was bewegt mich heute? Wofür und für wen will ich Worte finden? Je nach meiner aktuellen Gestimmtheit finde ich für mich in dieser kleinen Schrift eine spirituelle Anregung für den Augenblick oder auch darüber hinaus.

Dann folgt das eigentliche Tagesgebet:

Mein kleines Ritual für den Tag:
Ehre sei dem Vater und dem Sohn und dem Heiligen Geist. Wie im Anfang, so auch jetzt und allezeit und in Ewigkeit. Amen.
Ich bin einzigartig und Teil einer Gemeinschaft. Vor Gott kann ich mit allen meinen Gedanken und Gefühlen da sein – ohne Bedingungen zu erfüllen.

Hier folgen nun farblich abgesetzte »Icons«, die mit Emotionen oder Tageszeiten beschriftet sind:

morgens	glücklich	lebendig
besorgt	mittags	gestresst
dankbar	traurig	abends

Die Betenden können nun eine der folgenden Doppelseiten aufschlagen, welche zu dem Farbcode der Icons passen und welche ihren momentanen Bedürfnissen entsprechen. Links sind dort jeweils ein Psalm (abwechselnd in neuer Luther- oder Einheitsübersetzung), Luthers Morgensegen und ein Gebet von Papst Franziskus abgedruckt, rechts historische und zeitgenössische geistliche Prosa – quasi als Proprium. Danach kehren die Betenden in das Ordinarium zurück und beenden das Tagesgebet:

> Gott spricht zu mir. An seinem Wort kann ich mich orientieren und meinen Weg finden. Mein Denken und Tun kann gelingen, jede Stunde neu.
> Vater unser im Himmel, geheiligt werde dein Name. Dein Reich komme. Dein Wille geschehe, wie im Himmel so auf Erden. Unser tägliches Brot gib uns heute. Und vergib uns unsere Schuld, wie auch wir vergeben unsern Schuldigern. Und führe uns nicht in Versuchung, sondern erlöse und von dem Bösen. Denn dein ist das Reich und die Kraft und die Herrlichkeit in Ewigkeit. Amen.
> Gott schenkt sich im Heiligen Geist allen Menschen. Ich bitte um ihn, erspüre ihn und lasse ihn wirken. So bin ich gesegnet und werde frei, mir und anderen in Liebe zu begegnen.
> Der Herr segne dich und behüte dich. Der Herr lasse sein Angesicht über dir leuchten und sei dir gnädig. Der Herr wende sein Angesicht dir zu und schenke dir Frieden. Amen.

Eine MikroSite der »Gedanken« ist unter www.gebetslaeuten.de abrufbar, welche das Ritual elektronisch verfügbar macht. Daran anschließen wird eine App, welche die Aufforderung zum Tagesgebet mit vielfältigen Angeboten für Nutzer und Nutzerinnen mit unterschiedlichsten Erfahrungen und Anliegen verknüpft.

2. #createsoundscape – Klingende Glockendatenbank zum Mitmachen

Ein weiterer großer Baustein der Initiative »Hörst du nicht die Glocken?« trägt das Thema zusätzlich weit in die Öffentlichkeit: Im Rahmen des Europäischen Kulturerbejahres 2018 wird eine Nationale Klingende Glockendatenbank entstehen.

»Hörst du nicht die Glocken?« will mit diesem Baustein das Kulturerbe »Glocken« in der Öffentlichkeit wieder ins Bewusstsein rufen, präsent und nutzbar machen. Jugendgruppen sollen unter Anleitung die Geschichte der Glocken in ihrer Nachbarschaft erforschen, diese in Bild und Ton aufnehmen und an einen Webmaster senden. Dieser stellt die gesammelten Daten in eine digitale Landkarte ein, von der aus alle Informationen, also auch Bilder und Klänge, abrufbar sind.

Läutende, also schwingende Glocken in Türmen oder anderen Mauerwerkskonstruktionen sind ein historisches, kulturelles Alleinstellungsmerkmal für Europa, welches von dort weltweit exportiert wurde. In anderen Ländern, in denen in vergangenen Jahrhunderten und Jahrtausenden Glocken genutzt wurden, sind diese dagegen meist fest aufgehängt und werden angeschlagen. Die Mehrzahl von ihnen hängt in den Glockentürmen von Kirchen, es gibt aber auch zahlreiche Glocken in kommunalen Einrichtungen – seien es Rathäuser, Schulen, Stadttore oder Friedhöfe. Auch kleine und große Glockenspiele sind verbreitet. Bundesweit sind schätzungsweise deutlich mehr als 100.000 Glocken aufgehängt. Die meisten dieser Glocken werden regelmäßig geläutet oder angeschlagen.

Gemeinschaftliches Herstellen einer Klangdatenbank aller Glocken und Geläute in Deutschland als Modell für Glocken-Europa; Die Zielformulierung im Europäischen Kulturerbejahr und zwar »Förderung und Identifikation mit dem kulturellen Erbe und die Bereitschaft zu seiner Bewahrung sowie dessen Wahrnehmung als Teil eines kulturell übergreifenden, allen gemeinsamen europäischen Erbes« lässt sich mit der Klingenden Glockendatenbank in geradezu idealer Weise erfüllen, da die Kampagne sowohl dem Kennenlernen und Begreifen des Glockenklang-Erbes dient als auch seiner dauerhaften Vermittlung und Tradierung durch die Klangdatenbank.

Es sollen vorrangig Jugendliche zum Mitmachen gewonnen werden. Jugendliche nutzen ihre mobilen Endgeräte kreativ zur Informationsbeschaffung, zum Aufnehmen von Bild- und Klangdateien. Dies kommt dem Projekt in vollem Umfang zugute. Gleichzeitig lernen die Jugendlichen die Grenzen der digitalen Informationsbeschaffung und werden, um erfolgreich am Projekt teilnehmen zu können, um einen guten Eintrag in die Datenbank zustande zu bringen, Kontakt zu kundigen Personen aufnehmen bzw. in einem Archiv nach Informationen suchen.

Eine gesamtstaatliche Bedeutung ist sowohl durch die gezielte Ansprache von Multiplikatoren-Gruppierungen im gesamten Bundesgebiet als auch durch die angestrebte flächendeckende Erfassung des Glockenklangs und seiner jeweiligen Bedeutung gegeben. Eine systematische

Erfassung des Kulturerbes »Glockenklang« gibt es bislang auf nationaler Ebene nicht.

2.1 Ziele des Projektes

- Förderung der Identifikation mit dem baulichen und archäologischen Erbe und der Bereitschaft zu seiner Bewahrung: Glockentürme und die Glocken selbst sind normalerweise nicht zugänglich. Durch das Projekt befassen sich die Projektgruppen mit der Geschichte der Objekte und lernen sie zu deuten. Die Gruppen erhalten geführten und beaufsichtigten Zugang zu den bis dahin oft nur gehörten Klangdenkmälern. Mit dem Verständnis der untersuchten und besprochenen Bau- und Kunstwerke kann Verständnis für das Erbe und eine Beziehung zu dessen Bewahrung entstehen und wachsen.
- Hervorhebung und Weiterentwicklung von auf europäische Vernetzung und Austausch zielenden Aktivitäten im Kontext des kulturellen Erbes: Die durch das Projekt gemeinschaftlich entstehende Glockenklang-Datenbank macht vor Grenzen nicht halt. So wie der Glockenklang Grenzen von Städten, Ländern, Konfessionen oder Ideologien überwindet, ist die Datenbank offen für Klang-, Bild- und Textdaten aus allen europäischen Ländern. Über die unterschiedlichen Traditionen, Klangzusammenstellungen oder Widmungen des Läutens kann ein regionaler oder internationaler Austausch erfolgen.
- Schaffen von Möglichkeiten des gemeinsamen Austausches und der vermittelnden Ansprache von breiten Teilen der Gesellschaft: In den Projektgruppen soll sich intensiv über das Thema Glocken, ihre Tradition und Funktion, ausgetauscht werden. Die Projektgruppen sind gleichzeitig Multiplikatoren für ein Weitertragen der Themen in die Gesellschaft.

2.2 Bezüge zu den Leitthemen des Kulturerbejahres

Mit der Nationalen Klingenden Glockendatenbank zum Mitmachen lassen sich Bezüge zu den Leitthemen des Kulturerbejahres »Die Europäische Stadt«, »Europa: Erinnern und Aufbruch«, »Europa: Gelebtes Erbe« und »Europa: Austausch und Bewegung« herstellen.

2.2.1 Die europäische Stadt

Das Klangbild europäischer Städte ist stark mitgeprägt von Glockenklängen. Gerade im städtischen Umfeld ist die Vielfalt von Glocken wahrnehmbar: Am Rathaus spielt zur vollen Stunde ein Glockenspiel, zur Mittagszeit wird an verschiedenen Orten gleichzeitig zum Friedensgebet aufgerufen, das Festgeläute zu einer Hochzeit ruft die Erinnerung an eigene biografische Stationen wach, der Stundenschlag der Glocken und die Totenglocke auf dem Friedhof erinnern an die Vergänglichkeit des Lebens. Der Alltag wird durch den Stundenschlag und das Läutesignal (z. B. »Mittagszeit«) rhythmisiert und geordnet. Glockenklang ist in der Stadt Hintergrund und Aufforderung zugleich, steht im Dialog zwischen Besinnung und Betriebsamkeit.

2.2.2 Europa: Erinnern und Aufbruch

Von der Vergangenheit bis heute ist Glockenklang ein Zeichen für Frieden. In Kriegszeiten wurden immer wieder die Glocken abgehängt und die Bronze zu Kanonen oder Munition umgeschmolzen (z. B. Glockenfriedhof im Hamburger Hafen 1945). In Friedenszeiten durften dann wieder Glocken gegossen werden. Kanonengießer waren oft mit Glockengießern identisch. An diese Zusammenhänge kann erinnert werden, beispielsweise durch Erfassen und Diskutieren von Glockeninschriften, in denen häufig auf vergangene schwere Zeiten und auf die Bewahrung vor Unheil hingewiesen wird. Es können auch Vorschläge für neue Glockeninschriften gesammelt werden, die den Zeitgeist spiegeln und die in der Vorstellung der Projektgruppen Bestand haben sollen.

2.2.3 Europa: Gelebtes Erbe

Viele Glocken in den Türmen sind seit Jahrhunderten in Betrieb und verkünden ihre Botschaften, manche seit dem frühen Mittelalter. Für viele Menschen ist es erhebend, wenn beispielsweise der »Dicke Pitter« in Köln zu besonderen Anlässen geläutet wird. An vielen Orten wird regelmäßiges Läuten seit Jahrzehnten praktiziert.

2.2.4 Europa: Austausch und Bewegung

Glockengießer waren und sind überregional und grenzüberschreitend tätig. So hängen hier in Deutschland viele Glocken aus Frankreich, den Niederlanden, aus der Schweiz und Österreich, aus Italien und einigen osteuropäischen Ländern. Deutsche Glockengießereien exportieren weltweit. Jedes Land, jede Gießerei hat dabei ihre eigenen Klangvorlieben und -eigenarten. Die Idee der läutenden Glocken wurde von irischen Wandermönchen im 8. Jahrhundert von Süd- nach Nordeuropa gebracht, ist also eine von Süd nach Nord bestens rezipierte Kulturbotschaft mit transnationalem Charakter.

Alle Gemeinden (kirchlich und politisch) sowie die Leitungsorgane und Regionalvertretungen der Jugendgruppen werden informiert und zum Mitmachen eingeladen. Im Internet sind dann bereits schon Best-Practice-Beispiele und ein YouTube-Tutorial eingestellt, über die man sich informieren kann, was zu beachten ist und wie in etwa ein Ergebnis eines Eintrages aussehen könnte. Merkblätter für die Gruppenleiter/-innen informieren über die Bausteine der Kampagne und mögliche Vorgehensweisen. Sicherheitshinweise für das Begehen der Türme werden mitversandt.

2.3 Projektdurchführung

- Die Jugendlichen recherchieren im Netz, im Gemeindearchiv, beim zuständigen Glockensachverständigen oder in Interviews Angaben zu dokumentierenden Glocken in Kirchen und anderen Gebäuden.
- Die Jugendlichen machen ansprechende Fotos des zu dokumentierenden Gebäudes (innen/außen). Die Gruppe entscheidet, welche besten Fotos weitergeleitet werden.
- Die Jugendlichen erstellen von außen brauchbare Tonaufnahmen (mp3-Format) der zu dokumentierenden Glocken (nach rechtzeitiger Absprache mit den für das Läuten verantwortlichen Personen). Auch hier entscheiden die Gruppen über die weiterzuleitende Qualität der Aufnahmen.
- Kleine Gruppen besteigen unter Leitung eingewiesener Personen (Projektmitarbeitende/Küster/Sicherheitsbeauftragte/Feuerwehr) bei Beachtung aller Sicherheitsbestimmungen geeignete Türme und machen Fotos von den Glocken und ihren Inschriften.
- Aus den vorhandenen/historischen Inschriften entwickeln/formulieren die Jugendlichen eigene, aktuelle Texte, die als Anliegen künftig mit den jeweiligen Glocken verbunden werden (Homepage der Gemeinde/Mitteilungsblatt/Monitor, Wandzeitung im Gebäude/einstellbare, persönliche Erinnerung am Mobiltelefon).

- Alle Materialien werden an einen Webmaster gesandt (unter Verwendung von Online-Eingabehilfen), der sie auswertet, formatiert und in die Datenbank einstellt.

2.4 Motivation

- Die Urheber-Gruppierung der Einträge wird in der Datenbank bei jedem Objekt gut sichtbar genannt (eventuell auch mit Foto) und damit dauerhaft öffentlich gewürdigt.
- Die teilnehmenden Gemeinden und Institutionen präsentieren sich als aktuell, jugend- und technikaffin und machen traditionelle Kulturpflege für die Zukunft fit. Sie erhalten das (zu entwerfende) »Hörst du nicht die Glocken?« -Kulturerbe-Logo und können damit ein Plakat oder ein Signet am Gebäude gestalten und sich so als Teil des Netzwerkes präsentieren.

2.5 Nachhaltigkeit

- Die innerhalb der Projektzeit in die Datenbank integrierten Glocken/Geläute/Gebäude/Kirchen und der damit verbundene Nutzen üben eine starke Faszination auf weitere Glocken-Besitzende aus, sodass die Mitmach-Datenbank auf Dauer Nachfrage erfährt. Nach Projektende zahlen Interessierte einen Selbstkosten-Beitrag für das Beschaffen/die Einstellung der Daten an den Webmaster und ggfls. Hilfskräfte.
- Die Datenbankstruktur wird auf Wunsch anderen Institutionen (staatlich/kirchlich) in europäischen Ländern zur Verfügung gestellt/wird für Einträge aus diesen Ländern geöffnet.

2.6 Zielgruppen

- Jugendorganisationen/-gruppen der Kirchen (Pfadfinder, CVJM, Ministranten, Konfirmanden, Firmlinge, Jugendchöre, Jungbläser), Jugendfeuerwehr, NABU-Jugend, Jugendliche aus Heimat- und Sportvereinen, Auszubildende in Kommunen etc., die Daten und Aufnahmen sammeln.
- Nutzer/-innen, die weltweit ihre Heimatglocken hören wollen.
- Heimatkundler und Kulturwissenschaftlerinnen, welche die Entwicklung von Glocken-Klanglandschaften in Deutschland erforschen und auswerten wollen.

Die große Aufgabe des Projektteams wird nun sein, inner- und außerkirchliche Jugendorganisationen und -verbände bzw. Arbeitsfelder wie die Konfirmandenarbeit 2018 und 2019 zum Mitmachen zu bewegen. Dies soll vor allem durch attraktiv gestaltete Social-Media-Aktionen geschehen, aber auch durch Textbeiträge in Printmedien und andere Kanäle. Dazu wird eine Kommunikationsagentur mit einbezogen.

Es ist ein Geschenk, dass auf dem Wege einer staatlichen Förderung kirchliches Kulturerbe in das Bewusstsein einer nachwachsenden Generation kommt, die auf diese Weise einen neuen Bezug zu kirchlichen Traditionen und zur Gebetspraxis erhält.

Martin Kares

Bell-Ringing in the Course of the Day

An initiative of the Ecumenical Advisory Committee for German Bell-ringing

I. Bell-ringing in the course of the day

Our initiative is based on the observation that in many congregations the knowledge about right, function and content of bell-ringing over the course of the day has dramatically decreased and that even persons responsible for bell-ringing are unable to give accurate information. Despite the nationwide, omnipresent and unmistakable call to prayer, it is hardly acknowledged any more in Christian congregations.

If you ask local people about the different times of the day when bells are rung, you are surprised by their answers: »They toll at 11 o'clock in order to call the peasants from the field« was one of the more common answers; others had heard somewhere that this hour was used to ring the bells »against the Turks«. Leaving aside all aspects of an awareness of reality (the farmer in his sound-proof tractor is more likely to listen to heavy metal music, not bells …) and political correctness, this situation is not without problems: Imagine an expert is sent to the place of a bell dispute in the framework of court proceedings. This expert asks a random selection of people who live in the vicinity of the bells – including representatives of the congregation in question. He might ask the following questions:

- Do you know why bells are rung outside of service hours, and can you explain this to people in your town?
- Do you know the dedications of »your« bells, and is there any connection to the occasion of their ringing?
- Do you know that bell-ringing is legally protected only for very specific occasions and actions?

Even full-time staff of congregations are often incapable of answering these questions plausibly and correctly. For volunteers – who may even programme the clock which controls the ringing – the situation seems even worse: »It has always been like this that bells are rung at 11 o'clock«; »My predecessor told me to do it this way«; or »Midday – that's political bell-ringing«.

It would be naive to believe that a judge would acknowledge a special right of churches for such occasions in the context of free exercise of religion. A hastily agreed and submitted order of bell-ringing would not survive such proceedings, either.

However, the »Morning bells are ringing!« campaign aims to do more than educate church representatives about the answers to critical questions. It is meant to help rediscover and spread the power and potential which Christian congregations have enjoyed for centuries with bells as a means of communication. Its purpose is to remind us of the opportunities given to us in an agreed, regular orientation towards God in prayer. The campaign uses the spreading desire for individual piousness and spirituality, putting it into a larger context and, taking up the concept of concentric circles, aims at integrating individuality back into the community.

Of course there are still places with a vivid and rich prayer tradition, where a self-affirmation or re-positioning of bell-ringing in social life is not (yet) a necessity, because content and occasions are communicated with newcomers and new community members, or because the percentage of people without a connection to the church is small; but the number of towns and neighbourhoods is dramatically increasing where the loud signals of a Christian spiritual life are no longer understood and cause discussions on the question of tolerance. This applies to all denominations. On the other hand, new prayer groups or networks like the Ecumenical Liturgy of the Hours provide new hope. In these initiatives, people regularly come together to celebrate »the basic liturgy of the people of God«.

The Ecumenical Advisory Committee for German Bell-ringing is aware of the fact that this campaign may also rouse those who object to bell-ringing: Their reaction to »Morning bells are ringing!« is likely to be: »Yes, I can hear them – and they are quite a nuisance!« Even members of church leadership worried in this respect and recommended dropping the subject. In a comprehensive SWOT analysis, strengths and weaknesses, opportunities and threats of the initiative were collected, discussed and evaluated. A day workshop with participants from different areas of work in church and society supplied us with additional important insights. The result was to plan and implement the campaign in two stages: The first stage is meant to raise awareness in congregations, in church administration and amongst PR workers and to increase their knowledge. This is achieved through a »Guideline for congregations, their leaders and members«. It starts with the three above mentioned questions on bells for people in charge and gives the following answer:

> If you can answer all three questions with yes: Congratulations, you are well prepared for any future inquiries! If not, this brochure can tell you more about the purpose of bell-ringing, so you can enjoy their sound even more.

The first double page tells us more about the history and culture of bells:

> **5000 years – and still going strong …**
> Bells have been around for more than 5000 years. For 1500 years, they have been used in Christianity as a means of calling and signal for liturgical action. With their global sounds, they establish a connection to the cultural history of mankind and speak to people – irrespective of skin colour, ethnic origin or nation.
> Bells call us to prayer and to intercessions, they indicate time and hour and remind us of eternity. For their services in the church, they are consecrated in a service. Their canonical dedication determines and limits their use. The congregations define occasions for bell-ringing.
> Over the centuries, the use of bells has developed differently in different cultures. Regional customs of bell-ringing should be preserved and revived. In some places, however, bell-ringing needs a new impulse to be perceived and accepted as a positive message in the hustle and bustle of the world.

The second topic concerns concepts and orders, because there are quite a lot of misconceptions:

»… for they know what they are doing.«

Frequently, the chime of the clock is mistaken for bell-ringing. The chime of the clock indicates the time, but it should also be understood as a reminder of transience and the progress of time – »My times are in your hand«.

The ringing of several bells as a call to come to service is still widely understood. If a single bell is rung, it is either meant as an accompaniment of liturgical action (blessing, prayer, transubstantiation), or it is a call to prayer outside of regular service hours. The call to come to service, liturgical bell-ringing and prayer or angelus bell-ringing are the only legitimate reasons for a congregation to ring bells. For this reason, the leaders of a congregation must decide on occasions and times for bell-ringing and define them in a bell-ringing order, especially if there are no other documents in this respect available.

Before taking a decision on when to ring bells for prayer, you have the opportunity to take some time reviewing times, occasions and dedications of bell-ringing in your own and in neighbouring congregations. In many places, times of bell-ringing are not mutually agreed between congregations, partly because of an old sense of competition between different denominations. This is an issue that we should overcome today. Similarly, it is no longer realistic to call »peasants from their fields« by ringing bells at 11 o'clock. Without a clear purpose and defined times of bell-ringing, congregations can be accused of using the bells devoid of sense.

In the section »Daily life and rhythm«, traditional and new times for bell-ringing are discussed.

The pulse of the times

It is a centuries-old tradition going back to the early civilisations to divide the day into sections of three hours. Monks in monasteries translated this concept into the liturgy of the hours that is still practiced today. Angelus bells are rung in the morning, at midday and in the evening. Interestingly, we hear that a burnout may be prevented by giving the day some structure. The bell-ringing times at 9, 12, 3 and 6 o'clock result in a cross on the face of the clock. The discussions about early morning bell-ringing in some places could be solved by switching it to 9 o'clock. This could then be taken up in kindergartens and schools (in religious education) as a signal to join the prayer or as a blessing for the day.

Having an increased awareness for bell-ringing in the course of the day means: not more bell-ringing, but more purpose in it. If in one congregation

for example bells are traditionally rung for midday or evening prayer, this is quite sufficient. It has a special value if bell-ringing is happening at the same time(s) at several places: This can help create a sense of fellowship among Christians. Prayer happens in the knowledge that throughout the country people are turning towards God at this time.
Common prayers can build relationships and change things – they have even played a part in preparing the ground for German reunification.

The section »Dedication and message« deals with the prayer requests connected with the bells when they are cast or dedicated.

Heavy Metal
Most bells received a dedication when they were cast. They contain a Bible quote or are dedicated to persons from the Bible, from church history or to saints. Some inscriptions let bells proclaim messages even if we are not present or are not paying attention: »Ora pro nobis – pray for us« or »Oh country, hear the word of the Lord«.
The primary purpose of a ringing bell is to call us to service or to prayer. It proclaims an invitation, motivates for action, reminds us of God's action in our life and our service to God. It interrupts our daily life, our indifference, it admonishes and reminds us. Bells proclaim loud »heavy metal« messages. They are meant to be heard in the hustle and bustle of the world. Direct neighbours are protected by legal decibel limits and tower acoustics; occasions for and the duration of each bell-ringing are limited and justified.

The chapter »Distance and closeness« describes possible attitudes and approaches when hearing bells.

Carried away
So far, the meaning of bell-ringing is only known to a group of church »insiders«; however the ringing itself is heard by everybody. The ringing of a bell can serve as a reminder to have a break, for reflection, for an individual relationship with God, but also include an impulse for encounter and community. Depending on the situation and individual Christian/church history, it can accompany a possible inner journey – a model of spiritual growth:
- Hearing the bell – »Midday ringing«
- Pause – Break in the course of the day in the knowledge that many people are now thinking of the world and its needs (e. g. peace, justice, care of creation)

- Remembrance – Pause with remembrance of people I know, e.g. with request for health
- Prayer – Turning to God as recipient or companion for personal or communal concerns
- Pray together in the form of an agreed rite at a specific place (liturgy of the hours).

The section »Tolerance and respect« reflects on how prayer-specific bell-ringing can be explained to believers of other faiths and how we can invite participation. Muslims reacted consistently positively to the perspective that bell-ringing over the course of the day should again be understood as a call to prayer. A public display of worship in Germany in the course of the day is quite rare in any case.

Shout it from the rooftops

Even people who have no connection to the church or the Christian religion can understand the ringing of a bell as a positive signal. Of course it helps to convey its purpose: Midday ringing as a plea for peace and evening ringing as a plea for the integrity of creation can probably be accepted or at least tolerated by most people. To think about the common good and the world and to act accordingly is essential to most religions and ideologies.

Society's latent positive attitude towards bells – they remind us of biographical events, received blessings, peace, home – enables us to continue to perceive bell-ringing as a normal part of living together. In rural areas, bell-ringing is practiced when the death of a person of that village becomes known – in many cases irrespective of the person's religious affiliation. In this situation, all are equal.

A justified approach to public, distinctive signals of Christian life can be convincing and invite discussion. Questions like: »Why are bells rung during the day?« or »Does the church have to cause such a racket?« could be answered by the invitation: »We pray to God and for the world – maybe you could at least tolerate it or, even better, join us«.

The section »Creativity and implementation« describes a range of actions and events connected to bells that can be used by congregations to tap into the potential of the topic.

The section »Liturgical year and occasions« contains general remarks on bell-ringing, especially for services.

Ding-dong merrily on high

Selection of a bell for use as a prayer bell should be in line with its dedication/inscription. It does not make much sense to use the baptismal or death bell for this purpose.

So far, we have provided you with some ideas on bell-ringing with single bells for prayer in everyday life. Since we receive a lot of questions in this respect, we add a couple of basic rules on the ringing of several bells for services:

- If there are more than two bells, you can and should ring different bells for different occasions, in a way that suits the liturgical calendar. An organist does not pull out all the stops for all songs, either.
- Advent and Lent are fasting periods. This can be acknowledged by ringing fewer bells than for »normal« Sundays. From Maundy Thursday till Easter morning the bells are silent; Protestant churches should only ring the biggest or the Christ bell for service on Good Friday.
- Also in case of funeral and memorial services, bells should indicate that something is missing, that we are in grief, by using fewer bells or ringing in a minor chord.
- Christ celebrations are the highlights of the church year. For these occasions, be sure to ring everything you've got. Festive bell-ringing can also be used for special events in the congregation (communion, confirmation, visit of the bishop …).

At the end, the chapter »Obligation and choice« sums up what congregations need to take into account and what action they may take if need be.

The brochure is complemented by a leaflet for church helpers, sextons, sacristans. It says:

Correct bell-ringing is a great responsibility. Bell-ringing has to be filled with purpose, otherwise it is »a noisy gong or a clanging cymbal«. Electric ringing systems and computers make the work easier for those responsible for bell-ringing. Still, it is important to use these technical aids for the glory of God and with the right frame of mind.

Bells in the course of the church year

For parishes with three or more bells, it should become natural to ring different bells for services, depending on the season and occasion. An organist does not pull out all the stops for all songs, either. For the fasting periods of

Advent or Lent, some bells may »fast« too by remaining silent. For the birth and resurrection of Christ, our joy is then again mirrored in the sound of the bells. These and other possible variations are defined in a bell-ringing order, which is decided by the congregation's leadership. It has to take heed of the bells' dedications and musical harmony.

Switching the bells on and off
Unfortunately, bells are frequently switched on far too quickly one after the other or nearly at the same time. The starting of the bells should resemble the way to church; you don't usually run or stumble to service. Each bell from small to big should ring at least for a minute and be allowed to develop its sound before you add another one. This delayed start can be easily programmed in the automatic ringing system. Stopping the bells is also done from small to big: The sound of the biggest bell is the one left over at the end.

Duration of ringing
- How long is a Lord's Prayer? If you pray it slowly, maybe a minute. So the ringing of a prayer bell can be limited to three minutes; this way it will not be perceived as a nuisance.
- To herald the start of a Sunday, 5 minutes are a good measure. Bell-ringing before a service should never last longer than 10 minutes – especially in bigger cities hardly anyone will start out for church only after hearing the bells.
- If a bell accompanies the journey of a coffin to the grave, it may only stop once the coffin has reached its destination.

Bell care
Correct and differentiated use of bells also reduces wear and tear of the system. The German professional association stipulates maintenance by specialists once a year. It should be self-evident that staircase and belfry must be kept clean – especially in the corners, where rust and decay easily take hold and can cause great damage. A damaged protection against birds or a lack of safety in the staircase can cause the professional association to close down the belfry.

What good is it if guideline brochure and leaflet help explain and remember the framework of bell-ringing, but new impulse for a revival of the Christian tradition of the liturgy of the hours is missing?

As a first building block, a truly ecumenical prayer booklet in A7 format was developed to be carried in your pocket; it invites us to individual, spiritual breaks. This booklet is meant to support the desire that the sound of the prayer bell may incite more people to join the prayer; it offers a mini ritual for an individual break. The short ritual of »Thoughts during the day« is included here; it can be enriched depending on the specific situation. It starts with a short preparatory text, which can be skipped later:

> A break in daily life – for me and for you:
> A bell is ringing and catches my attention. I accept the invitation to stop what I'm currently doing and give room to me, my thoughts and feelings. I calm down, seek a sheltered space – maybe simply by closing my eyes. Or I light a candle, look at a symbol that helps me gather my thoughts, take an object into my hand that incites me to meditate. I feel connected to myself and to others. I listen inside me and open up for an encounter with God, who penetrates everything, including me.
> What moves me today? For what and for whom do I want to find words? Depending on my current mood, I search for a spiritual impulse in this booklet for this moment or this day.

This is followed by the prayer for the day:

> My short prayer for the day:
> Glory be to the Father and the Son and the Holy Spirit. As it was in the beginning, is now and ever shall be, world without end. Amen.
> I am unique and part of a community. Before God, I can be present with all my thoughts and feelings – without having to fulfil any conditions.

This is followed by colour-coded icons for emotions and times of the day:

morning	happy	alive
worried	midday	stressed
thankful	sad	evening

With this guide, the person praying can turn to one of the following double pages marked with icons that fit their current state of mind or the time of day. On the left page, there is always a psalm (alternating between revised Luther and Ecumenical Translation), Luther's morning blessing and a prayer of Pope Francis; the right page includes traditional and contemporary spiritual prose, serving as the proper. After that, the prayer returns to the ordinary to complete the prayer of the day:

> God speaks to me. I can follow his word and find my way. My thoughts and action can succeed, every hour anew.
> Our Father in heaven, hallowed be your name. Your kingdom come. Your will be done, on earth as it is in heaven. Give us this day our daily bread. And forgive us our debts, as we also have forgiven our debtors. And do not bring us to the time of trial, but rescue us from evil. For the kingdom, the power, and the glory are yours now and forever. Amen.
> In the Holy Spirit, God gives himself to all people. I ask for it, feel it and let it take hold. Thus, I am blessed and free to encounter myself and others in love.
> May the Lord bless you and keep you. May the Lord make his face to shine upon you, and be gracious to you. May the Lord lift up his countenance upon you, and give you peace. Amen.

On www.gebetslaeuten.de you can find a pdf version of the »Thoughts« booklet to make the ritual electronically accessible. The next step will be an app to connect the call to prayer with various offers for users with different experiences and concerns.

2. #createsoundscape – Bell database with sounds for open participation

Another important module of the campaign »Morning bells are ringing!« is intended to raise more public awareness for the topic. In the framework of the European Year of Cultural Heritage 2018, a national bell database with sounds will be set up.

»Morning bells are ringing!« aims at reminding the general public of bells as a cultural heritage that is present and should be used. Youth groups can be instructed to research the history of the bells in their neighbourhood, take pictures and sound samples and send these to a webmaster. These data will then be included in a digital map from which all data, including pictures and sounds, can be accessed.

Ringing, swinging bells in towers or other brickwork constructions are a historical and cultural feature unique to Europe, from where it was exported to the whole world. In other countries which used bells in past centuries and millennia, bells were usually installed to hang fixed and were merely struck. The majority of bells hang in church belfries, but there are also a variety of bells in communal institutions, such as town halls, schools, city gates or cemeteries.[1] Small and big chimes are quite common. In the whole of Germany, there are probably more than 100,000 bells. Most of them are rung or struck regularly.

Contributions to a sound database of all bells in Germany as a model for the bells of Europe: The aim of the European Year of Cultural Heritage »to promote identification with the cultural heritage and the willingness to preserve it as well as its perception as part of a cross-cultural, common European heritage« can easily be achieved by the bell database with sounds, since it serves the purpose of getting to know and understanding the heritage of bells as well as its continuous communication and passing on via the database.

Mostly youth are the target group for participation. Young people use their mobile devices in a creative way to gather information, to take pictures or to create audio files. This can all be used for the project. At the same time, youth learn the limits of digital information gathering and will have to establish contact to experts or go to an archive in order to produce a good entry for the database and successfully participate in the project.

The relevance to Germany as a whole is assured through a targeted approach to multiplier groups in the whole country as well as the desired nation-wide register of bell sounds and their respective meaning. So far, there has been no systematic register of the cultural heritage of bell sounds on a national level.

2.1 Goals of the project

- Promote identification with the architectural and archaeological heritage and the willingness to preserve it: Belfries and bells are usually not accessible to the public. With the help of this project, groups learn about the history of the objects and what they stand for. The groups

1 For Gutenberg-Gymnasium in Erfurt, a new school bell was cast in 2017 to remember the shooting that took place there.

are given guided and monitored access to the cultural monuments of which they only know the sound. With a new understanding of the visited and discussed monuments and works of art, they can develop and grow an understanding of the heritage and form a connection to its preservation.

- Highlighting and further development of activities aimed at European networking and exchange in the context of cultural heritage: The bell database resulting from the project does not stop at country borders. Just like the sound of bells transcends borders of cities, countries, confessions or ideologies, the database is open for sound, picture and text files from all European countries. It enables a regional and international exchange and sharing of different traditions, sounds and dedications of bell-ringing.
- Create opportunities for mutual sharing and outreach to large groups of society: The project groups are meant to discuss in depth the topic of bells, their tradition as well as their function. At the same time, project groups are multipliers for passing on the topic into society at large.

2.2 Links to the guiding themes of the Year of Cultural Heritage

The national bell database that is open for general participation can be linked to the following guiding themes of the Year of Cultural Heritage: »The European City«, »Europe: Remembrance and New Start«, »Europe: Living Heritage« and »Europe: Exchange and Movement«.

2.2.1 The European City

The soundscape of European cities is strongly influenced by the sound of bells. Especially in an urban setting, the diversity of bells can be heard: At the town hall there is a carillon every hour, at midday several bells ring to call people to a prayer for peace, wedding bells remind us of similar events in our own life, bells strike the hour, and the death bell at the cemetery reminds us of the transience of life. The day is structured by hourly bells and ringing signals (e. g. for midday). In cities, bells are background noise and requests at the same time, in a dialogue between reflection and activity.

2.2.2 Europe: Remembrance and New Start

Over the centuries, the sound of bells has been a sign of peace. In times of war, bells were often taken down and the bronze used for cannons or ammunition (e.g. the bell cemetery in Hamburg's harbour, 1945). After the war, bells were cast again. Frequently, cannon casters also acted as bell casters. These links can be remembered, e.g. by noting and discussing bell inscriptions, which often tell us of hard times or the deliverance from evil. Project groups can also collect suggestions for new bell inscriptions to mirror and preserve sentiments of current times.

2.2.3 Europe: Living Heritage

A lot of bells in their towers have been in use for centuries, telling us their message – some of them since the early Middle Ages. For many people it is a special moment when historic bells like the »Dicker Pitter« in Cologne are rung for special occasions. Regular bell-ringing has been practiced for decades at many places.

2.2.4 Europe: Exchange and Movement

Bell founders have always been active across regions and borders. In Germany, many bells have their origins in France, the Netherlands, Switzerland and Austria, Italy and a couple of Eastern European countries. German bell founders export their bells into the whole world. Each country, each foundry has their own sound preferences and characteristics. The concept of ringing bells was brought from Southern to Northern Europe by Irish itinerant monks in the 8th century. This makes it a well-received cultural message with a transnational character.

All congregations and municipalities as well as their governing bodies and regional representatives of youth groups are informed about the campaign and invited to participate. They can find best practice examples and a Youtube tutorial online to help them plan their project and have a look at what a final entry might look like. Leaflets for group leaders give information on the modules of the campaign and possible ways of action. We also include safety instructions for the climbing of the belfries.

2.3 Project implementation

- Participating youth research online, in their local archive, ask their local bell expert or read interviews to find out more about bells in churches and other buildings to be documented.
- They take photos of the building (inside and outside). The group decides which photos should be submitted.
- Outside, the youth record acceptable audio files (mp3 format) of the bells they want to document (after consultation with the person responsible for their ringing). Again, the group decides on the quality of the files they want to submit.
- Monitored by authorised personnel (project participant, sexton, safety officer, fire fighter) and respecting all safety regulations, small groups go up to the belfry and take photos of the bells and their inscriptions.
- Based on the existing/historical inscriptions, the youth develop/create new texts to be linked as a concern to the respective bell (website of the congregation, newsletter, notice board in the building, individual reminder on mobile phone).
- All materials are sent to a webmaster (using online upload tools), who evaluates, formats and enters them into the database.

2.4 Motivation

- The submitting group is mentioned in the database for each entry in a visible way (maybe even with a photo), so the contribution is permanently acknowledged.
- Participating congregations and institutions can show that they are up-to-date, open for youth and technology and capable of finding a modern way of preserving cultural heritage. They receive the campaign logo »Morning bells are ringing!« (to be designed) for use on a poster or sign at the building to indicate their participation in the network.

2.5 Sustainability

- All bells/buildings/churches registered in the database during the project and the resulting benefit increase the interest of other bell owners, thus giving the database a boost over time. After the project has ended, interested groups pay a modest fee (cost price) for the procurement/registration of their data to the webmaster and any assistants, if need be.

- If so desired, the database structure will be made accessible/opened up for other institutions (church or government) in European countries.

2.6 Target groups

- Youth organisations/groups of churches (scouts, YMCA, altar boys, confirmation groups, youth choirs/orchestras), youth fire brigade, environmental groups, youth from regional associations or sports clubs, apprentices in the municipality, etc., who collect data and audio files.
- Users who want to hear their home bells in the whole world.
- Local historians and cultural scientists who want to research and assess the development of bell soundscapes in Germany.

The project team's main task is now going to be to get church and other youth organisations and associations or fields of work like confirmation groups to participate in 2018 and 2019. This is mainly intended to happen through attractive social media campaigns, but also with the help of texts in print media and other communication channels. A communication agency has been employed to this end.

It is a gift that cultural heritage of the church can be brought to a young generation with the help of public funding; this way they can develop new ties to church traditions and the practice of praying.

Holger Eschmann

Die Feier zur Erneuerung des Bundes mit Gott

Eine Liturgie der Evangelisch-methodistischen Kirche

1. Vorwort zur Feier aus der Agende von 1993

Das Evangelium weist uns ein in den neuen Bund in Jesus Christus. Die christliche Kirche ist Bundesgemeinschaft, Gemeinschaft derer, die sich durch den Gebrauch der Gnadenmittel im Glaubensgehorsam in Gottes Gnadenbund einfügen ließen. In der Geschichte der Evangelisch-methodistischen Kirche hat der Bundesgedanke eine wichtige Rolle gespielt. Die vorliegende gottesdienstliche Ordnung ist ein Angebot zur Feier der Erneuerung des Bundes mit Gott in der Gemeinde. Wir antworten hier auf die Verkündigung des Evangeliums, indem wir unser Leben in feierlicher Form Gott aufs Neue zur Verfügung stellen. Denn Gottes Bund mit uns und unser Bund mit ihm, beides gehört untrennbar zusammen.

So forderte John Wesley am 25. Dezember 1747 die Mitglieder seiner Gemeinschaften auf, ihren Bund mit Gott zu erneuern. Sein erster Bunderneuerungsgottesdienst wurde am 11. August 1755 gehalten. Wesley veröffentlichte ihn im Jahr 1780. Diese Form wurde fast 100 Jahre lang ohne Veränderung gebraucht. Dann wurde sie mehrmals verändert, bis eine Gestalt gefunden war, die die Gemeinde stärker beteiligte. Im Wissen um die Bedeutung dieses Gottesdienstes wurde der vorliegende Text geschaffen.

Der Bundeserneuerungsgottesdienst wurde ursprünglich bei der Jahresschlussfeier, am ersten Sonntag des Jahres oder bei andern markanten Einschnitten im Gemeindeleben gefeiert, später auch bei Konferenzen und Tagungen. Dadurch sollte ein besonderer Akzent gesetzt werden: »Wir wollen uns in neuer Hingabe unsrem Herrn anvertrauen. Aus diesem Vertrauen heraus sind wir bereit, aufs Neue in seinem Dienst Verantwortung zu übernehmen.« – Heute lässt sich diese Gottesdienstform bei entsprechendem Anlass in der Gemeinde einsetzen, wie zum Beispiel vor dem Beginn einer evangelistischen Aktion. Einzelne Bausteine lassen sich auch als Teile anderer gottesdienstlicher Feiern verwenden.

Die Erneuerung dieses Bundes mit Gott gründet ausschließlich auf Gottes neuem Bund mit uns. Deshalb erinnern wir uns in dieser Feier dankbar daran, dass wir auf diesen Bund in Christus getauft wurden und uns bei der Aufnahme in die Kirchengliedschaft dazu bekannt haben. In diesem Sinn feiern wir hier Taufgedächtnis.

Der neue Bund findet seinen tiefsten gottesdienstlichen Ausdruck in der Feier des Abendmahls. Deshalb wird der Gottesdienst zur Erneuerung unsres Bundes mit Gott mit einer Mahlfeier verbunden. Er kann aber auch ohne eine solche gefeiert werden.

Anstelle der Fassung der Agende von 1993 ist im Folgenden »Die Feier zur Erneuerung des Bundes mit Gott« abgedruckt, wie sie im Gesangbuch der Evangelisch-methodistischen Kirche von 2002 unter der Nummer 776 zu finden ist und von den Gemeinden heute gefeiert wird.

2. Liturgie

Eingangswort

P Im Namen Gottes, des Vaters, des Sohnes und des Heiligen Geistes. Amen.

Bitte um ein reines Herz

A Allmächtiger Gott! Du siehst das Herz an. All unsere Wünsche sind dir bekannt. Kein Geheimnis ist vor dir verborgen. Reinige unsere Herzen und Gedanken und durchdringe sie mit deinem Heiligen Geist, damit wir dich vollkommen lieben und deinen heiligen Namen in Dankbarkeit ehren; durch Jesus Christus, unseren Herrn. Amen.

Lied

Dankgebet

P Gott, unser Vater, Quelle aller Güter. Alle Jahre unseres Lebens bist du uns gnädig gewesen. Wir danken dir für deine Liebe und Freundlichkeit, durch die du unsere Tage erfüllt und uns bis hierher geleitet hast.

G Du hast uns Leben und Verstand gegeben und uns in eine Welt gestellt, die erfüllt ist von deiner Herrlichkeit. Du hast uns erfreut und getröstet durch Angehörige und Freunde. Durch die Hände unserer Schwestern und Brüder hast du uns gedient.

P Du hast in unseren Herzen einen Hunger nach dir geweckt und uns deinen Frieden verliehen. Du hast uns erlöst und uns in Jesus Christus zu einem hohen Dienst berufen. Du hast uns in der Gemeinschaft deines Geistes und im Zeugendienst deiner Kirche unseren Platz gegeben.

G In Finsternis warst du uns Licht, in Not und Anfechtung Fels und Halt, in frohen Stunden der Geist der Freude, in unseren Mühen der reiche Lohn.

P Du hast an uns gedacht, wenn wir dich vergaßen. Du bist uns nachgegangen, selbst wenn wir vor dir flohen. Du bist uns mit Vergebung begegnet, wenn wir zu dir zurückkehrten.

P Für all deine Langmut und die Fülle deiner Gnade preisen wir deinen heiligen Namen.

A Amen.

Lied
Sündenbekenntnis

P Gott, unser Vater, du hast uns den Weg des Lebens in deinem Sohn gezeigt. Wir bekennen, wie schwer wir von ihm lernen und wie zögernd wir ihm nachfolgen. Du hast uns gerufen und wir haben nicht auf dich gehört. Deine Herrlichkeit ist erschienen und wir sind blind gewesen. Du hast deine Hand nach uns ausgestreckt und wir sind davor zurückgewichen. Wir haben viel empfangen und wenig gedankt. Wir sind deiner Liebe nicht würdig.

G Erbarme dich unser und vergib uns, Herr.
(kann auch gesungen werden)

P Vergib uns, wenn wir unsere Zeit vergeudet und unsere Gaben missbraucht haben. Vergib uns, wenn wir unsere eigenen Versäumnisse entschuldigt oder unsere Verantwortung abgelehnt haben. Vergib uns, wenn wir andere so wenig von deiner Liebe spüren ließen.

G Erbarme dich unser und vergib uns, Herr.
(kann auch gesungen werden)

Zusage der Vergebung

P Wenn wir unsere Sünden bekennen, so ist er treu und gerecht, dass er uns die Sünden vergibt und reinigt uns von aller Ungerechtigkeit (1 Joh 1,9). Im Namen Jesu Christi sind euch eure Sünden vergeben.

G Amen. Dank sei Gott!

Lied

Verkündigung

Alttestamentliche Schriftlesung

E Siehe, es kommt die Zeit, spricht der Herr, da will ich mit dem Hause Israel und mit dem Hause Juda einen neuen Bund schließen, nicht wie der Bund gewesen ist, den ich mit ihren Vätern schloss, als ich sie bei der Hand nahm, um sie aus Ägyptenland zu führen, ein Bund, den sie nicht gehalten haben, ob ich gleich ihr Herr war, spricht der Herr; sondern das soll der Bund sein, den ich mit dem Hause Israel schließen will nach dieser Zeit, spricht der Herr: »Ich will mein Gesetz in ihr Herz geben und in ihren Sinn schreiben, und sie sollen mein Volk sein und ich will ihr Gott sein. Und es wird keiner den andern noch ein Bruder den andern lehren und sagen: Erkenne den Herrn, sondern sie sollen mich alle erkennen, beide, Klein und Groß, spricht der Herr; denn ich will ihnen ihre Missetat vergeben und ihrer Sünde nimmermehr gedenken« (Jer 31, 31–34).

Lobpreis

Neutestamentliche Schriftlesung

E Jesus Christus spricht: Ich bin der Weinstock, ihr seid die Reben. Wer in mir bleibt und ich in ihm, der bringt viel Frucht; denn ohne mich könnt ihr nichts tun. Wer nicht in mir bleibt, der wird weggeworfen wie eine Rebe und verdorrt, und man sammelt sie und wirft sie ins Feuer und sie müssen brennen. Wenn ihr in mir bleibt und meine Worte in euch bleiben, werdet ihr bitten, was ihr wollt, und es wird euch widerfahren. Darin wird mein Vater verherrlicht, dass ihr viel Frucht bringt und werdet meine Jünger (Joh 15, 5–8).

Lobpreis
Predigt/Zeugnisse
Chorlied/Musikstück
Hinführung zur Erneuerung des Bundes

E Liebe Schwestern und Brüder: Christus ist der Mittler des neuen Bundes, den Gott mit uns geschlossen hat. Mit seinem eigenen Blut hat er ihn für immer besiegelt. Christus hat uns damit zu einem Leben berufen, das durch ihn von der Sünde befreit und Gott geweiht ist.

E Die eine Seite des Bundes ist Gottes Verheißung, dass er in uns und durch uns all das erfüllen will, was er in Jesus Christus, dem Anfänger und Vollender unseres Glaubens, zugesagt hat. Sichtbarer Ausdruck der Zuwendung Gottes zu uns ist die Taufe. Wir sind gewiss, dass seine Zusage auch jetzt gilt; denn Tag für Tag haben wir seine Güte erfahren und die Zuverlässigkeit seiner Gnade erlebt.

E Die andere Seite des Bundes ist unsere Verpflichtung, nicht mehr für uns selbst, sondern für ihn zu leben; denn er hat uns geliebt und sich für uns dahingegeben. Er hat uns berufen, ihm zu dienen, damit die Absicht seines Kommens erfüllt wird.

E Bei verschiedenen Gelegenheiten bekräftigen wir unsere Hingabe an Gott, vor allem, wenn wir uns am Tisch des Herrn versammeln. Heute sind wir, wie Generationen vor uns, mit der ausdrücklichen Absicht zusammengekommen, freudig und feierlich diesen Bund zu erneuern, den Gott mit ihnen und uns geschlossen hat.

Lied
Erneuerung des Bundes

P Liebe Schwestern und Brüder: Wir wollen jetzt diesen Bund befestigen und den Weg Christi gehen. Wir sind bereit, uns von ihm unseren Platz und Dienst zuweisen zu lassen. Er selbst ist unser Lohn.
Christus hat viele Dienste, die getan werden müssen; einige sind leicht, andere sind schwer; einige bringen Ehre, andere bringen Schmach; einige entsprechen unseren natürlichen Neigungen und Begabungen, andere widersprechen ihnen. In einigen können wir Christus und uns selbst gefallen; in anderen können wir Christus nur gefallen, wenn wir uns selbst verleugnen. Die Kraft aber, all dies

zu erfüllen, ist uns verheißen in Christus, der uns stärkt. Deshalb wollen wir uns erneut Gott hingeben, auf seine Verheißungen vertrauen und uns auf seine Gnade verlassen.

Ewiger Gott, du hast uns in Jesus Christus berufen, an deinem Bund teilzuhaben. Mit Freude gehen wir den Weg des Gehorsams. Wir verpflichten uns aus Liebe zu dir, deinen vollkommenen Willen zu suchen und zu tun. Wir gehören nicht mehr uns selbst, sondern dir.

A Ich gehöre nicht mehr mir, sondern dir. Stelle mich, wohin du willst. Geselle mich, zu wem du willst. Lass mich wirken, lass mich dulden. Brauche mich für dich, oder stelle mich für dich beiseite. Erhöhe mich für dich, erniedrige mich für dich. Lass mich erfüllt sein, lass mich leer sein. Lass mich alles haben, lass mich nichts haben. In freier Entscheidung und von ganzem Herzen überlasse ich alles deinem Willen und Wohlgefallen.

Herrlicher und erhabener Gott, Vater, Sohn und Heiliger Geist: Du bist mein, und ich bin dein. So soll es sein. Bestätige im Himmel den Bund, den ich jetzt auf Erden erneuert habe. Amen.

Lied

Es folgt das Abendmahl, beginnend mit den Einsetzungsworten.

Holger Eschmann

Celebration of the Renewal of God's Covenant

A worship of the United Methodist Church

1. Preface to the celebration from the 1993 order of worship

The gospel introduces us to the new covenant in Jesus Christ. The Christian church is a fellowship of the covenant; it is the community of all who were admitted to God's covenant of grace by use of the means of grace in obedience of faith. In the history of the Methodist Church, the idea of the covenant has played an important role. This order of worship is an offer to celebrate the renewal of God's covenant with the congregation. It is our answer to the proclamation of the gospel, offering our life once more to God in a celebratory form. For God's covenant with us and our covenant with him are inseparable.

On 25 December 1747, John Wesley urged the members of his communities to renew their covenant with God. His first Covenant Service was celebrated on 11 August 1755. Wesley published it in 1780. This form was used for nearly 100 years without any change. Then it was heavily amended, until a version was found which included more participation of the congregation. Knowing the importance of this service, the present text was created.

Originally, the service for the renewal of the covenant was celebrated at the end of year, on the first Sunday of the new year or on other relevant occasions in the life of the congregation, later also at conferences and meetings. This was meant to emphasize: »We want to turn to our Lord with renewed commitment. Based on this trust, we are ready to take on responsibility in his service.« Today, this form of service can be used for suitable occasions in the congregation, such as at the beginning of an evangelistic initiative. Parts of it can also be used in the framework of other celebrations.

The renewal of this covenant with God is exclusively based on God's new covenant with us. For this reason, we remember with gratitude that we have been baptized into this covenant in Christ and have confessed to it when we became members of the church. In this sense, we celebrate a form of baptismal remembrance.

The new covenant is best expressed in the celebration of communion. This is why it is included in our service for the renewal of the covenant. However, it can also be celebrated without communion.

Instead of the version of 1993, we present the »Celebration of the Renewal of God's Covenant« as printed in the worship book of the United Methodist Church in Germany, Austria and Switzerland/France of 2002 under no. 776, currently in use by the congregations.

2. Liturgy

Gathering

P In the name of God the Father, the Son and the Holy Spirit. Amen.

Plea for a clean heart

C 'Almighty God! You see our heart. All our desires are known to you. No secret is hidden from you. Cleanse our hearts and thoughts and imbue them with your Holy Spirit so that we may love you wholly and honour your holy name in gratitude; through Jesus Christ, our Lord. Amen.

Song

Prayer of thanksgiving

P God, our Father, source of all things. You have been gracious to us through all the years of our lives. We thank you for your loving care, which has filled our days and brought us to this time and place.

C You have given us life and reason, and set us in a world filled with your glory. You have comforted us with family and friends, and ministered to us through the hands of our sisters and brothers.

P You have filled our hearts with a hunger after you, and have given us your peace. You have redeemed us, and called us to a high calling in Christ Jesus. You have given us a place in the fellowship of your Spirit and the witness of your Church.

C You have been our light in darkness and a rock of strength in adversity and temptation. You have been the very Spirit of joy in our joys and the all-sufficient reward in all our labours.

P You remembered us when we forgot you. You followed us even when we tried to flee from you. You met us with forgiveness when we returned to you.

For all your patience and overflowing grace, we praise your holy name, oh God.

A Amen.

Song

Confession of sin

P God, our Father, you have shown us the way of life in your Son. We confess that we struggle to learn from him and hesitate to follow him. You have called us, and we have not paid heed. Your glory has appeared, and we have been blind. You have reached out to us, and we have receded. We have received a lot and given little thanks. We do not deserve your love.

C Lord, have mercy on us and forgive us.

(may also be sung)

P Forgive us if we have wasted our time and misused our gifts. Forgive us if we have found excuses for our own failures or refused our responsibility. Forgive us if we did not let others feel your love.

C Lord, have mercy on us and forgive us.

(may also be sung)

Promise of forgiveness

P If we confess our sins, he who is faithful and just will forgive us our sins and cleanse us from all unrighteousness (1 John 1:9). In the name of Jesus Christ, your sins are forgiven.

C Amen. Thanks be to God.

Song
Proclamation
Old Testament reading

L The days are surely coming, says the Lord, when I will make a new covenant with the house of Israel and the house of Judah. It will not be like the covenant that I made with their ancestors when I took them by the hand to bring them out of the land of Egypt – a covenant that they broke, though I was their husband, says the Lord. But this is the covenant that I will make with the house of Israel after those days, says the Lord: I will put my law within them, and I will write it on their hearts; and I will be their God, and they shall be my people. No longer shall they teach one another, or say to each other, »Know the Lord,« for they shall all know me, from the least of them to the greatest, says the Lord; for I will forgive their iniquity, and remember their sin no more (Jeremiah 31:31–34).

Worship
New Testament reading

L Jesus Christ says: I am the vine, you are the branches. Those who abide in me and I in them bear much fruit, because apart from me you can do nothing. Whoever does not abide in me is thrown away like a branch and withers; such branches are gathered, thrown into the fire, and burned. If you abide in me, and my words abide in you, ask for whatever you wish, and it will be done for you. My Father is glorified by this, that you bear much fruit and become my disciples (John 15:5–8).

Worship
Sermon/Witness
Choir/Music
Introduction to the renewal of the covenant

L Brothers and sisters: Jesus Christ is the mediator of the new covenant that God has made with us. He sealed it with his own blood, that it

might last forever. Thus Christ has called us to a life which is redeemed from sin through him and consecrated to God.
On the one side, God promises to give us new life in Christ, the source and perfecter of our faith. Baptism is the visible expression of God's love for us. We are certain that his promise is still valid, for we have experienced his graciousness day by day, and have seen the faithfulness of his grace.
On the other side, we are pledged to live no more for ourselves but only for Jesus Christ, who loved us and gave himself for us. He has called us to serve him, so the purpose of his coming may be fulfilled.
From time to time we renew our covenant with God, especially when we gather at the Lord's table. Today, however, we meet, as the generations before us have met, to joyfully and solemnly renew the covenant that binds us to God.

Song
Renewal of the covenant

P Brothers and sisters: We shall now renew this covenant and walk the path of Christ. We are ready to be given our place and work by him. He himself is our reward.
Christ has many services to be done. Some are more easy and honourable, others are more difficult and disgraceful. Some are suitable to our inclinations and interests, others are contrary to both. In some we may please Christ and please ourselves. But then there are other works where we cannot please Christ except by denying ourselves. The strength to do all this is promised to us in Christ. Therefore we want to give us again to God, to trust his promise and rely on his graciousness.
Eternal God, you have called us in Jesus Christ to partake in your covenant. We walk the path of obedience with joy. Out of love to you, we pledge to seek and do your perfect will. We are no longer our own, but yours.

A I am no longer mine, but yours. Put me where you want me to be. Put me with whom you want me to be with. Put me to doing, put me to suffering. Let me be employed for you, or laid aside for you. Rise me up for you, humble me for you. Let me be full, let me be empty. Let

me have all things, let me have nothing. I freely and with a willing heart give it all to your pleasure and disposal.
Glorious and exalted God, Father, Son and Holy Spirit: You are mine, and I am yours. So be it. And let the covenant I have made on earth be ratified in heaven. Amen.

Song
Words of institution and Communion

Duncan MacLaren / Susan Mansfield

Refugio: A Contemplative Eucharist

Protestant Eucharistic practice and Ignatian spirituality

Refugio is an inter-denominational Eucharist which takes place in Edinburgh every month. It celebrates the Eucharist in the context of reflective prayer. According to one description:

»Refugio takes its name from the shelters where pilgrims on the ancient route to Santiago de Compostela stop and find rest on their journey. Refugio is a stopping place for today's pilgrims, a monthly Communion set in the context of silence, symbol, and reflective prayer. It is led by a team drawn from a variety of backgrounds, and is open to all who seek quietness amid the busyness of life.«[1]

1. Origins

Refugio grew out of the experience of a group of friends, most of whom had been trained around the same time in Spiritual Accompaniment and Spiritual Direction in the Ignatian tradition. This training course took place over three years in Edinburgh, and was offered by the Epiphany Group, a community of practitioners working from the living tradition of Ignatian spirituality. They describe their aim as »[to help people] discover their identity in Christ and to live it more fully in the faith community that nurtures them«[2]. It was the chance comment of one of the teachers on this course – expressing a longing for a Eucharist set in the context of reflective prayer – which led to the beginning of Refugio.

---

[1] Refugio advertising flyer, unpublished, 2013, showing monthly dates January-June.

[2] http://www.epiphanygroup.org.uk/about-us/ (accessed 18.02.2018).

This comment captured a thirst among some of the course attenders to see contemplative approaches to prayer become more integrated into the regular worship of the Church and, at the same time, for our experience of corporate reflective prayer to be enhanced or ›completed‹ by Eucharistic worship.

Refugio began in February 2010 as a Sunday evening Eucharist at St James Episcopal Church, Leith, a district of Edinburgh. The original planning group included two Anglican priests, Duncan MacLaren and James Stewart, and four lay people trained, to different degrees, in reflective spirituality: Catherine Garrod, Susan Mansfield, Mollie Paterson and Elizabeth White.

The Anglican (Scottish Episcopal) origins of Refugio are perhaps not surprising. In the Scottish context, by far the largest denominations are the Roman Catholic Church and the (Presbyterian) Church of Scotland. The Catholic Church has arguably less freedom than the Anglicans to innovate around the Eucharist, and the Church of Scotland does not have a tradition of frequent celebration of the Eucharist. The Scottish Episcopal Church has a tradition of weekly communion, and a developing commitment to sharing this ecumenically, through, for example, the European Lutheran and Anglican Churches that come under the Porvoo Agreement.

That said, within a year Refugio had moved premises from St James Leith to the historic Greyfriars Church in Edinburgh, a Church of Scotland congregation that were themselves experimenting with innovative forms of reflective prayer, creating projects such as Nitekirk[3]. As well as giving Refugio a city-centre home, and a more dramatic setting, this welcome into a Church of Scotland building underlined the ecumenical nature of Refugio and the right of Eucharistic ministers from more than one denomination to take part.

As the years passed, the original team of six who started Refugio began to move on to different projects. Others stepped in to help, coming mostly from Anglican or Presbyterian traditions. More recently, Refugio was taken more formally under the organisational umbrella of Greyfriars Kirk, but continues to be offered by and for people from a range of traditions.

3 https://nitekirk.org/about/ (accessed 18.02.2018).

2. Distinctives

Although not unique in its approach, Refugio is perhaps unusual (and innovative) in a number of ways. For one, it does not claim to offer the worship of any one denomination. In practice its Eucharist is rooted in the Protestant tradition, while its contemplative dimension is inspired by (Catholic) Ignatian spirituality.

Secondly, the liturgical context for the Eucharist does not follow the patterns of any one prayer book, but takes its inspiration from contemporary expressions of contemplative prayer. This means it makes use of extended periods of silence, guided meditations, pre-recorded music, poetry, art and even body-work. These aspects form the bulk of the service, and are usually led by lay people skilled in contemplative approaches.

Thirdly, the physical setting of Refugio has been shaped by practices in reflective prayer, rather than by the historic norms of church architecture. Typically, those attending will sit in a circle, gathered around a symbolic focal point, which has been constructed for that event.

Fourthly, Refugio may, or may not, draw upon the lectionary themes for that week; but it does tend to offer a thematic focus, and this is presented in the symbolic centre-piece, guided meditation, prayers, and so on.

Lastly, the inter-denominational nature of this Eucharist means that priests and ministers from a variety of denominations are able to preside. This inevitably brings up questions of authority, and points up possible tensions between the policies of specific denominations, and the actions of their ministers. However, it is a tacit conviction of those who founded Refugio that the Eucharist does not belong to any one denomination, but to the whole Church.

3. Creating Refugio

In creating a typical Refugio meeting, we would begin by preparing the space. We learned, implicitly, during our training in reflective spirituality the value of creating a contemplative space into which we could welcome people. The chairs would be arranged in a circle – as numbers at Refugio remained quite small, we never had to address the issue of what to do if the circle became too large! While Greyfriars Kirk is a large gothic-style building with a seating capacity of several hundred, we found that lighting could be used effectively to create an intimate space for a smaller group in the heart of the building.

A further act of preparation was to build a visual centrepiece to reflect the theme of the service. Candles and coloured cloth would be arranged on a low table, or on the floor. Sometimes, an icon or painting would be used, or material relating to the seasons – daffodils for spring, for example, or coloured leaves for autumn. In September 2011, we realised that the date for that month's Refugio fell on the tenth anniversary of 9/11. One member of the group brought a centrepiece of broken and charred wood, and we placed candles amongst this »wreckage«. For the reflection that evening, we used words from 9/11 survivors and others affected by the disaster, about how they found hope in this darkest of times.

Once people arrived and were seated, we would *welcome* them and *explain the format of the service*; we did this every month because there were always new faces, and we knew that this style of service would be new for most people. At the beginning of the service, one of the team would guide the group in a stilling exercise. This might take the form of a body awareness exercise, a focus on breathing, or simply being in the moment. We recognised that it is not always easy to step out of the busyness of life into a place of stillness and quietness; our minds usually need help to slow down and lay aside the distractions.

Typically, the next step would be to offer a *guided meditation*. We found it helpful to split the tasks between us as a team so that no one person had the workload of preparing an entire service. The reflections would vary a great deal depending on the theme and the style of the person leading. Sometimes, we would structure our reflection around one of the traditional forms of prayer from the Benedictine or Ignatian traditions, such as Lectio Divina or Imaginative Contemplation. Rather than assume people were familiar with these traditions, we would offer prompts and questions, reading the relevant passage of Scripture aloud so they didn't need to refer to a Bible. The emphasis was not on giving a homily or directing people's thoughts, but on creating a space which allowed each person to explore the aspect of the material they felt drawn to, and ask how it might speak to them.

We often took *creative approaches* to themes. Poetry might be used –

George Herbert, Mary Oliver and T S Eliot all featured, and we drew on the spiritual writings of figures such as G. K. Chesterton, Henri Nouwen and Thomas Merton. We used music from a range of traditions, from classical and Celtic to Taize chants. One evening, the person leading the reflection brought along a plate of lemons which she passed around the group. We were each invited to examine our lemon in detail, appreciating the features which made it unique. Later, she invited us to take our lemons home to make gin and tonic!

One of the things we became aware of in creating Refugio was how church services are often full of words: hymns and prayers, church notices and homilies – words, words, words. In aiming to create a reflective service, we wanted to guard against simply replacing one kind of talking with another. We always made space for silence, sometimes a block of silence of about ten minutes, at other times, shorter intermittent silences. As leaders, we learned about »holding« a group in a period of silence. Reflective music was also used as another way of inviting people into a wordless space.

The traditional Anglican Eucharist also involves many words – just consider how many pages it takes up in the average service book! In thinking about how to offer a Eucharist more reflectively, we would sometimes use elements of the traditional Episcopal liturgies alongside periods of silence. We also found other liturgical material to draw on, such as the creative liturgies written by the Iona Community.

Sometimes the *bread and wine* would be served by the celebrant to those seated in the circle; often people would serve one another. The welcome at the beginning of the service always included an explanation about the Eucharist and the tradition from which it was offered, allowing people the choice to take part or not, as they felt comfortable. On a handful occasions, no ordained person was available and we offered a »bread and wine sharing« by lay people, again signaling this clearly at the outset. The service would end with a *closing blessing*, and an invitation to remain seated in the circle (a place of quietness) or to join us for tea and coffee.

We found the congregation at Refugio was a fluid group, a mixture of visitors and regulars, which is perhaps of a reflection of its role as a »stopping place on the journey«. Sitting outside a specific denomination, it drew people from a range of backgrounds. Some were members of »busier« churches but enjoyed the opportunity to experience quietness in an evening service. Others came from contemplative traditions such as Quakerism. It was also a sheltering place for some who were not able to find a home within existing congregations. One person wrote, after an early service: »It was great to realise I was actually in a ›proper church service‹ and feeling comfortable.«

Many told us that Refugio »filled a niche«. The fact that it continues to run, eight years after it began, is perhaps testament to this. Attendance is not large, but for some people, it continues to be the right place at the right time. We believe that it indicates that the potential for a reflective approach to Eucharistic worship is worthy of further investigation, and could be a valuable component if further integrated into the ongoing practices of the Churches.

Susanna Meyer

Berner West-Gottesdienst

Liturgie vom 2. November 2017[1]

1. Die Zielgruppe

30.000 Menschen, 17.000 Arbeitsplätze – das ist der Westen von Bern, der Hauptstadt der Schweiz. Von diesen Menschen aus etwa 130 Ländern gehören 11.000 zu einer der beiden evangelisch-reformierten Kirchengemeinden Bethlehem und Bümpliz. Der Berner West-Gottesdienst ist von Gemeindegliedern getragen – theologische Amateure und andere –, die sich beteiligen und zur Beteiligung locken möchten. Junge Musiker rhythmisieren die Feier mit Pop, Soul und Kirchenliedern. Im »Tränenteil« stehen fünf Möglichkeiten zur Wahl. Im Abendmahl und im anschließenden Nachtessen teilen wir, was wir mitbringen.

Der West-Gottesdienst entstand aus dem Bedürfnis einer Gemeindegruppe, Gottesdienste so zu feiern, dass »ihre« Musik vorkommt. So ist denn der eigentliche rote Faden dieser Feiern ein Musikteam, das mit Liedern und Musik die Stimmung prägt.

Zielgruppe sind Menschen der Altersgruppe 40–60, und zwar jene Menschen, die sich von traditionellen Gottesdiensten weniger angesprochen fühlen oder die mal Abwechslung wünschen: eine andere Form, wo sie Nähe und Distanz im Rahmen der Feier anders gestalten können als im »normalen« Gottesdienst. Seit 2012 wird dieser Gottesdienst viermal

[1] Vorbereitungsteam: Bernhard Christen, Martha Felber, Brigitte Fuchs, Christoph Furer, Elisabeth Gerber, Annekäthi Graf, Daniel Infanger, Silvia Kernen, Philipp Koenig, Marianne Locher, Christine Marending, Judith Pörksen, Stefan Ramseier, Hans Martin Roder, Eric Rolli, Maya Rolli, Ursula Schuster, Christine Schwab, Anna Schroeder, Urs Steinemann, Eveline Wagner, Beatrice Weichelt und Matthias Zürcher.

jährlich gefeiert und ist bei Menschen unterschiedlichen Alters und verschiedener Herkunft beliebt. Partizipation, Zusammenarbeit mit der Nachbarkirchgemeinde, lockere Atmosphäre, Zeitpunkt, erfrischend andere Musik – diese Merkpunkte unterscheiden ihn von anderen Gottesdiensten.

2. Die Vorbereitung

Zwei oder drei Wochen vorher treffen sich fünf bis zehn Leute aus dem Berner Westen, um den Gottesdienst gemeinsam vorzubereiten. Der Rahmen der Liturgie steht fest und ist immer gleich; das Thema wird jeweils an einem Jahrestreffen gemeinsam gewählt. So diskutieren wir ausführlich, vielfältig und kontrovers über das vorgeschlagene Thema wie »Schamlos«, »Weiter Raum«, »Gehorche!«, »Salz der Gesellschaft«, »Sich selber vergeben«, »Zusammenspiel« oder über die Jahreslosung, die am 1. Januar jeweils das Thema vorgibt. Unsere je persönlichen Zugänge zu Thema und Bibeltext stehen im Vordergrund. Eine Pfarrperson moderiert das Treffen, streut historisch-kritisches und theologisches Wissen ein und wählt die erwachsenenbildnerischen Methoden für den Austausch. Am Schluss des Treffens werden die Aufgaben für den Gottesdienst verteilt; alle wählen ihre Rolle selbst: Begrüsser, Salbender, Fürbitter, Tischdecker, Verkündiger und Segnender. Beim Abendmahl wirken vier bis sechs Leute mit, Ordinierte und Nicht-Ordinierte gemeinsam. Die Musikgruppe, bestehend aus zwei oder drei jungen Musikern, wird über alle Entscheide informiert und gebeten, passende Songs und Lieder einzuüben.

3. Die Rolle der Pfarrperson

Der Berner West-Gottesdienst ist ein Beteiligungs-Gottesdienst. Er wird getragen von engagierten Menschen aus der Gemeinde. Die Rolle der Pfarrperson verändert sich dadurch. Sie ist

- Erwachsenenbildnerin: Sie strukturiert das vorbereitende Treffen methodisch-didaktisch und gestaltet Lern- und Diskussionsorte.

- Liturgin: Sie coacht die beteiligten Gemeindeglieder rhetorisch, theologisch und liturgisch und befähigt sie dazu, ihre Rolle in der Liturgie authentisch auszufüllen und der Gemeinde zu dienen.
- Seelsorgerin: Die Teilete (das gemeinsame Essen) nach dem Gottesdienst ermöglicht viele Begegnungen mit der Gemeinde; es ist gut möglich, dass Menschen von der Feier berührt oder aufgewühlt sind und seelsorgerliche Begleitung - auch in der Zeit nach der Feier - gern in Anspruch nehmen.

4. Die Einstimmung

Eineinhalb Stunden vor Gottesdienstbeginn, sonntags um 15.30 Uhr, treffen sich alle, die den Gottesdienst mitverantworten, um die jeweilige Kirche einzurichten. Wir wechseln zwischen der reformierten Kirche in Bern-Bethlehem und der reformierten Kirche in Bern-Bümpliz ab. Zusammen mit der Sigristin stellen wir die Tische für die Teilete auf, stellen Teller und Besteck bereit, dekorieren die Tische, oft dem Thema des Gottesdienstes entsprechend. Wir stellen Brot und Traubensaft für das Abendmahl bereit, richten den Ort für die Kerzen, für den Tränenkrug, für die Fürbitten und für das Salben ein. Wir streben schlichte Schönheit an und wollen eine Übermöblierung des Kirchenraums vermeiden. Auch die Musikgruppe braucht einen Ort im Chor; der Pianist, die Sängerin, die Kontrabassistin sind für alle sichtbar.
Gemeinsam üben wir das Abendmahl: Wer spricht welche Sätze? Wer steht wo? Wie teilen wir das Brot genau? Und am Schluss: Wer gibt wem Becher und Brot?

5. Ablauf des Gottesdienstes

Die Einstimmung
Alle, die Zeit und Lust haben, treffen sich etwa eine halbe Stunde vor dem Gottesdienst in der Sakristei zu einer einfachen geistlichen Einstimmung:

- *Singen*: Wir singen ein Lied, das später auch im Gottesdienst gesungen wird.

- *Still werden*: Eingeführt z. B. mit den Worten: Wir genießen, dass wir da sind. Wir genießen, dass wir zusammen sind. Wir genießen, dass wir vor Gott sind in einer kurzen Stille. Du in mir – Ich in dir.
- *Anschauen*: Eingeführt z. B. mit den Worten: Wir schauen einander in die Augen. Schön, dass du da bist! Schön, dass ich da bin! Zusammen feiern wir diesen West-Gottesdienst. Zusammen feiern wir ein Fest. Zusammen mit allen Menschen, die dazukommen und sich anstecken lassen von dem, was wir ausstrahlen und Gott uns schenken will.
- *Salben*: Immer zwei, die nebeneinander stehen, segnen einander mit Öl und den Worten: N. N., du bist gesegnet von Gott, dem Vater (ein Kreuz mit Öl auf die Stirn malen), von Gott, dem Sohn (ein Kreuz mit Öl in die linke Handfläche) und von Gott, der heiligen Geistkraft (ein Kreuz mit Öl in die rechte Handfläche). Amen.
- *Segnen*: Wir stehen im Kreis, öffnen die linke Hand zum Empfangen, halten die rechte Hand über die Schulter der Nachbarin zum Weiterschenken und sprechen gemeinsam: »Segne uns, Gott, und behüte uns an Leib und Seele. Bewahre uns in deiner Liebe. Erfülle uns mit deiner Kraft. Amen.« Dieser Segen schließt jeweils auch den West-Gottesdienst ab.

Die Begrüßung

Zwei Mitglieder des Gottesdienst-Teams stehen mit schmalen Kerzen an der Eingangstür zur Kirche und begrüßen alle Mitfeiernden persönlich. Wenn die Glocken um 17 Uhr verklingen, und alle sitzen, gehen die beiden durch den Mittelgang durch die stille Kirche und zünden die Osterkerze mit ihren brennenden Kerzen an. Die schmalen Kerzen stecken sie in den Sand der Kerzenschale. Erst jetzt beginnt die Musik, oft mit einem Song, der ins Thema einstimmt. Die Begrüßung mit Worten enthält stets ein Bibelwort und macht neugierig auf das Thema des Gottesdienstes.

Die Tränen

Nach einem Gemeindelied und dem Gebet zur Sammlung laden wir ein zum »Tränenteil«:

»Wir dürfen unser Danken, Klagen und Bitten vor Gott bringen. Sie können eine Kerze anzünden. Sie können eine Träne in den Glaskrug fallen lassen – symbolisch – mit einer Glasmurmel. Sie können eine Bitte aufschreiben, die später im Fürbittengebet gelesen wird. Sie können sich segnen und salben lassen. Mit etwas Öl werden Sie beschenkt mit einem Zeichen der Zuwendung Gottes: ein Kreuz auf Ihre Stirn und/oder auf Ihre Handflächen. Sie können aber auch am Platz bleiben, die Musik genießen oder mitsingen.«

Währenddessen werden meditative Lieder gesungen.

Es gibt folgende Stationen:

- Tränenkrug – Trauer und Angst, aber auch Freude und Hoffnung zulassen und adressieren: Ein großer Krug aus Glas steht auf einem blauen Tuch, daneben eine Schale mit Glasmurmeln in verschiedenen Farben. Dazu steht in schöner Schrift auf einer Karte: Sammle meine Tränen in deinen Krug, denn bei dir sind sie aufgehoben (nach Psalm 56,9).
- Kerzen anzünden – an Menschen oder Situationen denken: In einer großen Sandschale brennen die beiden Kerzen von der Einstimmung. Jemand vom Team steht mit neuen Kerzen da und verteilt sie ohne Worte an alle, die eine Kerze anzünden wollen.
- Fürbitten – Gebete und Bitten notieren: Auf zwei Stehtischen, bedeckt mit einfarbigen Tüchern, stehen zwei Körbe: Ein Korb mit leeren A6-Karten und Stiften, daneben ein leerer Korb und eine Karte mit dem Satz: »Bitten, die im Fürbittengebet vorgelesen werden.« Eine Person aus dem Team steht dabei, sammelt anschließend die Fürbitten und ordnet sie in eine sinnvolle Reihenfolge; dazu gehört auch die Gruppierung der Bitten und die Rhythmisierung durch einen Kyrie-Ruf der Gemeinde.
- Salben – Belastendes aussprechen und Zuwendung erleben: Zwei bis drei Orte stehen für die Salbung bereit. Zwei Stühle, einander zugewandt, ein dritter Stuhl als Tisch für das kleine Salbengefäß. Die Salbungsorte stehen hinten in der Kirche, damit die Salbenden möglichst ungestört sind von entblößenden Blicken – aber im selben Raum. Wir begrüßen, wer sich auf einen der Stühle setzt, stellen uns vor und fragen nach dem Namen und dem Anliegen. Wir klären, ob sie eine Berührung wünschen, Stirn, Hände oder beides. Wir beten kurz für das erwähnte Anliegen und segnen dann die Person mit Öl (trinitarischer Segen, siehe oben).

Zurückkommen und in den Gesang mit einstimmen; das gemeinsame Singen markiert den Abschluss dieses Teils. Die Musik endet erst, wenn alle vom Salbungsteil wieder am Platz sind.

Die Verkündigung

Die Verkündigungsgruppe besteht aus zwei bis acht Personen und wählt die Formen frei: eine Theaterszene, ein Bild, das projiziert wird, ein Rundgang für die Gemeinde zu verschiedenen Stationen in der Kirche, ein Bibliolog, Cartoons auf Stellwänden, ein Hindernis-Parcours, drei Kurzpredigten, ein Interview, unterbrochen von Flüstergesprächen unter Banknachbarn, ein Ritual, bei dem alle frisches Wasser trinken …; der Fantasie sind keine Grenzen gesetzt, das Experimentieren ist erwünscht. Kriterien sind: Dient die Form den Menschen, die da sind? Hat die Form Platz im Raum? Dauert sie nicht länger als zwanzig oder fünfundzwanzig Minuten? Dient sie der Verkündigung? Sind wir als Verkündigende selbst überzeugt von Inhalt und Form?

Die Fürbitten

Nach einem Lied holt die Fürbitterin den Tränenkrug und stellt ihn auf den Abendmahlstisch. Sie betet die von der Gemeinde notierten Fürbitten im Wechsel mit einem Kyrie-Ruf der Gemeinde.

Das Teilen: Wir feiern Gottes Freundlichkeit
Einleiten

Wir feiern miteinander das Abendmahl.
Wir feiern die Freundschaft Gottes.
Wir teilen Brot und Traubensaft.
Alle sind dazu eingeladen.
Singen: Aus vielen Körnern gibt es Brot (Reformiertes Gesangbuch der Schweiz 321,1–3)
Oder: Santo, santo, santo (freiTöne 159)

Einsetzen

»Immer wenn ihr Brot teilt, immer wenn ihr aus dem gleichen Becher trinkt, denkt an mich«, hat Jesus gesagt.
Wir erinnern uns an Jesus von Nazareth. Er aß gern, er trank gern. Mit seinen Freundinnen und Freunden, mit Zöllnern und Sündern.

Als Jesus ermordet worden war in Jerusalem, gingen seine Freundinnen und Freunde zurück an den See Genezareth. Sie wollten Fische fangen. In dieser Nacht aber fingen sie nichts. Als der Morgen graute, erschien ihnen der auferstandene Jesus am Ufer und sagte: »Kommt, esst«. Ähnlich wie bei seinem letzten Passah-Essen, als er Brot nahm und sagte: »Das ist mein Leib, der für euch gegeben wird. Dies tut zu meinem Gedächtnis!«
(Brot zeigen, kurze Pause) Das ist sein Leben, es kommt uns zugute.

Ebenso nahm er den Becher nach dem Essen und sagte: »Dieser Becher ist der neue Bund in meinem Blut, das für euch vergossen wird.«

(Becher zeigen, kurze Pause) Das ist sein Sterben, es kommt uns zugute. Dies soll das Abendmahl heute auch für uns sein:

Es soll uns stärken für den Weg, der vor uns liegt. Es soll uns klarmachen: Wir sind nicht allein. Gott ist mit uns, auch wenn wir ihn nicht sehen. Genauso erging es den Jüngern: Sie wussten nicht, wie es weitergehen sollte; aber Gott war mit ihnen und hatte noch viel Großes mit ihnen vor. Im Feiern des Abendmahls will Gott uns schon heute etwas von der künftigen Gemeinschaft aller Menschen in seiner Nähe spüren lassen.

Beten
Geheimnisvoller Gott,
wir erinnern uns an Jesus von Nazaret.
Er hat die Menschen zu sich gerufen,
er hat sie geheilt,
seine Worte haben berührt,
getröstet und ermutigt.
Wir erinnern uns daran, wie Jesus Brot und Wein,
aber auch Freude und Kummer geteilt und verwandelt hat.
Wenn wir uns an sein Leiden und Sterben erinnern,
werden wir hellsichtig für die Leiden und das Elend heute.
Seine Auferstehung schenkt uns Hoffnung:
Dieses Brot und dieser Kelch verbinden uns mit allen,
die auf Gottes Verheißungen vertrauen und miteinander unterwegs sind.

Unser Vater im Himmel (beten in der bekannten Form)
Komm, schöpferische Geistkraft,
zu uns, zu diesem Brot, zu diesem Traubensaft.
Wir geben uns ein Zeichen des Friedens. (Friedensgruß)

Teilen
Kommt und esst vom Brot des Lebens. Kommt und trinkt vom Kelch der Freude.

Während des Abendmahls Instrumentalmusik oder Taizé-Lieder.
Danken
Wir danken dir, Gott, dass du dein Leben geteilt hast.
Wir danken dir, dass wir miteinander essen, trinken und teilen können.
Du richtest uns auf und gibst uns Kraft, schenkst Hoffnung und Lebensfreude.
Amen.

Einladung zur Teilete
Lied
Segen

Segne uns, Gott,
und behüte uns an Leib und Seele.
Bewahre uns in deiner Liebe,
erfülle uns mit deiner Kraft.
Amen.

Musik
Den Segen sprechen die beiden selben Personen, die am Anfang die Kerzen hineingetragen haben; beide stehen auch wieder am Ausgang und verabschieden die Gemeinde persönlich.

Das Essen
Alle, die wollen, können eine Speise für das gemeinsame Nachtessen mitbringen, ein kleines Brot, ein Stück Käse, einen Salat, einen Früchtekuchen oder eine Packung Kekse. Alles wird im Saal schön arrangiert und alle können sich von allem bedienen.

Susanna Meyer

Berner West Service

Liturgy of 2 November 2017[1]

1. Target group

30,000 people, 17,000 jobs – this is the West side of Bern, Switzerland's capital. Out of these people from about 130 different countries, 11,000 belong to one of the two Protestant Reformed congregations Bethlehem and Bümpliz. The Berner West service is supported by members of the congregation – theological amateurs and others – who wish to contribute and to encourage participation. Young musicians accompany the service with pop, soul and church hymns. There are five different possibilities for the »tears section«. In the Communion and the following dinner we share with each other what we have brought.

The Berner West service resulted from the wish of a congregational group to celebrate a service with »their« kind of music. The common thread of this service is the band creating the specific atmosphere with their songs and music.

The target group is comprised of people aged 40–60, people who do not feel involved in traditional services or who welcome a change: a different form where they can experience closeness and distance in a different way from a regular service setting. Since 2012, this service has been celebrated four times a year; it is popular among people of different

---

[1] Members of the team: Bernhard Christen, Martha Felber, Brigitte Fuchs, Christoph Furer, Elisabeth Gerber, Annekäthi Graf, Daniel Infanger, Silvia Kernen, Philipp Koenig, Marianne Locher, Christine Marending, Judith Pörksen, Stefan Ramseier, Hans Martin Roder, Eric Rolli, Maya Rolli, Ursula Schuster, Christine Schwab, Anna Schroeder, Urs Steinemann, Eveline Wagner, Beatrice Weichelt and Matthias Zürcher.

age groups and backgrounds. Participation, cooperation with the neighbouring congregation, a casual atmosphere, time, refreshingly different music – these aspects are what differentiates this service from other services.

2. Preparation

Two to three weeks in advance, five to ten people from the West side of Bern meet to prepare the service together. The liturgical framework is fixed and always the same; the topics are chosen by everybody in an annual meeting. These discussions are comprehensive, diverse and controversial; suggested topics include »Shameless«, »Broad place«, »Obey!«, »Salt of the society«, »Forgiving yourself«, »Interaction« or the Bible quote for the year, which is always the topic for 1 January. Our individual approach to the topic and Bible text is in the foreground. A pastor moderates the meeting, helps with historical-critical and theological background information and selects the pedagogical methodology for our discussions. At the end, everybody chooses their preferred role for the service: Welcome, anointing, intercessions, setting the table, proclamation or blessing. Four to six people help with Communion, ordained and laypeople together. The band, which is comprised of two or three young musicians, is informed about the planned service and asked to select appropriate songs.

3. The role of the pastor

Berner West Service is based on participation. It is conducted by committed members of the congregation. This changes the role of the pastor. He or she provides:

- Pedagogy: He/she is responsible for the methodological and didactic structure of the preparatory meeting and prepares a space for learning and discussion.
- Liturgy: He/she teaches the participating laypeople the necessary rhetorical, theological and liturgical skills and enables them to authentically serve the congregation in this liturgical capacity.

- Pastoral care: The shared meal after the service enables many encounters with the congregation; it is possible that people are touched or emotional after the service and gladly accept pastoral accompaniment, also in the time after the service.

4. Attunement

One and a half hours before the service, at 3:30 pm on a Sunday, the team meets to prepare the church for the service. We alternate between the Reformed Church in Bern-Bethlehem and the Reformed Church in Bern-Bümpliz. Together with the sexton, we set up the tables for the shared meal, supply plates and cutlery and decorate the tables, often according to the theme of the service. We put bread and grape juice for Communion in place and prepare corners for candles, for the jug of tears, for intercessions and for the anointment. We strive for simple beauty and try to avoid overcrowding the church. The band needs a space at the front, too; the pianist, the singer and the bass player are visible to everybody.

Together we practice the Communion sequence: Who speaks which lines? Who stands where? How exactly do we share the bread? And at the end: Who gives cup and bread to whom?

5. Structure of the service

Attunement

All who are interested and have the time meet half an hour before the service starts in the vestry for a simple spiritual attunement:

- *Singing:* We sing a song which will also be sung later in the service.
- *Silence:* Introduced by words like: We enjoy being here. We enjoy being together. We enjoy being before God in a brief silence. You in me – I in you.
- *Looking:* Introduced by words like: We look into each other's eyes. It is good that you are here! It is good that I am here! We celebrate this service together. Together with all people who join us and want to be touched by what we radiate and what God wants to give us.

- *Anointment*: In pairs, we bless each other with oil and the following words: »[Name], you are blessed by God the Father (draw a cross of oil onto the forehead), by God the Son, (a cross of oil onto the left palm) and God the Holy Spirit (a cross of oil onto the right palm). Amen.«
- *Blessing:* We stand in a circle, open the left hand for receiving, hold the right hand over the neighbour's shoulder for giving and speak the following words together: »Bless us, God, and watch over our body and soul. Keep us in your love. Fill us with your strength. Amen.« This blessing also concludes each service.

Welcome

Two team members welcome all participants in person at the entrance of the church, holding thin candles in their hands. Once the bells have rung at 5 pm and everybody is seated, the two walk through the middle aisle of the silent church and light the Paschal candle with the candles they are carrying. They stick their thin candles into the sand of the candle bowl. Only now does the music begin, usually with a song that fits the topic. The greeting always includes a Bible quote and introduces the topic of the service.

The tears

After a song and the collect we invite everybody to participate in the »tears section«:

»We may bring our thanks, laments and pleas before God. You can light a candle. You can drop a glass marble into the glass jug to symbolize a tear. You can write down a plea, which will be read later during the intercessions. You can come forward to be blessed and anointed. You will receive an oil cross on your forehead and/or your palms as a sign of God's love. But you can also stay seated, enjoy the music or sing along.« During this part, meditative songs are sung.
We have the following corners:

- *Jug of tears* – permit and address grief and fear, but also joy and hope: A big glass jug is placed on a blue cloth. Next to it is a bowl with glass marbles and different colours. A card says in beautiful writing: Put my tears in your bottle. Are they not in your record? (Psalm 56:9)

- *Light a candle* – thinking of people or situations: The two candles used for the welcome are burning in a big bowl of sand. A team member silently distributes new candles to all who want to light a candle.
- *Intercessions* – write down prayers and pleas: On two standing tables we have two baskets sitting on unicoloured cloths: One basket with small index cards and pens, one empty basket with a card that says: »Pleas to be read during intercessions«. One team member is at the tables, collects the intercessions and structures them into the order that will be read later; this includes grouping several pleas together and deciding when to include the congregation's Kyrie call in between.
- *Anointment* – speak of your troubles and be heard: There are two or three places for anointment. Two chairs are placed opposite each other, with a third chair serving as table for the ointment vessel. The places for anointment are at the back of the church to give those seeking anointment some privacy, but in a way that they are still in the same room. We greet whoever sits down on the chair, introduce ourselves and ask about the person's name and their concern. We ask whether they wish to be touched, on the forehead, on the hands or both. We pray briefly for the person's concern and then bless the person with oil (Trinitarian blessing, see above).

Come back and join the singing; the common song marks the end of this part. The music stops only once everybody is back in their seat.

Proclamation

The proclamation group is comprised of two to eight people and is free to choose their means of proclamation: A drama scene, a projected image, a walk through several stations in the church, bibliodrama, cartoons on screens, an obstacle course, three short sermons, an interview, whispering with your neighbours in the pew, a ritual where everybody drinks fresh water … There are no limits to your fantasy, experimentation is welcome. The criteria are: Does this form serve the people who are present? Is there enough space? Can it be completed in 20–25 minutes? Does it serve the purpose of proclamation? Are we as proclaimers convinced of content and form?

Intercessions
After a song, the person reading the intercessions places the jug of tears on the Communion table. He/she reads the intercessions written down by the congregation earlier, alternating with a Kyrie by the congregation.

Sharing: We celebrate God's kindness.
Introduction

We celebrate Communion together.
We celebrate God's friendship.
We share bread and grape juice.
Everybody is invited.

Song
Words of institution

»Each time you share bread, each time you drink from the same cup, think of me«, said Jesus.
We remember Jesus of Nazareth. He liked to eat, he liked to drink. With his friends, with tax collectors, with sinners.
When Jesus had been murdered in Jerusalem, his friends went back to the Sea of Galilee. They wanted to catch fish. But they did not catch any fish that night. When morning came, the risen Jesus appeared at the banks and said: »Come, eat.« Like at his last Passover supper, when he took bread and said:
»This is my body which is given for you. Do this in remembrance of me.«
(Show bread, brief pause) This is his life, it does us good.
Likewise he took the cup after supper and said: »This cup is the new covenant in my blood which is shed for you.«
(Show cup, brief pause) This is his death, it does us good.
This is to be our Communion for us today:
It will give us strength for the path ahead of us.
It will make us understand: We are not alone.
God is with us, even if we do not see him. The disciples felt the same:
They did not know how to continue, but God was with them and had great plans for them.

In celebrating Communion, God wants us to feel something of the future communion with all people at his side.

Prayer
Mysterious God,
we remember Jesus of Nazareth.
He called people to him,
he healed them,
his words touched, comforted and encouraged them.
We remember how Jesus shared and transformed bread and wine,
but also joy and sorrow.
In remembering his suffering and death,
we become attentive to today's suffering and hardship.
His resurrection gives us hope:
This bread and this cup connect us with all who have faith in God's promise and walk together.

Our Father … (pray in the form you are used to).
Come, creator Spirit, to us, to this bread, to this grape juice.
We give each other a sign of peace. (Greeting of peace)

Sharing
Come and eat the bread of life.
Come and drink the cup of joy.

Instrumental music or Taizé songs during Communion
Thanksgiving
We thank you, God, that you have shared your life.
We thank you that we can eat, drink and share together.
You lift us up and give us strength, hope and joy of life.
Amen.

Invitation to the shared meal
Song
Blessing

Bless us, God,
and watch over our body and soul.
Keep us in your love.
Fill us with your strength.
Amen.

Music

The blessing is given by the two people who have carried the candles into the church at the beginning; they now return to their place at the exit to say goodbye to everybody.

Shared meal

All who want to can bring one thing for the shared meal, like a loaf of bread, a piece of cheese, a salad, a fruit cake or a packet of biscuits. Everything is nicely arranged in the room, and everybody is free to help themselves.

Lisbeth Zogg Hohn

Das Tal im Nebel

Modell für einen generationenverbindenden Gottesdienst[1]

1. Kontext

Das Modell wurde im Rahmen des »Kirchensonntags« 2010 zum Thema: »Generationen gemeinsam unterwegs« entwickelt. Der Kirchensonntag wird im Evangelisch-reformierten Synodalverband Bern-Jura-Solothurn, Schweiz, jährlich seit 1912 im Februar gefeiert. Die Landeskirche bietet zu einem vorgegebenen Thema Materialien und Weiterbildungstagungen an. An einer solchen Tagung wurde das Modell vorgestellt, gefeiert und in die einzelnen Kirchgemeinden mitgenommen.

2. Leitung, Mitwirkende, Zielgruppe

Der Kirchensonntag wird von Freiwilligen gestaltet – mit oder ohne Beteiligung von Pfarrpersonen. Zielgruppen des vorliegenden Modells sind alle Generationen, mit Schwerpunkt Kinder und Erwachsene.

3. Zum Modell

Das Modell bietet eine Grundstruktur mit Thema, liturgischen Elementen und dem Herzstück, der Erzählung. Diese ist auch für ein Laienteam realisierbar und kann je nach Situation vor Ort angepasst werden.

Verkündigung ist weit verstanden. Sie geschieht durch Ort, Zeit, Anwesende, Stimmen, Erzählung, Liturgie. Eine Predigt ist nicht zwingend.

---

1 www.generationenwelten.ch.

Wenn doch, sollte sie an die Erzählung anknüpfen und kurz und bündig sein, während die Kinder in dieser Zeit aktiv sein können, zum Beispiel mit einer Gestaltungsarbeit, die sich aus der Geschichte ergibt.

4. Vorbereitung und Aufwand

An zwei Zusammenkünften des Teams wird das Modell zur Kenntnis genommen und der konkrete Gottesdienst entsprechend dem aktuellen Kontext ausgearbeitet. Vorschlag für die Verteilung der Rollen: Liturg, Erzähler und Bezugsperson für die Kinder, Sprecher, Verantwortliche für Musik und Raumgestaltung.

5. Texte

- Du stellst meine Füße in weiten Raum (Psalm 31,9).
- Und danach wird es geschehen, dass ich meinen Geist ausgieße über alles Fleisch; und eure Söhne und Töchter werden weissagen, eure Greise werden Träume träumen, eure Jünglinge werden Gesichte sehen. Auch über die Knechte und Mägde will ich in jenen Tagen meinen Geist ausgießen (Joel 2,28).
- »Das Licht ist an und für sich nicht zu sehen, nur an den Dingen, und auch die Dinge sind aus sich selber nicht zu sehen, sondern nur im Licht« (Martin Wagenschein)

6. Raumgestaltung

Mittelblaues Tuch für den Himmel, mit großer Sonne und Mondsichel (evtl. als Projektion). Davor Tisch mit Kerzen in den Farben des Regenbogens, jede Kerze steht für eine Generation, evtl. ergänzt mit altersentsprechenden Schuhen. Dies ergibt visuell den Generationenbogen. Kissen im Chor für die Kinder.

7. Ablauf

Empfang: Die Ankommenden werden am Eingang empfangen. Der Erzähler wendet sich an die Kinder und überreicht ihnen einen Folienstern.

Begrüßung und Grußwort: Du stellst meine Füße in weiten Raum (Psalm 31).

Unser Thema: Weiter Raum für alle Generationen, für den ganzen Generationenbogen, sodass sich Generationenfriede ausbreiten kann.

Musik: Nimmt Motive aus der Erzählung auf: Traum, Farbe, Licht, Raum

Thematische Einleitung: Liebe Kinder, jetzt sage ich gleich etwas zu den Erwachsenen. Währenddessen könnt ihr mit euren Fingernägeln die Sterne verzieren.

Liebe Erwachsene: Das Zusammenleben der Generationen ist eine schöne Vision, aber auch herausfordernd.

Es lebt vom weiten Raum

- des Miteinanders: Die Lebensalter inspirieren und bereichern einander. Jede Generation ist auf die anderen angewiesen. Sie hat gegenüber den anderen Aufgaben und Verantwortung – besonders die Erwachsenen.
- des Nebeneinanders: Jede Generation will und braucht etwas anderes. Sie muss sich selbst erfinden und bestehen. Sie braucht Raum fur sich selbst.
- des Nacheinanders: Jede und jeder von uns durchläuft die verschiedenen Lebensalter selbst: als Kinder, Jugendliche, junge Erwachsene, Mittelalterliche, Senioren.

Jede und jeder von uns hütet den Generationenbogen in sich selbst.

Gebet: Du, Gott, Du stellst meine Füße in weiten Raum. Jeder und jede soll Raum haben – zu wachsen und mit den anderen zusammen unterwegs zu sein. Wir danken dir dafür. Amen.

Lied

Einladung: Jetzt werde ich euch die Geschichte von Simon und Hannah, seiner Großmutter, erzählen. Stellt euch vor: Beide haben noch nie die Sonne, den Mond, die Sterne gesehen. Aber sie träumen davon. Deshalb steht Simon mitten in der Nacht auf, um Sonne, Mond und Sterne zu suchen. Liebe Kinder, ihr könnt ihm dabei helfen. Wir schmücken für ihn den Himmel. Kommt und hängt (klebt) eure Sterne daran. Wenn ihr möchtet, könnt ihr dann auf den Kissen hier vorne Platz nehmen.

Erzählung: Die Erzählung kann mit Klangmotiven gestaltet werden – sei es durch Instrumentalisten oder mit Beteiligung einer Kindergruppe: Wie tönt der Traum von Hannah und von Simon? Der Nebel? Wenn Simon Angst hat …? Der Fluss, die Eule? Als Simon die Sonnenwelt zum ersten Mal sieht? Das »Nein« der Regierenden? Die Verfolgungsjagd den Turm hinauf?

Eule und Fluss: Evtl. als Erzählfiguren

Das Tal im Nebel

Weit weg von hier gibt es ein Tal, eingebettet zwischen hohen Bergen.

In diesem Tal liegt eine kleine Stadt. Sie heisst Bruma.

Dort hat es immer Nebel. Tag und Nacht, jahrein, jahraus.

Es ist, wie wenn die Wolken vom Himmel auf die Erde gefallen wären.

Wenn die Leute ihr Haus verlassen, schauen sie in dickes Grau.

Der Nebel hat das Rot, das Blau und das Gelb einfach verschluckt.

Die grünen Bäume sehen aus wie schwarze Schatten.

Nur die Töne kann man durch den Nebel gut hören: das Rauschen des Bachs, den Ruf der Eule im Wald.

Die Leute, die in Bruma leben, sitzen darum am liebsten zusammen in ihren Stuben.

Dort ist es gemütlich, warm und manchmal sogar lustig.

Aber stellt euch vor: Noch nie hat ein Mensch von dort die Sonne gesehen! Noch nie!

Auch nicht den Mond. Auch nicht die Sterne.

Aber das stört die Menschen dort nicht. Sie sind zufrieden.

Und noch nie hat sich jemand gefragt, ob es vielleicht hinter dem Nebel noch eine andere Welt gäbe.

Das wäre wohl immer so geblieben, wenn da nicht Hannah gewesen wäre, eine alte Frau.

Und Simon, ihr Enkelkind.

Die beiden wohnen zusammen in einem kleinen Häuschen am Rand der Stadt.

Eines Morgens steht Hannah mit Simon in ihrem Garten.

Sie schaut hinauf zum grauen Himmel.

Ihre Augen strahlen.

»Heute Nacht hat mir geträumt, dass es jenseits der Berge noch eine andere Welt gebe.

Hell, weit und voller Farben!«
Eine andere Welt? Weit! Hell! Farbig!
Es kommt Simon vor wie sein eigener Traum.
Er nimmt seine Großmutter an der Hand: »Komm, Groma, wir suchen diese Welt.«
Doch Hannah seufzt: »Wäre das schön! Aber schau, ich bin alt – viel zu alt, um nochmals aufzubrechen.
Aber du – du bist jung und stark und mutig.
Vielleicht wirst du eines Tages auf die Berge steigen und das Licht entdecken.«
Simon ist so begeistert, dass er gleich allen Leuten von Hannahs Traum erzählt.
»Hannah hat eine andere Welt gesehen, voller Licht und Farben.
Man muss nur auf die Berge steigen.«
Doch die Leute lachen ihn nur aus:
»Was du nicht alles erzählst. Und das glaubst du deiner alten Großmutter?
Die spinnt doch. Die ist nicht mehr richtig im Kopf.«
Da wird Simon ganz still.
Warum hören die Leute nicht auf seine Großmutter?
Warum glauben sie ihm, Simon, nicht?
Enttäuscht kehrt er nach Hause zurück.
Er erzählt Hannah nichts. Aber sie merkt sofort, dass etwas nicht stimmt.
Am anderen Morgen steht Hannah wieder im Garten und schaut in den Himmel.
»Heute Nacht habe ich die Sonne gesehen.
Stell dir vor: Eine leuchtende Kugel! Ein Feuer am Himmel!
Sie ist wunderschön! Und sie gibt Wärme!«
Simon sagt nichts. Aber ihm ist, wie wenn er das selbst träumte.
Am nächsten Morgen steht sie schon wieder draußen:
»Sogar wenn es dunkel ist, stehen Lichter am Himmel.
Heute Nacht habe ich den Mond gesehen.
Er sieht aus wie ein großer Zitronenschnitz.
Und da ist ein Meer von Sternen.«
Da beschließt Simon, diese andere Welt zu suchen, mit den Farben, der Sonne, dem Mond und den Sternen.
Er muss es jetzt selbst sehen!
Vielleicht findet er sogar einen Weg,
wie auch seine geliebte Hannah die Sonne noch sehen kann, bevor sie stirbt.
Jetzt, heute.
Es wird Abend, es wird Nacht.

Simon schlüpft wie immer in sein Bett, aber er schläft nicht.
Als alles ganz ruhig ist, steht er auf, zieht sich warm an, nimmt seine Laterne und schleicht sich aus dem Haus, ganz leise.
Draußen ist es stockfinster.
Das Licht seiner Laterne wird vom Dunkel und vom Nebel verschluckt.
Es bekommt Angst.
Soll er nicht besser umkehren und wieder in sein Bett schlüpfen?
Vielleicht haben die Leute ja Recht und es ist – nichts, einfach nichts.
Aber was ist das?
Er hört ein feines Flüstern.
Der Fluss! – Er spricht ja mit ihm:
»Simon, komm, geh, weiter, weiter. Ich komme mit dir mit.
Hör einfach auf mein Rauschen. Hab keine Angst.
Du kannst mich immer hören, auch wenn du hoch oben in den Bergen bist.«
Da wagt sich Simon weiter.
Plötzlich – krrschsch, krrkk. Es knirscht und knackt.
Sind das die wilden Tiere?
Sein Herz klopft wild: Togg, zurück, togg, zurück.
Er dreht sich um, will zurück.
Aber was ist das?
Da – vor ihm leuchten zwei große runde Lichter. Er bleibt stehen.
Sind das die Sterne?
Nein, es sind die Augen der Eule.
»Uhu, Simon, hab keine Angst.
Alles ist gut. Geh weiter, ich fliege mit und wache über dich.«
Da wagt sich Simon weiter, durch den dunklen Wald, immer höher den Berg hinauf.
Der Nebel wird durchsichtiger.
Da – ein Zipfel des dunkelblauen Himmels.
Da, ein heller Streifen am Horizont.
Sein Herz klopft wild – vor Freude.
Er rennt.
Und dann erreicht Simon den Gipfel.
Die Sonne geht gerade auf.
Einige Sterne blinzeln ihm zu.
Und die Mondsichel, hoch am Himmel.
Zum ersten Mal in seinem Leben sieht er über die Bergspitzen hinaus, weit ins Land.
Es schaut zu, wie das Sonnenlicht den Wäldern, Wiesen, Blumen ihre Farben gibt.

Er sieht andere Dörfer und Städte.
Er sieht das Nebelmeer von oben.
Und er sieht die hohen Türme des Stadtpalastes.
Die ragen nämlich über den Nebel hinaus.
Er jubelt: »Hannah, du hast es gewusst! Und ich auch!«
So schnell er kann, rennt er zurück in die Stadt, direkt in den Palast.
Dort tagt gerade die Stadtregierung.
»Ich habe sie gesehen, es gibt sie, die andere Welt, voller Farben, jenseits der Berge.
Kommt, schaut!«
Doch die mächtigen Leute schauen ihn nur böse an.
»Das kann nicht sein! Einfach so in unsere Sitzung hineinzuplatzen! Frechdachs!«
Jemand sagt: »Der spinnt wohl genauso wie seine Großmutter.« Sie lachen!
Da stampft Simon auf; »Ich habe es aber gesehen! Und ihr könnt es auch sehen!
Ihr müsst nur auf eure hohen Türme steigen.
Die sind nämlich höher als der Nebel!«
»Auf die Türme hinaufsteigen ist verboten, schon immer«, schreit da der Präsident.
»Warte nur, jetzt packen wir dich und sperren dich ins Gefängnis!«
Da rennt Simon fort, hinaus.
Er rennt zum größten Turm und dort die Treppen hoch.
Die Männer hinter ihm her: »Halt! Polizei!«
Doch Simon ist jung und schnell und mutig.
Er rennt ihnen einfach davon.
Die anderen rennen hinterher. Es ist ein richtiger Umzug.
Zuvorderst Simon. Dann die Polizisten.
Und zuhinderst – außer Atem, keuchend – die ganze Stadtregierung.
Als sie oben ankommen, ist es einen Moment lang – einfach – still.
Jetzt sehen sie es selber.
Wie über dem Nebel die Sonne scheint.
Dass es noch eine andere Welt gibt als jene, die sie kennen: reich, farbig, weit.
Simon aber lässt die Leute einfach stehen.
Er rennt heim zu seiner Großmutter.
»Hannah! Ich habe sie gesehen, die Sonne, den Mond, die Sterne und die andere Welt.
Wie in deinen Träumen!«
Dann ist er plötzlich müde, sooo müde.

Er schlüpft in sein warmes Bett und schläft auf der Stelle ein.
Hannah bleibt neben ihm sitzen und schaut ihn an.
»Simon. Mein geliebter, mutiger Enkel. Ich bin so glücklich über dich!«
Als Simon wieder aufwacht, nimmt er sie bei der Hand.
»Jetzt will ich dir die andere Welt zeigen.
Dass du sie auch mit deinen Tag-Augen sehen kannst.
Es ist gar nicht weit. Komm!«
Wie es weitergegangen ist?
Die Leute blieben in Bruma wohnen.
Hie und da machten sie einen Ausflug auf die Berge.
Und sie feierten jedes Jahr ein Sonnen- und ein Mondfest.
Hannah und Simon aber sind umgezogen, in ein Häuschen direkt an der Nebelgrenze.
So hatten sie beides: ihre Stadt und die weite, farbige Sonnenwelt.

Musik

Kurzpredigt zur Erzählung und zu Joel 2,2.8: Unterdessen verzieren die Kinder eine Eule, eine Schablone mit beweglichen Flügeln, so kann sie mitfliegen, als gute Begleiterin. Nach der Predigt ziehen die Kinder durch die Kirche, zeigen allen ihre Eule und nehmen bei ihren Angehörigen wieder Platz.

Hannahs Traum: Nach Innen schauen

Hannah ist alt. Sie hat einen großen Teil ihrer Wegstrecke bereits gelebt und hinter sich. Irgendwann wird sie sterben. Sie steht an einem anderen Ort als Simon, der im Begriff ist, ins Leben aufzubrechen.

Die Formulierung »Das Leben hinter sich haben« trifft nur aus der Perspektive eines zeitlich linearen Denkmodells zu. Man kann das Alter auch anders betrachten: Wer alt ist, hat viel Lebenserfahrung gesammelt und trägt alles Gelebte in sich: das Kind, den Jugendlichen, den jungen Erwachsenen, das mittlere Alter. Ein alter Mensch hat sein Potenzial bereits verwirklicht und dabei die Ambivalenz des Lebens erfahren. Mit allem Geglückten, mit allen Brüchen und Grenzen. Die Lebenserfahrung verleiht die Fähigkeit zu träumen. Träumend wird das Erfahrende nochmals geschaut und das, was trägt und fruchtet, in Bildern verdichtet. Was man selbst geschaffen hat und was andere schaffen, kann jetzt gewürdigt werden.

Alt sein: die Weite der Welt in sich aufgenommen haben – als innere Quelle, um aus der Fülle zu leben und zu träumen.

Im Alter nehmen die körperlichen Kräfte ab. Hannah kann nicht mehr auf die Berge steigen. Aber sie lebt mit tiefer Spiritualität. Sie träumt die Verbindung zum ganzen Kosmos: zu den Bergen, zur weiten Welt, zu Farben, Licht, Sonne, Mond und Sternen. Sie hat sich umorientiert: vom Machen zum Sein, vom Individuellen zur Allverbundenheit.

Besonders verbunden ist sie mit Simon, ihrem Enkelkind. Sie lässt ihn Anteil haben an dem, was sie beseelt und an ihren inneren Bildern. »Eure Greise werden Träume träumen.«

Die alte Hannah ist eigensinnig und unabhängig. Sie kennt die Leute ihrer Stadt und muss damit rechnen, in deren Perspektive als Spinnerin zu gelten. Trotzdem bleibt sie bei sich selbst und ihrem eigenen inneren Weg. Diese Eigensinnigkeit ist eine große Qualität – und verbindet sie mit den Jungen.

Die alte Hannah ist weise: Zwischen ihr und den Naturkräften (Fluss und Eile) besteht ein enger Bezug. Es ist, wie wenn sie mit dem Fluss und der Eule kommunizieren und im gleichen Rhythmus schwingen würde. Fluss und Eule werden zu ihren Stellvertretern – oder ist es umgekehrt? Vielleicht hat sie im jahrelangen Lauschen auf das Flussgemurmel und den Eulenruf deren stärkenden und geerdeten Energien in sich aufgenommen.

Simons Vision: Verwirklichen, gestalten, verändern

Simon ist jung, stark, mutig und beseelt von einem unwiderstehlichen Drang zum Leben, Entdecken, Forschen.

Er lässt sich von Hannahs Träumen anstecken. Mehr noch: Es ist, wie wenn er diese selbst geträumt hätte. Es berührt etwas in ihm, das Form und Ausdruck werden will.

Hier treffen sich Alt und Jung: in der Sehnsucht nach der Fülle des Lebens.

Doch Simon begnügt sich nicht damit, die schönen Bilder nur nach innen zu schauen. Er muss sie im Außen erleben, mit allen Sinnen: auf der Haut spüren, sehen, fühlen, riechen. Als junger Mensch hat er die Kraft zum Machen, Aufbrechen, Handeln. Das ist – mehr als ein Traum – seine Vision: Die Welt erfahren und gestalten mit ihren reichen und farbigen Möglichkeiten. »Eure Söhne und Töchter werden Gesichte sehen.«

Simon bringt sich aktiv ein ins Spiel der Welt. Er hat Zugang zu einer schöpferischen, visionären Lebenskraft, die die Kräfte der Älteren überschreitet. Visionen sind innere ungestüme Bilder, die im Unterschied zu den Träumen der Alten mit großer Energie geladen sind und auf Verwirklichung drängen. Mit ihrer Hilfe gestalten die Jungen ihre eigene Zukunft und die Zukunft der nachfolgenden Generationen (im Unterschied zum vereinnahmenden Satz: »Die Jungen sind unsere Zukunft«). In ihrer schöpferischen Kraft sind die Jungen Gott näher als die Älteren und ihnen immer einen Schritt voraus. Diese biblische Sicht der jungen Generation ist radikal und provozierend –

für die Kirche, die Schule, die Gesellschaft – und nicht zuletzt für die Jugendlichen selbst. Was für eine Herausforderung und Chance, sich selbst so sehen und verstehen zu lernen.

Auslösend für den Aufbruch von Simon ist die Zuneigung zu seiner Großmutter. Er wünscht sich, dass sie die Welt jenseits der Berge vor ihrem Tod auch noch sehen könne. Er stellt sich vor, wie er seiner Großmutter ihren Wunsch erfüllt. Die Verbundenheit und Liebe zu Hannah ist für ihn eine Art Rückanbindung (re-ligio). Sie gibt ihm den Boden, den Halt und die Motivation, den Aufbruch zu wagen.

Umgekehrt wird er von Hannah unterstützt – und wie sich zeigt, auch von Verbündeten in der Natur. Diese sind für ihn Begleiter, Wächter, »Schutzengel« auf seinem persönlichen Weg. Sie helfen ihm, bei sich selbst zu bleiben, oder wenn er zweifelt, Ziel und Mitte wiederzufinden.

So geerdet, folgt Simon seinen Zukunftsgesichtern. Er erobert die Welt jenseits des Gewohnten. Und er hat die Kraft, der ganzen Stadt die Stirn zu bieten und sie – gegen den Willen der Regierenden – ihn das Neue, Weite, Farbige hereinzuziehen. Alle erfahren es, wenn sie es nur wollen.

Raum-Traum: Lebensräume mit Weite, Licht und Farben.

Ein wichtiges Thema der Geschichte ist der Kontrast zwischen der engen, grauen Nebelwelt und der Welt voller Weite, Vielfalt, Licht und Farben. Die Sehnsucht von Hannah und Simon nach einer anderen Welt entspricht ziemlich genau den Raum-Träumen vieler Kinder und Erwachsenen. Der Alltag und die modernen Gebäude in heutigen Lebens-Umfeldern sind leider nur allzu oft eher in der Nähe der grauen Welt.

Ritual zum Generationenbogen: Die Sonne macht die Welt weit. In ihrem Licht werden Farben, Formen, Bäume, Blumen, Tiere und Menschen sichtbar.

So ist auch das Gotteslicht – Es gibt dem Himmel, der Erde und jedem Lebewesen seine Farbe.

Und umgekehrt: In jedem Lebewesen spiegelt sich das Gotteslicht – Wie sonst könnte es sichtbar werden?

In Simon und in Hannah spiegelt sich das Gotteslicht!

Auch in dir! In deinem Alter, in deiner Art, wie du im Leben stehst, was dir wichtig ist, wie du glaubst und zweifelst. Wovon du träumst.

Auch in deinen Nächsten. Hören wir jetzt verschiedene Stimmen von Jung bis Alt, zu folgenden Fragen: Wie sie sich eine Kirche mit verschiedenen Generationen träumen; was sie im Alltag stärkt.

Die Zitate werden z. B. von zwei Zielgruppenvertretern vorgetragen. Sie kommen mit zur Altersgruppe passender Musik nach vorne und lesen die Aussagen abwechselnd vor. Schlusspunkt: Kerze anzünden, evtl. zitieren des Psalms. Die Vorlesenden kehren begleitet mit Musik zurück. Stille. Danach die nächste Altersgruppe.

Hören wir die Aussagen von Mädchen und Buben zwischen 4–13:

- Im großen Saal ist es schön. Dort ist viel Platz zum Laufen. Es hat Fenster und die Sonne scheint herein. Und der Pfarrer erzählt so schön Geschichten. Ich bin glücklich, wenn ich spielen kann, bis der Mond scheint.
- Ich trau mich nicht so recht in die Kirche. Ich würde gerne Kerzen anzünden. Und einmal möchte ich gerne in der Kirche übernachten. Ich würde die Räume viel farbiger machen. Und Blumen müsste es haben.
- Gelbe Kerze anzünden: »Du stellst unsere Füße in weiten Raum.«

Aussagen Jugendliche zwischen 14–19:
- Irgendwie müsste es in der Kirche mehr leben, ich weiß nicht genau, wie. In einem Raum, wo man sieht, dass Leben drin ist, bin ich lieber.
- Ich denke, es ist interessant, mit Erwachsenen darüber zu reden, was ich gerade erlebe. Mit Erwachsenen diskutieren, beide Meinungen hören, dann lernt man voneinander.
- Orange Kerze anzünden: »Du stellst unsere Füße in weiten Raum.«

Aussagen junge Erwachsene von 20–30:
- Ich habe gute Freunde und eine Familie, die mich unterstützt und mir vertraut. In der Freizeit mache ich Sport und Musik. Belastend finde ich Prüfungsstress, Zeitdruck und alles unter einen Hut zu bringen.
- Was ich in der Kirchgemeinde tun möchte? Verweilen, Ruhe und Wärme finden, meditieren, Kerzen anzünden, Menschen treffen, Gemeinschaft, Kameradschaft, Zusammenhalt.
- Rote Kerze anzünden: »Du stellst unsere Füße in weiten Raum.«

Aussagen Erwachsene von 31–50:
- Mir liegt viel an der Kirche, aber so wie sie sich ausdrückt, kommt sie bei mir als alleinerziehende Mutter manchmal etwas altertümlich, nicht

so lebensnah oder ganzheitlich an. Die Kirche darf nicht werten, sie soll offen sein für die verschiedensten Bedürfnisse.
- Die Kirche der Zukunft ist für mich ein interkulturell offener Ort der Begegnung, auch ein Treffpunkt mit Spielraum für Kinder und Jugendliche. Gut finde ich den Suppenmittag, Anlässe von gemeinnützigen und kulturellen Vereinen, Ausstellungen, Konzerte, Kultur.
- Violette Kerze anzünden: »Du stellst unsere Füße in weiten Raum.«

Aussagen Erwachsene von 50–65:
- Ich stelle mir die Generationenkirche so vor: Es hat Nischen zum Alleinsein und ausruhen, lesen etc. Und Orte, wo man miteinander reden, lachen, essen und spielen kann. Für Groß und Klein.
- Generationenkirche: Das ist schwierig umzusetzen: Ein Umdenken ist notwendig. Toleranz ist die Voraussetzung. Ich würde schon einmal eine Lesung lesen, bei einem Thema mithelfen, Anlässe unterstützen – ohne dabei nur ausgenutzt zu werden.
- Blaue Kerze anzünden: »Du stellst unsere Füße in weiten Raum.«

Aussagen Erwachsene von 66–80:
- Die Generationen mischen sich und es herrscht eine gute Stimmung. Dazu gehört z. B. Kuchen essen, geselliges Beisammensein, Hobbys ausüben (singen, malen etc.), gemeinsam feiern, Gott begegnen.
- Ich möchte mit meinen Enkeln hierher kommen können, so dass es ihnen wohl ist. Es sollte auch für Jugendliche einen Treffpunkt geben.
- Türkise Kerze anzünden: »Du stellst unsere Füße in weiten Raum.«

Aussagen Erwachsene 80+:
- Ich nehme jeden Tag, wie er kommt. Ich gehe raus und treffe meine Bekannten. Aber mich beschäftigt das schon, dass das Leben einmal ein Ende hat. Die Freunde sterben weg. Wie verläuft mein Lebensende?
- Das wäre ideal, wenn alle Generationen näher zusammenkämen. Das ist Gemeinschaft, volles Leben. Mir gefällt die Lebendigkeit der Kinder.
- Grüne Kerze anzünden: »Du stellst unsere Füße in weiten Raum.«

Jede und jeder hat seine eigene Farbe und Stimme.

Zusammen ergibt das den farbigen Generationenbogen – im Licht der Sonne, des Mondes, der Sterne. Im Gotteslicht. Das ist unsere Vision.

Musik
Gebet nach Psalm 31,9:

Du, Gott, Du stellst meine Fuße in weiten Raum.
Ja, das kenne ich doch:
Wenn ich als Kind zum ersten Mal aufstehe, auf beide Füße, um die Welt zu erkunden.
Wenn ich meine eigene Meinung und Kraft entdeckte, den aufrechten Gang.
Wenn ich als junger Mensch die Herkunftsfamilie verlasse, um mein eigenes Lebenshaus zu bauen.
Wenn ich nach einer Krise wieder Fuß fasse, um neu zu beginnen.
Wird es auch so sein, wenn ich sterbe?
DU, Gott, Du stellst meine Füße in weiten Raum.

Lied: Jubilate[2]
Aber, Du, Gott, was mutest du mir da zu!
Du weißt doch, wie oft auch das geschieht:
Meine Füße folgen mir nicht.
Falle hin.
Tu mir weh.
Nehme mir meinen Raum nicht.
Beschneide anderen den Raum.
Hab Angst vor der Weite, der leeren, dunkeln.
Bin einsam und mutlos.
Schließe mich ein im engen Zimmer.

Lied: Kyrie eleison[3]
Du, Gott, stellst meine Füße in weiten Raum.
Heißt das:

---

2 Z. B. freiTöne 73.
3 Z. B. freiTöne 39.

Freust du Dich, wenn ich ins Weite aufbreche? Immer wieder neu?
Werde ich dort Freunde, Freundinnen und gute Begleiter finden?
Vielleicht sogar Dich?
Ist dort mein Zuhause – unser aller Zuhause?
Amen.

Lied/Musik

Segen: Gott segne dich und deinen Weg.
Woher du kommst, wo du stehst, wohin es dich zieht.
Auf dass du JA sagen kannst – zu dir und deinem Leben.
Vielleicht sogar manchmal darüber jubeln, dass es glückt.
Gott segne die Menschen um dich herum, von Jung bis Alt:
deine Familie, Verwandten und Wahlverwandten,
deine Freunde und Freundinnen,
und all die Menschen, denen du täglich begegnest.
Auf dass ihr euch freuen könnt über euer Miteinander und Nebeneinander.
Gott segne jene Menschen, die dir fremd sind
und mit denen du nichts anfangen kannst.
Auf dass ihr einen Weg des Auskommens findet. Amen.

Lied

8. Kommentar zur Erzählung

Die Erzählvorlage basiert auf dem Bilderbuch von Arcado Lobado: Das Tal im Nebel.

Ich habe die Bilderbuchgeschichte in wesentlichen Punkten verändert:

- Der Großvater wurde durch Großmutter Hannah ersetzt, sodass beide Geschlechter vorkommen (Gendergerechtigkeit).
- In der Geschichte von Lobado versuchen Fluss und Eule Simon Angst einzujagen und ihn zurückzuhalten. Sie sind dort verbündet mit den bremsenden, »engstirnigen« Kräften. In meiner Erzählversion haben

die Naturwesen die Seite gewechselt: Sie unterstützen und begleiten Simon bei seiner Entdeckungsreise.
- Die Erzählung ist für verschiedene Generationen konzipiert. Sie arbeitet mit Erzählbildern und einem sich steigernden Spannungsaufbau. Sie eignet sich für Kinder ab ca. vier Jahren und Kinder der Unterstufe, aber auch für generationenverbindende Feiern und Events.

Literatur

Die Erzählung ist eine Adaption des Bilderbuches:
Lobado, Arcado: Das Tal im Nebel
© 1986, bohem press, Zürich. Vergriffen.
ISBN 10: 3855811776 ISBN 13: 9783855811779
Verlag: Bohem Press, 1986
Neuauflage: © 2000, SJW Schweiz. Jugendschriftenwerk SJW-Buch Nr. B17, 2000
ISBN (13): 978-3-7269-0017-5.

Christoph Jungen / Hans Martin Stähli / Katharina Stähli-Kehrli / Ueli Schupbach / Lisbeth Zogg Hohn, Familiengottesdienste in Thurnen 2001, Reformierte Kirchen Bern-Jura-Solothurn, Katechetik, Bern Neuauflage 2008.
find: refbejuso Thurner Modelle, http://www.refbejuso.ch/fileadmin/user_upload/Downloads/Katechetik/KA_Publikationen__Modelle/KA_MOD_d_Thurner-Modelle.pdf.

Lisbeth Zogg Hohn

The Foggy Valley

Concept for a cross-generational service[1]

1. Context

This concept was developed in the framework of the 2010 »Church Sunday« with the topic »Generations walk together«. Since 1912, the Evangelical Reformed Church Synod Bern-Jura-Solothurn (Switzerland) has been celebrating Church Sunday every February. The regional church offers materials and further education seminars on a defined topic. This concept was presented, celebrated and taken up by congregations at such a meeting.

2. Direction, participants, target group

Church Sunday is conducted by volunteers, with or without the involvement of pastors. The target group of this concept includes all generations, with the focus on children and adults.

3. Concept

The concept features a basic structure with a topic, liturgical elements and its core, the narration. This can also be realised by laypeople and can be adapted to the specific local situation.

Proclamation is understood in a wider sense. It happens through place, time, people present, voices, narration, liturgy. A sermon is not

1 www.generationenwelten.ch.

necessary. If there is a sermon, it should link to the narration and be short and concise; children should be able to be active during this time, e.g. with a drawing or crafting work connected to the story.

4. Preparation and effort

In two team meetings, the concept is acknowledged and the specific service planned according to the given context. Suggestion for the different roles: officiant, narrator and contact person for the children, speakers, persons responsible for music and church decoration/setup.

5. Texts

- You have set my feet in a broad place (Psalm 31:8).
- Then afterward I will pour out my spirit on all flesh; your sons and your daughters shall prophesy, your old men shall dream dreams, and your young men shall see visions. Even on the male and female slaves, in those days, I will pour out my spirit (Joel 2:28–29).
- »Light itself cannot be seen, only on things, and the things themselves cannot be seen either, only in the light« (Martin Wagenschein).

6. Church setup

Sky-blue cloth with a big sun and moon (maybe projected). In front of it, a table with candles in all colours of the rainbow; each candle stands for one generation, maybe together with age-specific shoes. This is the visualisation of the arc of generations. Cushions at the front for the children.

7. Service order

Welcome: Everybody is welcomed at the entrance. The narrator welcomes the children and gives them a star made from foil.

Gathering and Greeting: You have set my feet in a broad place (Psalm 31).

Our topic: A broad place for all generations, for the whole arc of generations, for peace among the generations.

Music: Takes up elements from the narration: Dream, colour, light, space

Introduction to the topic: Dear children, I am about to tell the adults something. During this time, you can decorate the stars with your fingertips.

Dear adults: Generations living together is a beautiful vision, but also a challenge.

It needs

- The broad place of being with each other: Different age groups inspire and enrich each other. Each generation depends on the others. Each generation has specific tasks and responsibilities towards the others – especially adults.
- The broad place of living next to each other: Each generation wants and needs something different – it must invent itself and persist. It needs room to itself.
- The broad place of living one after the other: Each one of us experiences the different periods of life themselves: being a child, an adolescent, a young adult, middle-aged, elderly.

Each and every one of us carries the arc of generations in themselves.

Prayer: You, God, You have set my feet in a broad place. Each one should have a broad place – to grow and to walk together with the others. We give you thanks for it. Amen.

Song

Invitation: Now I am going to tell you the story of Simon and his grandmother Hannah. Imagine: Both have never seen the sun, the moon and the stars. But they dream about it. This is why Simon gets up in the middle of the night in order to look for the sun, the moon and the stars. Dear children, you can help him. Let's decorate the sky for him. Come and attach your stars here. If you like, you can then sit on the cushions here at the front.

Narration: The narration can be supported by sounds: either by musicians or with the participation of children: How does the dream of Hannah and Simon sound? The fog? When Simon is afraid? The river, the owl?

When Simon sees the sun world for the first time? The »No« of the town council? The chase up the tower?

Owl and river: Maybe as narrating figures

The Foggy Valley
Far, far away, there is a valley in the midst of high mountains.
In this valley, there is a town. Its name is Bruma.
It is always foggy there. Day and night, year after year.
It is as if the clouds had dropped from the sky to earth.
When people leave their house, all they see is a thick grey.
The fog has swallowed the red, the blue and the yellow.
The green trees look like black shadows.
Only sounds can be heard well through the fog: the rush of a creek, the call of an owl in the woods.
So the people living in Bruma prefer to sit together in their homes.
It's warm there, comfortable and sometimes quite funny.
But imagine: Never has any person of that town seen the sun!
Not once!
Neither the moon. Neither the stars.
But the people of that town do not mind. They are content.
And nobody has ever questioned whether there might be a different world beyond all the fog.
This might have continued forever, if it hadn't been for Hannah, an old woman.
And Simon, her grandson.
The two of them live together in a small house on the fringe of the town.
One morning, Hannah is in the garden with Simon.
She looks up to the grey sky.
Her eyes are bright.
»This night I dreamed that there is another world beyond the mountains.
Bright, wide and full of colours!«
Another world? Wide! Bright! Colours!
To Simon, it seems like his own dream.
He takes his grandmother by the hand: »Come, granny, we'll go looking for this world.«
But Hannah sighs: »That would be nice! But look, I am too old – much too old to go on a journey.
But you – you are young and strong and courageous.
Maybe you'll climb the mountains one day and discover the light.«

Simon is so enthusiastic that he tells everybody about Hannah's dream.
»Hannah has seen another world, full of light and colours.
All you have to do is climb the mountains.«
But the people laugh at him:
»Nonsense. You believe your old grandmother?
She doesn't know what she's saying. She's no longer right in her head.«
Simon becomes quiet.
Why are people not listening to his grandmother?
Why don't they believe him?
Disappointed, he returns home.
He doesn't say anything about it to Hannah. But she notices immediately that something is wrong.
The next morning, Hannah is in her garden again, looking at the sky.
»This night I have seen the sun.
Imagine: A glowing sphere! A fire in the sky!
It is beautiful! And it radiates warmth!«
Simon doesn't respond. But it feels like he was dreaming the same dream.
The next morning, she is out again:
»Even when it's dark, there are lights in the sky.
This night I have seen the moon.
It looks like a big slice of lemon.
And there's a sea of stars.«
So Simon decides to go looking for this other world, with colours, sun, moon and stars.
He has to see for himself!
Perhaps he'll even find a way
for his beloved Hannah to see the sun herself before she dies.
Now, today.
Evening comes, night falls.
Simon goes to bed as usual, but he doesn't sleep.
When everything is quiet, he gets up, dresses warmly, takes his lantern and sneaks out of the house, very quietly.
Outside it is pitch-black.
The light of his lantern is swallowed by the darkness and the fog.
He is frightened.
Maybe he should return and go back to bed?
Maybe people are right and there is – nothing, just nothing.
But what is that?
He hears a soft whisper.
The river! It talks to him:

»Simon, come, go on, continue your journey. I am coming with you.
Just listen to my rushing. Don't be afraid.
You can always hear me, even when you're high up in the mountains.«
So Simon dares to go on.
Suddenly – a noise. Crunching, cracking.
Is this the sound of wild animals?
His heart is beating fast: Beat, go back, beat, go back.
He turns around, wants to go back.
But what is this?
There – in front of him, two big round lights. He stands still.
Are these the stars?
No, it's the eyes of an owl.
»Hoot, Simon, don't be afraid.
All is good. Go on, I'll fly with you and watch over you.«
So Simon dares to go on, through the dark forest, higher and higher up the mountain.
The fog becomes thinner.
Finally – a streak of dark-blue sky.
There, a silver lining on the horizon.
His heart is beating fast, joyfully.
He starts to run.
And then Simon reaches the summit.
The sun is rising.
A couple of stars twinkle at him.
And the crescent moon, high up in the sky.
For the first time in his life, he looks beyond the mountain tops, far into the land.
He watches the sunlight give colour to forests, meadows, flowers.
He sees other villages and towns.
He sees the foggy valley from above.
And he sees the high towers of the town's palace.
For they are higher than the fog.
He rejoices: »Hannah, you were right! And me too!«
As fast as he can, he runs back into town, directly into the palace.
The town council is in the middle of its meeting.
»I've seen it, it exists, the other world, full of colours, beyond the mountains. Come, look!«
But the powerful town councillors just stare at him angrily.
»This can't be right! You can't just disturb our meeting like this! Rascal!«

Somebody says: »He's just as bonkers as his grandmother.« They laugh at him!
Simon stamps his foot: »But I've seen it! And you can see it, too!
All you need to do is climb your high towers.
Because they are higher than the fog!«
»It is forbidden to climb the towers, as it always has been«, the President cries.
»Wait and see, we'll get you and put you in prison!«
So Simon runs away, outside.
He runs to the highest tower and up the stairs.
The men are behind him: »Stop! Police!«
But Simon is young, fast and brave.
He just keeps running.
The others run behind him. It's a long line.
First, Simon. Then the police.
And at the end – out of breath, panting – the whole town council.
When they reach the top, there's a brief silence.
Now they see it for themselves.
The sun shining above the fog.
A world different to the one they know: Rich, colourful, wide.
But Simon lets them stand and stare.
He runs home to his grandmother.
»Hannah! I have seen it, the sun, the moon, the stars and the other world.
Like in your dreams!«
Then he is suddenly tired, very tired.
He snuggles up in his bed and immediately falls asleep.
Hannah sits down next to him and watches him sleep.
»Simon. My beloved, brave grandson. I am so happy for you!«
When Simon awakes, he takes her by the hand.
»Now I want to show you the other world.
So you can see it with your day eyes, too.
It's not that far. Come!«
Do you want to know the end?
The people continued to live in Bruma.
Sometimes they went up to the mountains.
And each year they celebrated a sun festival and a moon festival.
But Hannah and Simon have moved into a small house directly at the border of the fog.
This way they could have both: Their town and the wide, colourful world of sun.

Music

Short sermon linked to the narration and to Joel 2:2-8: Meanwhile, the children decorate an owl, a stencil with moveable wings, so the owl can fly as a good companion. After the sermon, the children go through the church, show everybody their owl and go back to their families.

Hannah's dream: Introspection

Hannah is old. She has already lived the biggest part of her life. She will die some day. She is in a different place than Simon, who is about to start his life.

The idea of »having lived your life« only applies from the perspective of a linear way of thinking about time. You can look at age in a different way: Old people have gained a lot of life experience and carry it all inside them: the child, the youth, the young adult, middle age. An old person has already realised their potential and experienced the ambivalence of life. With all their successes, their disruptions and limits. Their life experience enables them to dream. When dreaming, past experiences are re-evaluated, and what has marked us is condensed into images. Now we can appreciate what we have created ourselves and what others are creating.

Being old: having taken up the broad place of the world inside oneself – as an inner source to live and dream from.

Ageing, we lose our physical strength. Hannah can't climb the mountains any more. But she lives with a deep spirituality. She dreams her connection with the whole cosmos: mountains, the wide world, colours, light, sun, moon and stars. She has shifted her focus: from doing to being, from the individual to interconnectedness.

She has a special connection to her grandson Simon. She lets him participate in what moves her, in her inner images. »Your old men shall dream dreams.«

Old Hannah is stubborn and independent. She knows the people of her town and that they think she's crazy. Despite this, she stays true to herself and her own path. This stubbornness is a good quality and links her to the boy.

Old Hannah is wise: There is a close connection between her and the forces of nature (river and owl). She seems to communicate with river and owl and swings in the same rhythm as them. River and owl take her place – or is it the other way round? Maybe she has taken up their strengthening and grounded energies over the years of listening to the river murmuring and the owl calling.

Simon's vision: Realise, shape, change

Simon is young, strong, courageous and characterized by the irresistible need to live, discover, research.

He becomes infected by Hannah's dreams. Even more: He feels like he had dreamed her dreams himself. They touch something inside him, something that wants to be formed and expressed.

Old and young meet here: in the desire to have a full life.

But Simon is not content just to watch the beautiful images inside him. He has to experience them outside him, with all senses: Sense on his skin, see, feel, smell. As a young person, he has the strength to do, to move, to act. This is more than a dream, it is his vision: To see the world and shape it with its rich and colourful possibilities. »Your sons and your daughters shall prophesy.«

Simon actively participates in the goings-on of the world. He has access to a creative, visionary force of life, which surpasses the strength of the older woman. Visions are internal, wild images, which in contrast to the dreams of the old woman burst with energy and urge him to be realised. With their help, the young people shape their own future and the future of following generations (in contrast to the patronising statement: »The youth are our future«). In their creative force, the young people are closer to God than the old ones, and always one step ahead. This biblical perspective of the young generation is radical and provocative – for the church, for the school and for society – but also for the youth themselves. What a challenge and what an opportunity to learn to see and understand oneself this way.

The trigger for Simon's departure is his affection to his grandmother. He wants her to see the world beyond the mountains before her death, too. He imagines fulfilling his grandmother's wish. His connection and love for Hannah is his form of attachment (re-ligio). It gives him the basis, the strength and the motivation to risk the journey.

But he is also supported by Hannah – and as we see later, also by allies in nature. They become companions, guardians, guardian angels on his personal quest. They help him stay with himself, find his target and focus again in case of doubt.

Grounded like this, Simon follows his dream. He conquers a world beyond everything he is used to. And he has the strength to confront the whole town and draw it – against the will of those in power – to the new, wide, colourful world. Everybody experiences it, if they wish to.

Dream of space: Life spaces with wideness, light and colours

Another important aspect of this story is the contrast of the narrow, grey, foggy world and the world full of space, diversity, light and colours. Hannah's and Simon's desire for another world corresponds quite exactly to the dreams of spaces many children and adults have. Our daily routine and the modern buildings in our current living environments unfortunately resemble all too often the grey world.

Arc of generations ritual: The sun makes the world wide. In its light, colours, shapes, trees, flowers, animals and human beings become visible.

The same is true for God's light: it gives the sky, the earth and each living creature their colour.

And the other way round: Each living creature mirrors God's light – how else could it be visible?

God's light is also mirrored in Simon and Hannah!

And in you, too! In your age, in your way, in your position in life, in what is important to you, how you believe and doubt. In what you dream.

In your neighbour, too. Let's hear different voices from young to old, on the following questions: How they dream about a church with several generations; what strengthens them in their daily life.

The quotes can be read by two representatives of each target group. They come to the front, accompanied by music suitable to their age group, and take turns to read the statements. At the end: Light a candle, maybe quote the psalm. The representatives go back to their seats, accompanied by music. Silence. Then the next age group.

Let's hear the statements of girls and boys between 4 and 13:

- The big room is nice. There's a lot of space to run. It has windows and the sun shines in. The pastor tells good stories. I am happy when I can play until the moon is up.
- I am a little bit afraid to go into the church. I would like to light candles. I want to stay overnight in the church once. I would make the rooms much more colourful. There should be flowers.
- Light a yellow candle: »You have set my feet in a broad place.«

Statements of adolescents 14–19:

- Somehow there should be more life in the church, I don't know exactly how. I prefer to be in a room where you see that there's life inside.

- I think it is interesting to talk with adults about what I am experiencing. Discuss with adults, listen to both opinions, then you learn from each other.
- Light an orange candle: »You have set my feet in a broad place.«

Statements of young adults 20–30:
- I have good friends and a family who support and trust me. In my free time, I do sports and make music. I struggle to accommodate exam stress, time pressure and everything.
- What I would like to do in the congregation? Spend some time, find some quiet and warmth, meditate, light a candle, meet people, fellowship, camaraderie, solidarity.
- Light a red candle: »You have set my feet in a broad place.«

Statements of adults 31–50:
- I appreciate the church, but the way it expresses itself seems to me as a single mum a bit old-fashioned, not really true-to-life or holistic. The church should not judge; it should be open for different needs.
- For me, the church of the future is an intercultural, open space of encounter, but also a meeting place with a play area for children and adolescents. I like the soup lunch, events of non-profit or cultural associations, exhibitions, concerts, culture.
- Light a violet candle: »You have set my feet in a broad place.«

Statements of adults 50–65:
- This is how I imagine a cross-generational church: It has corners to be alone and rest, read, etc. And spaces to talk to each other, laugh, eat and play. For old and young.
- A cross-generational church: That's hard to implement. We need to think differently. Tolerance is a precondition. I would be willing to help with a reading, or prepare a topic, support an event – without being exploited.
- Light a blue candle: »You have set my feet in a broad place.«

Statements of adults 66–80:
- Generations mix, and there's a good mood. This includes e. g. eating cake, spending time together, pursue a hobby (singing, painting, etc.), celebrate together, encounter God.

- I want to be able to come here with my grandchildren, and they should feel alright here. There should also be a meeting place for youth.
- Light a turquoise candle: »You have set my feet in a broad place.«

Statements of adults 80+:
- I take every day as it is. I go out and meet my acquaintances. But I do think about the fact that life will come to an end. Friends are dying. What will the end of my life be like?
- It would be ideal if all generations could get closer to each other. This is community, the full life. I like the liveliness of the children.
- Light a green candle: »You have set my feet in a broad place.«

Everyone has their own colour and mood.
Together, they make up the arc of generations – in the light of the sun, the moon, the stars. In the light of God. This is our vision.

Music
Prayer on Psalm 31:8:

You, God, have set my feet in a broad place.
Yes, I know that:
When I get up as a child on my feet for the first time, to explore the world.
When I discover my own opinion, my strength, walk upright.
When I leave my parents' home as a young adult in order to build my own house of life.
When I recover after a crisis to start anew.
Will it be so when I die?
You, God, have set my feet in a broad place.

Song: Jubilate

But God, what do you ask of me?
You know how often this happens:
My feet won't follow me.
I stumble.
I get hurt.

Don't take my space away from me.
Cut other people's space.
I am afraid of the empty, dark, broad place.
I am lonely and frightened.
I lock myself up in a narrow room.

Song: Kyrie eleison

You, God, have set my feet in a broad place.
Does that mean:
You are happy when I leave for a wide place? Again and again?
Will I find friends and good companions?
Maybe even you?
Is this my home – the home of all of us?
Amen.

Song/music
Blessing: May God bless you and your journey.
Where you come from, where you are right now, where you are going.
So you can say yes – to you and your life.
Maybe you can even rejoice that it is good.

May God bless the people around you, young and old:
Your family and relatives;
your friends and people you chose;
and all people you encounter day by day.
May you be able to be happy about your being together.

May God bless the people who are strange to you
and to whom you find no connection.
May you find a way to get along. Amen.
Song

8. Comments on the narration

This narration is based on the picture book by Arcado Lobado: Das Tal im Nebel (The Foggy Valley).

I have changed this story in several respects:

- The grandfather has become a grandmother in order to include both sexes in the story (gender justice).
- In Lobado's story, the river and the owl try to frighten Simon and hold him back. They are in league with the limiting, narrow-minded forces. In my version, these two creatures have changed sides: They support and accompany Simon on his journey of discovery.
- The story is suitable for several generations. It works with narrative images and an arc of suspense. It can be told to children from the age of 4 and schoolchildren, but also used for cross-generational celebrations and events.

References

This narration is adapted from the picture book:
Lobado, Arcado: Das Tal im Nebel
© 1986, bohem press, Zürich. Out of print.
ISBN 10: 3855811776, ISBN 13: 9783855811779
Publisher: Bohem Press, 1986
New edition: © 2000, SJW Schweiz. Jugendschriftenwerk SJW-Buch Nr. B17, 2000
ISBN (13): 978-3-7269-0017-5.

Christoph Jungen / Hans Martin Stähli / Katharina Stähli-Kehrli / Ueli Schupbach / Lisbeth Zogg Hohn, Familiengottesdienste in Thurnen 2001, Reformierte Kirchen Bern-Jura-Solothurn, Katechetik, Bern New edition 2008.
find: refbejuso Thurner Modelle, http://www.refbejuso.ch/fileadmin/user_upload/Downloads/Katechetik/KA_Publikationen__Modelle/KA_MOD_d_ThurnerModelle.pdf.

Susanna Meyer

Gottesdienst mit Abendmahl nach der Emmauserzählung

Die Emmaus-Liturgie wurde von der Deutschschweizer Liturgiekommission unter der Leitung von Prof. Dr. Andreas Marti als Beispiel einer formal selbständigen Feier entwickelt, um eine prinzipielle Alternative zu den auf dem »letzten Abendmahl« gegründeten Modellen der Tradition zu haben. Dabei wird die Geschichte der beiden Jünger auf dem Weg von Jerusalem nach Emmaus in Lukas 24 mit dem gemeinsamen Mahl mit dem Auferstandenen als gleichwertige Ursprungslegende betrachtet, die einen weiteren Raum öffnet als die auf dem letzten Mahl mit den Jüngern basierenden Abendmahlserzählungen. Der Impuls kam von Andreas Marti, angeregt durch die Mosaiken in Monreale (https://www.gottesdienst-ref.ch/liturgie/gottesdienst-im-kirchenjahr/karwoche-und-ostern/ostermorgen-und-osterzeit). Das Modell wurde in einer von Katrin Kusmierz, Hansueli Walt und Susanna Meyer bearbeiteten Fassung an der 2. Gottesdienstkonsultation in Wien vom 9.–11. November 2016 gefeiert. Allerdings wurden dort – im Unterschied zur Vorlage – die traditionellen Einsetzungsworte aus 1. Kor 11, 23b–26 eingefügt. Diese Einsetzungsworte fehlen in der Vorlage der Liturgiekommission, was in der Schweiz sehr umstritten war und dazu geführt hatte, dass das Modell nicht in die Taschenliturgie von 2011 aufgenommen wurde.

1. Station: Krypta
Musik zum Anfang
Liturgische Eröffnung

L: Die Gnade unseres Herrn Jesus Christus
Und die Liebe Gottes,
und die Gemeinschaft des Heiligen Geistes
sei mit uns allen.

Jesus Christus spricht:
Ich bin das Brot des Lebens,
wer zu mir kommt, den wird nicht hungern;
und wer an mich glaubt, den wird nimmermehr dürsten.

Begrüßung
Lied (stehend): freiTöne 2, Schweige und höre
Schriftlesung 1: Lukas 24,13–16

Und da waren am selben Tag zwei von ihnen unterwegs zu einem Dorf namens Emmaus, das sechzig Stadien von Jerusalem entfernt ist. Und sie redeten miteinander über all das, was vorgefallen war. Und es geschah, während sie miteinander redeten und sich besprachen, dass Jesus selbst sich zu ihnen gesellte und sie begleitete. Doch ihre Augen waren gehalten, so dass sie ihn nicht erkannten.

Gebet mit Schuldbekenntnis und Zuspruch:
L: Wir beten:
Gott, Du Quelle des Lebens!
Unterwegs im Leben
sehnen wir uns nach Deiner Gegenwart;
Deine Gegenwart,
die uns umhüllt,
die uns Geborgenheit und Sicherheit schenkt,
die uns heil werden lässt.
Du hast Dich Deinen Menschen geschenkt,
bist ihnen nahe gekommen
in den Boten, die Abraham besuchten
oder im leichten Windhauch, der Elija gestreift hat;
und in Deinem Sohn, der Deiner Liebe Gestalt verliehen hat.

Alle: Wir bekennen:
Unterwegs im Hier und Jetzt,
zwischen Auferstehung und Vollendung,
verlieren wir Dich manchmal aus den Augen.
Wir verlieren uns in uns selber
und in den Geschäftigkeiten des Alltags.

Unsere Augen sind gehalten, der Blick verstellt für die Zeichen Deiner Gegenwart.
Unterwegs im Hier und Jetzt,
wird unser Vertrauen in die Kraft der Auferstehung immer wieder brüchig,
und wir vergessen, dass der Kerker des Todes aufgeschlossen
und das Tor zum Leben weit offen ist.
Gott erbarme dich!
Alle: Kyrie eleison (Nr. 194 aus dem Reformierten Gesangbuch der Schweiz) (Kehrvers)
Liturg/Kantor singt über den ausgehaltenen Noten in der Zeile:
Öffne uns die Augen, dass wir dich erkennen, wenn du mit uns gehst.
Alle: Kyrie eleison (Kehrvers)
L/K: Öffne uns die Ohren, dass wir dich vernehmen, wenn du zu uns sprichst.
Alle: Kyrie eleison (Kehrvers)
L/K: Öffne uns das Herz, dass wir dir begegnen, wenn wir Brot und Wein teilen.
Alle: Kyrie eleison (Kehrvers)

Zuspruch
L: Es sollen wohl Berge weichen und Hügel hinfallen,
aber meine Gnade soll nicht von dir weichen,
und der Bund meines Friedens soll nicht hinfallen,
spricht der Herr, dein Erbarmer (Jesaja 54,10).

Aufbruch zur 2. Station: Kirchenschiff
Verkündigung
Schriftlesung II: Lukas 24,17–27

Er aber sagte zu ihnen: Was sind das für Worte, die ihr da unterwegs miteinander wechselt? Da blieben sie mit düsterer Miene stehen. Der eine aber, mit Namen Klopas, antwortete ihm: Du bist wohl der Einzige, der sich in Jerusalem aufhält und nicht erfahren hat, was sich in diesen Tagen dort zugetragen hat. Und er sagte zu ihnen: Was denn? Sie sagten zu ihm: Das mit Jesus von Nazaret, der ein Prophet war, mächtig in Tat und Wort vor Gott und dem ganzen Volk, und wie unsere Hohen Priester und führenden Männer ihn ausgeliefert haben, damit er zum Tod verurteilt würde, und wie sie ihn gekreuzigt haben. Wir aber hofften, er sei es, der Israel erlösen werde; doch jetzt ist es schon drei Tage her, seit dies geschehen ist. Doch dann haben uns einige Frauen, die zu uns gehören, in Schrecken versetzt. Sie waren frühmorgens am Grab, und als sie den Leib nicht fanden, kamen sie und sagten, sie hätten gar eine Erscheinung von Engeln gehabt, die gesagt hätten, er lebe. Da gingen einige der Unsrigen zum Grab und fanden es so, wie die Frauen gesagt hatten; ihn aber haben sie nicht gesehen. Da sagte er zu ihnen: Wie unverständig seid ihr doch und trägen Herzens! Dass ihr nicht glaubt nach allem, was die Propheten gesagt haben! Musste der Gesalbte nicht solches erleiden und so in seine Herrlichkeit eingehen? Und er fing an bei Mose und allen Propheten und legte ihnen aus, was in allen Schriften über ihn steht.

Predigt Teil I
Zwischenspiel
Schriftlesung III: Lukas 24,28–29

Und sie näherten sich dem Dorf, wohin sie unterwegs waren, und er tat so, als wolle er weitergehen. Doch sie bedrängten ihn und sagten: Bleibe bei uns, denn es will Abend werden, und der Tag hat sich schon geneigt. Und er ging hinein und blieb bei ihnen.

Fürbitte:
L: Wir beten:
Bleibe bei uns – Du, Auferstandener, der uns ins Leben vorausgeht.
Manchmal gehen wir uns selbst verloren. Wir verlieren die Orientierung und das Ziel aus den Augen. Wir bitten dich: halte die Gewissheit in uns lebendig, dass du mit uns gehst. Auch dann, wenn wir mutlos und verzagt sind.
Wir bitten, bleibe bei uns: Manchmal gehst du uns verloren, in alledem was unser Leben so mit sich bringt. Lass uns aufmerksam sein für die Zeichen deiner Gegenwart. Öffne unser Herz für Spuren deiner Liebe und Zuwendung zu uns und allen Menschen.
Wir bitten, sei mit allen Menschen, über die sich das Dunkel von Krieg und Gewalt senkt. Sei mit allen Menschen, denen die Nacht nicht die er-

sehnte Ruhe bringt, weil sie nicht in Sicherheit sind. Wir denken besonders an:

… *Tagesaktuelles einfügen*
Wir bitten, bleibe bei uns und bei deiner ganzen Kirche. Öffne uns die Augen, um dich dort zu erkennen, wo wir nicht mit dir gerechnet haben. Lass uns aufbrechen und dir nachfolgen, und mach uns zu Werkzeugen deines Friedens.
Amen.

Lied (stehend): freiTöne 162, Ich bin bei euch
Schriftlesung IV: Lukas 24,30–44
Und es geschah, als er sich mit ihnen zu Tisch gesetzt hatte, dass er das Brot nahm, den Lobpreis sprach, es brach und ihnen gab. Da wurden ihnen die Augen aufgetan, und sie erkannten ihn. Und schon war er nicht mehr zu sehen. Und sie sagten zueinander: Brannte nicht unser Herz, als er unterwegs mit uns redete, als er uns die Schriften aufschloss? Und noch zur selben Stunde standen sie auf und kehrten nach Jerusalem zurück und fanden die elf versammelt und die, welche zu ihnen gehörten; die sagten: Der Herr ist tatsächlich auferweckt worden und dem Simon erschienen. Und auch sie erzählten, was unterwegs geschehen war, und wie er von ihnen am Brechen des Brotes erkannt worden war.
Während sie noch darüber redeten, trat er selbst in ihre Mitte, und er sagt zu ihnen: Friede sei mit euch! Da gerieten sie in Angst und Schrecken und meinten, einen Geist zu sehen. Und er sagte zu ihnen: Was seid ihr so verstört, und warum steigen solche Gedanken in euch auf? Seht meine Hände und Füße: Ich selbst bin es. Fasst mich an und seht! Ein Geist hat kein Fleisch und keine Knochen, wie ihr es an mir seht. Und während er das sagte, zeigte er ihnen seine Hände und Füße. Da sie aber vor lauter Freude noch immer ungläubig waren und staunten, sagte er zu ihnen: Habt ihr etwas zu essen hier? Da gaben sie ihm ein Stück gebratenen Fisch; und er nahm es und aß es vor ihren Augen. Dann sagte er zu ihnen: Das sind meine Worte, die ich zu euch gesagt habe, als ich noch mit euch zusammen war: Alles muss erfüllt werden, was im Gesetz des Mose und bei den Propheten und in den Psalmen über mich geschrieben steht.

Predigt, Teil II und Überleitung zum Abendmahl
3. Station: sitzend im Kreis um den Abendmahlstisch
Abendmahl
L: Wie die beiden Jünger, so lädt Jesus Christus auch uns an seinen Tisch:
Zum Fest der Erinnerung an Gottes Wege mit seiner Welt,
zum Fest der Gemeinschaft untereinander und mit Gott,
zum Fest der Hoffnung auf eine neue Erde und einen neuen Himmel.

Wir preisen dich, du lebendiger Gott.
Alle Dinge hast du ins Dasein gerufen.
Wir danken dir, dass wir leben, lieben und geliebt werden.
Wir danken dir für den Sinn, den du uns zeigst in Jesus,
dem neuen Menschen, dem Auferstandenen.
Dich preisen die Mächte des Alls,
die ganze Schöpfung singt dein Lob.
Lass unsere Stimmen sich vereinen zum Hochgesang von deiner Herrlichkeit.

Sanctus (Lied): freitöne 153, Du bist heilig
Wenn wir Abendmahl feiern, ist er bei uns mit seinen Worten und Taten, seiner Liebe zu Gott und zu seinen Mitmenschen, mit seinem Leiden und Sterben und seiner Auferstehung. Wir erwarten seine Wiederkunft, da er Recht schaffen wird für die Lebenden und die Toten.
Der Herr, Jesus, nahm in der Nacht, da er ausgeliefert wurde, Brot, dankte, brach es und sprach: Dies ist mein Leib für euch. Das tut zu meinem Gedächtnis.
Ebenso nahm er nach dem Essen den Kelch und sprach: Dieser Kelch ist der neue Bund in meinem Blut. Das tut, sooft Ihr daraus trinkt, zu meinem Gedächtnis.
Denn sooft ihr dieses Brot esst und den Kelch trinkt, verkündigt ihr den Tod des Herrn, bis dass er kommt.

Epiklese
Und so bitten wir dich, Vater Jesu Christi:
Segne dieses Brot und diesen Wein,
Früchte dieser Erde und der Arbeit von Menschen.
Sende deinen Heiligen Geist auf uns und diese Gaben,

damit er uns erneuere
und uns die Kraft und Ausdauer gebe
zum Aufbau deiner Kirche,
zur Gestaltung unserer Welt in Frieden und Gerechtigkeit
und zur Bewahrung deiner guten Schöpfung.

Unser Vater (stehend, wir bleiben stehen bis und während des Dankgebets):
Wir heißen deine Kinder und sind es, darum beten wir voller Vertrauen
mit den Worten, die Jesus uns gelehrt hat:
Unser Vater im Himmel …

Lied: freitöne 151, Christus, Antlitz Gottes
Wir teilen, was uns geschenkt ist:
Wir essen vom Brot des Lebens
Und trinken vom Kelch des Friedens.
Kommt, schmeckt und seht, wie freundlich unser Gott ist.

Austeilung mit Musik: Die Austeilung erfolgt stehend im Kreis. Das Brot wird von den Liturgen ausgeteilt; der Kelch im Kreis von Person zu Person weitergereicht mit den Worten: »Kelch des Heils«.

Dankgebet (aus Psalm 103), gemeinsam gesprochen.
Alle: Lobe den Herrn, meine Seele,
und alles, was in mir ist, seinen heiligen Namen.
Lobe den Herrn meine Seele,
und vergiss nicht, was er dir Gutes getan hat.
Der dich krönt mit Gnade und Erbarmen,
der dich mit gutem sättigt dein Leben lang.

Kollekte und Mitteilungen
Lied (stehend): freiTöne 194, Go Gently, Go lightly.
Sendung

L: Geht hin
in dem Vertrauen,
dass es die Kraft Gottes ist,
die in euch ruft.

Geht hin,
in dem Glauben,
dass es die Liebe Jesu ist,
die euch hinaustreibt.
Geht hin,
in der Gewissheit,
dass Gottes Geist
euch lebendig erhält.

Segen
L: Der Segen des Gottes von Sara und Abraham,
der Segen des Sohnes, von Maria geboren,
der Segen des Heiligen Geistes, der über uns wacht wie Mutter und Vater über ihre Kinder,
sei mit euch allen.
Alle: Amen.

Musik zum Ausgang

Susanna Meyer

Service with Communion Following the Emmaus Story

The Emmaus Liturgy was developed by the German-speaking Swiss Reformed Liturgical Commission chaired by Prof. Dr. Andreas Marti. It is an example of a formally complete service that provides a fundamental alternative to the traditional models based on the »last supper«. The liturgy focuses on the story in Luke 24 of the two disciples journeying from Jerusalem to Emmaus and their supper with the risen Christ, regarding it as a foundational legend of equal value. This story opens up a wider space than the last supper narratives based on Jesus' final meal with his disciples. The idea came from Andreas Marti, who was inspired by the mosaics in Monreale, Sicily (https://www.gottesdienst-ref.ch/liturgie/gottesdienst-im-kirchenjahr/karwoche-und-ostern/ostermorgen-und-osterzeit). Katrin Kusmierz, Hansueli Walt and Susanna Meyer arranged a service based on this model at the 2nd Worship Consultation in Vienna from 9 to 11 November 2016. This service included the traditional words of institution from 1Cor 11:23b–26, however, thereby diverging from the original idea. The Liturgical Commission had omitted the words of institution, which provoked a heated debate in Switzerland. As a consequence, the Emmaus Liturgy was not included in the *Taschenausgabe Liturgie* (pocket edition) of 2011.

1st Station: Crypt
Introductory music
Liturgical opening

L: May the grace of our Lord Jesus Christ
and the lovc of God
and the fellowship of the Holy Spirit
be with us all.

Jesus Christ says:
I am the bread of life,
whoever comes to me shall not hunger,
and whoever believes in me shall never thirst.

Welcome
Hymn (standing)
Reading I: Luke 24:13–16

Now that same day two of them were going to a village called Emmaus, about seven miles from Jerusalem. They were talking with each other about everything that had happened. As they talked and discussed these things with each other, Jesus himself came up and walked along with them; but they were kept from recognizing him.

Prayer with confession of sin and assurance
L: We pray:
God, source of life!
On our journey through life
we long for your presence;
your presence,
which envelops us,
which makes us feel safe and secure;
which makes us whole.
You have given yourself to your people,
you have reached out to them
through the messengers who visited Abraham
or the light breeze that touched Elijah;
and in your Son, who embodies your love.
All: We confess:
On our journey in the here and now,
between resurrection and completion,
we sometimes lose sight of you.
We get lost in ourselves
and in our day-to-day activities.
We are kept from seeing
the signs of your presence.

On our journey in the here and now,
our faith in the power of the resurrection often becomes brittle,
and we forget that the prison of death has been opened
and that the gateway to life is wide open.
Lord, have mercy!

All: Kyrie eleison (Refrain)
The leader or cantor sings over the sustained notes in the line:
Open our eyes so that we may recognize you when you walk with us.
All: Kyrie eleison (Refrain)
L/C: Open our ears so that we may hear you when you talk to us.
All: Kyrie eleison (Refrain)
L/C: Open our hearts so that we may encounter you when we share bread and wine.
All: Kyrie eleison (Refrain)

Assurance
L: Though the mountains be shaken and the hills be removed,
yet my unfailing love for you will not be shaken,
nor my covenant of peace be removed,
says the Lord, who has compassion on you (Isaiah 54:10).

Walk to the 2nd station: Nave
Proclamation
Reading II: Luke 24:17–27

He asked them, »What are you discussing together as you walk along?« They stood still, their faces downcast. One of them, named Cleopas, asked him, »Are you the only one visiting Jerusalem who does not know the things that have happened there in these days?« »What things?« he asked. »About Jesus of Nazareth,« they replied. »He was a prophet, powerful in word and deed before God and all the people. The chief priests and our rulers handed him over to be sentenced to death, and they crucified him; but we had hoped that he was the one who was going to redeem Israel. And what is more, it is the third day since all this took place. In addition, some of our women amazed us. They went to the tomb early this morning but didn't find his body. They came and told us that they had seen a vision of angels, who said he was alive. Then some of our companions went to the tomb and found it just as the women had said, but they did not see Jesus.« He said to them, »How foolish you are, and how slow to believe all that the prophets have spoken! Did not the Messiah have to suffer these things and then enter his glory?« And beginning with Moses and all the Prophets, he explained to them what was said in all the Scriptures concerning himself.

Sermon: Part I
Interlude
Reading III: Luke 24:28–29

As they approached the village to which they were going, Jesus continued on as if he were going farther. But they urged him strongly, »Stay with us, for it is nearly evening; the day is almost over.« So he went in to stay with them.

Intercessions
L: We pray:
Stay with us – you, the resurrected one, who precedes us into life.
Sometimes we lose ourselves. We lose orientation and sight of our goal.
We pray: Keep the knowledge in us alive that you walk with us. Also in times when we feel discouraged and disheartened.
We pray: Stay with us. Sometimes we lose you in all that our life involves. Let us pay attention to the signs of your presence. Open our heart for the traces of your love and affection for us and all people.
We pray: Be with all who find themselves in the darkness of war and violence. Be with all people who do not find peace at night because they are not safe. We especially think of:

Include current affairs
We pray: Stay with us and with your whole church. Open our eyes so that we may recognize you in places where we did not expect to find you. Let us go forth and follow you, and make us instruments of your peace. Amen.

Hymn (standing)

Reading IV: Luke 24:30–44

When he was at the table with them, he took bread, gave thanks, broke it and began to give it to them. Then their eyes were opened and they recognized him, and he disappeared from their sight. They asked each other, »Were not our hearts burning within us while he talked with us on the road and opened the Scriptures to us?« They got up and returned at once to Jerusalem. There they found the Eleven and those with them, assembled together and saying, »It is true! The Lord has risen and has appeared to Simon.« Then the two told what had happened on the way, and how Jesus was recognized by them when he broke the bread.

While they were still talking about this, Jesus himself stood among them and said to them, »Peace be with you.« They were startled and frightened, thinking they saw a ghost. He said to them, »Why are you troubled, and why do doubts rise in your minds? Look at my hands and my feet. It is I myself! Touch me and see; a ghost does not have flesh and bones, as you see I have.« When he had said this, he showed them his hands and feet. And while they still did not believe it because of joy and amazement, he asked them, »Do you have anything here to eat?« They gave him a piece of broiled fish, and he took it and ate it in their presence. He said to them, »This is what I told you while I was still with you: Everything must be fulfilled that is written about me in the Law of Moses, the Prophets and the Psalms.«

Sermon: Part II and transition to Communion

3rd Station: Sitting in a circle around the communion table

Communion

L: Like the two disciples, Jesus Christ invites us to his table:
For the celebration of remembrance of God's ways with his world,
for the celebration of fellowship with each other and with God,
for the celebration of hope for a new earth and a new Heaven.
We praise you, living God.
You have called all things into existence.
We thank you that we live, love and are loved.
We thank you for the purpose that you show us in Jesus,
the new human being, the resurrected one.

The powers of Heaven praise you,
the whole creation sings your praise.
Let us join our voices in the praise of your glory.

Sanctus (hymn)

Whenever we celebrate Communion, he is with us with his words and deeds, his love for God and the people, with his suffering and death and his resurrection. We await his second coming, when he will bring justice to the living and the dead.

The Lord Jesus Christ, on the night when he was betrayed, took bread, and when he had given thanks, he broke it and said: this is my body which is given for you. Do this in remembrance of me.

In the same way he also took the cup after the supper, and said: This cup is the covenant in my blood. Do this, as often as you drink it, in remembrance of me.

For as often as you eat this bread and drink the cup, you proclaim the Lord's death until he comes.

Epiclesis

And so we pray to you, father of Jesus Christ:
Bless this bread and this wine,
fruits of the earth and of people's work.
Send your Holy Spirit upon us and these gifts,
so that it may renew us,
and give us the strength and perseverance
to build your church,
to shape our world in peace and justice,
and to preserve your good creation.

The Lord's Prayer (standing; we remain standing up to and including the prayer of thanksgiving):

We are called your children, and that is what we are. Therefore we pray in complete faith with the words Jesus taught us:
Our father in heaven …

Hymn
We share what has been given to us:
We eat the bread of life
and drink from the cup of peace.
Come, taste and see how friendly our God is.

Administration with music: Communion is administered standing in a circle. The bread is distributed by the liturgists; the cup is handed from one person to the next with the words: »Cup of salvation«.
Prayer of thanksgiving (based on Psalm 103), spoken together.
All: Praise the Lord, my soul;
all my inmost being, praise his holy name.
Praise the Lord, my soul;
and forget not all his benefits –
who crowns you with love and compassion,
who satisfies your desires with good things all through your life.

Collection and announcements
Hymn (standing)
Sending forth

L: Go forth
in the faith
that it is the power of God
that calls within you.
Go forth
in the faith
that it is the love of Jesus
that sends you out into the world.
Go forth
in the certainty
that the Spirit of God
keeps you alive.

Blessing
L: May the blessing of the God of Sara and Abraham,
the blessing of the Son, born of Mary,

the blessing of the Holy Spirit, who watches over us like mother and father over their children,
be with you all.
All: Amen.

Musical ending